RESOLVING
ETHICAL
DILEMMAS

A GUIDE FOR CLINICIANS

THIRD EDITION

RESOLVING ETHICAL DILEMMAS

A GUIDE FOR CLINICIANS

Bernard Lo, M.D., F.A.C.P.

Professor of Medicine
Director, Program in Medical Ethics
University of California, San Francisco
Attending Physician, Moffitt-Long Hospital
School of Medicine,
San Francisco, California

 LIPPINCOTT WILLIAMS & WILKINS
A **Wolters Kluwer** Company
Philadelphia • Baltimore • New York • London
Buenos Aires • Hong Kong • Sydney • Tokyo

Acquisitions Editor: Sonya Seigafuse
Developmental Editor: LuzSelenia Loeb
Project Manager: Alicia Jackson
Senior Manufacturing Manager: Benjamin Rivera
Marketing Manager: Kathy Neely
Designer: Christine Jenny
Production Service: nSight, Inc.
Printer: Edwards Brothers

© 2005 by LIPPINCOTT WILLIAMS & WILKINS
530 Walnut Street
Philadelphia, PA 19106 USA
LWW.com

Printed in the USA

Second Edition, 2000 © Lippincott Williams & Wilkins

Library of Congress Cataloging-in-Publication Data
Lo, Bernard.
  Resolving ethical dilemmas : a guide for clinicians / Bernard Lo.—3rd ed.
    p. ; cm.
  Includes bibliographical references and index.
  ISBN 0-7817-5357-0
  1. Medical ethics. 2. Medicine—Decision making. 3. Clinical
medicine—Moral and ethical aspects. I. Title. [DNLM: 1. Ethics,
Clinical—Case Reports.]
  R724.L59 2005
  174.2--dc22

2005000146

Care has been taken to confirm the accuracy of the information presented and to describe generally accepted practices. However, the authors, editors, and publisher are not responsible for errors or omissions or for any consequences from application of the information in this book and make no warranty, expressed or implied, with respect to the currency, completeness, or accuracy of the contents of the publication. Application of the information in a particular situation remains the professional responsibility of the practitioner.

The authors, editors, and publisher have exerted every effort to ensure that drug selection and dosage set forth in this text are in accordance with current recommendations and practice at the time of publication. However, in view of ongoing research, changes in government regulations, and the constant flow of information relating to drug therapy and drug reactions, the reader is urged to check the package insert for each drug for any change in indications and dosage and for added warnings and precautions. This is particularly important when the recommended agent is a new or infrequently employed drug.

Some drugs and medical devices presented in the publication have Food and Drug Administration (FDA) clearance for limited use in restricted research settings. It is the responsibility of health care providers to ascertain the FDA status of each drug or device planned for use in their clinical practice.

10 9 8 7 6 5 4 3 2

Contents

Preface to the First Edition

As a resident, I was paged by the intensive care unit late one night. I recognized the patient, a 17-year-old boy who had undergone bone marrow transplantation for leukemia and now had chronic interstitial fibrosis. The shy, bright smile I remembered from a previous admission was gone. According to the chart, he had developed progressive respiratory failure. His thin intubated body was squirming restlessly in the bed. The patient's father grabbed my hand and pointed to the ventilator, saying, "Stop, it's enough. He doesn't want this." I phoned the attending physician, an eminent hematologist, who said that the patient was expected to die in the next few days. I asked whether we should extubate the patient, as his father had requested, and sedate him. The hematologist said that the bone marrow transplant service wanted to continue intensive care; although he did not defend their decision, he deferred to it. We did agree on a Do Not Resuscitate (DNR) order. I gave some sedation to the patient and tried to comfort him and his family. The boy died just before I went off duty the next morning, more comfortable perhaps but by no means peaceful. The father asked me, "Why didn't they stop? Why?" Later, the attending physician told me that after my phone call, he couldn't get back to sleep. He said that he wanted to call me back to tell me to extubate the patient.

Like this boy's father, I kept asking, "Why?" Why were we so insistent on imposing our medical technology on dying patients? Why were decisions driven by physicians' personalities, hospital politics, research priorities, or staffing problems rather than by what was best for the patient? Why were we comfortable withholding cardiopulmonary resuscitation (CPR) but uneasy administering high doses of narcotics to a patient with intractable ventilatory failure? Although we spent much time on rounds talking about the use of immunosuppressive agents, antibiotics, ventilators, and a vast array of treatments, why did we avoid discussing what to do when such interventions were no longer helpful or appropriate?

My interest in medical ethics, and ultimately this book, grew from such perplexing cases as this and from the illnesses of family members and friends. From visiting my favorite aunt, who had developed multi-infarct dementia, I learned how hard it is to say that life is no longer worth living. She had become almost immobile, dependent on others for all her needs, and would often moan and shout when moved. But she would smile when I held her hands or stroked her cheek. Although mute most of the day, she laughed when I showed her pictures of my son and would ask me, "How old?" We could spend an hour looking at the same pictures over and over, with her repeating the same questions. But even as her family and I despaired over her deteriorating condition, it was not yet time to let her go. Life was still a precious gift, not yet an intolerable burden.

As I began writing and speaking about medical ethics, I learned that many colleagues shared my concerns. At professional meetings practitioners often tell me about cases whose ethical dilemmas still bother them. I have tried to keep in mind such physicians struggling to do what was right in difficult situations. This book features realistic cases that physicians can relate to their own experience. The goal of *Resolving Ethical Dilemmas* is to help clinicians resolve the mundane ethical issues in patient care as well as the dilemmas that keep them awake at night. In some cases there are persuasive reasons for a course of action, but in others the countervailing arguments are equally compelling. Yet even when the philosophic debate is closely balanced, physicians must act, choosing one plan of care or another.

This book grew in several ways beyond my initial work on decisions regarding life-sustaining interventions. First, over the years I realized that physicians need help with many ethical issues. Friends and colleagues often asked me why no one has written about impaired colleagues, about patients' requests to deceive insurance companies, and about the ethical problems in managed care.

Second, as the AIDS epidemic ravaged San Francisco, we grappled with new ethical dilemmas, such as the duty to provide care, access to experimental therapies, and the fear of nosocomial HIV infection. Third, a personal calamity broadened the issues of this book. On October 20, 1991, a firestorm raged through the Oakland hills. Our house and more than 2,000 others burned to the ground in a few hours. My wife and I felt sad, angry, frustrated, and overwhelmed by the task of putting our lives back together. It was hard to make any choices, much less informed or rational ones. Gradually I realized I was struggling with the same issues in this book as in life. Issues of autonomy, informed consent, and fiduciary responsibility took on increasing prominence. How can people make informed decisions when they are emotionally overwhelmed? Why must physicians act in their patients' best interests, even to their personal financial disadvantage, when insurance companies and other businesses have no such obligation?

Colleagues sometimes ask me why I work on such "depressing" topics. Although the issues are indeed somber, it is also a special privilege when patients and their families trust us with their grief, anger, and tranquility and show us how to endure turmoil and sorrow. An elderly patient who had hidden for months the severity of her bone cancer pain was delighted when I made a home visit, saying, "I am so glad I could show you my garden. Now you know why I want to die here, looking at my flowers." Another of my patients died from breast cancer and recurrent pleural effusions. She always cried and moaned as we tapped her effusions, even though she knew that her breathing would be easier. I wondered whether we were hurting her rather than helping her. After her death, I said to her son that it must have been hard for him to care for her. He replied softly, "Doc, it made me a better man." As physicians, we see the worst and the best of people. At times they are helpless and angry and make foolish decisions. But when confronting problems that are too large for them, people often become heroes. Ultimately I hope this book will help patients who struggle with such problems by guiding the physicians who care for them.

Bernard Lo

Preface to the Third Edition

Clinical ethics needs to keep up with dramatic changes in medical practice, with new research on ethical issues, and new ways of thinking about them. This third edition addresses many new developments.

- New federal health privacy regulations have created new legal obligations and have heightened attention to confidentiality. However, misunderstandings about these regulations have impeded good patient care.
- New research and reports about medical errors have led to new ways of thinking about mistakes, responsibility for errors, and disclosure of errors to patients or families.
- In transplantation the use of live donors (and unrelated live donors) has increased. Although these changes might increase the supply of organs for transplantation, they also heighten concerns about inadequate consent or excessive risk.
- In the wake of the SARS epidemic and anthrax outbreaks, clinicians can expect to face dilemmas when patients refuse to comply with public health recommendations.
- New regulations limiting residents' working hours have led to new dilemmas in teaching hospitals.
- A highly publicized legal case about withdrawing a feeding tube from a woman in a persistent vegetative state has highlighted disagreements over who is the appropriate surrogate for patients who lack decision-making capacity.

This edition also contains important revisions regarding genetic testing, gifts from drug companies, advance directives, and futile interventions. Important new material has been added to the chapters on specialties other than internal medicine. Chapter 37 has more discussion of adolescent confidentiality and consent for care. Chapter 38 discusses disclosure of provider-specific outcomes. Chapter 40 has new material on outpatient commitment and on use of psychiatric medications to enhance mental and social functioning in persons who do not have major psychiatric illness. Finally, the cases for discussion and the accompanying questions have been expanded.

It is a pleasure to thank the many colleagues and friends who have helped me better understand these difficult topics. I owe a special thanks to Leslie Wolf, Steve Pantilat, Sara Swenson, and Doug White, who through many discussions have shared their clear thinking, common sense, and expertise. Patti Zettler provided invaluable background research and skilled editing. David Cox, Elena Gates, and Kim Kirkwood have helped me better understand their respective specialties. Collaborations with Ann Alpers, Tom Bodenheimer, Tom Gallagher, Angela Holder, Mitchell Katz, Timothy Quill, and James Tulsky have enabled me to explore new territory and fresh ideas. Over the years, Nancy Dubler and Robert Steinbrook have been extraordinary friends and colleagues. I have been fortunate to work with thoughtful colleagues on the Greenwall Foundation Faculty Scholars Program, the Recombinant DNA Advisory Committee at the National Institutes of Health, the Institute of Medicine, the National Bioethics Advisory Commission, and the American College of Physicians Ethics Committee and End-of-life Care Panel. I am grateful for the opportunity to learn from them. At UCSF, I have benefited from residents, medical students, and fellows who ask hard questions and share their tough cases. My department chairman, Lee Goldman, has given unstinting support and encouragement. I am grateful to the Greenwall Foundation and the National Institutes of Mental Health for supporting some of the work that formed the basis of this revision.

To my family, I owe my greatest thanks. I am ever grateful to my parents, C.P. and Lucy Lo, and my aunt, Edith Chu, for the values they imparted to me. The physicians in my family, my sister and brother-in-law, Anna and Peter Davol, and my wife, Laurie Dornbrand, have provided shining examples of dedication to patients, in the face of tightening managed care constraints. Laurie is my best friend and my toughest critic, and she keeps me focused on the human stories behind the dilemmas. Our son Aaron keeps the computers at home functioning smoothly and doesn't hesitate to give definitive and thoughtful answers to the questions I agonize over. Our daughter, Maya, reminds me that good teachers need to be interesting and have pizazz. Her flair for the dramatic makes every day sparkle.

Bernard Lo

Fundamentals of Clinical Ethics

CHAPTER 1

An Approach to Ethical Dilemmas in Patient Care

"This case is really bothering me. I haven't been able to stop worrying about it. I'm just not sure what the right thing to do is." Cases that have no easy answers can perplex physicians. Strong reasons for a course of action might be balanced by cogent countervailing arguments. Common sense, clinical experience, being a good person, and having good intentions do not guarantee that physicians will respond appropriately to such dilemmas. Ethical dilemmas provoke powerful emotional responses, and strong emotions are often a clue to the presence of an unresolved ethical issue. However, emotions alone are not a satisfactory way of resolving ethical dilemmas. The following cases illustrate the range of ethical issues in clinical medicine.

CASE 1.1 Decisions about life-sustaining interventions.

An elderly woman with severe dementia develops pneumonia. Her daughter insists that hospitalization and administration of antibiotics would be pointless and that the patient would not want such "heroics." However, her son demands that she be treated because he believes that life is sacred. In this case the physician can be criticized no matter what she does, either for imposing unwanted interventions or for withholding beneficial therapy.

CASE 1.2 Confidentiality of HIV test results.

A 32-year-old man with a positive test for human immunodeficiency virus (HIV) antibodies refuses to notify his wife. "If she finds out, it would destroy our marriage." Should the physician notify the wife despite the patient's objections? Although maintaining patient confidentiality is important, it seems cruel not to warn the wife that she is at risk for a fatal infection.

CASE 1.3 Referrals in a managed care system.

A high-school basketball star suffers a knee injury and a probable meniscus tear. She belongs to a particular health maintenance organization (HMO) whose orthopedic surgeons have little experience with arthroscopic surgery. Should the physician tell the patient that more experienced surgeons are available outside the HMO? In this situation the HMO's financial interest and the physician's self-interest conflict with the physician's obligation to act in the patient's best interests.

In such cases physicians cannot avoid difficult decisions. This chapter describes how clinical ethics can help physicians deal with such dilemmas and presents an approach to resolving them. Specific ethical problems are discussed in detail in subsequent chapters.

WHAT IS CLINICAL ETHICS?

SOURCES OF MORAL GUIDANCE

Personal Moral Values

Physicians, like everyone, draw on many sources of moral guidance, including parental and family values, cultural traditions, and religious beliefs. These are the roots of a person's moral values and create a disposition to do the right actions. However, there are several reasons why they cannot be the only guidance for dilemmas in clinical ethics.

First, these personal moral values might not address important issues in clinical ethics: Often, doctors face many difficult ethical issues for the first time during their training and clinical practice. As shown in Case 1.1, laypeople have little education about such topics as life-sustaining treatment or surrogate decision making. In addition, personal moral values might offer conflicting advice on a particular situation. People often hold several fundamental beliefs that are in conflict. A physician might want both to alleviate the suffering of a dying patient and to respect the sacredness of life. For physicians to be perplexed about a dilemma in clinical ethics is not a blot on their characters or backgrounds.

Second, physicians have role-specific ethical obligations that go beyond their obligations as good citizens and good persons. Doctors have special duties to maintain confidentiality, as seen in Case 1.2, and to disclose information to patients during the informed consent process, as seen in Case 1.3. The moral values and upbringing that guide physicians' personal lives usually do not address special professional roles.

Third, physicians need to persuade others of their plans to resolve ethical dilemmas in patient care. Other health care workers, patients, and family members might have different religious or cultural backgrounds than the patient. Also, patients and their relatives might not understand the physician's professional codes of behavior. Clinical ethics analyzes the reasons that justify a particular course of action. People can be persuaded by cogent arguments, and people with different worldviews can reach an agreement in specific cases. Frequently, positions on ethical issues can be shown to be untenable because they are internally inconsistent or do not take into account countervailing arguments.

We next discuss the general types of justifications commonly offered for actions. Subsequent chapters analyze specific justifications for actions in various situations.

Claims of Conscience

Sometimes people explain their actions as a matter of conscience: to act otherwise would make them feel ashamed or guilty or violate their sense of wholeness or integrity. Conscience involves self-reflection and judgment about whether an action is right or wrong (1). For example, in Case 1.2, a physician might declare, "I couldn't live with myself if I didn't notify his wife."

Deeply held claims of conscience are generally honored. It would be dehumanizing to compel people to act in ways that violate their sense of integrity and responsibility. Claims of conscience, however, might not always resolve a dispute. Other people might cite their own conscience as a countervailing argument. Also, people might sometimes appeal to the conscience to rationalize a selfish or immoral action.

Claims of Rights

To explain their positions on ethical issues, people often appeal to rights, such as a "right to die," or a "right to health care." To philosophers, rights are justified claims that a person can make on others or on society (2). The language of rights is widespread in U.S. culture, yet appeals to rights are often controversial. Other people might deny that the right exists, or they might assert conflicting rights. For example, in Case 1.2, even if the seropositive patient has a right to confidentiality, the wife might have a countervailing right to know that she is at risk for a fatal infectious disease. Claims of rights are often used to end debates; however, the crucial issue is whether persuasive arguments support the existence of the right.

Distinguishing Morality and Ethics

The terms "morality" and "ethics" are often used interchangeably to refer to standards of right and wrong behavior. However, it is helpful to draw some distinctions. Moral choices ultimately rest on values or beliefs that cannot be proved but are simply accepted. Morality usually refers to conduct that conforms "to the accepted customs or conventions of a people (3)." A child usually learns from parents and religious leaders what a particular culture or group regards as correct and might accept it without deliberation. Ultimately, such fundamental moral beliefs are part of a person's character. Yet ordinary moral rules, which usually provide an adequate guide for daily conduct, might fail to provide clear direction in many clinical situations. For instance, moral precepts to respect the sanctity of life can be used in Case 1.1 to justify both continuing and withholding antibiotics.

In contrast to morality, ethics connotes deliberation and explicit arguments to justify particular actions. Ethics also refers to a branch of philosophy that deals with the "principles governing ideal human character" or to a professional code of conduct (3). To philosophers, ethics focuses on the reasons *why* an action is considered right or wrong. It asks people to justify their positions and beliefs by rational arguments that can persuade others.

HOW DOES CLINICAL ETHICS DIFFER FROM LAW?

The law, through statutes, regulations, and decisions in specific cases, also provides guidance on what physicians may or may not do. On many issues the law reflects an ethical consensus in society. Moreover, rulings by courts give reasons for decisions and therefore provide an analysis of pertinent issues. Hence, physicians should be familiar with what the law says regarding issues in clinical ethics. However, the law cannot provide definitive answers to ethical dilemmas.

First, the law, particularly the criminal law, sets only a minimally acceptable standard of conduct. It indicates what acts are so *wrong* that the physician will be held legally liable for committing them. In contrast, ethics focuses on the *right* or the best decision in a situation. From a legal perspective, pediatricians need only obtain the authorization of the parent or guardian to treat a child. However, professional ethics requires pediatricians to provide pediatric patients with pertinent information in ways that are developmentally appropriate and to obtain their assent for care (*see* Chapter 37). Furthermore, ethical standards require pediatricians to act with compassion and integrity; it is impossible for the law to enforce such standards. Second, the law explicitly grants physicians discretion in some situations. For instance, most states allow physicians to determine when a patient lacks decision-making capacity and, thus, when a surrogate should take over the role of making decisions with the physician (*see* Chapter 13). In these states, physicians must act on ethical and clinical considerations, not legal ones. Third, the law might provide no clear guide to action on certain topics. For example, the law provides scant guidance on the issue of disclosing genetic information to relatives when the patient objects to disclosure. Finally, law and ethics might conflict. Abortion is legal throughout the United States, and physician-assisted suicide is legal in the state of Oregon. However, both practices continue to be controversial ethically.

Furthermore, many people might regard actions that are prohibited by law to be ethical. In a few states the courts have rejected family decision making for incompetent patients who have not provided written advance directives or very specific oral directives. Ethically, however, the consensus is to respect surrogate decision making by concerned family members (*see* Chapter 12). In such conflicts, most physicians feel uncomfortable about simply following the letter of the law.

HOW DOES CLINICAL ETHICS DIFFER FROM PROFESSIONAL OATHS AND CODES?

Many physicians seek ethical guidance from professional codes, such as the Hippocratic Oath or the modern codes of ethics of the American Medical Association or the American College of Physicians (4,5). Although professional oaths and codes might provide helpful guidance for physician behavior, they have several shortcomings (6). First, they are unilateral declarations by groups of physicians, without any input from patients or the public. Codes of ethics and professional oaths do not acknowledge that society has granted autonomy and privileges to physicians and, therefore, has the right to insist on certain expectations. Second, the content of professional codes has been criticized. The Hippocratic tradition is highly paternalistic, granting patients little role in making decisions. For instance, it does not require physicians to disclose information to patients or allow them to make informed choices. Nor does the Hippocratic Oath enjoin physicians to be truthful with patients. Third, oaths and codes are often terse documents that articulate general precepts but fail to address many specific ethical issues. Resolving difficult cases generally requires additional analysis beyond such general guidance.

HOW CLINICAL ETHICS CAN HELP PHYSICIANS

Certain situations commonly recur in clinical practice. Physicians learn to recognize individual cases as examples of syndromes, such as "angina" or "hyponatremia (7)." Placing cases into categories allows physicians to organize relevant data and draw on experiences with similar cases. For each type of case, the physician learns to gather additional information, to anticipate associated problems or complications, and to develop an approach to the class of cases. To be sure, the approach needs to be modified in specific cases, because no two cases are identical and there are always exceptional cases. Nonetheless, a standard approach can manage the vast majority of cases. The more categories of cases physicians have studied, the better prepared they are for clinical practice.

Learning about clinical ethics can help physicians identify, understand, and resolve common ethical issues in patient care. By studying "teaching cases," physicians can gain vicarious experience in resolving specific dilemmas (8,9). Doctors can learn how to interpret ethical guidelines in particular situations, how to identify features of a case that distinguish it from other apparently similar cases, and how to know when exceptions to guidelines are justified.

IDENTIFY ETHICAL ISSUES

By studying realistic cases that illustrate common ethical problems, physicians may better recognize the ethical issues in their own cases. In some cases physicians might have only a vague uneasiness that important ethical issues are at stake. In other situations health care workers might be perplexed about difficult decisions but fail to identify problems as specifically ethical in nature, as opposed to issues of clinical management or interpersonal conflict. Thus, physicians need to be able to identify such fundamental ethical issues as assessment of decision-making capacity, advance directives, or confidentiality and to develop an approach to each issue.

UNDERSTAND AREAS OF ETHICAL CONSENSUS AND CONTROVERSY

On many issues, physicians, philosophers, and the courts agree on what should be done (6,10–12). Such agreement is often possible even when people disagree on the reasons for their actions (13). For example, it is well established that competent, informed patients may refuse interventions recommended by their physicians and that certain exceptions to confidentiality of medical information are appropriate both ethically and legally. Subsequent chapters point out areas of widespread ethical agreement as well as those areas of ongoing controversy.

Clinical ethics can indicate which actions are clearly right or wrong and which are controversial. Philosophers distinguish among actions that are obligatory, permissible, and wrong (14). In Case 1.3, it would be *obligatory* for physicians to tell the patient about other options for care (*see* Chapter 40). At the other extreme, it would be *wrong* for physicians to lie and tell the patient that the orthopedic care in this HMO is as good as the care elsewhere. Still other actions might be ethically *permissible* but not required. Some acts may be optional because the arguments for and against them are so evenly balanced that reasonable people may disagree. Other actions are optional in a different sense: It would be praiseworthy to perform them, but failure to do so would not be blameworthy. For instance, it would be heroic for a busy physician in Case 1.3 to devote extensive time to convincing the HMO to pay for orthopedic care outside the system, but he could not be blamed if he merely wrote a letter and made some phone calls on the athlete's behalf.

AN APPROACH TO ETHICAL DILEMMAS IN CLINICAL MEDICINE

A systematic approach to ethical problems helps ensure that no important considerations are overlooked and that similar cases are resolved consistently. The approach outlined in Table 1-1 includes three general steps: clarifying the facts of the case, analyzing the ethical issues, and resolving the dilemma. For any particular case, an experienced physician may modify the general approach.

TABLE 1-1

An Approach to Ethical Dilemmas in Clinical Medicine

Clarify the facts of the case.
    What is the clinical situation?
    Who is the primary decision maker?
    What are the concerns, values, and preferences of stakeholders?
Analyze the ethical issues.
    What are the pertinent ethical issues?
    How should ethical guidelines be applied to these issues?
Address psychosocial issues.
    What pragmatic issues complicate the case?
    Hold a team meeting.
    Meet with the patient or family.
Negotiate to reach agreement.
Seek assistance as needed.

CLARIFY THE FACTS OF THE CASE

Physicians first need to gather pertinent information about the medical situation and the ethical issues in the case.

What Is the Clinical Situation?

Sound ethical decision making requires accurate clinical information about the patient's diagnosis and prognosis, the options for care, and the benefits and risks of each alternative. In addition, psychosocial information is essential, such as the relationships among patient, son, and daughter in Case 1.1 or between the husband and wife in Case 1.2.

Who Is the Primary Decision Maker?

If the patient is competent, he or she makes decisions jointly with the physician, choosing among feasible alternatives. If the patient lacks decision-making capacity, an appropriate surrogate needs to be identified, generally a family member. Case 1.1 illustrates disagreements over who should serve as surrogate. Physicians need to understand the preferences of the patient or surrogate, as well as the reasoning behind their choices.

What Are the Concerns, Values, and Preferences of Stakeholders?

Other health care workers who provide direct care to the patient need to be involved in decisions. Nurses, house staff, and medical students are responsible for their actions when carrying out the attending physician's "orders." In addition, these health care workers have close relationships with patients and families, answer their questions, and explain plans for care. Other people might also have a stake in decisions. In Case 1.2, the patient's wife will be directly affected by the decision. Her viewpoint needs to be taken into account.

ANALYZE THE ETHICAL ISSUES

What Are the Pertinent Ethical Issues?

As with clinical medicine, how a case is framed often determines how it is resolved. Case 1.1 could be framed as a family disagreement. However, it is more fruitful to focus on more specific ethical issues:

- Has the patient provided trustworthy advance directives? (*See* Chapter 12.)
- Who should serve as surrogate decision maker for incompetent patients? (*See* Chapter 13.)

How Should Ethical Guidelines Be Applied to These Issues?

Framing ethical issues properly often suggests considerations to be taken into account and an approach to the situation. In Case 1.1, there are well-established guidelines to help the physicians and family determine what weight to give the patient's previous statements. If the patient had given trustworthy advance directives, they should be respected. People might agree on ethical guidelines but disagree over how to interpret them. For example, the son might agree with respecting the patient's choices but argue that her previous statements were too ambiguous to direct care. In Case 1.2, maintaining patient confidentiality conflicts with preventing harm to another person. Existing guidelines help the physician determine whether overriding confidentiality is justified in this situation (*see* Chapter 5). In Case 1.3, if the physician's arrangement with a managed care plan includes a "gag clause" that forbids her from disclosing interventions not covered by the plan, such clauses are considered unethical (*see* Chapter 6).

Difficult cases cannot be resolved by mechanically applying formal rules. Discretion and practical judgment are needed to interpret general guidelines in the particular circumstances of a case or to consider other factors.

ADDRESS PSYCHOSOCIAL ISSUES

Although analysis of ethical issues is essential, few dilemmas in clinical ethics are resolved solely by philosophical arguments. Good communication and interpersonal skills are also needed.

What Pragmatic Issues Complicate the Case?

Emotions, misunderstandings, interpersonal conflicts, and time pressures often complicate clinical dilemmas. Physicians need to identify and address such complicating factors. Indeed, many "ethical" dilemmas are settled by addressing these issues rather than through philosophical debate. Showing respect, concern, and compassion builds trust and helps resolve dilemmas.

Hold a Team Meeting

Team meetings can provide additional information about the patient's medical condition and the views of stakeholders. Health care workers from different clinical, personal, and cultural backgrounds can frequently point out hidden assumptions and value judgments, call attention to neglected issues, and suggest fresh alternatives. Moreover, a team meeting offers the opportunity to forge agreement on recommendations for care.

Meet with the Patient or Family

Physicians need to talk to patients and families to understand their concerns, needs, and values. Open-ended questions can elicit their perspective. In Case 1.1, the physician can ask, "As you think about your mother's condition, what concerns you the most? What do you hope for?" If such concerns can be addressed directly, the patient or family often accepts the physician's recommendations.

Patients or families might become confused if they hear mixed messages from different clinicians. Family conferences with all health care workers enhance consistent communication. If the health care team cannot agree on recommendations, the areas of agreement and disagreement need to be articulated carefully.

NEGOTIATE TO REACH AGREEMENT

Physicians need to try to reach a decision that is acceptable to both them and the patient or surrogate. Decisions also need to be consistent with the ethical guidelines discussed in this book and in the medical literature. To achieve this, physicians need to be flexible and be willing to compromise.

SEEK ASSISTANCE AS NEEDED

In difficult cases the physician may seek assistance from the hospital ethics committee or an ethics consultant (*see* Chapter 16). A second opinion from another physician not directly involved in the case might also be helpful. A chaplain, social worker, or nurse might have better rapport with the patient or family than the physician and be able to facilitate discussions.

In summary, physicians commonly face difficult ethical issues in clinical practice. Reading about such issues, thinking about them, and discussing them with colleagues can help physicians resolve ethical dilemmas. As with any clinical problem, following a systematic approach helps ensure that all pertinent considerations are taken into account. The important steps include gathering information about the medical situation and the preferences of the patient or surrogate and clarifying the salient ethical and pragmatic issues.

REFERENCES

1. Beauchamp TL, Childress JF. *Principles of biomedical ethics*, 4th ed. New York: Oxford University Press, 1994: 474–483.
2. Beauchamp TL, Childress JF. *Principles of biomedical ethics*, 4th ed. New York: Oxford University Press, 1994: 69–77.
3. *Webster's new dictionary of synonyms*. Springfield: Merriam-Webster Inc, 1984:547.
4. Council on Ethical and Judicial Affairs. *Code of medical ethics: current opinions with annotations*. Chicago: American Medical Association, 1998.
5. American College of Physicians. American college of physicians ethics manual. *Ann Intern Med* 1998;128: 576–594.
6. Veatch RM. *A theory of medical ethics*. New York: Basic Books Inc, 1981.
7. Kassirer JP. Diagnostic reasoning. *Ann Intern Med* 1989;110:893–900.
8. Lo B, Jonsen AR. Ethical dilemmas and the clinician. *Ann Intern Med* 1980;92:116–117.
9. Lo B, Quill T, Tulsky J. Discussing palliative care with patients. *Ann Intern Med* 1999;130:744–749.
10. President's Commission for the Study of Ethical Problems in Medicine and Biomedical and Behavioral Research. *Deciding to forego life-sustaining treatment*. Washington, DC: U.S. Government Printing Office, 1983.
11. Beauchamp TL, Childress JF. *Principles of biomedical ethics*, 4th ed. New York: Oxford University Press, 1994.
12. American College of Physicians. American college of physicians ethics manual. *Ann Intern Med* 1992; 117:947–960.
13. Jonsen AR, Toulmin S. *The abuse of casuistry: a history of moral reasoning*. Berkeley: University of California Press, 1988.
14. Beauchamp TL, Childress JF. *Principles of biomedical ethics*, 4th ed. New York: Oxford University Press, 1994:211.

CHAPTER 2

Overview of Ethical Guidelines

In clinical medicine ethical dilemmas arise because there are sound reasons for conflicting courses of action. In resolving ethical dilemmas, physicians need to refer to general maxims that inform choices and justify actions. This chapter provides an overview of guidelines in clinical ethics. Subsequent chapters discuss these ethical guidelines in detail and apply them to specific cases.

RESPECT FOR PERSONS

Treating patients with respect entails several ethical obligations. First, physicians must respect the medical decisions of persons who are autonomous (1). The term *autonomy* literally means "self-rule." Autonomous people act intentionally, are informed, and are free from interference and control by others. They should be allowed to shape their lives and control their destinies. The concept of autonomy includes the ideas of self-determination, independence, and freedom. In addition to respecting the decisions of autonomous patients, doctors should take steps to promote patient autonomy, as by disclosing information and helping patients deliberate.

With regard to health care, autonomy justifies the doctrine of informed consent (*see* Chapter 3). Informed consent has several specific aspects. Informed, competent patients may refuse unwanted medical interventions. In the case of surgery and invasive procedures, such refusals respect patients' bodily integrity. In addition, patients may choose among medically feasible alternatives. Important clinical choices need not involve a major bodily invasion. For instance, choosing whether to have an x-ray or choosing among several drugs for a condition do not implicate the patient's bodily integrity in a manner similar to surgery. Competent, informed patients have the right to make choices that conflict with the wishes of family members or the recommendations of their physicians.

A person's autonomy is not absolute and may be justifiably restricted for several reasons. If a person is incapable of making informed decisions, trying to respect his or her autonomy might be less important than acting in his or her best interests. Autonomy might also be constrained by the needs of other individuals or society at large. A person is not free to act in ways that violate other people's autonomy, harm others, or impose unfair claims on society's resources.

A second meaning of respect for persons goes beyond respecting autonomy. Many patients are not autonomous because illness or medication impairs their decision-making capacity. Physicians should still treat them as persons with individual characteristics, preferences, and values. Decisions should respect their preferences and values, so far as they are known. In addition, all patients, whether autonomous or not, should be treated with compassion and dignity. Thus, respect for persons includes responding to the patient's suffering with caring, empathy, and attention.

Third, respect for persons is related to other ethical guidelines, such as avoiding misrepresentation, maintaining confidentiality, and keeping promises. Breaches of these other guidelines show disrespect for patients and also compromise their self-determination. There are additional reasons for these other guidelines, as we will discuss.

MAINTAIN CONFIDENTIALITY

Maintaining the confidentiality of medical information respects patient privacy. It also encourages people to seek treatment and to discuss their problems frankly. In addition, confidentiality protects patients from harms that might occur if information about psychiatric illness, sexual preference, or alcohol or drug use were widely known. Patients and the public expect physicians to keep medical information confidential. Maintaining confidentiality, however, is not an absolute duty. In some situations physicians need to override confidentiality in order to protect third parties from harm (*see* Chapter 5).

AVOID DECEPTION AND NONDISCLOSURE

Truth telling—avoiding lies—is a cornerstone of social interaction. If people cannot depend on others to tell the truth, no one will make agreements or contracts. Physicians also might mislead patients without technically lying, for example, by giving partial information that is literally true but deceptive. Deception violates the autonomy of people who are deceived because it causes them to make decisions on the basis of false premises. To cover these broader issues, this book uses the term "deception" rather than "lying." In addition, physicians may withhold from patients information about their diagnosis or prognosis. Physicians may withhold information to protect patients from bad news. However, patients cannot make informed decisions about their medical care if they do not receive the information about their condition that they would like to have.

KEEP PROMISES

Promises generate expectations in other people, who in turn modify their plans on the assumption that promises will be kept. The very concept of promises is undermined if people are free to break them. It is unfair for someone to expect others to honor their promises, but to break his or her own. Keeping promises also enhances trust in both the individual physician and the medical profession. Furthermore, promises relieve patients' anxiety about the future by providing reassurance that doctors will not abandon them.

ACT IN THE BEST INTERESTS OF PATIENTS

The guideline of nonmaleficence, or "do no harm," forbids physicians from providing ineffective therapies or from acting selfishly or maliciously (2). This oft-cited precept, however, provides only limited guidance, because many beneficial interventions also entail serious risks and side effects. Literally, doing no harm would preclude such treatments as surgery and cancer chemotherapy.

The guideline of *beneficence* requires physicians to take positive actions for the benefit of patients (*see* Chapter 4). Because patients do not possess medical expertise and might be vulnerable owing to illnesses, they rely on physicians to provide sound advice and to promote their well-being. Physicians encourage such trust. For these reasons, physicians have a fiduciary duty to act in the best interests of their patients.

UNWISE DECISIONS BY PATIENTS

Acting in patients' best interests might conflict with respecting their informed choices, as when patients' refusals of care might thwart their own goals or cause them serious harm. For example, a young man with asthma may refuse mechanical ventilation for reversible respiratory failure. Simply accepting such refusals, in the name of respecting autonomy, would constitute a constricted view of responsibility. Physicians need to listen to patients, educate them, try to persuade them to accept beneficial treatment, or negotiate a mutually acceptable compromise. If disagreements persist, the patient's informed choices and view of best interests should prevail.

PATIENTS WHO LACK DECISION-MAKING CAPACITY

The choices and preferences of many patients who lack decision-making capacity are unknown or unclear. In this situation, respecting autonomy is not pertinent. Instead, physicians should be guided by the patient's best interests (*see* Chapter 4).

CONFLICTS OF INTEREST

Physicians should act in the patient's best interests rather than in their own self-interest when conflicts of interest occur (*see* Chapters 29–36). Patients trust their physicians to act on their behalf and feel betrayed if that trust is abused. In a potential conflict of interest, physicians should consider how patients, the public, and colleagues would react if they knew about the situation. Even the appearance of a conflict of interest might damage trust in the individual physician and in the profession.

ALLOCATE RESOURCES JUSTLY

The term "justice" is used in a general sense to mean fairness—that is, people should get what they deserve. In addition, people who are situated equally should also be treated equally. It is important to act consistently in cases that are similar in ethically relevant ways. Otherwise, decisions would be arbitrary, biased, and unfair. More precisely, people who are similar in ethically relevant respects should be treated similarly, and people who differ in ethically significant ways should be treated differently. To make this formal statement of justice operational, the physician would need to specify what counts as an ethically relevant distinction and what it means to treat people similarly.

In health care settings, "justice" usually refers to the allocation of health care resources. Allocation decisions are unavoidable because resources are limited and could be spent on other social goods, such as education or the environment, instead of on health care. Ideally, allocation decisions should be made as public policy and set by government officials or judges, according to appropriate procedures. Physicians should participate in public debates about allocation and help set policies. In general, however, rationing medical care at the bedside should be avoided because it might be inconsistent, discriminatory, and ineffective. At the bedside, physicians usually should act as patient advocates within constraints set by society and sound practice (*see* Chapter 30). In some cases, however, two patients might compete for the same limited resources, such as physician time or a bed in intensive care. When this occurs, physicians should ration their time and resources according to patients' medical needs and the probability and degree of benefit.

THE USE OF ETHICAL GUIDELINES

Having summarized guidelines for clinical ethics, we next discuss how physicians should use them in specific cases. This book uses the term *guidelines* to connote that ethical generalizations cannot be mechanically or rigidly applied but need to be used in particular cases with discretion and judgment. Guidelines are derived from decisions made in specific cases as well as from moral theories (3,4). In turn, guidelines shape decisions in similar cases in the future. However, guidelines might be difficult to apply in new cases for several reasons.

GUIDELINES NEED TO BE INTERPRETED IN THE CONTEXT OF SPECIFIC CASES

The meaning or force of a guideline might not be clear in a particular case. Uncertainty and case-by-case variation are inherent in clinical medicine. Furthermore, patients have different priorities and goals for care. A crucial issue is whether the case to be decided can be distinguished in ethically meaningful ways from previous cases to which the guideline was applied. Unforeseen or novel cases might point out the shortcomings of an existing guideline and suggest that it needs to be modified or an exception made.

EXCEPTIONS TO GUIDELINES MIGHT BE APPROPRIATE

Guidelines are not absolute. A particular case, particularly unforeseen or novel cases, might have distinctive features that justify making an exception to a guideline (3). To ensure fairness, physicians who make an exception to a guideline should justify their decisions. The justification should apply not only to the specific case under consideration but also to all similar cases faced by other physicians. Some philosophers regard guidelines simply as rules of thumb that provide advice but are not binding. However, if people can set aside guidelines too easily, decisions might be inconsistent. Many philosophers regard ethical guidelines as *prima facie* binding: They should be followed unless they conflict with stronger obligations or guidelines or unless there are compelling reasons to make an exception (5). *Prima facie* guidelines are more binding than mere rules of thumb. The burden of proof is on those who claim that an exception to the guideline is warranted. Furthermore, when *prima facie* guidelines are overridden, they are not simply ignored. People often experience regret or even remorse that guidelines are being broken. Thus, people should minimize the extent to which *prima facie* guidelines are violated and mitigate the adverse consequences of doing so.

DIFFERENT GUIDELINES MIGHT CONFLICT

In many situations following one ethical guideline would require the physician to compromise another guideline. Respecting a patient's refusal of treatment might clash with acting in the patient's best interests. Maintaining confidentiality might conflict with protecting third parties from harm. Allocating resources equitably might conflict with doing what is best for an individual patient. The practice of medicine would be much easier if there were a fixed hierarchy of ethical guidelines—for example, if patient autonomy always took priority over beneficence. However, life is not so simple. In some clinical situations, respecting a patient's wishes should be paramount, whereas in others a patient's best interests should prevail. Physicians need to understand why an ethical guideline should take priority in some situations but not in others.

The ability to make prudent decisions in specific situations has been described as *discernment* or *practical wisdom*. Discernment involves an understanding of how ethical guidelines are relevant in a variety of situations and to the particular case at hand (6).

PRINCIPLES, RULES, AND DUTIES

This book uses the term guidelines to refer to ethical generalizations that guide action, because other terms, such as principles, rules, and duties, have undesirable connotations. According to the dictionary, *principle* connotes a "basis for reasoning or a guide for conduct or procedure (7)." Many philosophers, however, use the term in a more restricted sense, to refer only to a comprehensive ethical theory that explains how to resolve conflicts among different precepts (8,9). A unified theory would also presumably provide clear, specific rules for action and a justification of those rules (8).

Philosophers have devoted considerable effort to developing comprehensive ethical theories. The two main types of ethical theory are consequentialist and deontological. *Consequentialist* theories judge the rightness or wrongness of actions by their consequences. Utilitarianism, the most prominent consequentialist theory, considers actions and rules appropriate when the overall benefits to all parties outweigh the overall harms. For instance, a utilitarian would consider it justified to tell a lie, breach confidentiality, or break a promise if, on the whole, the benefits of doing so outweigh the harms. In contrast, *deontological* theories claim that the rightness or wrongness of an action depends on more factors than the consequences of an action. To a deontologist, actions such as telling a lie, breaching confidentiality, and breaking promises are inherently wrong. They would be morally suspect even if they produced no harmful consequences or led to beneficial ones.

Comprehensive theories of clinical ethics, however, are problematic (10). Utilitarian theories are flawed because they condone seemingly harmful actions that are not detected. For example, utilitarians might condone breaking a promise when no one else knows it is broken. Furthermore, acts that maximize the benefits for society as a whole may be considered acceptable even though they impose grave harms on individual persons. In a utilitarian analysis, harms to individuals might be outweighed by a sufficiently large benefit to society. Such an inequitable distribution of benefits and harms might be unfair.

Deontological theories can be criticized because they cannot provide a satisfactory account of which principles or rules take priority over others in cases of conflict. For example, deontological theories would have difficulty determining whether beneficence or confidentiality would prevail when a patient with human immunodeficiency virus (HIV) infection refused to notify his wife that she is at risk.

Detailed and lucid expositions of ethical theories as well as their critiques are available (10). Many writers, myself included, believe that a comprehensive and consistent theory of clinical ethics cannot be developed (11). This book avoids reference to ethical theories and to the term principle not only because of these conceptual problems but also because ethical theories and principles are too abstract to provide guidance to physicians in specific cases.

The term *rule* is used in ethics to refer to generalizations that are narrower in scope than principles. The term is helpful because it focuses on individual conduct in specific situations, rather than on abstract generalizations. However, rules are generally regarded as binding, often prohibiting certain behaviors (3). In common language, "rule" might imply restrictions on individual conduct in order to maintain order in the group or for the sake of a goal (7). For example, we speak of rules for a game or for an institution. The implication might be that rules can be applied in a straightforward manner, as when disputes in a game are settled by referring to the rules. In this sense, rules may be arbitrarily imposed in order to establish clear expectations for everyone. For example, rules for visiting hours may be established in a hospital to provide clear guidance for conduct, without any claim that one choice of hours is superior to another. However, the term "rule" is misleading in clinical ethics, because exceptions need to be made and because guidelines are not arbitrary conventions but reflect deeply held values.

Finally, this book avoids the term *duty*, which might connote legal as well as ethical obligations. Ethical obligations, however, differ from legal duties imposed by legislation, regulations, or court rulings, as Chapter 22 discusses.

OTHER APPROACHES TO ETHICS

Because ethical theories and principles often do not help people resolve conflicts, other approaches to clinical ethics have been suggested (10,11).

CASUISTRY

Instead of constructing or relying on theories, some writers focus on how to resolve specific cases (3,12–14). According to these writers, people resolve dilemmas in everyday life by "looking at the concrete details of particular cases (15)." In this view, moral rules are not absolute; they merely create presumptions that may be rebutted, depending on the particular circumstances. The strategy is to compare a given case with clear-cut, paradigmatic cases. The key issue is whether the given case so closely resembles the paradigmatic case that it should be resolved in a similar manner or whether it can be distinguished and therefore treated differently (3). In some cases the application of ethical maxims will be clear-cut. In more difficult cases it might be unclear whether a guideline applies or different guidelines might provide conflicting advice. Proponents of case-based ethics emphasize the need for what Aristotle called practical wisdom, the ability to make appropriate decisions given the particular circumstances of the case. The essential issue is "how closely the present circumstances resemble those of the earlier precedent cases for which this type of argument was originally devised (16)." In educational terms, casuistry teaches by case analyses, starting with paradigmatic cases in which principles clearly apply and moving to complex, ambiguous cases over which reasonable people may disagree.

A case-based approach to clinical ethics takes into account the complexity of real-life decisions and offers readers a vicarious experience in resolving ethical problems (17). Dilemmas in clinical ethics generally present as specific decisions in patient care, not as clashes of abstract philosophical principles. This book emphasizes how to approach difficult cases and how to weigh different considerations in reaching a decision.

Case-based analyses, however, face a serious challenge: to provide a convincing basis for weighing some factors more heavily than others in reaching a decision. Indeed, casuistry runs the risk of *ad hoc* reasoning and inconsistent decisions. To avoid such pitfalls, this book will continually refer back to the ethical guidelines described in this chapter and explain why particular factors will be decisive in some situations, while different considerations will weigh most heavily in other circumstances.

AN ETHIC OF CARING

Feminist writers argue that principles and rules provide an incomplete and inadequate conception of ethics (18,19). In this perspective, rule-based morality gives insufficient attention to maintaining or restoring relationships among individuals and avoiding interpersonal conflicts. In this view, responding to the needs and welfare of specific individuals might be more important than acting in accord with abstract standards. For example, when family members make decisions for an incompetent patient, traditional ethics might undervalue the need for the family members to get along with one another and live with the consequences of their decisions (20). In some situations it might be more important to prevent serious family disputes than to follow the patient's prior directives. Such caring and responsiveness is often claimed to be a typically "feminine" orientation, as contrasted with a "masculine" orientation toward rules and principles. Empirical studies, however, do not support the hypothesis of gender-related orientations to ethics (21).

The emphasis on caring and on the well-being of others is welcome in medicine and other helping professions. Caring is essential in the doctor–patient relationship, and sympathy and compassion might be more important in clinical practice than following ethical guidelines mechanically. However, it is also important to move beyond a sensitivity to these issues to a detailed description of how caring should impact on decisions in specific clinical situations. Furthermore, attending to the welfare of others might conflict with other important ethical imperatives, such as respecting the patient's autonomy.

VIRTUE ETHICS

Some writers point out that merely following guidelines might lead to a thin view of ethics. Physicians might perform the right actions but lack the spirit that should animate the medical profession. Virtue ethics emphasizes that the physician's characteristics are ultimately more important than the doctor's specific actions and their congruence with ethical principles (17). In this perspective the essential questions are: Is the doctor a good physician? A good person? In one such view, the virtues of a good physician include fidelity, compassion, fortitude, temperance, integrity, and self-effacement (17).

Virtue ethics is helpful because it emphasizes the importance of such qualities as compassion, dedication, and altruism in physicians. Furthermore, in some extremely complicated or unique situations, the physician's integrity might be a crucial factor in resolving dilemmas. However, virtue ethics also has serious limitations because it lacks specifics on what the doctor should do in particular circumstances. A virtuous person might still commit wrong actions. Also, virtues might conflict with each other. In a given case, some people may believe that following a general guideline demonstrates the physician's integrity, while others believe that it would be compassionate to make an exception to the guideline.

In summary, ethical guidelines include showing respect for persons, avoiding deception, maintaining confidentiality, keeping promises, acting in the best interests of patients, and allocating resources justly. These guidelines need to be applied to particular cases with discretion and judgment. Subsequent chapters discuss these guidelines in detail.

REFERENCES

1. Beauchamp TL, Childress JF. *Principles of biomedical ethics*, 4th ed. New York: Oxford University Press, 1994:120–132.
2. Jonsen AR. Do no harm. *Ann Intern Med* 1978;88:827–832.
3. Sunnstein CR. *Legal reasoning and political conflict*. New York: Oxford University Press, 1996.

4. Beauchamp TL, Childress JF. *Principles of biomedical ethics*, 4th ed. New York: Oxford University Press, 1994:3–43.
5. Beauchamp TL, Childress JF. *Principles of biomedical ethics*, 4th ed. New York: Oxford University Press, 1994:33–34.
6. Beauchamp TL, Childress JF. *Principles of biomedical ethics*, 4th ed. New York: Oxford University Press, 1994:468–469.
7. *Webster's new dictionary of synonyms*. Springfield: Merriam-Webster Inc., 1984:638.
8. Clouser KD, Gert B. A critique of principlism. *J Med Philos* 1990;15:219–236.
9. Beauchamp TL, Childress JF. *Principles of biomedical ethics*, 4th ed. New York: Oxford University Press, 1994:100–109.
10. Beauchamp TL, Childress JF. *Principles of biomedical ethics*, 4th ed. New York: Oxford University Press, 1994:44–119.
11. Pellegrino ED. The metamorphosis of medical ethics: a 30-year retrospective. *JAMA* 1992;269:1158–1162.
12. Toulmin S. The tyranny of principles. *Hastings Center Rep* 1981;11:31–39.
13. Jonsen AR, Toulmin S. *The abuse of casuistry: a history of moral reasoning*. Berkeley: University of California Press, 1988.
14. Arras JD. Getting down to cases: the revival of casuistry in bioethics. *J Med Philos* 1991;16:29–51.
15. Jonsen AR, Toulmin S. *The abuse of casuistry: a history of moral reasoning*. Berkeley: University of California Press, 1988:30.
16. Jonsen AR, Toulmin S. *The abuse of casuistry: a history of moral reasoning*. Berkeley: University of California Press, 1988:35.
17. Lo B, Jonsen AR. Ethical dilemmas and the clinician. *Ann Intern Med* 1980;92:116–117.
18. Gilligan C. *In a different voice: psychological theory and women's development*. Cambridge: Harvard University Press, 1982.
19. Gilligan C, Ward JV, Taylor JM, eds. *Mapping the moral domain: a contribution of women's thinking to psychological theory and education*. Cambridge: Harvard University Press, 1988.
20. Alpers A, Lo B. Avoiding family feuds: responding to surrogates' demands for life-sustaining treatment. *J Law, Med Ethics* 1999;27:69–73.
21. Bebeau MJ, Brabeck M. Ethical sensitivity and moral reasoning among men and women in the professions. In: Brabeck MM, ed. *Who cares? Theory, research, and educational implications of the ethic of care*. New York: Praeger, 1989:144–163.

ANNOTATED BIBLIOGRAPHY

1. Beauchamp TL, Childress JF. *Principles of biomedical ethics*, 5th ed. New York: Oxford University Press, 2001. Comprehensive and lucid presentation of the philosophical foundations of biomedical ethics. Excellent references for further reading in the philosophical literature.
2. Pellegrino ED. The metamorphosis of medical ethics: a 30-year retrospective. *JAMA* 1992;269:1158–1162. Insightful review and critique of various approaches to medical ethics.
3. Jonsen AR, Toulmin S. *The abuse of casuistry: a history of moral reasoning*. Berkeley: University of California Press, 1988. Offers a cogent rationale for a case-based approach to ethics and provides an overview of the accomplishments and downfall of casuistry.

CHAPTER 3

Informed Consent

Informed consent requires physicians to share decision-making power with patients. Many physicians, however, are skeptical about informed consent or are even hostile to it. Some believe that it is impossible because patients can never understand medical situations as well as doctors. Other physicians regard informed consent as a meaningless legal ritual because they can almost always persuade patients to follow their recommendations. In addition, some patients do not want to participate in decision making, as in the following case.

CASE 3.1 Reluctance to make a decision.

Mr. T was an 88-year-old man with severe chronic obstructive pulmonary disease *(COPD), coronary artery disease, and peptic ulcer disease. He developed an adenocarcinoma of the lung, which could be treated with surgery or radiation therapy. His physician was reluctant to recommend surgery because of the patient's increased operative risk. In addition, his COPD was so severe that he might be dyspneic after a pneumonectomy. When his doctor discussed alternatives for treatment, Mr. T said, "Do what you think is best. You're the doctor."*

In this case only Mr. T can determine if the chance of being cured of cancer is worth the risk of severe dyspnea, but Mr. T apparently does not want to make decisions. How should the physician proceed? This chapter discusses the definition of informed consent, its justification, its requirements, problems with informed consent, and ways in which physicians can promote shared decision making with patients.

WHAT IS INFORMED CONSENT?

Discussions about informed consent are often confusing because people use this term in different senses.

AGREEMENT WITH THE PHYSICIAN'S RECOMMENDATIONS

Patients usually agree with physicians' recommendations. Such an agreement is particularly common in an acute illness, when the goals of care are clear, one option is superior, the benefits are great, and the risks are small. For example, a patient who suffers a wrist fracture almost always agrees to a cast. In such situations informed consent seems tantamount to obtaining the patient's agreement to the proposed intervention. Physicians often speak of "consenting the patient," implying that it is a foregone conclusion that the patient will agree.

RIGHT TO REFUSE INTERVENTIONS

Another view of informed consent is that patients have an ethical and legal right to be free of unwanted medical interventions. Hence, competent patients have the power to reject their physicians' recommendations about care.

CHOICE AMONG ALTERNATIVES

A broader view of informed consent holds that patients should have the positive right to choose among feasible options in addition to the negative right to refuse unwanted interventions. For instance, Case 3.1 involves not only the right to refuse surgery but also a choice between surgery and radiation therapy.

SHARED DECISION MAKING

A still more comprehensive view is that informed consent is a process of shared decision making by the physician and patient (1). Both parties need to discuss the issues and reach a mutually acceptable decision. Through repeated discussions, physicians can educate patients about their conditions and the alternatives for care, help them deliberate, make recommendations, and to try to persuade them to accept the recommendations (2).

REASONS FOR INFORMED CONSENT AND SHARED DECISION MAKING

Several ethical and pragmatic reasons justify a broader conception of informed consent (3–5).

RESPECT PATIENT SELF-DETERMINATION

People want to make decisions about their bodies and health care in accordance with their values and goals. Decision-making power in health care is important because the stakes can be high. One court expressed this idea in sweeping terms, declaring, "Every human being of adult years and sound mind has a right to determine what shall be done with his own body (6)."

Patient choice should be promoted because in most clinical settings, different goals and approaches are possible, outcomes are uncertain, and an intervention might cause both benefit and harm (7). Individuals place different values on health, medical care, and risk. Some patients are wary about the side effects of medication, while others want to try risky therapies that promise better outcomes. Lung cancer patients are generally concerned about the short-term morbidity and mortality of surgery as well as long-term survival and cure (8). Older patients often prefer radiation therapy, which has a lower 5-year survival rate but also a lower likelihood of death during treatment. Physicians cannot accurately predict patients' preferences. For example, patients with newly diagnosed cancer are more likely than physicians, nurses, and the general public to prefer intensive chemotherapy with little chance of cure (9).

ENHANCE THE PATIENT'S WELL-BEING

The goal of medical care is to enhance patient well-being, which can be judged only in terms of the patient's goals and values. The patient's values are particularly important when various treatment approaches have very different characteristics or complications and involve trade-offs between short-term and long-term outcomes, when one of the options carries a small chance of a grave outcome, when the patient has unusual aversions toward risk or certain outcomes, and when there is uncertainty and disagreement among physicians (10). The choice between surgery and radiation in Case 3.1 has many of these characteristics. In addition, participation in decisions might have other beneficial consequences for patients, such as increased sense of control, self-efficacy, and adherence to plans for care.

FULFILL LEGAL REQUIREMENTS

Physicians might consider informed consent "a nuisance, an alien imposition of the legal system that must be tolerated . . . but can be dealt with in relatively mechanical ways, such as making sure patients sign consent forms before major procedures (11)." Similarly, many patients are cynical about informed consent. In one study nearly 80% of patients said that the purpose of informed consent was to protect the physician (12).

REQUIREMENTS FOR INFORMED CONSENT

Ethically and legally, informed consent requires discussions of pertinent information, obtaining the patient's agreement to the plan of care, and freedom from coercion (5).

INFORMATION TO DISCUSS WITH PATIENTS

Physicians need to discuss with patients information that is relevant to the decision at hand (Table 3-1). Most court decisions and legal commentaries use the term "disclose," and, when summarizing legal doctrine, this book also uses this term. In general, however, we prefer the term "discuss" to emphasize that a dialogue between the physician and patient is preferable to a monologue by the physician.

Patients need to know the *nature* of the intervention, the expected *benefits*, the *risks*, and the likely *consequences*. In general, risks that are common knowledge, already known to the patient, of trivial impact, or very infrequent do not need to be discussed. For instance, patients do not need to be told about the nature of venipuncture, the rare risk of infection, or the minor discomfort of hematomas. On the other hand, for invasive interventions, courts have ruled that physicians need to discuss serious but rare risks, such as death or stroke. In Case 3.1, the physician should discuss with Mr. T the risks of surgical mortality, prolonged hospitalization, and long-term shortness of breath following surgery.

The risks of an intervention might include psychosocial as well as biomedical risks. For human immunodeficiency virus (HIV) and genetic testing, the pertinent risks are not the risks of venipuncture, but the risks of stigma and discrimination in employment or health insurance. Many states have enacted special provisions, requiring written informed consent and pretest counseling for HIV testing (13).

Patients also need to understand the *alternatives* to the proposed test or treatment and their risks, benefits, and consequences. In particular, the alternative of no intervention needs to be discussed. If a patient declines the recommended intervention, the physician needs to explain the adverse consequences of the refusal. In one case a court ruled that when a woman refuses a Pap smear, the physician needs to discuss how the test could diagnose cancer at an early stage and avert death through early treatment (14).

It is controversial whether physicians need to disclose information about themselves that affect patient outcomes (*see* Chapter 38). For example, patients might find it pertinent to know the *outcomes* of a surgical procedure at a given institution or by a particular surgeon, as contrasted to outcomes reported in the literature. Some states make such individualized outcome data for cardiac surgeons available to the public. In addition, the surgeon's *experience* might be pertinent, because increased volume is associated with better outcomes for some operations and surgeons have a "learning curve" for new procedures. Another issue that patients might find pertinent is the *role of trainees* in their care, particularly with invasive or surgical procedures. As Chapter 36 discusses in detail, most patients want to know about the role of trainees and agree to their participation. The physician's own health might also be pertinent to patient decisions. For instance, a patient might wish to seek a different provider if a physician is impaired because of alcoholism, dementia, or other medical conditions.

TABLE 3-1

Information to Discuss with Patients

The nature of the test or treatment.
The benefits, risks, and consequences of the intervention.
The alternatives and their benefits, risks, and consequences.

Although some courts have ruled that physician-specific experience needs to be disclosed for some operations, other courts have not (15). If disclosure is guided by what a reasonable physician would disclose, disclosure of such information would not be legally required. However, from the ethical perspective of providing patients pertinent information to make informed decisions, such disclosure is desirable.

Physicians must take the initiative in discussing information rather than wait for patients to ask questions. Patients, who have far less medical knowledge than physicians, might not even know what questions to pose. Empirical studies show that physicians often fail to provide sufficient information for patients to make informed decisions (16).

The extent of the disclosure will depend on the clinical context. For conditions such as appendicitis or pneumonia, or if there is only one realistic option and it is highly effective, relatively safe, and strongly recommended, a detailed consent process might be of little benefit to patients (17).

It is controversial whether physicians need to inform patients of alternatives for care that they do not believe are medically indicated. Obviously, physicians do not need to mention treatments that have no scientific rationale, would provide no medical benefit, or are known to be ineffective or harmful, such as laetrile for cancer; nor do physicians need to discuss complementary or alternative medicines that they do not accept as valid. However, physicians should inform patients of alternatives that other reasonable physicians would recommend. Thus, a physician who believed that surgery was the best approach to Mr. T's lung cancer still ought to inform him about the option of radiation therapy.

Discussions about the proposed test or treatment and the alternatives should be conducted by the attending physician or by the physician performing the intervention, the proposed test or treatment, and the alternatives (18). Such discussions should not be delegated to nurses, medical students, or house officers. Some busy physicians who have already discussed an intervention with the patient during an office visit will ask a nurse or house officer to obtain the patient's signature on a consent form in the hospital. Although this approach is understandable because it saves time, it might be problematic if the patient has questions that an inexperienced physician or a nurse cannot answer.

PATIENT AGREEMENT WITH THE TREATMENT PLAN

Patients must agree with the intended plan of care. For major interventions, such as surgery, obtaining explicit written authorization is standard. Written consent signals the patient that the decision is important. In ambulatory care, oral agreement to the plan of care is usual because the risks are lower and because patients can choose to discontinue medications (19,20).

AGREEMENT SHOULD BE VOLUNTARY

Coercion and manipulation invalidate consent because they preclude free choices by patients. Coercion involves threats that are intended to control patients' behavior and that patients find irresistible (21). An example is a threat to discharge a patient from the hospital if he does not agree with the recommended care. Manipulation of information might also thwart informed decisions. For example, physicians might misrepresent the patient's condition or the nature of the proposed intervention. Coercion and manipulation contrast with persuasion, which is an attempt to convince the patient to act in a certain way by providing rational arguments and accurate data (21). Persuasion respects patient autonomy and, indeed, enhances it by improving the patient's understanding of the situation and the options.

Certain constraints on patients' choices are not coercive (4). The patient's prognosis might be so grim that all alternatives are undesirable and the patient has no "real choice." Warnings by the physician about the outcomes of choices or about the natural history of the illness are also not coercive because the physician makes no threat to bring about undesirable outcomes. Indeed, physicians would be remiss if they did not point out to patients the consequences of unwise choices.

Patients might lack the capacity to make informed decisions, as discussed in Chapter 10. For such patients, advance directives or appropriate surrogates should guide decisions (*see* Chapters 12 and 13).

OBJECTIONS TO INFORMED CONSENT

PATIENTS DO NOT UNDERSTAND MEDICAL INFORMATION

Patients often do not recall information they have discussed with physicians, even basic information about the proposed treatment. In a study of cancer patients who had just consented to treatment, only 60% understood the purpose and nature of the treatment, 55% could name any complication, and 27% could name an alternative treatment. Furthermore, just 40% had read the consent form carefully (22). Many physicians have had similar experiences with patients and conclude that patients are unable to make decisions in an informed way.

Physicians, however, are partly to blame for patients' poor comprehension. Doctors often use technical jargon that is incomprehensible to laypeople. Informed consent forms are usually difficult to read and understand (23). More importantly, physicians often fail to provide patients with basic information about interventions (19,24,25).

PATIENTS DO NOT WANT TO MAKE DECISIONS

As shown in Case 3.1, some patients might not want to make decisions but instead defer to physicians or family members. This might be particularly true of patients from cultures where informed consent and autonomy are not as important as in the United States. Several older empirical studies indicate that although patients generally want information about their condition and treatment, many do not want to make decisions. In one study almost all hospitalized patients regarded the physician as the decision maker (24). Patients wanted information about plans for care in order to know what was going to happen and how to carry out those plans effectively. However, the only patients playing an active role in decision making were those with chronic diseases who needed to take medications regularly and to report changes in their condition. In ambulatory settings, although most patients want information about their illness, approximately one-half of the patients want to defer decisions to physicians (12,26). Many patients, however, want to play a more active role in decisions later, after they have experience with the prescribed medications (26). More recent studies suggest that about two-thirds of patients want to share decision making with physicians (27,28).

PATIENTS MAKE DECISIONS THAT CONTRADICT THEIR BEST INTERESTS

A common criticism of informed consent is that patients might make unwise or harmful choices. Some physicians fear that information about risks might cause patients to refuse medically beneficial interventions. Empirical studies, however, do not support these concerns. In one study of 104 refusals of inpatient treatment, none were attributed to disclosure of information (29). Fourteen patients, however, refused care because of inadequate information about tests or treatments.

PATIENTS OFTEN DECIDE WITHOUT DELIBERATING ABOUT RISKS AND BENEFITS

Informed consent assumes rational, deliberate patient decision making. However, patients might make important decisions without such deliberation. For example, people who donate a kidney or part of their liver for transplantation often decide to do so as soon as they learn of the opportunity. For example, donors might say that they had to do it or that they had no choice. Moreover, they commonly decide to donate before learning about the risks of the procedure. Instead, their decision is driven by a commitment to specific people and to helping others.

Although patients might not use all disclosed information, it is nonetheless important that physicians give patients pertinent information. Even if a patient decided to pursue a course of medical care upon first hearing about it, that patient may still reconsider upon learning more information.

PATIENTS MIGHT NOT WANT TO MAKE DECISIONS INDIVIDUALLY

In some cultures patients might be expected to involve their families in medical decisions rather than make decisions as individuals (5). In some cultures women might traditionally be expected to defer decisions to their husbands or fathers. Clearly, physicians need to allow patients to involve others in their medical decisions if they choose to do so. However, physicians must avoid creating an expectation that patients must involve others in decisions, because not all patients from a given culture might agree with traditional decision-making practices.

LEGAL ASPECTS OF INFORMED CONSENT

Court rulings have shaped the doctrine of informed consent, with particular focus on what information must be disclosed to patients.

MALPRACTICE

Physicians who do not obtain informed consent might be found liable in civil suits for battery or negligence (5). *Battery* is the harmful or offensive touching of another person. Physicians might commit battery if they carry out surgery without the patient's consent or if the surgery exceeds the scope of patient consent (30). For instance, a physician might be liable for performing a mastectomy on a patient who had consented to only a biopsy, even if the intervention was medically appropriate, skillfully performed, and beneficial. This battery model, however, fits medicine poorly. Many cases do not involve physical touching of the patient, as when physicians prescribe drugs, fail to consider alternative approaches, or do not disclose information to the patient. In addition, battery requires that the physician intended to provide care without the patient's consent. Most cases of malpractice, however, involve unintentional actions.

The modern approach to malpractice, which has supplanted the battery model, is to hold physicians liable for *negligence*. To be found negligent, the physician must breach a duty to the patient, the patient must suffer a harm, and the breach of duty must cause the harm. With regard to informed consent, the patient needs to prove that the physician failed to disclose a risk that should have been disclosed, that the patient would not have consented had the risk been discussed, and that the risk occurred and caused harm. A crucial issue in malpractice law, therefore, is what risks should be discussed.

STANDARDS FOR DISCLOSURE

Full or complete disclosure of all information that physicians know about a particular condition is impossible. Thus, the issue is not *whether* physicians should limit the amount and types of information they discuss with patients, but rather *what* information should be discussed or omitted.

Courts have used several standards to determine what information to disclose to the patient (5). A slight majority of states have adopted a *professional standard*: The physician must disclose what a reasonable physician of ordinary skill would disclose in the same or similar circumstances. This is equivalent to providing the information that colleagues customarily provide. The professional standard has been criticized because patients generally want more information than physicians customarily discuss.

Many states have adopted a patient-oriented standard for disclosure: Physicians should disclose what a *reasonable patient* in the same or similar situations would find relevant to the medical decision. Generally, this standard requires more disclosure than the professional standard and is more consistent with the goal of promoting patient decision making and choices.

Some individuals, however, might desire more information than the standard "reasonable" patient. For example, a carpenter might be particularly concerned that a new medication might impair his or her dexterity or alertness. To accommodate individual patient needs fully, a few states have adopted a subjective standard for disclosure: The physician must provide information that the *individual patient* would find pertinent to the decision. This subjective standard for disclosure is problematic in malpractice litigation. If a rare, undisclosed complication occurs, the patient might claim that he would not have consented to the intervention if the physician had mentioned that particular risk. In hindsight, it might be difficult to decide whether this assertion is plausible.

In some states statutes specify that certain risks need to be disclosed—for example, "brain damage" or "loss of function of any organ or limb (5)." State courts have also ruled on issues of disclosure. A California court ruled that a physician did not have to give a quantitative estimate of life expectancy to a patient with pancreatic cancer. His widow claimed that if he had known such information, he would have declined chemotherapy and arranged his business affairs (31).

CONSENT FORMS

The consent form documents that the patient agreed to treatment. In some states a signed consent form provides a legal presumption of valid consent (32). However, a signed consent form is not tantamount to informed consent because the discussion of the risks, benefits, alternatives, and consequences might be inadequate (5).

EXCEPTIONS TO INFORMED CONSENT

Several exceptions to informed consent illustrate how acting in the patient's best interests might supersede patient self-determination. These exceptions need to be carefully limited so that they do not undermine informed consent.

LACK OF DECISION-MAKING CAPACITY

When patients lack decision-making capacity, an appropriate surrogate should give consent or refusal, following the patient's previously stated preferences or his or her best interests (*see* Chapter 4).

EMERGENCIES

In an emergency, delaying treatment to obtain informed consent might jeopardize the patient's health or life. Legally, the courts have recognized a doctrine of *implied consent*: Because reasonable persons would consent to treatment in such emergency circumstances, physicians may presume that the patient in question also would consent. Few people would object to treating life-threatening emergencies, such as an impending airway obstruction in anaphylaxis, without the patient's explicit consent. It is often possible to abbreviate the process of disclosure and consent in an urgent situation, rather than dispense with it altogether. In addition, the process of informed consent can often be initiated while the treatment is being started.

The emergency exception should not be used when informed consent is feasible or if it is known that a particular patient does not want the treatment. For example, terminally ill patients might have indicated that they do not want cardiopulmonary resuscitation (CPR). If such patients seek emergency care, the usual presumption that CPR should be initiated in case of cardiac arrest would not be valid.

Some physicians claim that consent is implied when a patient seeks care from a hospital or signs a general consent form upon admission. The implication is that informed consent for specific tests or treatments is unnecessary. However, this use of "implied consent" is unacceptable, because it allows physicians to administer any type of care they choose. When patients come to a hospital, they do not give physicians *carte blanche*. Most patients would probably agree to certain interventions, such as diagnostic testing, but would want to base further decisions on new information.

THERAPEUTIC PRIVILEGE

Physicians may withhold information when disclosure would severely harm the patient or undermine informed decision making by the patient (1). For example, a patient might be depressed and have a history of previous suicide attempts in response to serious medical diagnoses. Telling such a patient he has cancer might provoke another suicide attempt. However, the concept of therapeutic privilege needs to be sharply circumscribed. The likelihood that the patient will feel sad does not justify withholding a serious diagnosis. Therapeutic privilege also does not allow the physician to "remain silent simply because divulgence might prompt the patient to forego therapy the physician feels the patient really needs (33)."

WAIVER

Patients like Mr. T in Case 3.1 might not want to participate in making decisions about their care. Ethically and legally, patients' requests to waive the right of informed consent should be respected. Self-determination would be undermined if patients were forced to participate in decision making against their wishes. Shared decision making entitles patients to participate actively in health care decisions but does not require them to do so (4). To be ethically valid, a waiver of informed consent must itself be informed. Patients must appreciate that they have the right to receive information and to make decisions about their care. Physicians can give patients the option to not receive information or make a decision without thereby suggesting that they should do so. Physicians must keep in mind that patients might later want to participate more actively in decisions.

PROMOTING SHARED DECISION MAKING

The process of shared decision making generally requires multiple discussions between the physician and patient (Table 3-2) (34).

ENCOURAGE THE PATIENT TO PLAY AN ACTIVE ROLE IN MAKING DECISIONS

Physicians can encourage patient involvement in decisions, even with patients like Mr. T in Case 3.1 who defer to their judgment. Mr. T's doctor might say, "I'd be glad to tell you what I think is best for you. But first I need to understand what is important to you."

Elicit the Patient's Perspective about the Illness

Physicians can elicit the patient's concerns, expectations, and values regarding medical care through open-ended questions. When Mr. T's physician asked him what was most important to him over the next few years, Mr. T replied that he wanted to continue to care for his sister, who had stomach cancer. Another useful question is "What concerns you the most about your health?"

Build a Partnership with the Patient

Physicians can acknowledge that the decision is complex and difficult (34). Moreover, doctors can affirm their dedication to working for the patient's well-being: "We'll work together to make the best decisions for you."

ENSURE THAT PATIENTS ARE INFORMED

Provide Comprehensible Information

To enhance patient understanding, physicians should use simple language and avoid medical jargon. Innovative ways of presenting information include videotapes, interactive videodiscs, and discussions with patients who have had the intervention (34,35).

TABLE 3-2

Promoting Shared Decision Making

Encourage the patient to play an active role in decisions.
    Elicit the patient's perspective about the illness.
    Build a partnership with the patient.
Ensure that patients are informed.
    Provide comprehensible information.
    Try to frame issues without bias.
    Interpret the alternatives in light of the patient's goals.
    Check that patients have understood information.
Protect the patient's best interests.
    Help the patient deliberate.
    Make a recommendation.
    Try to persuade patients.

Try to Frame Issues without Bias

People are more likely to accept a treatment if the outcomes are phrased in terms of survival, rather than in terms of death (36). Lung cancer patients are more likely to prefer surgery to radiation therapy if outcomes are framed as the probability of living rather than the probability of dying (36). Moreover, surgery is more attractive when survival data are presented as the average number of years lived rather than as the probability of surviving a given time period. To minimize bias, Mr. T's physician should describe the likelihood of both surviving and dying after surgery and radiation therapy.

Physicians also need to consider how to frame the disclosure of rare but serious risks, such as the risk of an anaphylactic reaction to radiographic contrast material (37). Patients might infer incorrectly that a risk is significant because the physician has mentioned it. Physicians should put the risk in context, for example, by saying, "I believe that this is a very small risk, compared with the information we would gain from the test."

Interpret the Alternatives in Light of the Patient's Goals

In some clinical situations alternative courses of care have strikingly different benefits and burdens for the patient. Examples include surgery, hormonal treatment, or watchful waiting for benign prostatic hypertrophy and lumpectomy plus radiation or mastectomy for localized breast cancer. In these situations, which have been called *toss-ups*, the patient's goals and values are decisive. In Case 3.1, Mr. T's physician explained that he would be unable to care for his sister while recuperating from surgery and also that he might die from the operation.

Check That Patients Have Understood Information

Disclosure by the physician is not equivalent to comprehension by the patient. It is helpful to ask patients to repeat the information in their own words.

PROMOTE THE PATIENT'S BEST INTERESTS

The guideline of beneficence requires physicians to help patients make decisions that are in their best interests (*see* Chapter 4). In addition to providing information, physicians should help patients deliberate about their choices.

Help Patients Deliberate

Patients often clarify their values and preferences only in the context of an actual decision, rather than having firm preexisting values that they apply to the decision. Thus, patients commonly need to spend time deciding what option they prefer. In some situations the decision is a close call; the balance of benefits and risks of the various options are not far apart. Sometimes patients need to compare a risky treatment that promises benefit against foregoing the treatment and accepting the risk of a complication as part of the natural history of the disease. For example, in deciding whether to start anticoagulation for atrial fibrillation, patients differ in how they balance the risk of serious bleeding against the risk of an embolic complication (38,39). The physician can help the patient frame such decisions by asking whether the patient is the kind of person who wants to try everything to prevent a complication or the kind of person who would rather suffer the natural course of illness rather than the adverse effects of interventions.

Make a Recommendation

Physicians should not merely list the alternatives and leave it up to the patient to decide (40–42). Patients commonly seek a recommendation regarding what plan is most likely to fulfill their goals. Physicians should offer a recommendation on the basis of the patient's values. In light of Mr. T's desire to care for his sister, his doctor recommended radiation therapy.

Try to Persuade Patients

Physicians should also try to dissuade patients from choices that are clearly contrary to their best interests, as judged by their own values (2).

In summary, shared decision making respects patient self-determination. In order for patients to make informed choices, physicians must discuss with them the alternatives for care and the benefits, risks, and consequences of each alternative. Physicians also need to encourage patients to play an active role in decision making and to ensure that patients are informed.

REFERENCES

1. Meisel A, Kuczewski M. Legal myths about informed consent. *Arch Intern Med* 1996;156(22):2521–2526.
2. Emanuel EJ, Emanuel LL. Four models of the physician-patient relationship. *JAMA* 1992;267:2221–2226.
3. President's Commission for the Study of Ethical Problems in Medicine and Biomedical and Behavioral Research. *Making health care decisions.* Washington, DC: U.S. Government Printing Office, 1982.
4. Brock DW. *Life and death.* New York: Cambridge University Press, 1993:21–54.
5. Berg JW, Lidz CW, Appelbaum PS. *Informed consent: legal theory and clinical practice,* 2nd ed. New York: Oxford University Press, 2001.
6. Schloendorff v. Society of New York Hospitals. 211 N.Y. 125, 105 N.E. 92, 1914.
7. Shultz MM. From informed consent to patient choice: a new protected interest. *Yale Law J* 1985;95:219–299.
8. McNeil BJ, Weichselbaum R, Pauker SG. Fallacy of the five-year survival in lung cancer. *N Engl J Med* 1978;299:307–401.
9. Slevin ML, Stubbs L, Plant HJ, et al. Attitudes toward chemotherapy: comparing views of patients with cancer with those of doctors, nurses, and general public. *Br Med J* 1990;300:1458–1460.
10. Kassirer JP. Incorporating patient preferences into medical decisions. *N Engl J Med* 1994;330:1895–1896.
11. Appelbaum PS, Lidz CW, Meisel A. *Informed consent: legal theory and clinical practice.* New York: Oxford University Press, 1987.
12. Cassileth BR, Zupkis RV, Sutton-Smith K, et al. Information and participation preferences among cancer patients. *Ann Intern Med* 1980;92:832–836.
13. Lo B, Steinbrook RL, Coates T, et al. Voluntary HIV screening: weighing the benefits and harms. *Ann Intern Med* 1989;110:727–733.
14. Truman v. Thomas. 27 Cal.3d 285, 165 Cal.Rptr. 308, 611 P.2d 902 (Cal. 1980).
15. Howard v. University. 172 N.J. 537, 800 A.2d 73 (N.J. 2002).
16. Braddock CH III, Edwards KA, Hasenberg NM, et al. Informed decision making in outpatient practice: time to get back to basics. *JAMA* 1999;282(24):2313–2320.
17. Whitney SN, McGuire AL, McCullough LB. A typology of shared decision making, informed consent, and simple consent. *Ann Intern Med* 2004;140(1):54–59.
18. Rozovsky FA. *Consent to treatment: a practical guide,* 2nd ed. Boston: Little, Brown and Company, 1990:721–727.
19. Braddock CH, Fihn SD, Levinson W, et al. How doctors and patients discuss routine clinical decisions: informed decision making in the outpatient setting. *J Gen Intern Med* 1997;12:339–345.
20. Diem SJ. How and when should physicians discuss clinical decisions with patients? *J Gen Intern Med* 1997;12:397–398.
21. Faden RR, Beauchamp TL. *A history and theory of informed consent.* New York: Oxford University Press, 1986:337–381.
22. Cassileth BR, Zupkis RV, Sutton-Smith K, et al. Informed consent – why are its goals imperfectly realized? *N Engl J Med* 1980;302:896–900.
23. Grundner TM. On the readability of surgical consent forms. *N Engl J Med* 1980;302:900–902.
24. Lidz CW, Meisel A, Osterweis M, et al. Barriers to informed consent. *Ann Intern Med* 1983;99:539–543.
25. Wu WC, Pearlman RA. Consent in medical decision-making: the role of communication. *J Gen Intern Med* 1988;3:9–14.
26. Strull WM, Lo B, Charles G. Do patients want to participate in decision making? *JAMA* 1984;252:2990–2994.
27. Deber RB, Kraetschmer N, Irvine J. What role do patients wish to play in treatment decision-making? *Arch Intern Med* 1996;156:1414–1420.
28. Mazur DJ, Hickam DH. Patients' preferences for risk disclosure and role in decision making for invasive medical procedures. *J Gen Intern Med* 1997;12:114–117.
29. Appelbaum PS, Roth LH. Patients who refuse treatment in medical hospitals. *JAMA* 1983;250:1296–1301.
30. Rozovsky FA. *Consent to treatment: a practical guide,* 2nd ed. Boston: Little, Brown and Company, 1990:24–29.
31. Annas GJ. Informed consent, cancer, and truth in prognosis. *N Engl J Med* 1994;330:223–225.
32. Annas GJ, Law SA, Rosenblatt RA, et al. *American health law.* Boston: Little, Brown and Company, 1990: 601–612.
33. Canterbury v. Spence. 464 F.2d 772 (D.C. Cir. 1972).
34. Epstein RM, Alper BS, Quill TE. Communicating evidence for participatory decision making. *JAMA* 2004; 291(19):2359–2366.
35. Barry MJ, Fowler FJ, Mulley AG, et al. Patient reactions to a program designed to facilitate patient participation in treatment decisions for benign prostatic hyperplasia. *Med Care* 1995;33:771–782.
36. McNeil BJ, Pauker SG, Sox H, Tversky A. On the elicitation of preferences for alternative therapies. *N Engl J Med* 1982;306:1259.
37. Brody H. *The healer's power.* New Haven: Yale University Press, 1992.
38. Protheroe J, Fahey T, Montgomery AA, et al. The impact of patients' preferences on the treatment of atrial fibrillation: observational study of patient based decision analysis. *Br Med J* 2000;320(7246):1380–1384.
39. Devereaux PJ, Anderson DR, Gardner MJ, et al. Differences between perspectives of physicians and patients on anticoagulation in patients with atrial fibrillation: observational study. *Br Med J* 2001;323(7323):1218–1222.

40. Ingelfinger FJ. Arrogance. *N Engl J Med* 1980;303:1507–1511.
41. Quill TE, Brody H. Physician recommendations and patient autonomy: finding a balance between physician power and patient choice. *Ann Intern Med* 1996;126:763–769.
42. Ubel PA. "What should I do, doc?": Some psychologic benefits of physician recommendations. *Arch Intern Med* 2002;162(9):977–980.

ANNOTATED BIBLIOGRAPHY

1. Berg JW, Lidz CW, Appelbaum PS. *Informed consent: legal theory and clinical practice*, 2nd ed.. New York: Oxford University Press, 2001.
   Comprehensive and lucid book, covering ethical, legal, and practical aspects of informed consent. Stresses the need for dialogue between doctors and patients.
2. Meisel A, Kuczewski M. Legal and ethical myths about informed consent. *Arch Intern Med* 1996;156: 2521–2526.
   Corrects several common misunderstandings about informed consent.
3. Whitney SN, McGuire AL, McCullough LB. A typology of shared decision making, informed consent, and simple consent. *Ann Intern Med* 2004;140(1):54–59.
   Argues that detailed informed consent is not required when there is only one medically feasible option; however, shared decision making is important whenever several options exist.
4. Epstein RM, Alper BS, Quill TE. Communicating evidence for participatory decision making. *JAMA* 2004;291(19): 2359–2366.
   Suggests how physicians can communicate information to patients in ways that enhance shared decision making.

CHAPTER 4

Promoting the Patient's Best Interests

Patients may reject the recommendations of their physicians, refusing beneficial interventions or insisting on interventions that are not indicated. In such cases physicians are torn between respecting patient autonomy and acting in the patients' best interests. If physicians simply accept unwise patient decisions in the name of respecting patient autonomy, their role seems morally constricted. This chapter discusses how physicians can protect the well-being of patients while avoiding the pitfalls of paternalism.

PATIENT REFUSAL OF BENEFICIAL INTERVENTIONS

The following case illustrates how patients may refuse beneficial interventions.

CASE 4.1 Refusal of surgery for critical aortic stenosis.

Mrs. N is a 76-year-old widow with aortic stenosis. For several years she has been refusing further evaluation, saying that she would not want surgery. After an episode of near-syncope, she agrees to echocardiography, mostly to humor her physician. Critical aortic outflow obstruction is found. Her primary care physician strongly recommends valve replacement. The risks of surgery are unacceptable to her, particularly the risk of prolonged hospitalization or neurologic or cognitive impairment. Having lived a full life, she says she welcomes a sudden death rather than a prolonged decline. In the past she has been reluctant to visit physicians, undergo tests, or take medications. She leads an active life, writing a resource book for senior citizens, leading several volunteer organizations, and enjoying concerts.

Mrs. N's physicians believe that her refusal conflicts with her best interests. With valve replacement she is likely to live longer and avoid debilitating symptoms such as chest pain and dyspnea. Refusal of surgery might result in what she fears most: progressive decline and loss of independence.

How can physicians respond to Mrs. N's refusal? On the one hand, it would be disrespectful and impractical to override her refusal and operate without her consent. On the other hand, accepting her refusal without further discussion might result in an adverse outcome that could have been averted. What attempts by physicians to persuade Mrs. N to agree to surgery are warranted? To address these issues, physicians need to understand the ethical guidelines of doing no harm and acting in their patients' best interests.

DOING NO HARM TO PATIENTS

The ethical guideline of nonmaleficence requires people to refrain from inflicting harm on others. Prohibiting harmful actions is the core of morality (1). For instance, the Ten Commandments prohibit killing, lying, and stealing. Avoiding harm is generally considered a more stringent ethical obligation than providing benefit (1).

The widely quoted maxim "Do no harm" has several distinct meanings (2,3). First, physicians should not provide interventions that are known to be ineffective. Second, physicians should not act maliciously, as by providing substandard care because they dislike the patient's ethnic background or political views. Third, doctors should also act with due care and diligence. Fourth, the maxim sometimes is cited as "Above all, do no harm," or, more impressively in Latin, *Primum non nocere*. If physicians cannot benefit patients, they should at least not harm them or make the situation worse. Fifth, when benefits and burdens are evenly balanced, physicians should err on the side of not intervening.

However, the precept "do no harm" provides only limited guidance. Many medical interventions, such as the aortic valve replacement mentioned in Case 4.1, offer both great benefits and serious risks and side effects. Doing no harm would literally preclude such interventions, yet some patients may accept substantial risks to gain medical benefits (4). Furthermore, as we discuss next, merely doing no harm seems a limited view of the physician's role (5).

PROMOTING THE PATIENT'S BEST INTERESTS

The ethical guideline of beneficence requires physicians to promote patients' "important and legitimate interests (5)." This guideline arises from the nature of the doctor–patient relationship and of medical professionalism.

THE FIDUCIARY NATURE OF THE DOCTOR–PATIENT RELATIONSHIP

Physicians have special responsibilities to act for the well-being of patients because patients are often impaired in significant ways by their illness (6,7). Furthermore, the stakes are high; poor decisions might place patients' health or lives at risk.

Reasons for the Fiduciary Relationship

Patients are vulnerable. Because illness might undermine patients' independence and judgment, people might be less able to look after their own interests when they are sick. Because of this vulnerability, patients often depend on physicians for advice and trust their recommendations.

Physicians have expertise that patients lack. Physicians have expert knowledge as well as the experience and judgment to apply it to the patient's individual circumstances.

Patients rely on their physicians. It is often difficult for patients to obtain information and advice other than through physicians. Often, they have no previous experience in making medical decisions. In serious illness, patients might have little time to seek second opinions. Similarly, it is hard for laypeople to determine whether a physician's advice is sound or to evaluate a physician's skills. Hence, patients rely on the advice of their physicians.

Definition of a Fiduciary Relationship

Legally, relationships between professionals and clients are characterized as fiduciary. The term fiduciary is derived from the Latin word *fidere*, to trust. Fiduciaries hold something in trust for another. They must act in the best interests of their patients or client, subordinating their self-interest. Fiduciaries are held to higher standards than ordinary citizens and businesspeople, who use their knowledge and skill for their own self-interest, rather than for the benefit of their customers (7). Ordinary business relationships are characterized by the phrase *caveat emptor*, "let the buyer beware," not by trust and reliance.

Many arrangements in managed care challenge the fiduciary nature of the doctor–patient relationship (*see* Chapter 34). Financial incentives under managed care encourage physicians to act in their own self-interest or in the interest of third parties such as hospitals, physician groups, or managed care plans, rather than in the best interests of patients. Utilization review and practice guidelines might limit physicians' freedom to act on behalf of their patients. Patients might fear that physicians no longer exercise independent clinical judgment but simply carry out bureaucratic policies set by administrators.

THE NATURE OF PROFESSIONALISM

In professional codes of ethics, physicians promise to serve the best interests of patients. Literally, physicians "profess" to use their skills to heal and comfort the sick, encouraging patients to rely on them and promising to act in a fiduciary manner (8). In return for physicians acting for the good of their patients, society grants physicians a great deal of autonomy in selecting applicants for medical schools and postgraduate training, in establishing standards for certification, and in disciplining practitioners (9).

PROBLEMS WITH BEST INTERESTS

The idea that physicians should act in the best interests of patients is indisputable. However, in any given case the actions that are in the patient's best interests might be controversial.

DISAGREEMENTS OVER WHAT IS BEST FOR A PATIENT

People may disagree over the goals of care or the assessment of the benefits and burdens of an intervention. In Case 4.1, the physicians' goal is to increase the patient's likelihood of survival. However, the patient's goal is to avoid physical and mental decline, particularly in the perioperative period. Furthermore, the physicians and patients may weigh the risks and benefits of surgery differently (10). Physicians tend to focus on the prospect of long-term survival, while Mrs. N is more concerned about the short-term risks of surgery and her quality of life (11).

QUALITY OF LIFE

The term *quality of life* is used in many ways. Factors that might be considered include:

* The symptoms of the illness and the side effects of treatment
* The patient's functional ability to perform basic activities of living such as walking, shopping, and preparing meals
* The patient's experiences of happiness, pleasure, pain, and suffering
* The patient's independence, privacy, and dignity

Competent patients usually consider their quality of life as well as the duration of life when making health care decisions. In some situations a patient with a serious illness may decide that her quality of life is so poor that interventions are unacceptably burdensome. The principle of autonomy requires respecting a patient's judgments about quality of life when that patient is competent and informed. More controversy exists if other persons are making the judgments.

Quality of Life Judgments by Others Might Be Problematic

Persons with chronic illness such as coronary artery disease and chronic obstructive lung disease rate their quality of life higher than their physicians do (12). Similarly, elderly patients who have survived a hospitalization in the intensive care unit (ICU) view their quality of life higher than their family members do (13). Such discrepancies are not surprising. Many patients learn to cope with chronic illness over time, develop support systems, and continue to find substantial pleasure in life. Furthermore, quality of life might improve substantially if in-home assistance or adaptive devices are provided. In addition, assessments of quality of life might be discriminatory if they are based on the patient's economic value to society or social worth. These considerations are not pertinent to medical decisions, which should be based on need and likely benefit (14). Thus, quality of life judgments by others might be inaccurate and biased unless they reflect the patient's own assessment of quality of life.

Quality of Life in Patients with Severe Neurologic Impairment

Consider a patient with severe Alzheimer disease who cannot respond to questions. He usually appears comfortable and smiles when music is played or when someone gives him a back rub. However, he has catastrophic reactions, shouting and striking people when asked to take a bath.

Some writers argue that a patient's quality of life falls below a minimal acceptable level if he lacks qualities that are considered essential to being a person (15,16). In this view patients in a persistent vegetative state or who cannot survive outside an ICU have an unacceptable quality of life. These authors contend that such lives are "useless" and "not worth living and that it is not a goal of medicine to sustain biological existence in such situations (15)."

Others reject such quality of life considerations. Some fear that such considerations will lead to discrimination against people with disabilities. Proponents of a "right to life" believe that biologic life should be prolonged, regardless of prognosis or quality of life. This position is often based on fundamentalist religious beliefs about the sacredness of life. These disagreements illustrate how determinations of quality of life by others might be problematic unless they are based on the patient's own judgments.

MEDICAL PATERNALISM

Historically, beneficence rather than respect for persons was the dominant ethical principle for physicians. Doctors made decisions for the patient on the basis of what they believed was the patient's best interest. This approach to decision making has been termed *medical paternalism* (17), analogous to how parents make decisions for their children. Deferring to the physician's recommendations is reasonable in many acute illnesses or emergencies: when cure is possible, when the benefits of therapy far outweigh the risks, and when treatment must be started promptly.

Definition of Paternalism

Philosophers define paternalism as intentionally overriding a person's known preferences or actions in order to benefit that person (17). They further distinguish two types of paternalism. In weak or soft paternalism, the patient's decisions are not informed or are not voluntary (17). If a patient's autonomy is impaired or in doubt, it is appropriate for physicians to intervene, at least temporarily. The justification is that patients should be protected from harming themselves through nonautonomous decisions and actions. Intervening to determine whether a patient is competent and informed is a minimal imposition on patient autonomy, compared to the possible harms of allowing an incompetent patient to act unwisely.

In strong or hard paternalism, a patient's autonomous choices are overridden. An example is withholding a diagnosis or a test result requested by a patient because the physician believes the information will greatly upset the patient. When writing about paternalism, philosophers generally mean strong or hard paternalism (17). Strong or hard paternalism has been sharply criticized, as we will discuss in the next section.

Problems with Medical Paternalism

Critics of (strong) paternalism raise several objections (17). First, value judgments are unavoidable in clinical medicine, and patients, not physicians, should make them. Physicians can define the burdens and benefits of an intervention, but only Mrs. N can decide whether the surgical risk and side effects are worth the chance for long-term survival and relief of symptoms.

Second, the belief that patients cannot make wise medical decisions is a self-fulfilling prophecy. If patients are not informed, they will not be able to make meaningful choices. Similarly, patients who sense that they have no decision-making power will become passive. In contrast, if patients are empowered to make decisions, they generally ask questions, seek information, and take responsibility for difficult choices.

Third, physicians might seek to override a patient's wishes because of their own psychological and emotional reactions to the case. Some physicians are affronted if patients reject their recommendations. "Refusal of treatment is seen by physicians as a rejection of an offer of help, which in turn may be seen as a rejection of the person making the offer. As a result, physicians may feel angry, frustrated, and unwilling to explore the underlying basis of refusal (18)."

PATIENT REQUESTS FOR INTERVENTIONS

Patients sometimes insist on medical interventions that physicians consider far more harmful than beneficial. Such insistence might frustrate and anger physicians. Disagreements over patient requests are often framed as conflicting rights: The patient claims the right to decide about his medical care while the physician asserts a countervailing right to follow her professional judgment. Framing the issues in this way, however, generally leads to stalemate. A more fruitful approach is to examine the benefits and burdens for the patient.

INTERVENTIONS OUTSIDE APPROPRIATE MEDICAL PRACTICE

CASE 4.2 Request to monitor side effects of a performance-enhancing drug.

A 22-year-old college swimmer is taking oral anabolic steroids, which she obtains through friends at the gym where she lifts weights. She is aware of the long-term side effects but plans to use the drugs only for the next year while she is competing. Many of her competitors are using steroids, and she cannot remain competitive unless she takes them also. She asks her physician to monitor her for side effects but not to prescribe the drugs.

In this case the patient is using drugs for enhancement, not for the treatment or prevention of illness. Many physicians believe that enhancement of normal function is not an appropriate goal of medicine. In this case the medical risks might be serious. There are additional reasons that the physician might decline this request. Using performance-enhancing drugs is unfair to other competitors and violates rules governing athletic competitions. Even though this patient is not asking the physician to prescribe the steroids, the physician might believe that monitoring for side effects condones the practice.

From another perspective, however, the physician can frame the request as preventing harm to the patient. Patients commonly use other substances that might harm their health, such as cigarettes and alcohol, which they obtain without prescription. However, physicians continue to follow patients using such substances, monitor them for adverse effects, and treat complications, while still urging them to stop. Indeed, by maintaining a supportive doctor–patient relationship, physicians might be better positioned to persuade patients to stop taking harmful substances.

INTERVENTIONS WHOSE BENEFIT CAN ONLY BE ASSESSED BY THE PATIENT

CASE 4.3 Request for controlled drug for pain.

A 56-year-old man has been disabled by chronic back pain for 10 years. Extensive evaluations, including a magnetic resonance (MR) scan, have been negative. Exercises and physical therapy have provided only minor improvement. After changing health insurance plans, the patient visits a new physician and requests a refill of a prescription for eight 160-mg tablets of oxycodone (Oxycontin) daily. He says that he has not changed the dosage in several years. His new physician does not prescribe opioids at this strength and dosage for chronic pain. She wants to wean the patient off opioids and to help him live an active life despite the pain. The patient refuses a referral to a pain clinic. "I know that Oxycontin works. Nothing else helps me."

In this case the risks of treatment are significant. Oxycodone has been abused, diverted to illegal sales, and implicated in local outbreaks of opioid abuse. Because only patients can assess the severity of pain, some physicians are uncomfortable prescribing opioids, particularly when the dosage seems high. In this case only the patient can assess the effects of treatment. Physicians might be uncomfortable adjusting the dosage of drugs on the basis of only the subjective report of the patient without objective signs or tests.

The benefits to the patient are also significant. Pain is undertreated by physicians and causes substantial suffering. Many experts in pain management believe that the regular use of opioids for chronic pain syndromes rarely leads to addiction and is effective in relieving pain and enhancing function (19). The fact that pain can only be assessed through the patient's self-report should not lead physicians to downplay the importance of treating it effectively.

The ethical guideline of respecting patient autonomy and the legal doctrine of informed consent give patients the *negative* right to refuse unwanted treatments (*see* Chapter 3). However, this patient claims the *positive* right to receive a specific drug. Some countries allow patients to buy many drugs, including antibiotics, without a physician's prescription. In the United States, however, only physicians are licensed to order tests or prescribe medications. Prescriptions for opioids such as oxycodone require special physician registration numbers from the Drug Enforcement Agency and, in some states, special triplicate prescription forms. These restrictions address the concern that opioids might be diverted to illegal uses or used to maintain an addiction. In California a physician may prescribe opioids and other controlled substances only if "in good faith he believes" that the patient's medical condition requires it (20).

INTERVENTION WITH SMALL BENEFIT BUT NO RISKS

CASE 4.4 Request for an expensive, low-yield test.

A 41-year-old bus driver has episodes of crampy abdominal pain and alternating diarrhea and constipation. One year ago, after an evaluation that included colonoscopy, she was diagnosed with irritable bowel syndrome (IBS). Dietary manipulations have been ineffective. On the advice of a friend, she asks her doctor to order an abdominal computed tomography (CT) scan because when the cramps are severe she fears something serious has been missed. She also says that "if doctors could only find out what is causing this, they would be able to do something about it." She refuses to discuss psychosocial issues about her illness or to try antidepressants that inhibit serotonin reuptake, saying that "my problems aren't in my head."

The physician's goal in Case 4.4 is to help the patient cope with a chronic medical condition and live an active life despite her symptoms. However, the patient's goals are relief of her symptoms and reassurance that her condition is not dangerous. Because of their divergent goals for care, it is understandable that the patient and physician disagree on weighing the benefits and burdens of the CT scan.

To the patient in Case 4.4, a scan has little medical risk and potentially great benefit. She believes that a negative scan would provide reassurance. In the unlikely event that the scan is abnormal, her course of care would be dramatically changed. In contrast, from the physician's perspective, a negative scan result is unlikely to lead to reassurance. Patients who seek "just another test" for reassurance often request further tests in a fruitless quest for a definitive diagnosis. Articles on IBS advise against additional diagnostic tests if a thorough initial work-up is negative and the clinical course is typical (21,22). In other situations the medical risks of the requested therapy might be serious. If the patient in Case 4.4 had requested exploratory surgery for reassurance or to establish a definitive diagnosis, the physicians should certainly have demurred.

ALLOCATING RESOURCES FAIRLY

Given the soaring cost of health care, physicians have a duty to allocate health care resources fairly and cannot ignore the costs of patient requests. Expensive high-technology procedures such as the CT scans noted in Case 4.4 drive up the cost of medical care. In addition, CT scans might reveal lesions that require further costly evaluation but ultimately prove to be clinically insignificant.

Cost, however, should not be the main reason for refusing patient requests. Under the current health care system, physicians have no explicit societal mandate to limit care in order to control costs. In managed care systems potential conflicts of interest make it problematic to limit highly beneficial care on the basis of cost (*see* Chapter 32).

The primary consideration should be the benefits and risks to the patient, rather than costs. If the intervention's medical risks outweigh any benefits for the patient, the patient's request can be refused without reference to costs. Patients who have financial incentives to control costs—through substantial copayments—are less likely to request such interventions. Thus, when patients and physicians both have financial incentives for cost-effective medicine, situations like Case 4.4 might be easier to resolve.

Cost might determine how much time and effort physicians should spend on trying to dissuade the patient. The physician should spend more time trying to discourage an expensive CT scan than in discouraging inexpensive tests. If the patient with IBS in Case 4.4 wanted a simple blood test that offered little benefit, few physicians would strongly object.

REACHING AGREEMENT ON BEST INTERESTS

Through continued discussions with patients, physicians can promote the best interests of patients while recognizing patients' ultimate power to decide (Table 4-1). Chapter 14 gives detailed recommendations for such discussions.

TABLE 4-1

Promoting the Patient's Best Interests

Understand the patient's perspective.
Address misunderstandings and concerns.
Try to persuade the patient.
Negotiate a mutually acceptable plan of care.
Ultimately let the patient decide.

Physicians should recommend what they believe is best for the patient from the perspective of the patient's values and preferences. In shared decision making, physicians should not merely present patients with a list of alternatives and leave them to decide.

Physicians should try to dissuade patients from unwise decisions. Persuasion respects patients and fosters their autonomy. Persuasion might include talking to the patient on several occasions and asking the patient to talk to family members, friends, other physicians, or other patients who have had the intervention. Persuasion needs to be distinguished from deception and threats. The latter are wrong because they undermine the patient's autonomy. Persuasion must also be distinguished from badgering the patient. Continual attempts to convince patients to change their minds might be counterproductive. It might be better to acknowledge that the choices are difficult, allow patients more time to decide, and give them more control over the decision-making process.

In summary, physicians need to respect patient autonomy and act in the patient's best interests simultaneously. Physicians have a fiduciary obligation to act for the well-being of patients as patients would define it. Physicians can satisfy the ethical guidelines of beneficence and autonomy by understanding the patient's perspective, by trying to persuade patients, and by negotiating a mutually acceptable plan.

REFERENCES

1. Beauchamp TL, Childress JF. *Principles of biomedical ethics*, 4th ed. New York: Oxford University Press, 1994:189–258.
2. Jonsen AR. Do no harm. *Ann Intern Med* 1978;88:827–832.
3. Brewin TB. Primum non nocere? *Lancet* 1994;344:1487–1488.
4. Delaney M. The case for patient access to experimental therapy. *J Infect Dis* 1989;159(3):416–419.
5. Beauchamp TL, Childress JF. *Principles of biomedical ethics*, 3rd ed. New York: Oxford University Press, 1989:194–227.
6. Hall MA, Berenson RA. Ethical practice in managed care: a dose of realism. *Ann Intern Med* 1998;128:395–402.
7. Rodwin MA. *Medicine, money, and morals: physicians' conflicts of interest*. New York: Oxford University Press, 1993.
8. Pellegrino ED, Thomasma DG. *For the patient's good: the restoration of beneficence in health care*. New York: Oxford University Press; 1988.
9. Veatch RM. *A theory of medical ethics*. New York: Basic Books, 1981.
10. Slevin ML, Stubbs L, Plant HJ, et al. Attitudes toward chemotherapy: comparing views of patients with cancer with those of doctors, nurses, and general public. *Br Med J* 1990;300:1458–1460.
11. McNeil BJ, Weichselbaum R, Pauker SG. Fallacy of the five-year survival in lung cancer. *N Engl J Med* 1978;299:307–401.
12. Pearlman RA, Uhlmann RF. Quality of life in chronic diseases: perceptions of elderly patients. *J Gerontol* 1988;43:M25–M30.
13. Danis M, Patrick DL, Southerland LI, et al. Patients' and families' preferences for medical intensive care. *JAMA* 1988;260:797–802.
14. Ziv TA, Lo B. Denial of care to illegal immigrants: proposition 187 in California. *N Engl J Med* 1995;335:1095–1098.
15. Schneiderman LJ, Jecker NS, Jonsen AR. Medical futility: its meaning and ethical implications. *Ann Intern Med* 1990;112:949–954.
16. Schneiderman LJ, Jecker NS, Jonsen AR. Medical futility: response to critiques. *Ann Intern Med* 1996;125:669–674.
17. Beauchamp TL, Childress JF. *Principles of biomedical ethics*, 4th ed. New York: Oxford University Press, 1994:271–287.

18. Appelbaum PS, Lidz CW, Meisel A. *Informed consent: legal theory and clinical practice*. New York: Oxford University Press, 1987:196.
19. Rosenthal E. Patients in pain find relief, not addiction, in narcotics. *New York Times* 1993 March 28; Sect. A1.
20. California Health & Safety Code. §11210.
21. Drossman DR. Irritable bowel syndrome. In: Dornbrand L, Hoole AJ, Pickard CG, eds. *Manual of clinical problems in adult ambulatory care*. Boston: Little, Brown and Company, 1992:206–209.
22. Longstreth GF. Irritable bowel syndrome: diagnosis in the managed care era. *Dig Dis Sci* 1997;42:1105–1111.

ANNOTATED BIBLIOGRAPHY

1. President's Commission for the Study of Ethical Problems in Medicine and Biomedical and Behavioral Research. *Making health care decisions*. Washington, DC: U.S. Government Printing Office, 1982.
   Lucid and thoughtful exposition of shared decision-making by physicians and patients.
2. Quill TE. Partnerships in patient care: a contractual approach. *Ann Intern Med* 1983;98:228–234.
   Practical suggestions on how to negotiate mutually acceptable decisions with patients.
3. Pellegrino ED, Thomasma DG. *For the patient's good: the restoration of beneficence in health care*. New York: Oxford University Press, 1988.
   Comprehensive exposition of the importance of beneficence in the doctor–patient relationship.

CHAPTER 5

Confidentiality

Patients reveal to physicians sensitive personal information about their medical and emotional problems, their alcohol and drug use, and their sexual activities. The presumption is that physicians should maintain confidentiality of patient information. However, exceptions to confidentiality might be warranted to prevent serious harm to third parties or to the patient (Table 5-1). The human immunodeficiency virus (HIV) epidemic, the development of computerized medical records, and the explosion of genetic information have sharpened controversies over confidentiality. In 2003 the federal government issued health privacy regulations, also known as HIPAA *regulations*, because the 1996 Health Insurance Portability and Accountability Act mandated them.

THE IMPORTANCE OF CONFIDENTIALITY IN MEDICINE

REASONS FOR CONFIDENTIALITY

Keeping medical information confidential shows respect for patients (1,2). Patients want to control access to sensitive personal information and expect physicians to maintain confidentiality. Maintaining confidentiality also has beneficial consequences for patients and for the doctor–patient relationship. It encourages people to seek medical care and discuss candidly sensitive issues, such as psychiatric illness, sexually transmitted diseases, and substance abuse. In turn, treatment for these conditions benefits both the individual patient and public health. Furthermore, confidentiality prevents harmful consequences to patients, such as stigmatization and discrimination. Patients might fear that employers will gain access to their health information and discriminate against them.

Respect for confidentiality is a strong tradition in medicine. The Hippocratic Oath enjoins physicians, "What I may see or hear in the course of the treatment...which on no account one must spread abroad, I will keep to myself, holding such things shameful to be spoken about (3)." Modern professional codes similarly urge physicians to maintain confidentiality. The legal system may also hold physicians liable for unwarranted disclosure of medical information (4).

DIFFICULTIES MAINTAINING CONFIDENTIALITY

Maintaining confidentiality is increasingly difficult in modern medicine. Many people have access to medical records, including the attending physician, house staff, students, consultants, nurses, social workers, pharmacists, billing staff, medical records personnel, insurance company employees, and quality-of-care reviewers (5). Computerized medical records, which improve access to medical information, also allow more serious breaches of confidentiality. Confidentiality can be violated at any computer station, extensive data on each patient is available, and information on a large number of patients can be accessed at once (6). Fax and e-mail also present opportunities for confidentiality to be broken (7).

TABLE 5-1

Exceptions to Confidentiality

Exceptions to protect third parties
    Reporting to public officials
        Infectious diseases
        Impaired drivers
    Injuries caused by weapons or crimes
    Partner notification by public health officials
    Warnings by physicians to persons at risk
    Violence by psychiatric patients
    Infectious diseases
Exceptions to protect patients
    Child abuse
    Elder abuse
    Domestic violence

Many breaches of confidentiality, however, result from health-care workers' indiscretions. Caregivers might discuss patients by name at parties or even in hospital elevators or cafeterias (8,9). Although many physicians take such discussions for granted, patients object to such breaches of confidentiality (8). As a court ruling asked pointedly, "What policy would be served by according the physician the right to gossip about a patient's health (4)?"

WAIVERS OF CONFIDENTIALITY

Patients commonly give physicians permission to disclose information about their condition, for example, to other physicians or to insurance companies. Patients might not appreciate that signing a general release allows the insurance company to further disseminate the information. Insurance companies generally place patients' diagnoses in a computerized database that is accessible to other insurance companies or to employers without further permission from the patient (10).

COUNTERVAILING ETHICAL GUIDELINES

Although confidentiality is important, it is not an absolute value. In some situations, overriding confidentiality might be justified in order to provide important benefits to patients or to prevent serious harm to third parties. Access to information might be needed to provide high-quality medical care to patients or to protect the public health. These exceptions require careful justification, because not every instance of benefit to patients or prevention of harm to others warrants overriding confidentiality.

FEDERAL HEALTH PRIVACY REGULATIONS

Under the HIPAA health policy regulations, health care providers are required to set policies and procedures about privacy, educate staff, and provide patients with notice about their privacy rights and how the organization uses and discloses personal health information (PHI) (11). Providers are permitted to use and disclose PHI without patient authorization for treatment, payment, and health care operations. Health care operations include training programs, quality improvement, and accreditation and licensing. Providers may disclose information as required by public health laws and regulations. Patients must give specific authorization to disclose psychotherapy notes. Specific patient authorization is required to use PHI for research and marketing, although important exceptions are permitted.

Providers are required to use the minimum PHI necessary to achieve these desired purposes. For patient care, the full medical record may be accessed. Providers must also take reasonable safeguards against prohibited or incidental use or disclosure of PHI. Patients are permitted to examine and copy their records, to request amendments to their records, to request to receive information by alternative means and locations (such as not leaving messages on an answering machine), and to obtain a list of disclosures of their information. Because the regulations set criminal penalties for intentional violations, many risk managers are interpreting the regulations conservatively. These federal regulations establish a minimum level of protection; state laws and organizational policies might be stricter.

Good patient care requires communication among various health care providers. In the course of care, incidental disclosure of information and breaches of confidentiality might occur. Physicians should take reasonable precautions to prevent inappropriate disclosures but should not forego communications that might be essential in patient care (11). For example, physicians might communicate with other providers by e-mail or fax without explicit patient authorization, but should take such precautions as keeping fax machines in areas where other patients cannot access them. Furthermore, physicians can discuss patients at the nursing station, provided that they keep their voices down and pause when someone or a patient or visitor approaches.

DISCLOSING THE PATIENT'S CONDITION TO OTHERS

Disclosure of patient information to family members, friends, or the press might raise ethical issues.

DISCLOSURE TO RELATIVES AND FRIENDS

Relatives and friends often ask about the patient's condition. Most patients want the physician to talk to their family, and usually physicians do not even ask the patient's permission to do so. In some cases, however, the patient might not want the information disclosed.

CASE 5.1 Estrangement from relatives.

A 32-year-old woman is admitted to the hospital after a serious automobile accident. She is disoriented and confused. The patient's sister requests that the patient's husband not be given any information. The patient has previously told the physician about her hostile divorce proceedings. The husband, however, learns that she is hospitalized and inquires about her condition.

The HIPAA privacy regulations establish a reasonable approach to this issue. Health care providers need to notify patients that relatives will be informed unless the patient requests that they not be. In ethical terms, the physician can presume that patients would want their relatives notified. In Case 5.1 the physician can conclude that this presumption no longer holds. Thus, the physician may give only minimal information to the husband in order to allay his fears about her condition but refer him to the patient's sister or other relatives for details. Similarly, physicians can provide information about a patient's condition and treatment to family members and other people involved in the patient's care, provided that the patient does not object. Often, such communication is needed to help monitor the patient, arrange follow-up care, or ensure that medications are taken as prescribed.

INFORMATION ABOUT PUBLIC FIGURES

The press might seek information about patients who are public figures or celebrities. The public and the news media might have legitimate reasons to know medical information about a public figure. For instance, a political candidate's health is an important concern to voters (12) yet famous people have a right to confidentiality, as do all people. The physician and hospital should ask the patient or appropriate surrogate what information, if any, should be released.

OMITTING SENSITIVE INFORMATION FROM MEDICAL RECORDS

Patients who are concerned about breaches of confidentiality may ask physicians to omit sensitive information from their medical records.

CASE 5.2　Omission of information from the medical record.

A nurse who is in excellent health has a routine checkup at the hospital where he works. He asks his physician not to write in the medical record that he had been severely depressed several years ago. He knows that many people in the hospital might see his record, and he does not want colleagues to know his psychiatric history. He also fears that he will have difficulty changing jobs if his history is known, even if he has no symptoms at the time.

Physicians might fear that omitting medical information from patient records might compromise the quality of care. Important clinical information might not be available in an emergency. In addition, documentation of the patient's current condition and treatment might be required for insurance payment or authorization for services. Furthermore, it might not be feasible to exclude information from an electronic medical record. Even if a diagnosis is omitted from the record, it might be inferred from the patient's laboratory tests or medications.

The purpose of the medical record is to enhance patient well-being and quality of care. Generally, the patient is the best judge of his or her best interests. Some patients might regard breaches of confidentiality as more threatening than the risk of suboptimal care resulting from incomplete medical records. Thus, a patient's informed preferences to exclude sensitive information from the medical record should be respected if feasible. Many psychiatrists keep their detailed psychotherapy notes separate from the rest of the patient's medical record.

OVERRIDING CONFIDENTIALITY TO PROTECT THIRD PARTIES

Overriding patient confidentiality might prevent serious harm to third parties, as the following case illustrates. HIPAA expressly permits these exceptions to confidentiality, which are often required by state law.

CASE 5.3　Risk of HIV transmission.

A 32-year-old accountant reveals to his physician that he had a positive test for HIV antibodies at an anonymous testing center. He asks his physician not to disclose the test results to anyone, because he is concerned about losing his job and health insurance. His physician encourages him to notify his wife so that she can be tested. After several discussions, the patient continues to refuse to notify his wife or allow others to do so. He declares, "If she finds out, it would destroy our marriage." Should the physician notify the wife despite the patient's objections?

The ethical guideline of nonmaleficence requires both patients and physicians to avoid harming other people and to prevent harm to others. Infected persons have a moral duty not to harm others and to notify persons whom they have placed at risk. This duty is particularly strong when trust is expected, as in marriage. The common law may also impose on infected persons a legal duty to notify partners whom they place at risk (13). In Case 5.3, the patient abrogates this responsibility. In addition, physicians might need to override confidentiality to prevent serious harm to third parties in some circumstances, as we discuss next.

JUSTIFICATIONS FOR OVERRIDING CONFIDENTIALITY

The balance between preventing harm to third parties and protecting confidentiality is ultimately set by society through statutes, public health regulations, and court decisions. Setting this balance as public policy allows all points of view to be represented and is preferable to decisions by the individual physicians in their offices or at the bedside. Laws on confidentiality vary from state to state. In general, exceptions to confidentiality are warranted when all the following conditions are met (Table 5-2):

- The potential harm to identifiable third parties is serious.
- The likelihood of harm is high.
- There is no less invasive, alternative means for warning or protecting those at risk.
- Breaching confidentiality allows the person at risk to take steps to prevent harm.
- Harm to the patient resulting from the breach of confidentiality is minimized and acceptable. Disclosure should be limited to information essential for the intended purpose, and only those persons with a need to know should receive information.

TABLE 5-2

Situations in Which Overriding Confidentiality Is Warranted

The potential harm to third parties is serious.

The likelihood of harm is high.

No alternative for warning or protecting those at risk exists.

Breaching confidentiality will prevent harm.

Harm to the patient is minimized and acceptable.

In these circumstances the overall harm to the third parties at risk is judged to be greater than the harm to the index case resulting from overriding confidentiality (14).

Confidentiality can be overridden in several ways. Physicians need to distinguish reporting to public officials, partner notification by public health officials, and direct warnings to third parties at risk.

REPORTING TO PUBLIC OFFICIALS

In certain situations physicians are legally required to break confidentiality and to report the name of a patient to appropriate public officials (Table 5-1).

Infectious Diseases

Physicians, clinical laboratories, and hospitals are required to report to public health officials the names of patients with specified infectious diseases, such as tuberculosis and gonorrhea. Such reporting allows accurate epidemiologic statistics and public health planning and facilitates partner notification. The goals of monitoring diseases and planning programs can be achieved without reporting the names of infected persons. However, partner notification requires reporting by name.

SPECIAL PROTECTIONS

Certain conditions might be considered particularly sensitive because the risk of stigma and discrimination is believed to be greater than in other illnesses. Earlier in the HIV epidemic, many states passed laws to strengthen the confidentiality of HIV test results and to require written informed consent for HIV testing (15). Furthermore, although the Centers for Disease Control and Prevention (CDC) required AIDS cases to be reported, HIV infection was not reportable in many states (16). Alternative test sites were established in which people could be tested for HIV antibodies anonymously.

Recently, reporting of HIV infection to public health officials has become more similar to reporting of other infectious diseases. Reporting of persons with HIV infections by name is now required in most states and has been recommended nationally (17–19). There are several reasons for this policy change (17,19). Because prognosis has improved dramatically with highly active antiretroviral therapy, there is a stronger rationale for partner notification. Also, reporting only AIDS cases gives an inaccurate picture of the epidemic, compromises public health planning, and leads to inequitable distribution of funding based on caseload. However, anonymous testing is still permitted (20).

IMPAIRED DRIVERS

Many states require physicians to report to the department of motor vehicles persons with specified medical conditions that impair their ability to drive safely. Such conditions include epilepsy, syncope, dementia, sleep apnea, and other conditions that impair consciousness (21–23). Even if the underlying condition is treated, the patient might not be able to drive safely. For example, after placement of an implantable cardiac defibrillator, about 10% of patients experience syncope or near-syncope associated with defibrillation in the first year (24). The physician's role is not to stop the patient from driving or to decide whether the patient should be permitted to drive. Such determinations are properly made by the department of motor vehicles. The physician only informs officials of persons who warrant investigation. Reporting is particularly important for patients who drive commercially and present greater risks because they spend more hours on the road, are responsible for third parties, and drive heavy vehicles (23,24).

Injuries Caused by Weapons or Crimes

Almost all states require physicians to report injuries involving a deadly weapon or criminal act (25). The rationale is to protect the public from further violence.

PARTNER NOTIFICATION BY PUBLIC HEALTH OFFICIALS

In partner notification, persons at risk for an infectious disease are warned that they have been exposed. More partners are notified when public health officials carry out the notification than when patients do it themselves (26). In the AIDS epidemic, the term *partner notification* has replaced the traditional term *contact tracing*. Many contagious diseases, such as tuberculosis, are spread through aerosolized particles and can be transmitted by casual contact. Many casual contacts might be located without the cooperation of the index case, as by going to the index case's workplace.

"Mandatory" Partner Notification

For all practical purposes, partner notification in HIV and other blood-borne and sexually transmitted diseases must be voluntary (27). In many cases sexual or drug-sharing partners cannot be identified without the infected person's cooperation. If patients do not wish to cooperate, they can deny that they have partners or give inaccurate names and addresses. Attempts to make partner notification "mandatory" are misguided and counterproductive. Any perception that partner notification programs are punitive or disrespectful to index cases will further reduce cooperation.

Minimizing Harm during Partner Notification

In partner notification, partners should only be told that they have been exposed. The identity of the index case is not revealed (27). However, index cases cannot be promised anonymity, because partners can often infer their identity.

WARNINGS BY PHYSICIANS TO PERSONS AT RISK

In addition to notifying public officials, physicians might have a legal duty or the legal option to warn identifiable persons whom a patient places at risk (Table 5-1).

Violence by Psychiatric Patients

Physicians have a legal responsibility to override confidentiality to protect persons who are potential targets of violence by psychiatric patients (*see* Chapter 42). The landmark Tarasoff ruling declared, "Protective privilege ends where public peril begins (28)." Although many physicians believe that the law requires them to *warn* the persons who are potential targets, in fact the law requires a broader duty to *protect* the person who is a potential target from harm (29). This duty to protect persons who are targets might involve more intensive therapy, voluntary or involuntary hospitalization, convincing the patient to give up weapons, or notifying the police. Many states have similar requirements.

INFECTIOUS DISEASES

Courts might require physicians to warn patients with infectious diseases to take precautions to prevent their infectious disease from afflicting others (30). In addition, some courts require physicians to notify identified persons whom their infected patients place at risk (31,32). These rulings involved conditions such as hepatitis, tuberculosis, and Rocky Mountain Spotted Fever. Generally, physicians can fulfill this duty by notifying public health officials.

PHYSICIAN JUDGMENT

Although society has set legal requirements for public health reporting, physicians might still face dilemmas. As in Case 5.3, patients might ask physicians not to disclose information as required by law. Such a patient might promise to use condoms but refuse to notify his wife. Physicians might be sympathetic to such requests. In one study more than 60% of physicians were willing to allow a patient with gonorrhea to tell his wife that he had nonspecific urethritis (33). This strategy, however, is ethically problematic. The wife would not know the nature of the infection, her long-term risk of infertility, or the need for follow-up. In addition, feminists object that male physicians apply an unfair double standard, protecting the man's interests rather than the woman's health and autonomy.

Some jurisdictions explicitly give physicians discretion on partner notification in some situations (34,35). For example, in California physicians are *permitted* but not *required* to notify partners of HIV-infected patients (or notify public health officials) (36). Physicians who decide to notify cannot be held liable in civil or criminal proceedings (36).

Sound medical ethics might require notification even though the law does not. In Case 5.3, physicians should try to persuade the patient to agree to public health measures. The physician also can try to elicit patients' concerns and address them. For example, if patients are concerned about job discrimination, physicians can reassure them that the Americans with Disabilities Act protects patients from discrimination based on illness. Physicians should notify patients if reporting will occur over their objections and take into account requests about carrying out the reporting. For instance, a patient may choose to notify his wife before public health reporting.

OVERRIDING CONFIDENTIALITY TO PROTECT PATIENTS

In several situations physicians are required to override confidentiality to protect the patient rather than third parties (Table 5-1). In these situations the ethical justification for intervening is that patients might not be able to protect themselves. The federal health privacy regulations allow physicians to comply with state requirements for such reporting.

CHILD ABUSE

All states require health care workers to report suspected child abuse or neglect to child protective services agencies (37). The parents' privacy is overridden in order to protect vulnerable children from a high probability of serious harm. More than 1,000 children die of neglect and abuse each year; most are under the age of 5 (37). Health care workers might be the only people outside the family to have close contact with preschool children. Physicians need only reasonable suspicion of abuse and neglect, not definitive proof, to justify a fuller investigation. To encourage reporting, most states grant immunity from civil and criminal liability when reporting is done in good faith. Intervention might enable parents to obtain enough assistance and support to prevent further abuse. In extreme cases the child might be removed from parental custody. In evaluating possible child abuse, pediatricians should treat parents with respect, keeping in mind that most parents are trying their best to deal with the challenges of childrearing.

ELDER ABUSE

Most states require health care workers to report cases of elder abuse to adult protective services (38). The goal is to identify persons who are incapable of seeking assistance on their own and to offer them help. Elderly persons who are dependent on their caretakers might be unwilling or unable to complain about physical or psychological abuse or neglect (39). Patients might not be aware of available in-home supportive services or might feel intimidated by caretakers. Patients might fear that if they complain, they will be worse off, perhaps placed in a nursing home. Most abusers of elderly persons are family members who are overwhelmed by caring for a frail elderly person. Thus, reporting and intervention might provide resources that allow the elderly person to continue to live safely at home. Elderly persons who are truly capable of making informed decisions and free of intimidation or coercion are free to decline offered assistance.

Specific laws for reporting elder abuse vary from state to state. Generally, reasonable suspicion of abuse is sufficient to trigger reporting. Health care workers must report abuse only when they obtain information about a patient in their professional roles. Thus, although physicians as private citizens *may* report an elderly neighbor whom they suspect is abused, they are not *required* to do so. Health care workers receive legal immunity when they make reports of suspected abuse in good faith.

DOMESTIC VIOLENCE

Domestic violence is physical, sexual, or psychological assault against intimate partners. The vast majority of people who are assaulted are women. Many states require health care workers to report suspected domestic violence or abuse (25). Persons who are assaulted often are unable to take steps on their own to escape further violence. Reporting is intended to protect the person assaulted and to hold perpetrators of violence accountable. However, it might be ineffective or even counterproductive (25). Mandatory reporting might put battered patients at risk of retaliation from their assailants. The police and courts often respond poorly to reports of abuse. Thus, physicians might face conflicting obligations: a legal mandate to report and the patient's desire not to report the abuse. Physicians should provide emotional support and refer patients to shelter, legal services, and counseling. Particular concerns about an increased risk of violence should be communicated to the police when making a report (25). Whenever possible, physicians should promote the abused person's autonomy—for example, respecting a request to delay reporting until the person can find shelter.

In conclusion, physicians should maintain confidentiality unless there are compelling reasons to override it. Physicians need to understand why society has determined that in some situations it is appropriate to override confidentiality. In some situations the law provides clear guidance for physicians about confidentiality. However, the law might be silent about other situations, or it might defer to the judgment of physicians. Finally, the physician might want to go beyond the law in some circumstances. Even if public health reporting is required by law, it is respectful to tell patients that reporting will occur, obtain their agreement if possible, and take steps to address their concerns and minimize harm to them.

REFERENCES

1. Beauchamp TL, Childress JF. *Principles of biomedical ethics*, 4th ed. New York: Oxford University Press, 1994: 418–429.
2. Bok S. *Secrets*. New York: Pantheon Books, 1982.
3. Beauchamp TL, Childress JF. *Principles of biomedical ethics*, 3rd ed. New York: Oxford University Press, 1989: 329–341.
4. Horne v. Patton, 287 So.2nd 824 (Ala. 1974).
5. Siegler M. Confidentiality in medicine—a decrepit concept. *N Engl J Med* 1982;307:1518–1521.
6. Committee on Maintaining Privacy and Security in Health Care Applications of the National Information Infrastructure. *For the record: protecting electronic health information*. Washington, DC: National Academy Press, 1997.
7. Rind DM, Kohane IS, Szolovits P. Maintaining the confidentiality of medical records shared over the Internet and the World Wide Web. *Ann Intern Med* 1997;127:138–141.
8. Weiss BD. Confidentiality expectations of patients, physicians, and medical students. *JAMA* 1982;247:2695–2697.
9. Ubel PA, Zell MM, Miller DJ. Elevator talk: observational study of inappropriate comments in a public space. *Am J Med* 1995;99:190–194.
10. Donaldson MS, Lohr KN, eds. *Health data in the information age*. Washington, DC: National Academy Press, 1994.
11. Department of Health and Human Services. Standards for privacy of individually identifiable health information; proposed rule. *Fed Reg* 2002;67(59):14793–14800.
12. Annas GJ. The health of the President and presidential candidates: the public's right to know. *N Engl J Med* 1995;333(14):945–949.
13. Kathleen K. v. Robert B., 150 Cal. App. 3d 992, 198 Cal Rptr. 273 (1984).
14. Beauchamp TL, Childress JF. *Principles of biomedical ethics*, 4th ed. New York: Oxford University Press, 1994:266–269, 282–284.
15. Rennert S. *AIDS/HIV and confidentiality: model policy and procedures*. Washington, DC: American Bar Association, 1991.

16. Gostin LO. The AIDS litigation project: a national review of court and human rights commission decisions, part I: the social impact of AIDS. *JAMA* 1990;263:1961–1970.
17. Gostin L, Ward JW, Baker AC. National HIV case reporting in the United States—a defining moment in the history of the epidemic. *N Engl J Med* 1997;337:1162–1167.
18. Gostin LO, Webber DW. HIV infection and AIDS in the public health and health care systems. *JAMA* 1998; 279:1108–1113.
19. CDC. CDC guidelines for national human immunodeficiency virus case surveillance, including monitoring for human immunodeficiency virus infection and acquired immunodeficiency syndrome. *MMWR* 1999;48:1–31.
20. CDC. HIV testing among populations at risk for HIV infection—nine states, November 1995–December 1996. *MMWR* 1998;47:1086–1091.
21. Strickberger SA, Cantillon CO, Friedman PL. When should patients with lethal ventricular arrhythmia resume driving? *Ann Intern Med* 1991;115:560–563.
22. Drachman DM. Who may drive? Who may not? Who shall decide? *Ann Neurol* 1988;24:787–788.
23. Suratt PM, Findley LJ. Driving with sleep apnea. *N Engl J Med* 1999;340:881–882.
24. Epstein AE, Miles WM, Benditt DG, et al. Personal and public safety issues related to arrhythmias that may affect consciousness: implications for regulation and physician recommendations. *Circulation* 1996;94: 1147–1166.
25. Hyman A, Schillinger D, Lo B. Laws mandating reporting of domestic violence: do they promote patient well-being? *JAMA* 1995;273:1781–1787.
26. Landis SE, Schoenbach VJ, Weber DJ, et al. Results of a randomized trial of partner notification in cases of HIV infection in North Carolina. *N Engl J Med* 1992;326:101–106.
27. Bayer R, Toomey KE. HIV prevention and the two faces of partner notification. *Am J Public Health* 1992;82:1158–1164.
28. Tarasoff v. Regents of the University of California, 551 P2d 334 (Cal 1976).
29. Anfang SA, Appelbaum PS. Twenty years after Tarasoff: reviewing the duty to protect. *Harv Rev Psychiatry* 1996;4(2):67–76.
30. Areen J, King PA, Goldberg S et al., eds. *Law, science and medicine*, 2nd ed. Westbury, New York: The Foundation Press, Inc, 1996.
31. Furrow BR, Johnson SH, Jost TS. *Health law: cases, materials, problems*, 3rd ed. St. Paul: West Publishing Co, 1997:385–388.
32. Bradshaw v. Daniel, 854 S.W.2d 865 (Tenn. 1993).
33. Novack DH, Detering BJ, Arnold R. Physicians' attitudes toward using deception to resolve difficult ethical problems. *JAMA* 1989;261:2980–2985.
34. Edgar H, Sandomire H. Medical privacy issues in the age of AIDS: legislative options. *Am J Law Med* 1990;16: 155–222.
35. Gostin LO, Lazzarini Z, Flaherty KM. Legislative survey of state confidentiality laws, with special emphasis on HIV and immunization. www.epi0c.org/privacy/medical/cdc_survey.html, 1997.
36. Cal. Health and Safety Code. §§120975-121020.
37. Wissow LS. Child abuse and neglect. *N Engl J Med* 1995;332:1425–1431.
38. Lachs MS, Pillemer K. Abuse and neglect of elderly persons. *N Engl J Med* 1995;332:437–443.
39. Aravanis SC, Adelman RD, Breckman R, et al. Diagnostic and treatment guidelines in elder abuse and neglect. *Arch Fam Med* 1993;2:371–388.

ANNOTATED BIBLIOGRAPHY

1. Lo B, Dornbrand L, Dubler NN. From Hippocrates to HIPAA: confidentiality, government regulations, and professional judgment. *JAMA* 2005;In press.
   Analyzes the federal confidentiality regulations (also known as HIPAA regulations) and how physician judgment is still required to determine what risk of a breach of confidentiality is acceptable when disclosing information to other health care workers caring for a patient.
2. Lo B, Alpers A. The uses and abuses of personal health information in pharmacy benefits management. *JAMA* 2000;283:801–806.
   Analyzes dilemmas regarding confidentiality and use of personal health information in computerized databases in health care organizations.
3. Bayer R, Toomey KE. HIV prevention and the two faces of partner notification. *Am J Public Health* 1992; 82:1158–1164.
   Argues that failure to distinguish between contact tracing and the duty to warn has led to serious confusion. Contact tracing cannot be compulsory and has traditionally protected the anonymity of the index case.
4. Hyman A, Schillinger D, Lo B. Laws mandating reporting of domestic violence: do they promote patient well-being? *JAMA* 1995;273:1781–1787.
   Explains that recent laws mandating reporting of domestic violence may place physicians in a dilemma if reporting is likely to lead to retaliation by the perpetrator.
5. Gostin LO. *Public health law: power, duty, restraint*. Berkeley: University of California Press, 2000:85–109.
   Lucid discussion of overriding confidentiality to protect the public health.

CHAPTER 6

Avoiding Deception and Nondisclosure

Children are taught to tell the truth and avoid lies. In clinical medicine, however, the distinction between telling the truth and lying can seem simplistic. Even doctors who condemn outright lying might consider withholding a grave diagnosis from a patient or exaggerating a patient's condition to secure that patient's insurance coverage. This chapter analyzes the ethical considerations regarding lying, deception, misrepresentation, and nondisclosure. Such actions might mislead either the patient or a third party, such as an insurance company or a disability agency.

DEFINITIONS

The following case illustrates some ways physicians might provide misleading information.

CASE 6.1 Family request not to tell the patient the diagnosis of cancer.

A 70-year-old Cantonese-speaking man with a change in bowel habits and weight loss is found to have a carcinoma of the colon. The daughter and son ask the physician not to tell their father he has cancer. They say that patients in his generation are not told they have cancer and that if he is told, he will lose hope.

Physicians might provide misleading information in different ways.

Lying refers to statements (a) that the speaker knows are false or believes to be false and (b) that are intended to mislead the listener. For example, the physician might tell the patient that the tests were normal.

Deception is more broadly defined than lying, and it includes all statements and actions that are intended to mislead the listener, whether or not they are literally true. An example would be telling the patient that he has a "growth," hoping that the patient will believe nothing is wrong. Other techniques used to mislead people include employing technical jargon, using ambiguous statements, omitting important qualifying information, and presenting misleading statistics.

Misrepresentation is a still broader category, including unintentional as well as intentional statements and actions. The statements might or might not be literally true. Unintentional misrepresentation might result from inexperience, poor interpersonal skills, or lack of diligence or knowledge. For instance, a physician might not tell a patient that he or she had cancer because the physician did not receive the biopsy report.

Nondisclosure means that the physician does not provide information about the diagnosis, prognosis, or plan of care. For example, a physician might not tell a patient that he or she has cancer unless the patient specifically asks.

Many writers on medical ethics use terms such as "truth-telling" or "veracity." This book, however, uses the terms *deception* and *misrepresentation* because ethically difficult cases usually involve deception or nondisclosure rather than outright lies.

ETHICAL OBJECTIONS TO LYING

Traditional religious and moral codes forbid lying. The Old Testament, for example, exhorts people not to bear false witness. Lying and deception also show disrespect for others. Those who are lied to or deceived generally feel betrayed or manipulated, even if the liar has benevolent motives. Lying also undermines social trust because listeners cannot be confident that other statements by the person will be truthful. This loss of trust is particularly grave in medicine because trust is essential in a doctor–patient relationship. In addition to undermining the speaker's integrity, lying is further condemned because a single lie often requires continued deception.

Lying and deception are considered prima facie wrong; the presumption is that they are inappropriate (1). Although some "white" lies may be accepted as customs that do not deceive anyone, lying generally requires a justification.

The ethical issue is whether general prohibitions on lying also apply to deception and nondisclosure in situations like Case 6.1.

DECEPTION OR NONDISCLOSURE TO THE PATIENT

Traditional codes of medical ethics did not require physicians to be truthful or forthcoming to patients (2). The writings of Hippocrates urge physicians to conceal "most things from the patient while you are attending him." Until recently, many physicians in the United States either did not tell patients about serious diagnoses such as cancer or deceived them (3). There are several reasons for such deception or nondisclosure.

REASONS FOR DECEPTION OR NONDISCLOSURE

Deception and Nondisclosure Prevent Serious Harm to Patients

Physicians might fear that disclosing a serious diagnosis might cause a patient to lose hope, refuse medically beneficial treatment, or become depressed. Few patients, however, refuse recommended treatment after learning a serious diagnosis (4). Although sadness and anxiety might be common, major depression or suicide attempts are rare. Some patients, however, currently have major depression or have attempted suicide previously. In such cases it would be justified to withhold the diagnosis while obtaining psychiatric consultation and assessing the likelihood of harm. In exceptional cases the risk of harm might be so serious that it would be justified to withhold the diagnosis until the patient's mental health improves.

Disclosure Is Not Culturally Appropriate

In many cultures patients traditionally are not told of a diagnosis of cancer or other serious illness. According to one study, although 87% of European-American patients and 89% of African-American patients want to be told if they have cancer, 65% of Mexican-Americans and 47% of Korean-Americans would not want to be told (5). Another study found that although 69% of European-American patients and 63% of African-American patients want to be told a terminal prognosis, only 48% of Mexican-Americans and 35% of Korean-Americans do. In some cultures disclosure of a grave diagnosis is believed to cause patients to suffer but withholding information gives serenity, security, and hope (6). Being direct and explicit might be considered insensitive and cruel. Families and physicians might try to protect the patient by taking on decision-making responsibility (7). Although it would be unfair to impose American standards of disclosure on patients who adhere to a different cultural standard, the crucial ethical issue is whether a patient wants to know the diagnosis, not what most people in their culture would want.

Patients Do Not Want to Be Told

If patients do not want to know their diagnoses, it would be autocratic to force them to receive information against their will, even in the name of promoting informed decisions. Indeed, it would violate patient autonomy to do so.

Disclosure Might Violate the Physician's Conscience

In some cases there might be additional, physician-centered reasons for nondisclosure.

CASE 6.2 Physician objection to disclosure.

On a routine check-up, a 25-year-old married woman asks about options for contraception. The gynecologist is a devout Catholic whose religious beliefs oppose contraception and abortion.

Some physicians might have personal moral objections to specific medical interventions, such as contraception, abortion, or some measures to reduce human immunodeficiency virus (HIV) transmission, such as condoms and needle exchange. As a matter of conscience, they do not prescribe or recommend these interventions. Moreover, they might believe that they would be complicit with an immoral action if they even discuss these options with patients.

REASONS AGAINST DECEPTION AND NONDISCLOSURE

Most Patients Want to Know Their Diagnosis and Options for Care

The vast majority of patients in the United States want to know if they have a serious diagnosis. In one survey, 94% of those asked said that they "would want to know everything" about their medical condition, "even if it is unfavorable (8)." Ninety-six percent wanted to know a diagnosis of cancer. The desire to be told a serious diagnosis is so strong in the United States that more than 90% of patients want radiologists to tell them of abnormal results at the time of the imaging study rather than waiting for their primary physician to give them the results (9). Even among patients from cultures in which nondisclosure is traditional, many want to be informed of their diagnosis (5).

Patients Need Information for Decisions

For patients to make informed decisions, physicians need to disclose pertinent information (*see* Chapter 3). It is problematical if physicians fail to inform patients of options that are medically acceptable. Under the doctrine of informed consent, doctors are expected to disclose such information without patients having to ask for it. In other clinical settings, physicians have a role-specific affirmative duty to disclose all medically appropriate options to patients, even if they would not personally recommend them, without patients' having to ask (*see* Chapter 3).

Physicians are not obligated to carry out actions that would violate their fundamental moral beliefs or their conscience. They are free to withdraw from the care of a patient as a last resort if a mutually acceptable plan cannot be negotiated. However, it is problematical if physicians provide care without informing patients of options that are medically acceptable because patients would not be able to make informed choices. Thus, respecting the physician's conscience might conflict with respecting the patient's autonomy.

Disclosure Has More Beneficial than Harmful Consequences

Disclosure of the diagnosis and prognosis can benefit patients. Patients are more likely to adhere to treatment regimens that they understand and have agreed to. Furthermore, many patients with a serious diagnosis already suspect it. If physicians and family members remain silent, patients might imagine that the situation is worse than it actually is. Patients often feel relieved when their illnesses are explained and they can focus on treatment options.

Deception and Nondisclosure Require More Deception

Deception and nondisclosure usually require additional, more elaborate deceptions. If a patient is not told the diagnosis of cancer, deception is needed to explain the reasons for surgery or other treatments.

Deception and Nondisclosure Might Be Impossible

In the long run it is usually unrealistic to keep patients from knowing their diagnoses. A nurse, house officer, or x-ray technician might disclose it. When patients belatedly find out their diagnoses, they generally feel angry and betrayed. Thus, the practical issue is not whether to tell the patient the diagnosis but rather how to tell the patient.

TABLE 6-1
Resolving Dilemmas about Deception and Nondisclosure to Patients

Anticipate dilemmas about disclosure.
Determine what the patient wants.
Elicit the family's concerns.
Focus on how to tell the diagnosis, not whether to tell.
If you are withholding information, plan for future contingencies.

RESOLVING DILEMMAS ABOUT MISREPRESENTATION AND NONDISCLOSURE TO PATIENTS

Physicians can respond to dilemmas about informing patients of serious diagnoses, without resorting to misrepresentation or nondisclosure (Table 6-1).

Anticipate Dilemmas Regarding Disclosure

Dilemmas can often be anticipated, for example, if the patient is from a culture in which serious diagnoses traditionally are not disclosed. When ordering tests, physicians can ask patients whether they wish to be informed of the results: "Many patients want to know their test results, while other patients want the doctor to tell a family member. I will do whatever you prefer. Do you want me to tell you the test results?" At this point, after the physician receives the test results, it might be too late to inquire about the patient's preferences for disclosure without revealing the diagnosis. Simply asking the question might signal that the results are abnormal because there is no reason to withhold normal results from the patient.

Determine What the Patient Wants

When a family requests that a patient not be told, the physician should assess whether this is the patient's wish or the family's. Has the patient explicitly said that he would not want to be told a serious diagnosis? Convincing evidence that the patient himself would not want to be told should be respected.

Elicit the Family's Concerns

The physician should elicit the family's concerns. "What do you fear most about telling your father he has cancer?" In such discussions the physician needs to validate the family's feelings as the natural reactions of loving relatives. The physician also needs to explain to the family how disclosure is usually beneficial, as discussed previously.

Focus on How to Tell the Diagnosis, Not Whether to Tell

Disclosing bad news usually can be done in supportive ways that help patients cope. Physicians can soften bad news by being compassionate, responding to the patient's concerns, offering empathy, and helping mobilize support (10–15). The Appendix discusses how to break bad news to patients.

If Withholding Information, Plan for Future Contingencies

If the physician deems it appropriate to withhold the diagnosis, the doctor should discuss plans for care with an appropriate surrogate, usually a close relative. Patients who do not want to be told their diagnosis might change their minds. Physicians should regularly ask patients if they have questions or want to discuss anything else about their condition.

Physicians should never promise family members that the patient will not learn a serious diagnosis. A nurse, an x-ray technician, or an insurance company representative might inadvertently disclose it. It is usually counterproductive to devise elaborate schemes to keep patients from the diagnosis instead of helping them cope with the bad news.

In some cases excellent care can be provided without explicitly talking about the diagnosis with the patient. If the family in Case 6.1 provides care and emotional support and helps the patient reach closure in life, little might be gained from making the prognosis explicit. Such cases illustrate that ethical values taken for granted in the United States are not the only basis for good medical care.

Responding to Conscientious Objection by Physicians

In caring for patients, physicians have role-specific responsibilities that might transcend their own personal views. As in any clinical situation, physicians need to respond to the patient's medical and emotional needs, inform the patient about alternatives for care, and promote informed decision-making. At a minimum, physicians should tell patients that there are options for care they will not discuss because of their own religious or moral beliefs but that other physicians are willing to discuss. For the sake of continuity of care, physicians should inform patients at the onset of their moral objections to these interventions. However, it is ethically problematic for physicians to use their role to impose their moral or religious views on patients.

Similar dilemmas arise when a health care organization, such as a Catholic hospital, does not provide family planning or abortion services (16). Although there are strong reasons to respect an institutional policy that is based on religious beliefs, it is also important to inform women who present for care or schedule appointments that certain options will not be provided at that institution.

Similar dilemmas arise when hospitals and third-party payers forbid individual physicians from providing information to patients about family planning or abortion, writing prescriptions, or referring patients to other organizations for such services (16). Individual physicians should have the scope to discuss and recommend interventions that in their judgment are medically appropriate. To restrict such communication on the basis of an organization's policies or religious mission is to impose its views on both patients and health care providers and to deny important information to patients. It is simplistic to believe that all patients who seek care at an institution share the moral beliefs that animate the institutional policy.

DECEPTION OR NONDISCLOSURE TO THIRD PARTIES

Patients who seek benefits, such as insurance coverage, disability, and excused absences from work, often need physicians to give information to third parties. Physicians might consider using deception to help them gain such benefits. Although such deception might be motivated by a desire to help the patient, it is ethically problematic. Throughout this section it is assumed that the patient has authorized disclosure to the third party.

REASONS FOR DECEPTION

Physicians might claim they are acting in the best interest of patients when using deception. In doing so, physicians might regard themselves as patient advocates, helping their patients gain medical and social benefits. In some situations the benefits of deception seem to outweigh the harms.

CASE 6.3 Insurance coverage.

A 42-year-old accountant presents with a 2-month history of lower back pain that has not responded to conservative therapy with rest, nonsteroidal antiinflammatory agents, and exercises. There are no neurological symptoms, and the physical examination is normal. His father had prostate cancer that presented as back pain, and he is concerned that he might have a serious disease causing his symptoms. The physician and patient agree that an MRI scan would reassure the patient. His health insurance policy requires preauthorization for MRI studies, which are usually authorized only if there are neurological findings or other findings suggesting a systemic disease. The physician considers putting on the requisition that he has numbness and weakness in his legs to facilitate approval of the study.

In one survey, 39% of physicians reported that during the past year they had exaggerated the severity of a patient's condition, changed a patient's billing diagnosis, or reported signs and symptoms the patient did not have in order to help the patient get needed care (17). Such deception is more common when physicians believe that it is unfair for the plan not to cover the intervention, when they believe that the insurer's appeals process was unwieldy, and when the patient's condition is more serious (18). The physician might believe that obtaining a drug for the patient is redressing a wrong rather than breaking an ethical guideline.

In Case 6.3 the benefits of deception for the patient seem large and greater than the costs of other alternatives. The physician believes that he and the patient have arrived at a mutually acceptable plan of care that addresses his concerns. The rationale for this plan, however, might be difficult for a busy practitioner to explain to a bureaucrat applying a standardized list of indications for the test. In other situations the harms of deception might seem very small, as in the following case.

CASE 6.4 Excuse from work.

A patient asks a physician to sign a form excusing an absence from work. He says that he had a severe upper respiratory infection but has now recovered. The physician did not see the patient while he was ill.

In Case 6.4 the physician might sign the form, even though the physician does not know whether the patient was actually sick or not. The doctor might consider the harm—inappropriate absenteeism—minor and better handled directly by the employer (19). It neither would be cost effective for patients to visit physicians for all self-limited illnesses that keep them from work nor would it be desirable to medicalize such conditions by encouraging patients to consult physicians. Even if the worker was not sick, perhaps he had a good reason to stay home—to care for a sick child, for example. For these reasons, physicians commonly certify work absences even when they have not examined the patient during the illness.

REASONS NOT TO DECEIVE

Deception Undermines Trust in Physicians

Physicians dealing with a specific case might not appreciate the impact of a practice of deception in these situations. Lying and deception undermine social trust because people cannot trust that other statements are truthful. It is especially problematic for physicians to lie or intentionally deceive others because the relationship between doctors and patients and society depends on trust. If physicians are known to use deception in some situations to help patients, they might also use it in other situations for other purposes.

It might seem unfair for the insurance company to deny coverage for care that is beneficial or to require physicians to assume heavy bureaucratic burdens. In situations like Case 6.3, physicians report that if the appeals process is cumbersome, they are more likely to use deception—for example, stating that the patient has numbness and tingling in his legs. The physician might argue that this statement is literally true; most people have such symptoms at some time in their lives.

Third parties expect truthful information. Physicians have an obligation to avoid misrepresentation to patients because of the fiduciary nature of the doctor–patient relationship (*see* Chapter 4). Physicians have similar obligations to avoid deception to these third parties, but for different reasons. The relationship between physicians and third parties is contractual rather than fiduciary. In contracts both parties are required to avoid deception and deal fairly (20). Insurers commonly require physicians to affirm that the information provided is accurate and complete. In Case 6.3 insurers consider such deception to be fraud and might bring legal charges.

It is unrealistic to expect that such deception to third parties will not be discovered. Computers help insurers to identify questionable claims. Similarly, other physicians review applications for disability from Social Security and worker's compensation (21). Once misled, third parties will mistrust other information from physicians and might require additional documentation. Physicians, who already complain of bureaucratic intrusions on the practice of medicine, might then face additional paperwork.

The Harms of Deception Outweigh the Benefits

When indirect and long-term harms are taken into account, the overall harms of deception outweigh the benefits (22). Deception about a patient's condition indirectly harms other people. Giving disability parking cards makes it more difficult for persons who are truly disabled to park. Deceptive claims for disability or insurance coverage force the public, workers, and employers to pay higher taxes or insurance premiums.

patient's underlying emotions. "This must be very hard for you." Gestures such as touching the patient on the forearm or hand might convey empathy more effectively than words. Another way to show concern is to help with immediate details, such as calling a family member. Expressions such as "I know what you're going through" might be counterproductive; the patient might feel that a healthy person could not imagine having a fatal diagnosis.

Repeat the discussion at subsequent visits to ensure that the patient has understood. Providing information is a process, not a single conversation. At each visit, asking how the patient is doing can allow the patient to raise issues.

Share uncertainty with the patient. When patients ask how much longer they have to live, physicians usually do not give straightforward responses (10). In the spirit of respecting patient autonomy, physicians need to give patients the best information possible. When physicians cite an average prognosis, they need to make clear that an individual might have a longer or shorter survival than the mean. In addition to answering questions about prognosis literally, physicians also need to address the patient's psychosocial concerns, such as fears of losing control, suffering unrelieved pain, and dying alone.

REFERENCES

1. Bok S. *Secrets*. New York: Pantheon Books, 1982.
2. Reiser SJ. Words as scalpels: transmitting evidence in the clinical dialogue. *Ann Intern Med* 1980;92:837–842.
3. Novack DH, Plumer, R, Smith, RL. Changes in physicians' attitudes toward telling the cancer patient. *JAMA* 1979;241(9):897–900.
4. Appelbaum PS, Roth LH. Patients who refuse treatment in medical hospitals. *JAMA* 1983;250:1296–1301.
5. Blackhall LJ, Murphy ST, Frank G. Ethnicity and attitudes toward patient autonomy. *JAMA* 1995;274:820–825.
6. Gordon DB, Paci E. Disclosure practices and cultural narratives: understanding concealment and silence around cancer in Tuscany, Italy. *Soc Sci Med* 1997;46:1433–1452.
7. Surbone A. Truth telling to the patient. *JAMA* 1992;268:1661–1662.
8. *President's Commission for the Study of Ethical Problems in Medicine and Biomedical and Behavioral Research. Making Health Care Decisions*. Washington, DC: U.S. Government Printing Office, 1982.
9. Schreiber MH, Leonard M, Rieniets CY. Disclosure of imaging findings to patients directly by radiologists: survey of patients' preferences. *Am J Roentgenol* 1995;165:467–469.
10. Fallowfield L. Giving sad and bad news. *Lancet* 1993;341:476–478.
11. Miranda J, Brody RV. Communicating bad news. *West J Med* 1992;156:83–85.
12. Brewin TB. Three ways of giving bad news. *Lancet* 1991;337:1207–1209.
13. Quill TE, Townsend P. Bad news: delivery, dialogue, and dilemma. *Arch Intern Med* 1991;151:463–470.
14. McLauchlan CAJ. Handling distressed relatives and breaking bad news. *Br Med J* 1990;301:1145–1149.
15. Ptacek JT, Eberhardt TL. Breaking bad news: a review of the literature. *JAMA* 1996;276:496–502.
16. Gallagher J. Religious freedom, reproductive health care, and hospital mergers. *J Am Med Womens Assoc* 1997; 52:65–68.
17. Wynia MK, Cummins DS, VanGeest JB. Should physicians manipulate reimbursement rules to benefit patients? *JAMA* 2000;284(11):1382–1383.
18. Werner RM, Alexander GC, Fagerlin A. The "Hassle Factor": What motivates physicians to manipulate reimbursement rules? *Arch Intern Med* 2002;162(10):1134–1139.
19. Holleman WL, Holleman MC. School and work release evaluations. *JAMA* 1988;260:3629–3634.
20. Farnsworth EA. *Contracts*, 2nd ed. Boston: Little, Brown and Company, 1990:249–272.
21. Carey TS, Hadler NM. The role of the primary physician in disability determination for Social Security and worker's compensation. *Ann Intern Med* 1986;104:706–710.
22. Bok S. *Lying: Moral Choices in Public and Private Life*. New York: Pantheon Books, 1978.
23. Nyberg D. *The Varnished Truth*. Chicago: University of Chicago Press, 1993.
24. Green MJ, Farber NJ, Ubel PA, et al. Lying to each other: when internal medicine residents use deception with their colleagues. *Arch Intern Med* 2000;160(15):2317–2323.

ANNOTATED BIBLIOGRAPHY

1. Bok S. *Lying: moral choices in public and private life*. New York: Pantheon Books, 1978.
   Offers a comprehensive discussion of lies, stressing that people who are lied to feel betrayed and consider lying more serious than the liar does.
2. Blackhall LJ, Murphy ST, Frank G, et al. Ethnicity and attitudes toward patient autonomy. *JAMA* 1995;274: 820–825.
   Reports that fewer Mexican-American and Korean-American patients want to be told a serious diagnosis or grave prognosis, compared to European-Americans and African-Americans.
3. Surbone A. Truth telling to the patient. *JAMA* 1992;268:1661–1662.
   Points out that in most other cultures it is customary for families and physicians to shield patients from disturbing information about their diagnosis or prognosis.

CHAPTER 7

Keeping Promises

Physicians, like all people, make promises and are sometimes tempted to break them. Once made, promises are generally regarded as binding. In retrospect, however, some promises might seem imprudent or mistaken. The following cases demonstrate that some promises can be kept only if important ethical guidelines are violated.

CASE 7.1 Promise not to tell the patient that she has cancer.

A 61-year-old Mexican American widow undergoes a needle aspiration of a breast mass. Her daughter and son ask the physician not to tell the patient if the mass is cancer because they fear that she would not be able to handle the bad news. They point out that it is not customary in Mexico to tell women of her age that they have cancer. After breast cancer is diagnosed, the physician refers the patient to a surgeon. The surgeon believes that patients need to be involved in decisions regarding mastectomy or lumpectomy. In addition, the patient asks a Spanish-speaking nurse, "Why do I need surgery? Do I have cancer?" The surgeon and nurse feel constrained by the primary physician's promise not to tell the patient her diagnosis.

CASE 7.2 Promise to schedule tests.

A 54-year-old man, a heavy smoker, is hospitalized for hemoptysis, weight loss, and angina pectoris. A chest x-ray shows a 2-cm proximal lung mass, with hilar adenopathy. A bronchoscopy is scheduled to obtain a biopsy. When the intern walks by his room, the patient shouts, "This is outrageous. I haven't had breakfast, I haven't had lunch. Now they say they don't know when the test will be done and that I might have to go through all this again tomorrow. If this is how the hospital is run, I'm leaving." The intern, eager to appease the patient and continue with his other work, promises the patient that the test will be done that afternoon. He tells the nurse to call the bronchoscopy suite to say that the procedure needs to be done that afternoon.

Making and keeping promises is ethically important because it reduces uncertainty and promotes trust. However, Case 7.1 illustrates that in some situations keeping promises might be problematic, and Case 7.2 shows that some promises might be ill-advised or unrealistic.

THE ETHICAL SIGNIFICANCE OF PROMISES

A promise is a commitment to act a certain way in the future, either to do something or to refrain from doing something. Promises generate expectations in others, who in turn modify their plans and actions on the assumption that promises will be kept (1). In everyday social interactions, people commonly make promises and expect others to keep the ones they make. Promises might be exchanged for other promises, as in a business contract. For example, a merchant might promise to deliver goods in exchange for the promise of payment on delivery.

Keeping promises is desirable for several reasons. It results in beneficial consequences by making the future more predictable, relieving anxiety, and promoting trust. Indeed, another definition of "promise" is "that which causes hope, expectation, or assurance (2)." Keeping promises is also important even if there are no short-term beneficial consequences. Promise-keeping is essential for harmonious social interactions. If promises are widely broken, people would be unwilling to rely on others to keep commitments.

If promises are broken, the person to whom the promise is made often suffers a setback (3). The resulting tangible harm might be inconvenience and monetary losses. Moreover, it seems unfair to allow people to break promises simply because it would be to their advantage to do so, particularly when the other person has relied on the promise. The very concept of promises is negated if people feel free to break them. It is manipulative to expect others to honor their promises, even to their detriment, but to break one's own promises when it is in one's self-interest (3).

Promise-keeping is especially important for physicians. Because the doctor–patient relationship is based on trust, patients often feel betrayed if physicians break promises. Once betrayed, patients might be less likely to trust the individual physician or the medical profession. Promises by physicians might help patients cope with the uncertainty and fears inherent in being sick. In addition, promises establish mutual expectations that benefit both physicians and patients. For example, physicians promise confidentiality of medical information; in return, patients are more candid about discussing sensitive issues pertaining to their health. Thus, the patient's well-being is enhanced, and the physician's work is facilitated.

PROBLEMS WITH KEEPING PROMISES

None of us want to keep all the promises we make. Some promises are made on the spur of the moment, under emotional stress, with inadequate information, or without proper deliberation (3). Foolish promises that put one at a great disadvantage are often retracted, particularly if they confer a gratuitous boon on the other person. People might excuse breaking such promises because the other person is no worse off than if the promise had never been made in the first place. With many retracted promises, the other person has taken no action in reliance on the promise.

Clinical dilemmas occur when keeping promises would require actions that violate other ethical guidelines. In Case 7.1 the surgeon and nurse believe the initial promise not to tell the patient violates the guideline of respecting patient autonomy.

In Case 7.2 the intern's promise was misleading because he could not guarantee that the test would take place that afternoon.

SUGGESTIONS FOR PHYSICIANS

DO NOT MAKE PROMISES LIGHTLY

A statement that the physician regards as kindly reassurance might be interpreted by the patient or family as a promise. Even if the physician does not think a promise is important, the patient is likely to. Patients typically are more upset when physicians break promises than the physicians are.

ADDRESS THE CONCERNS UNDERLYING THE REQUEST FOR A PROMISE

If someone asks the physician to make an unrealistic promise, the physician can elicit the underlying concerns and address them in other ways. Thus, in Case 7.1, the physician needs to understand the concerns underlying the family's request not to tell the patient her diagnosis (*see* Chapter 6). In Case 7.2 the physician needs to listen to and empathize with the patient's feelings of frustration and anger.

DO NOT PROMISE OUTCOMES THAT ARE OUT OF YOUR CONTROL

Physicians should avoid making promises that are beyond their control to keep. Because clinical outcomes are inherently uncertain, it is unrealistic to make a promise that guarantees a good outcome or the absence of complications after a procedure. Given the complex organization of modern medicine, it is misleading to make promises about the actions of other members of the health care team. After all, other physicians and nurses are autonomous agents who have free will and their own moral and professional values. Thus, in Case 7.1, even if the physician agrees not to disclose the diagnosis to the patient, another health care worker might disclose it. Furthermore, the physician should be clear that, if asked directly, she will tell the patient she has cancer.

In Case 7.2 physicians should not make promises about situations not under their direct control, such as the scheduling of bronchoscopy. In the short run it might seem easier to promise that the test will be done rather than to listen to the patient complain about problems. However, making a promise that might not be kept is likely to cause more problems in the long run. It might be better simply to listen and acknowledge that the patient has every right to be angry. Realistically, what the doctor can promise is to look into the matter and to do his or her best to make sure that such delays and inconvenience do not happen again. If the doctor makes such promises, the doctor needs to follow up on them appropriately—for instance, by calling the patient ombudsman or filing an incident report with the charge nurse.

DO NOT VIOLATE ETHICAL GUIDELINES BECAUSE OF AN ILL-CONSIDERED PROMISE

Although promise-keeping is important, it is not an absolute duty. Other ethical guidelines are also important and might take priority in some situations. In some cases breaking the promise might be the lesser of two evils. The strongest case for overriding the promise-keeping occurs when the following conditions are met:

- Keeping the promise would violate another important ethical guideline. In Case 7.1 keeping the promise would require deception by the physician and compromise the patient's autonomy.
- The countervailing ethical considerations were not taken into account when the promise was made.
- The clinical and ethical situation has changed significantly since the promise was made. In Case 7.1 the doctor promised not to tell the patient before she asked whether she had cancer.
- Someone else made the promise. Although a person's promise can bind his own future actions, that person has no authority to bind others, such as the surgeon in Case 7.1 or the consultant performing the bronchoscopy in Case 7.2.
- The promise was stated implicitly rather than explicitly.

In Case 7.1 respect for patient autonomy and avoiding deception should prevail over keeping a promise to third parties. It is usually better to admit that the promise was a mistake and to deal with the consequences as directly and compassionately as possible.

In summary, promises can allay patients' fears and uncertainty. It is important to keep promises because other people rely on them. Breaking promises undermines trust in the individual physician and in the medical profession, yet keeping promises is not an absolute ethical duty. Sometimes respecting a promise might require the physician to violate other important ethical guidelines. In exceptional situations breaking a promise might be justified as the lesser of two evils. ·

REFERENCES

1. Farnsworth EA. *Contracts*, 2nd ed. Boston: Little, Brown and Company, 1990:39–110.
2. *Webster's revised unabridged dictionary*, (http://www.dictionary.com).
3. Fuller LL, Eisenberg MA. *Basic contract law*, 4th ed. St. Paul: West Publishing Company, 1981:1–8.

Shared Decision Making

CHAPTER 8

An Approach to Decisions About Clinical Interventions

$\mathbf{M}$edical interventions might allow accurate diagnosis and effective treatment, but they might also be applied when their benefit is questionable or when patients would not want them. Physicians therefore must try to avoid two types of errors: withholding potentially beneficial tests and therapies that the patient would want and imposing interventions that are not beneficial or not wanted.

This brief chapter presents an approach to decisions about clinical interventions. The general approach to ethical issues in Chapter 1 can be adapted to such decisions (Fig. 8-1). The key questions are as follows:

IS THE INTERVENTION FUTILE IN A STRICT SENSE?
Sound ethical judgments require accurate medical information. Physicians are under no obligation to provide interventions that are futile in a strict sense (*see* Chapter 9).

DOES THE PATIENT HAVE ADEQUATE DECISION-MAKING CAPACITY?
This is a crucial branch point in decision-making. Chapter 10 discusses how to determine whether a patient lacks decision-making capacity.

IF THE PATIENT IS COMPETENT, WHAT IS THE PATIENTS INFORMED DECISION?
Competent, informed patients may refuse medical interventions (*see* Chapter 11). Patients frequently lack decision-making capacity when decisions about medical interventions must be made. If the patient lacks decision-making capacity, two additional questions need to be posed.

IF THE PATIENT IS NOT COMPETENT, HAS HE OR SHE GIVEN ADVANCE DIRECTIVES?
Clear and convincing advance directives should be respected (*see* Chapter 12). In the absence of such advance directives, decisions should be based on what the patient would want or what is in his or her best interests (*see* Chapter 12).

IF THE PATIENT HAS NOT CLEARLY INDICATED WHAT HE OR SHE WOULD WANT DONE IN THE SITUATION, WHO SHOULD SERVE AS SURROGATE?
Generally, the surrogate should be a person designated by the patient or a close family member (*see* Chapter 13).

This book then considers disagreements between doctors and patients over medical interventions. Chapter 14 analyzes insistence by patients or surrogates on interventions that physicians regard as inappropriate. Chapter 15 discusses conclusions about life-sustaining interventions that are commonly drawn but that prove misleading on closer analysis. Chapter 16 discusses how ethics committees or ethics consultants can help physicians resolve ethical dilemmas.

Next, this book analyzes life-sustaining interventions in specific situations. Chapter 17 discusses Do Not Resuscitate (DNR) orders. Often, discussions about DNR orders are the first step in

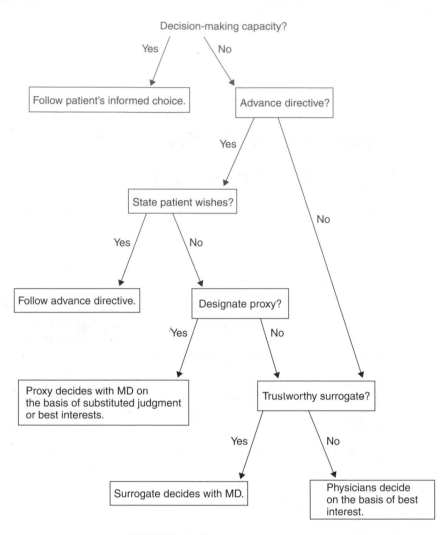

FIGURE 8-1 • Flow chart for clinical decisions.

a comprehensive evaluation of the goals and plans for care. Chapters 18-21 discuss physician-assisted suicide, tube feedings, the persistent vegetative state, and the determination of death.

Legal issues are then presented. Chapter 22 analyzes landmark legal cases that have dramatized dilemmas about life-sustaining interventions.

CHAPTER 9

Futile Interventions

Patients or surrogates sometimes request medical interventions that physicians consider irrational or pointless. The concept of futility seems an appealing way to resolve such disagreements. The term "futility" comes from a Latin word meaning "leaky (1)." In classical mythology the gods condemned the daughters of Danaus to carry water in leaky buckets (1). No matter how hard they tried, they could never achieve their goal of transporting water. By analogy, futile medical interventions would serve no meaningful purpose, no matter how often they are repeated.

Physicians claim that judgment of futility is a matter of professional expertise. In this view physicians may decide unilaterally to forego futile interventions rather than share with patients or surrogates. Because the term futility gives decision-making power to physicians, however, it must be used with caution. The term is fraught with confusion, inconsistency, and controversy.

STRICT DEFINITIONS OF FUTILITY

Physicians use the term in different ways (2–5). In three strictly defined senses, medical futility justifies unilateral decisions by physicians to withhold or withdraw interventions (Table 9-1).

INTERVENTION HAS NO PATHOPHYSIOLOGIC RATIONALE

CASE 9.1 Antibiotics not active against organism.
A 74-year-old woman has progressive septic shock with Staphylococcus infection despite treatment with appropriate antibiotics. The patient's family requests an antibiotic that they learned about on the Internet. The antibiotic is active only against gram-negative bacteria.

In this case there is no pathophysiological rationale for the antibiotic because it is not effective against the gram-positive bacteria causing this patient's illness. The antibiotic would provide no physiological benefit by raising the patient's blood pressure. Even if the family insists on the drug, there is no medical reason to administer it.

CARDIAC ARREST OCCURS BECAUSE OF REFRACTORY HYPOTENSION OR HYPOXEMIA

CASE 9.2 Patient with progressive septic shock.
A woman is comatose, on renal dialysis, and on a ventilator. On increasing doses of vasopressors, her mean arterial pressure falls to 60 mmHg. Her physicians want to write an order not to resuscitate in case of a cardiopulmonary arrest.

TABLE 9-1

When Is an Intervention Futile in a Strict Sense?

Intervention has no pathophysiologic rationale.

Cardiac arrest occurs because of refractory hypotension or hypoxemia.

The intervention has already failed in the patient.

In Case 9.2 cardiopulmonary arrest occurs because of progressive hypotension despite maximal support of the patient's circulation and oxygenation. Effective circulation cannot be sustained in this patient despite appropriate therapy. If her hypotension results in cardiopulmonary arrest, cardiopulmonary resuscitation (CPR) could not restore effective circulation. Even if cardiac rhythm were restored, she would again have refractory hypotension, which would again result in cardiopulmonary arrest.

THE INTERVENTION HAS ALREADY FAILED IN THE PATIENT

CASE 9.3 No response to CPR.

A 54-year-old man suffers a cardiac arrest in the emergency room. CPR and advanced cardiac support are initiated promptly. After 30 minutes all measures recommended in the American Heart Association guidelines have been attempted. He remains in asystole. His family insists that resuscitation be continued.

An adequate clinical attempt of CPR has failed to achieve the fundamental goal of restoring effective circulation and breathing. It is pointless to continue or repeat interventions that have already failed.

These three strict senses of "futility" are as plain as the root metaphor of carrying water in leaky buckets. A miraculous recovery might occur if such a futile intervention is attempted, but clinical decisions should not be based on the possibility of miracles. The determination that an intervention is futile in these strict senses is based on objective data or judgments within the expertise of physicians. Physicians have no ethical duty to provide interventions that are futile in these strict senses; indeed, they generally have an ethical obligation *not* to provide them.

LOOSE DEFINITIONS OF FUTILITY

The term "futility" is also used in several looser senses that are confusing, involve value judgments, and do not justify unilateral decisions by physicians to withhold interventions (4–6). Sometimes the phrase "not medically indicated" is used in similar ways.

CASE 9.4 Recurrent aspiration pneumonia and severe dementia.

A 74-year-old man with severe dementia is hospitalized for the third time in 6 months for aspiration pneumonia. At baseline he sometimes recognizes his daughter and smiles when watching television or listening to music. The daughter, his only surviving relative, insists that he be treated with antibiotics. The resident exclaims, "Treating him is futile! His dementia is not going to improve, and it's inhumane to keep alive someone with such a poor quality of life." The resident also argues that a Do Not Attempt Resuscitation (DNAR) order should be written on the basis of futility because CPR is so unlikely to succeed.

THE LIKELIHOOD OF SUCCESS IS VERY SMALL

Some physicians contend that an intervention should be considered futile if the likelihood of success in a given situation is extremely small—for example, no success in the last 100 attempts or less than a 1% chance of success (7). However, there are problems in setting a quantitative, probabilistic concept of futility. Why set the threshold at 1%? Some patients or families might consider a likelihood of success of 1% worth pursuing in some circumstances. On the other hand, some physicians might desire to make unilateral decisions to forego interventions whose likelihood of success is 2% or even 5%. Indeed, studies show that physicians commonly describe interventions as futile when the likelihood of success is far greater than 1% (8,9). Hence, even if agreement could be forged on a quantitative threshold for futility, in practice a much broader range of cases is characterized as futile.

NO WORTHWHILE GOALS OF CARE CAN BE ACHIEVED

Futility can be defined only in terms of the goals of care (10). Some ethicists contend that the proper goal of medicine is not simply to correct physiological derangements. For these writers it is inappropriate to prolong life if the patient will not regain consciousness or leave the intensive care unit (ICU) alive (1,7).

THE PATIENT'S QUALITY OF LIFE IS UNACCEPTABLE

In some situations physicians might declare an intervention futile because they believe that the patient's quality of life is unacceptable. For example, some ethicists consider interventions futile for patients in a persistent vegetative state (PVS), who will never regain consciousness or interact with other people (1). They argue that sustaining biological life is not an appropriate goal when the patient has no likelihood of regaining consciousness.

However, individual patients or the public might view the goals of care differently than physicians. Some people regard life as precious even if the patient will not leave the ICU alive, as in Case 9.4. Indeed, some states have public policies that favor prolonging life in patients who will not regain consciousness (11). At a minimum, physicians need to discuss goals with patients rather than attempt to define them unilaterally.

PROSPECTIVE BENEFIT IS NOT WORTH THE RESOURCES REQUIRED

An intervention might be termed futile because the expected outcomes are not considered worth the effort and resources required. However, society as a whole, not an individual physician acting unilaterally at the bedside, needs to decide the allocation of resources (*see* Chapter 30). Asserting that such interventions are futile closes off this difficult but essential debate (12).

PRACTICAL PROBLEMS WITH THE CONCEPT OF FUTILITY

Several problems occur in practice when physicians make unilateral decisions to withhold "futile" interventions.

JUDGMENTS OF FUTILITY ARE OFTEN MISTAKEN OR PROBLEMATIC

Physicians often err when they claim that an intervention has a very low probability of success. One study analyzed cases in which residents had written DNAR orders on the basis of a probabilistic definition of futility (9). In 32% of such cases residents estimated the probability of survival after CPR to be 5% or higher. In 20% of cases the estimated probability of survival after CPR was 10% or greater. Thus, the term "futility" was applied inappropriately when physicians believed the probability of success was much greater than the 1% threshold for futility proposed in the literature. Problems also occur when determinations of futility are based on quality of life. In the same study residents determined that CPR would be futile in this sense for 40 competent patients. Physicians discussed quality of life with only 65% of these patients, even though such discussions were feasible (9). It is ethically problematic for physicians to judge a competent patient's quality of life without talking to the patient directly. Many studies have found that physicians underestimate the extent to which patients believe their lives are worth living (13,14).

UNILATERAL DECISIONS BY PHYSICIANS POLARIZE DISAGREEMENTS

Attempts by physicians to resolve disputes by claiming the power to act unilaterally are likely to antagonize patients and surrogates. Furthermore, declaring one intervention futile might not settle other important issues in a case. For instance, CPR might be futile in a strict sense in a patient with multisystem failure in the ICU. However, a unilateral decision by physicians to withhold CPR would probably worsen disagreements about mechanical ventilation, vasopressor support, and antibiotics for infection.

PHYSICIANS CONFUSE FUTILITY AND BEST INTERESTS

Physicians commonly confuse futility and best interests as a basis for their decisions (10). Even if an intervention cannot be termed futile in a strict sense, physicians may recommend against it because the burdens outweigh the benefits to the patient. Furthermore, doctors may try to persuade the patient or surrogate that the intervention is not in the patient's best interests. Chapter 4 discusses in detail the concept of best interests.

SAFEGUARDS WHEN INTERVENTIONS ARE CONSIDERED FUTILE

Procedural safeguards are necessary to ensure that physicians' unilateral decisions to withhold "futile" interventions are appropriate (Table 9-2). Open discussions of medical futility help guard against errors and abuses. In the original meaning of "futile," there is no controversy that a leaky bucket will not hold water. Similarly, it should not be difficult for a physician to persuade colleagues, the patient or surrogate, or the public that a particular intervention is futile.

OBTAIN A SECOND OPINION

The physician who is considering a unilateral decision to forego a "futile" treatment should obtain a second opinion from a colleague or from the institutional ethics committee. Such second opinions are important because judgments of futility might be flawed.

DISCUSS THE INTERVENTION WITH THE PATIENT OR SURROGATE

Some physicians believe that they need not discuss futile interventions with the patient or surrogate. For example, in Case 9.3 a vast array of interventions would be futile in a strict sense, such as cancer chemotherapy. It would be pointless to tell patients or surrogates of interventions that are irrelevant to the illness at hand. In some cases, however, physicians might not discuss pertinent interventions because they fear that the patient or surrogate will disagree with their assessment that an intervention is futile. Physicians might use the idea of unilateral decisions about futility to avoid unpleasant discussions (15). However, the best approach to such situations is more discussion, not less.

Generally, discussing "futile" treatments with patients or surrogates is beneficial. It shows respect for patients and surrogates and clarifies their expectations, goals, concerns, and needs.

TABLE 9-2

Safeguards When Physicians Unilaterally Decide That an Intervention Is Futile

Obtain a second opinion.
Discuss the intervention with the patient or surrogate.
Establish explicit guidelines on futility.

Chapter 14 gives specific suggestions for such discussions. Moreover, such discussions help safeguard against improper uses of the term futility. Almost all patients or surrogates will eventually agree with physicians' judgments that interventions are futile (16).

ESTABLISH EXPLICIT GUIDELINES ON FUTILITY

Health care organizations should develop written guidelines about futile interventions (15,17). Written institutional guidelines demonstrate that unilateral decisions to forego futile interventions are made on the basis of carefully considered standards, not on *ad hoc* reasoning in particular cases. Several cities have developed policies and procedures for futility for a group of hospitals in a community (17–19). A recent Texas statute enacted many provisions of these policies and established an extrajudicial procedure for determining futility and discussing the matter with the patient or family (20). When physicians believe that an intervention is futile and the patient or family disagrees, the patient or family must be invited to meet with the hospital ethics committee. If the ethics committee agrees that the intervention is futile but the family does not, the hospital must try to work with the family to find another physician or institution willing to provide the intervention. After 10 days, if transfer of the patient cannot be arranged, the physician and hospital may withhold or withdraw the futile intervention. In early experience, the ethics committee agrees with the determination of futility in over 90% of cases, and in 86% of these cases the family accepts this judgment (20).

In conclusion, the concepts of futility and "not medically indicated" are intuitively appealing but need to be used extremely carefully. When futility is strictly defined, physicians may, and indeed should, make unilateral decisions to withhold interventions. However, it is problematic for physicians to use these concepts in looser ways to resolve disagreements with patients or families.

REFERENCES

1. Schneiderman LJ, Jecker NS, Jonsen AR. Medical futility: its meaning and ethical implications. *Ann Intern Med* 1990;112:949–954.
2. Youngner SJ. Who defines futility? *JAMA* 1988;260:2094–2095.
3. Lo B. Unanswered questions about DNR orders. *JAMA* 1991;265:1874–1875.
4. Truog RD, Brett AS, Frader J. The problem with futility. *N Engl J Med* 1992;326:1560–1564.
5. Helft PR, Siegler M, Lantos J. The rise and fall of the futility movement. *N Engl J Med* 2000;343(4):293–296.
6. Lantos JD, Singer PA, Walker RM, et al. The illusion of futility in clinical practice. *Am J Med* 1989;87:81–84.
7. Schneiderman LJ, Jecker NS, Jonsen AR. Medical futility: response to critiques. *Ann Intern Med* 1996;125: 669–674.
8. Prendergast TJ, Luce JM. Increasing incidence of withholding and withdrawal of life support from the critically ill. *Am Rev Resp Dis Crit Care Med* 1997;155:15–20.
9. Curtis JR, Park DR, Krone MR, et al. The use of the medical futility rationale in do not attempt resuscitation orders. *JAMA* 1995;273:124–128.
10. Kite S, Wilkinson S. Beyond futility: to what extent is the concept of futility useful in clinical decision-making about CPR? *Lancet Oncol* 2002;3:638–642.
11. Cruzan v. Harmon. 760 S.W.2d 408.
12. Alpers A, Lo B. Futility: not just a medical issue. *Law Med Health Care* 1992;20:327–329.
13. Pearlman RA, Uhlmann RF. Quality of life in chronic diseases: perceptions of elderly patients. *J Gerontol* 1988; 43:M25–M30.
14. Danis M, Patrick DL, Southerland LI, et al. Patients' and families' preferences for medical intensive care. *JAMA* 1988;260:797–802.
15. Council on Ethical and Judicial Affairs AMA. Medical futility in end-of-life care. *JAMA* 1999;281:937–941.
16. Smedira NG, Evans BH, Grais LS, et al. Withholding and withdrawing of life support from the critically ill. *N Engl J Med* 1990;322:309–315.
17. Halevy A, Brody B. A multi-institutional collaborative policy on medical futility. *JAMA* 1996;276:571–574.
18. Bay Area Network of Ethics Committees (BANEC) Nonbeneficial Treatment Working Group. Nonbeneficial or futile medical treatment: conflict resolution guidelines for the San Francisco Bay Area. *West J Med* 1999;170: 287–290.
19. Murphy DJ, Barbour E. GUIDe (Guidelines for the Use of Intensive Care in Denver): a community effort to define futile and inappropriate care. *New Horizons* 1994;2:326–331.
20. Fine RL, Mayo TW. Resolution of futility by due process: early experience with the Texas Advance Directives Act. *Ann Intern Med* 2003;138(9):743–746.

ANNOTATED BIBLIOGRAPHY

1. Kite S, Wilkinson S. Beyond futility: to what extent is the concept of futility useful in clinical decision-making about CPR? *Lancet Oncol* 2002;3:638–642.
   Helft PR, Siegler M, Lantos J. The rise and fall of the futility movement. *N Engl J Med* 2000;343:293–296.
   Two articles that argue that the concept of futility has limited usefulness in clinical practice.
2. Curtis JR, Park DR, Krone MR, et al. The use of the medical futility rationale in do not attempt resuscitation orders. *JAMA* 1995;273:124–128.
   Empirical study documenting problems and mistakes that occur when physicians claim that CPR would be futile.
3. Fine RL, Mayo TW. Resolution of futility by due process: early experience with the Texas Advance Directives Act. *Ann Intern Med* 2003;138:743–746.
   Describes a statewide futility policy that refers intractable disagreements over futility to the hospital ethics committee.

CHAPTER 10

Decision-making Capacity

Physicians must respect the autonomous choices of patients. However, illness or medications can impair the capacity of patients to make decisions about their health care. Such patients might be unable to make any decisions, or they might make decisions that contradict their best interests and cause them serious, even irreparable, harm. Decision-making ability falls along a continuum, with no natural threshold for adequate decision-making capacity, yet for any proposed intervention, a binary decision needs to be made: Either patients have adequate decision-making capacity and their choices should be respected or they do not and their preferences can be set aside (1). The following case illustrates how it might be difficult to decide whether decision-making power should be taken away from a patient.

CASE 10.1 Refusal to explain a decision.

Mrs. C, a 74-year-old widow with mild dementia, is admitted for congestive heart failure and angina pectoris that has progressed despite maximal medical therapy (2). In the past 3 years she has suffered two myocardial infarctions. Her physician recommends coronary angiography and, if possible, angioplasty.

Mrs. C recognizes her primary care physician but seldom knows the date or the name of the clinic. She has forgotten to come to several clinic appointments. Her mental functioning gets worse when she is hospitalized. A nephew, her only relative, pays a woman to shop, cook, and clean house for her. He reports that Mrs. C enjoys watching television, attending the senior center, and sitting in the park.

When asked about her wishes for care, Mrs. C says that she wants to go home. After many discussions, the cardiology team convinces her to have the angiogram. On the morning of the procedure, however, she changes her mind, saying that she doesn't want anyone to put a tube into her heart and that she has been in the hospital long enough. Her nephew believes that angioplasty would be best for her but is reluctant to contradict her wishes because she has always been independent and stubborn. Mrs. C is generally adverse to medical interventions. She refused mammography, even though she has a family history of breast cancer. She also refused treatment for a cholesterol level of 318 mg per dL.

The team asks a psychiatrist to see her. On a mental status examination, she does not know the date, the name of the hospital, or the city. She recalls only one of three objects and cannot perform serial subtraction. She refuses to talk further with the psychiatrist, saying that she is not crazy.

In this case Mrs. C's mental functioning is obviously impaired. Is it so impaired that her nephew should assume the authority to make medical decisions for her? Her refusal did not seem so unreasonable to some physicians and nurses. Furthermore, some nurses asked why her consent to angiography was not questioned, only her refusal.

This chapter analyzes how physicians should assess whether patients like Mrs. C have the capacity to make decisions about their care. This book uses the term *competent* to refer to patients who have the capacity to make informed decisions about medical interventions. Strictly speaking, all adults are considered competent to make such decisions unless a court has declared them *incompetent*. In everyday practice, however, physicians usually make *de facto* determinations that patients lack decision-making capacity and arrange for surrogates to make decisions, without involving the courts (3–6). This clinical approach has been defended because routine judicial intervention imposes unacceptable delays and generally involves only superficial hearings. Because legal competency hearings are far less common than informal determinations by physicians, this book does not use the legal term incompetent. Instead, we say that a patient *lacks decision-making capacity* if a physician rather than a court determines that the patient is unable to make informed decisions about health care (3).

ETHICAL IMPLICATIONS OF DECISION-MAKING CAPACITY

Caring for patients whose decision-making capacity is questionable involves two conflicting ethical guidelines. On the one hand, physicians must respect the authority of competent patients to make decisions that others might regard as foolish, unwise, or harmful (*see* Chapter 11). On the other hand, physicians should act in their patients' best interests (*see* Chapter 4). Patients who lack decision-making capacity are vulnerable and might be seriously harmed by decisions that are contrary to their best interests. Such persons need to be protected from harm (6,7). The patient's decision-making capacity is therefore crucial. If it is intact, the patient's decisions will be respected. If it is seriously impaired, decision-making power is taken from the patient and given to a surrogate.

Generally, a patient's decision-making capacity is not challenged if he or she agrees with the physician. On its face this practice suggests that patients are only incapacitated when they disagree with physicians. However, it makes sense to raise more questions about decision-making capacity when a patient refuses a beneficial intervention than when he or she consents to it. When Mrs. C accepts angiography, her care would be the same whether or not she has decision-making capacity. If she has adequate decision-making capacity, her consent to angioplasty would be valid. If she lacks it, the physician and her surrogate agree that angiography was necessary because it was in her best interests. Now consider Mrs. C's refusal of angiography (assuming that she had not previously given an informed refusal). If she has decision-making capacity, her refusal would have to be respected. If she lacks it, a surrogate would assume decision-making power. The physician and her nephew agree that angiography is in her best interests. Hence, if she refuses, her management hinges on whether her decision-making capacity is considered impaired. Thus, it is appropriate that Mrs. C's refusal of recommended interventions triggers questions about her capacity to make medical decisions. Such a refusal, however, does not by itself prove that she lacks such capacity.

LEGAL STANDARDS FOR COMPETENCE

The courts have not enunciated clear standards of competency to make medical decisions (4,8). A comprehensive legal treatise concludes that "the meanings of competence and incompetence are usually taken for granted or dealt with only in a cursory way by courts (8)." Many older legal cases viewed incompetence in general or global terms. Either the patient was competent in all aspects of life or the patient was not competent in any sphere. The courts inferred incompetence from a person's overall ability to function in life, medical diagnoses, general mental functioning, and personal appearance.

However, a person might be capable of performing some tasks adequately but not others (6). For example, a person might be capable of making informed medical decisions but not informed financial decisions. Thus, it would be more appropriate to consider a person competent or incompetent for specific tasks rather than in all aspects of life (5). The modern legal consensus is that a person should be considered competent to make medical decisions if he or she is capable of giving informed consent (5). More specifically, a patient is considered competent if he or she appreciates the diagnosis and prognosis, the nature of the tests or treatments proposed, the alternatives, the risks and benefits of each, and the probable consequences. Chapter 3 discusses informed consent in detail.

CLINICAL STANDARDS FOR DECISION-MAKING CAPACITY

A patient's decision-making capacity should be subjected to scrutiny in several situations. As in Case 10.1, the patient might refuse a treatment that the physician strongly recommends or vacillate in making a decision. In other cases patients might have conditions that commonly impair decision-making capacity, such as dementia, schizophrenia, or depression. Although these conditions justify closer scrutiny of the patient's decision-making capacity, they are not tantamount to impaired decision-making capacity. Physicians need to test directly the patient's ability to give informed consent for the proposed intervention (3,6,9). Decision-making capacity requires a cluster of abilities (Table 10-1), as outlined below.

THE PATIENT MAKES AND COMMUNICATES A CHOICE

A patient must appreciate that he or she—and not the physician or family members—has ultimate decision-making power. In addition, the patient must be willing to choose among the alternative courses of care. A patient who vacillates repeatedly between consent and refusal is incapable of making a decision, let alone an informed one. Such profound indecision must be distinguished from changing one's mind as the situation changes, as the patient receives more information or advice, or after the patient deliberates.

The patient must communicate his or her choice. A patient who is unable to speak, for example, because of being on a ventilator, does not necessarily lack decision-making capacity. That patient might be able to communicate through writing messages, using an alphabet board, or blinking or nodding in response to questions.

THE PATIENT UNDERSTANDS INFORMATION THAT IS PERTINENT TO THE DECISION AND APPRECIATES ITS RELEVANCE TO THE SITUATION

A patient needs to understand the medical situation and prognosis, the nature of the proposed intervention, the alternatives, the risks and benefits, and the likely consequences of each alternative. The patient needs this information to make an informed decision. In addition to comprehending this information, the patient needs to appreciate that he or she has the disorder and what the consequences of treatment would be. The patient needs to accept that the information that the physician discussed is relevant to his or her own situation. In Case 10.1 the health care team could not determine whether Mrs. C understood that angioplasty usually relieves chest pain but has certain risks.

DECISIONS ARE CONSISTENT WITH THE PATIENT'S VALUES AND GOALS

Choices should be consistent with the patient's character and core values. If Mrs. C wants to be more active without pain, refusing surgery or angioplasty would be inconsistent with her goals. However, many patients do not have well-articulated values and goals or might have multiple,

TABLE 10-1

Clinical Standards for Decision-making Capacity

The patient makes and communicates a choice.

The patient appreciates the following information:

- the medical situation and prognosis
- the nature of the recommended care
- alternative courses of care
- the risks, benefits, and consequences of each alternative.

Decisions are consistent with the patient's values and goals.

Decisions do not result from delusions.

The patient uses reasoning to make a choice.

conflicting goals. Mrs. C might want to return home but also to be more active and pain-free. A choice might be consistent with some goals but not with others. People do not necessarily have a fixed hierarchy of goals and values. Mrs. C might define her goals or set priorities only by deciding about angiography. Thus, physicians should not regard a patient as lacking decision-making capacity merely because that patient cannot articulate a set of general values or goals.

DECISIONS DO NOT RESULT FROM DELUSIONS OR DISTORTED VIEWS OF REALITY

Some patients have delusions that preclude informed decision-making. For instance, Mary Northern was an elderly woman who refused amputation of her gangrenous legs, denying that gangrene had caused her feet to be "dead, black, shriveled, rotting and stinking (10)." Instead, she believed that they were merely blackened by soot or dust. The court declared her incompetent because she was "incapable of recognizing facts which would be obvious to a person of normal perception (10)." The court said that if she had acknowledged that her legs were gangrenous but refused amputation because she preferred death to the loss of her feet, she would have been considered competent to refuse the surgery.

THE PATIENT USES REASONING TO MAKE A CHOICE

Processing information logically is another element of the capacity to make medical decisions. Patients should compare and weigh the various options for care (11). This requirement does not require the patient to choose what most people consider reasonable in the situation. Unconventional decisions do not necessarily imply lack of decision-making capacity. Expectations for reasoning must take into account that many people do not deliberate but instead rely on emotional or intuitive factors in making important decisions.

ASSESSMENTS OF DECISION-MAKING CAPACITY SHOULD TAKE INTO ACCOUNT THE CLINICAL CONTEXT

Assessments must consider the patient's functional abilities, the demands of the specific clinical situation, and the harm that might result from her choice. Some writers have suggested that a patient who chooses an option that has great risk and little prospect of benefit should meet higher standards for decision-making capacity than a patient who chooses an option that has great prospect of benefit and little risk (6,12,13). The benefits and risks of alternatives should also be taken into account; a patient who chooses an option that has less benefit and greater risk than the alternatives should be held to a stricter standard of decision-making capacity. Also, the nature of the intervention might be important. A patient might be given more leeway to refuse disfiguring surgery, such as amputation, than treatments with less drastic side effects. Such a sliding scale offers more protection to patients when the potential harm resulting from their decisions is greater. According to this view, it seems plausible in Case 10.1 to apply a more rigorous standard of capacity when Mrs. C refuses treatment for symptomatic, life-threatening cardiac disease than when she refuses screening tests or treatment for cardiac risk factors. Although such a sliding scale is intuitively appealing, it might be problematic in practice. People are likely to disagree over what risks are serious and over what standard should be required for a particular decision. A sliding scale might allow physicians to exercise inappropriate control over patients with whom they disagree. To guard against such problems, physicians need to define explicitly the criteria they are using in assessing a patient's decision-making capacity.

ASSESSING THE CAPACITY TO MAKE DECISIONS

Many helpful and practical suggestions for determining decision-making capacity have been offered (9,14). The assessment presupposes that the patient has received adequate information about his or her condition and the interventions. If there is any doubt, the physician needs to repeat the information.

DOES THE PATIENT UNDERSTAND THE DISCLOSED INFORMATION?

Helpful questions include:

- "Tell me what you believe is wrong with your health now."
- "What is angiography likely to do for you?"

DOES THE PATIENT APPRECIATE THE CONSEQUENCES OF HIS OR HER CHOICES?

The physician can ask:

- "What do you believe will happen if you do not have angiography?"
- "I've described the possible benefits and risks of angiography. If these benefits or risks occurred, how would your everyday activities be affected?"

DOES THE PATIENT USE REASONING TO MAKE A CHOICE?

The doctor can make such requests as:

- "Tell me how you reached your decision. . . ."
- "Help me understand how you decided to refuse the angiogram."
- "Tell me what makes angiography seem worse than the alternatives."

In addition, it is helpful to talk to family and friends, nurses, and other physicians caring for the patient, particularly when the physician does not know the patient well. These persons can clarify whether the patient's mental function or choices have changed over time.

THE ROLE OF MENTAL STATUS TESTING

Clinicians often use mental status tests to assess whether a patient has the capacity to make medical decisions. Such tests evaluate orientation of the subject to person, place, and time, attention span, immediate recall, short-term and long-term memory, ability to perform simple calculations, and language skills (15).

However, mental status tests are less useful than directly assessing whether the patient understands the nature of the intervention, the risks and benefits, the alternatives, and the consequences (16). For example, Mrs. C scored poorly on standard mental status tests, but if she appreciates that angioplasty would probably improve her chest pain and shortness of breath, she has the capacity to make an informed refusal.

In several court rulings patients with abnormal mental status tests were found competent to make decisions about health care. For example, a 72-year-old man who withdrew his consent for amputation of his gangrenous legs was found competent even though one psychiatrist found that he was disoriented to the place and to the people around him and had visual hallucinations (17). The probate judge found that "his conversation did wander occasionally but to no greater extent than would be expected of a 72-year-old man in his circumstances." The patient hoped "for a miracle" but realized that "there is no great likelihood of its occurrence."

In another case a 77-year-old woman was found competent to refuse amputation of her leg for gangrene (18). Testimony indicated that she was "lucid on some matters and confused on others," that her "train of thought sometimes wanders," and that "her conception of time is distorted." One psychiatrist claimed that her refusal to discuss the amputation with him indicated that "she was unable to face up to the problem." The court found that she understood that in "rejecting the amputation she is, in effect, choosing death over life."

CONSULTATION BY PSYCHIATRISTS

Psychiatrists might be helpful in evaluating patients whose decision-making capacity is questionable (4,14,19). Psychiatrists are skilled at interviewing patients with mental impairment. Compared to nonspecialists, they might be more successful at engaging the patient in discussions and better able to evaluate the patient's understanding of the proposed intervention. In addition, psychiatrists specialize in diagnosing and treating mental illnesses that might impair a patient's decision-making capacity. Psychiatrists are also skilled at identifying and resolving interpersonal and intrapsychic conflicts that impair decision making (19).

Attending physicians can readily acquire the skills to assess patients' decision-making capacity, and routine psychiatric consultation is not necessary (20). Ultimately, attending physicians are responsible for judging whether the patient lacks decision-making capacity.

ENHANCING THE CAPACITY OF PATIENTS TO MAKE DECISIONS

Impairments in decision-making capacity might be reversible if underlying medical or psychiatric conditions are treated. In addition, physicians can enhance patient understanding of pertinent information by presenting information in simple language, in small chunks, slowly and repeatedly over time. Diagrams and videotapes might improve comprehension. Furthermore, the presence of family members or friends can help reduce anxiety, correct misunderstandings, and focus on the salient issues.

ENGAGING THE PATIENT IN DISCUSSIONS

Patients like Mrs. C might refuse to answer questions or explain their decisions. They need to understand that lack of cooperation might lead to a determination of impaired decision-making capacity and loss of the power to make health care decisions. However, repeated attempts to assess decision-making capacity or to persuade them might be counterproductive. Patients might be angry at losing control or resent being badgered. In turn, health care workers might feel frustrated.

DECISION-MAKING CAPACITY IN SPECIFIC CLINICAL SITUATIONS

MENTAL ILLNESS AND DECISION-MAKING CAPACITY

Many patients with mental illness are competent to make decisions about their medical care. However, lack of decision-making capacity is more common in certain psychiatric conditions. Patients with schizophrenia or depression commonly fail to appreciate the relevance of information to their situation. According to one study, among inpatients with schizophrenia, 35% did not acknowledge their symptoms and diagnosis (21). Furthermore, 13% to 14% of patients with schizophrenia or major depression denied the potential benefit of treatment.

Psychiatric illness might also impair decision-making capacity more subtly (22). Patients who are depressed might overemphasize the risks of treatment, underestimate the benefits, believe that treatment is less likely to be successful for them than for others, or feel unworthy of the intervention.

Psychiatric patients might be so gravely disabled or unable to care for themselves that they might be involuntarily committed (*see* Chapter 40). However, involuntary commitment does not empower physicians to give whatever medical treatment they consider advisable. If such a patient refuses treatment for medical problems, an appropriate surrogate or a separate court order is needed to authorize treatment.

UNCONVENTIONAL DECISIONS BASED ON RELIGIOUS BELIEFS

Patients might refuse effective medical treatments because of religious beliefs. Religious beliefs are matters of faith; empirical evidence and reasoning are not pertinent. In the United States freedom of religion is deeply respected. Furthermore, it is troubling for physicians to label some religious beliefs as acceptable and others as not. Thus, refusals of treatment by competent adults on religious grounds are accepted. (Parental refusals of effective treatment for children may be overridden, as is discussed in Chapter 37.) Religious beliefs need not be articulated as formal or orthodox doctrines. As one court ruling declared, beliefs that others consider "unwise, foolish, or ridiculous" do not render a person incompetent (23). Indeed, informed consent would be meaningless if such individualistic refusals were not respected, even though they conflicted with medical or popular wisdom.

The physician's inquiry generally is limited to whether the religious beliefs are sincere in the sense that they antedate the illness and are consistent with prior actions (24) and whether other aspects of decision-making are problematic. Some patients have religious delusions or hallucinations. For example, a patient might believe that he is Christ, that the devil has caused his colon cancer, or that he should refuse surgery because it is God's will that he suffer. Because of his delusions, he is not capable of making informed decisions. It does not matter that his delusions are based on religious ideas.

EMERGENCIES

A patient with questionable decision-making capacity might present with an emergency condition that requires immediate treatment. Rather than evaluating the patient's decision-making capacity, physicians should provide emergency care unless it is known that the patient or surrogate would refuse such care. This approach is justified by implied consent to emergency care (*see* Chapter 3).

CARING FOR PATIENTS WHO LACK DECISION-MAKING CAPACITY

After physicians determine that a patient lacks decision-making capacity, advance directives or surrogate decision-making should guide further care (*see* Chapters 12 and 13).

Even if a patient lacks the capacity to make decisions, his or her stated preferences should be given substantial consideration. For instance, mentally incapacitated patients might balk at phlebotomy or x-rays, sometimes screaming their refusal. Even if the courts declared such a patient incompetent, it would be morally and emotionally repugnant to impose interventions on an unwilling patient. Health care workers might consider it inhumane to force a patient to undergo a highly invasive intervention when he or she cannot understand its purpose and benefits. Furthermore, future cooperation might be undermined. It is preferable if the patient assents to interventions decided on by a surrogate or court, even if that patient cannot give informed consent. Persuasion, cajoling, and asking family members and friends to talk to the patient are acceptable ways to try to gain the patient's cooperation. Often, a patient will agree to treatment after caregivers have listened to his or her objections, modified the treatment plans, or changed the hospital routine.

In summary, physicians commonly decide that patients lack the capacity to make informed decisions about their care without resorting to the courts. Physicians need to understand the clinical standards for decision-making capacity and be able to apply these standards in specific cases. Good communication skills are crucial for assessing decision-making capacity.

REFERENCES

1. Brock DW. *Life and Death*. New York: Cambridge University Press, 1993.
2. Lo B. Assessing decision-making capacity. *Law Med Health Care* 1990;18:193–201.
3. President's Commission for the Study of Ethical Problems in Medicine and Biomedical and Behavioral Research. *Making Health Care Decisions*. Washington, DC: U.S. Government Printing Office, 1982.
4. Appelbaum PS, Lidz CW, Meisel A. *Informed consent: legal theory and clinical practice*. New York: Oxford University Press, 1987:266.
5. Meisel A. *The right to die*. New York: John Wiley & Sons, 1989.
6. Buchanan AE, Brock DW. *Deciding for others*. Cambridge: Cambridge University Press, 1989.
7. Beauchamp TL, Childress JF. *Principles of biomedical ethics*, 4th ed. New York: Oxford University Press, 1994.
8. Meisel A. *The right to die*, 2nd ed. New York: John Wiley & Sons, 1995.
9. Grisso T, Appelbaum P. *Assessing competence to consent to treatment: a guide for physicians and other health professionals*. New York: Oxford University Press, 1998.
10. State Dep't of Human Resources v. Northern. 563 S.W.2d 197 (Tenn. Ct. App. 1978).
11. Grisso T, Appelbaum P. *Assessing competence to consent to treatment: a guide for physicians and other health professionals*. New York: Oxford University Press, 1998:52–58.
12. Grisso T, Appelbaum P. *Assessing competence to consent to treatment: a guide for physicians and other health professionals*. New York: Oxford University Press, 1998:22–26.
13. Drane JF. Competency to give an informed consent. *JAMA* 1984;252:925–927.
14. Appelbaum PS, Grisso T. Assessing patients' capacities to consent to treatment. *N Engl J Med* 1988;319: 1635–1638.
15. Kane RL, Ouslander JG, Ibrass IB. *Essentials of clinical geriatrics*, 2nd ed. New York: McGraw-Hill, 1989.
16. Grisso T, Appelbaum P. *Assessing competence to consent to treatment: a guide for physicians and other health professionals*. New York: Oxford University Press, 1998:90–91.
17. In re Quackenbush. 156 N.J. Super. 282, 383 A.2d 785 (1978).

18. Lane v. Candura. 6 Mass. App. 377,376 N.E.2d 1232 (1978).
19. Perl M, Shelp EE. Psychiatric consultation masking moral dilemmas in medicine. *N Engl J Med* 1982;307: 618–621.
20. Grisso T, Appelbaum P. *Assessing competence to consent to treatment: a guide for physicians and other health professionals.* New York: Oxford University Press, 1998:77–80.
21. Appelbaum PS, Grisso T. The MacArthur Treatment Competence Study, I: mental illness and competence to consent to treatment. *Law Hum Behav* 1995;19:105–126.
22. Bursztajn HJ, Gutheil TG, Brodsky A. *Affective disorders, competence, and decision making.* In Gutheil TG, Bursztajn HJ, Brodsky A, Alexander V, eds. *Decision making in psychiatry and the law.* Baltimore: Williams & Wilkins, 1991:153–170.
23. In re Brooks. 32 Ill.2d 361, 205 N.E.2d 435 (1965).
24. Grisso T, Appelbaum P. *Assessing competence to consent to treatment: a guide for physicians and other health professionals.* New York: Oxford University Press, 1998:47–48.

ANNOTATED BIBLIOGRAPHY

1. Grisso T, Appelbaum P. *Assessing competence to consent to treatment: a guide for physicians and other health professionals.* New York: Oxford University Press, 1998.
   Lucid, practical, and comprehensive discussion of how to assess decision-making capacity.
2. Buchanan AE, Brock DW. *Deciding for others.* Cambridge: Cambridge University Press, 1989.
   Comprehensive discussion of different definitions and standards for decision-making capacity.

CHAPTER 11

Refusal of Treatment by Competent, Informed Patients

Competent and informed patients may refuse interventions that their physicians recommend. In some cases physicians may hesitate to accept refusals that jeopardize the patient's life or health. Although concern for a patient's well-being is commendable, as discussed in Chapter 4, it is important for physicians to understand the strong ethical and legal reasons for respecting refusals made by informed, competent patients. This chapter discusses the reasons for respecting such refusals, the problems that result from refusals of transfusions by Jehovah's Witnesses, and restrictions on patient refusal.

REASONS FOR RESPECTING PATIENT REFUSALS

RESPECT FOR PATIENT AUTONOMY

Honoring refusal of treatment by competent, informed patients respects their self-determination and individuality. Ethically, physicians should respect the autonomy of persons to make decisions about their care (1–4). Patients should be free of unwanted medical interventions. The option of declining treatment is fundamental to the concept of informed consent. If patients must consent to treatment, then logically they have the right to decline treatment. The U.S. Supreme Court has suggested that the Constitution protects a competent patient's refusal of life-sustaining treatment (5). A large body of case law supports the right of competent, informed patients to refuse treatment (6).

IMPOSING MEDICAL INTERVENTIONS WOULD BE UNACCEPTABLE

On a practical level it is difficult to imagine imposing unwanted medical interventions on a competent patient. Sedating or restraining patients to impose treatment over their objections seems intrusive and inhumane. Most people would find such means repugnant, even if the original refusal of treatment was unwise.

SCOPE OF REFUSAL

Competent patients are permitted to refuse virtually any treatments, even highly beneficial ones with few side effects. The range of interventions includes surgery, mechanical ventilation, renal dialysis, antibiotics, cardiopulmonary resuscitation, and tube feedings (6). Competent patients have a right to refuse treatment even if such refusal might shorten their lives or lead to their deaths. They are not required to have a terminal illness as a condition for refusing treatment.

Competent patients may refuse treatment even if their family, friends, or physicians disagree with them. As one court ruling declared, even decisions that are "unwise, foolish, or ridiculous (7)" might need to be respected. Indeed, informed consent would be meaningless unless patients could refuse interventions for highly personal reasons or make decisions that conflict with medical or popular wisdom.

JEHOVAH'S WITNESS CASES

Jehovah's Witnesses do not accept blood transfusions, basing their refusal on an interpretation of the Bible (8). They believe that although a blood transfusion might save their corporeal life, it will deprive them of everlasting salvation. Their refusals are clearly articulated, are usually steadfast over time, and are supported by their family and friends. Refusals of blood transfusions by Jehovah's Witnesses might be distressing to physicians because, from a purely clinical perspective, the benefits of transfusion are great and the risks trivial. Many patients are young, previously healthy, and can be restored to perfect health.

REACTIONS OF HEALTH CARE PROVIDERS

Jehovah's Witnesses generally consent to other interventions, such as surgery, if transfusions are not used. Physicians might feel that Jehovah's Witnesses, by refusing transfusions but agreeing to other care, unnecessarily compromise medical outcomes, make their job more difficult, and require them to provide substandard care. Physicians might believe that they are being asked to accomplish the goal of saving the patient's life without using the best available means. Some surgeons complain that operating on a Jehovah's Witness without transfusions is like having to operate with one hand tied behind their back. They have less margin for error or complications. On a psychological level, some physicians resent the loss of control over the patient's care. Some health care workers might also blame the patient for making their jobs more complicated. Many surgeons and anesthesiologists prefer not to treat Jehovah's Witnesses. Often, however, transferring such patients to another institution or physician is impractical.

Frustrated health care workers might develop imaginative plans for administering blood to Jehovah's Witnesses. Some physicians suggest waiting until such patients are unconscious and then asking if they object to a transfusion. Because patients are then no longer able to refuse, these physicians would administer blood. Other physicians advocate simply giving transfusions after patients are under anesthesia and not telling them about it. Both such actions, however, are unacceptable because they are deceptive and undermine trust in physicians.

Health care workers need to appreciate that without transfusions medical outcomes for Jehovah's Witness are often quite good, even though care is more difficult. For example, operative mortality for open heart surgery on Jehovah's Witnesses has been reported as acceptably low, using intraoperative cell salvage and other blood conservation techniques (9).

LEGAL ISSUES

The courts have consistently upheld refusals of blood transfusions by competent adult Jehovah's Witnesses (10–13). Recent controversies have involved incompetent Jehovah's Witnesses. Some physicians object that wallet cards signed by Jehovah's Witnesses are not sufficient evidence that the patient made an informed decision (14).

PRACTICAL SUGGESTIONS

Physicians caring for Jehovah's Witnesses can take several steps to ensure that the patient's refusal of transfusions is informed and steadfast. First, the physician should ask the adult patient about transfusions when no family members, friends, or religious advisors are present. This lessens the chance that the patient feels coerced into refusing. When alone, some Jehovah's Witnesses will agree to transfusions. Second, the physician should ask patients whether they would accept transfusions if they are ordered by a court. Some Jehovah's Witnesses will accept a transfusion as long as they do not personally consent to it. Under these circumstances many judges are willing to order that transfusions be given. Third, some Jehovah's Witnesses will refuse all blood products but others will accept various blood components. Most will accept erythropoietin and fluorinated blood substitutes. Fourth, physicians should ask whether the patient has any other concerns about receiving blood, such as a risk of human immunodeficiency virus (HIV) infection or hepatitis. If the underlying reason for refusal is really a fear of infection, this concern should be addressed directly.

Having ensured that the refusal is steadfast and informed, health care workers should respect the patient's decision. From the point of view of a Jehovah's Witness, the decision to refuse transfusions is simple. They would be pleased to survive the hospitalization, but as one patient put it, "What good is a few years of life compared to everlasting damnation (15)?" Even if health care workers do not agree with this belief, they need to respect it. Continuing to try to convince a Jehovah's Witness shows disrespect. Furthermore, using deception to administer blood cannot be condoned.

When an adult Jehovah's Witness who requires a transfusion lacks decision-making capacity, the situation is more complicated. Advance directives that reflect informed decisions should be respected, as Chapter 12 discusses. Many Jehovah's Witnesses have completed wallet-sized "blood cards" declaring they would refuse transfusions. The ethical validity of these cards has been questioned because completion of the cards might have been coerced by peer pressure and because the patient might not have been informed about the risks and benefits of transfusions (14).

Physicians should respond differently if the patient is a minor and the parents are refusing a medically indicated transfusion (*see* Chapter 37). In this situation physicians should ask a court to approve the transfusion. As one court declared, parents are "not free to make martyrs of their children (16)."

RESTRICTIONS ON REFUSAL

The right of competent, informed patients to refuse medical treatment may be limited in certain situations.

COMMUNICABLE DISEASES

In certain circumstances competent patients may be required to undergo treatment against their wishes in order to prevent harm to third parties. The clearest examples are infectious diseases that can be transmitted by casual contact, such as tuberculosis (17,18). To reduce the risk of transmitting a serious disease to other persons, infected individuals may be required to be treated or else be quarantined until they no longer pose a risk to others.

COMPELLED TREATMENT OF PREGNANT WOMEN

In several cases the courts have ordered pregnant women to undergo cesarean sections or blood transfusions over their objections, allegedly to protect the health of the fetus. These rulings, however, have been sharply criticized for violating the woman's bodily integrity and right of self-determination. Recent court rulings have rejected interventions against the wishes of the pregnant woman (19–21).

Trying to prevent harm to the fetus that will be carried to term is praiseworthy (*see* Chapter 39). However, in most situations in pregnancy compelled treatment is not feasible. In diabetes or drug addiction, interventions must be continued over an extended period, the cooperation of the pregnant woman is needed, and the infringement of her autonomy caused by ongoing forced treatment is substantial.

TREATING COMPETENT PATIENTS FOR THEIR OWN BENEFIT

Providing interventions over the objections of a competent patient in order to prevent harm to third parties needs to be clearly distinguished from providing treatment in order to prevent harm to the patient. The physician's duty to prevent harm to competent patients is considered weaker than the duty to prevent harm to unsuspecting third parties. Physicians should try to persuade patients and to negotiate a mutually acceptable plan of care (*see* Chapter 4). They may not, however, override the informed decisions of a competent patient because they believe it would be better for that patient.

In some situations physicians might be tempted to administer treatment to prevent serious harm to patients. Jonsen et al. discuss the perplexing case of a young man with bacterial meningitis who refused antibiotics (22). The patient shows no indication of impaired decision-making capacity other than his "enigmatic refusal" of treatment. As they present the case, there is no time for prolonged discussion. Rather than allow the patient to die from such a readily treatable infection, these authors advocate administering antibiotics because they believe that "something essential is missing in the case." Indeed, the authors later disclose that earlier the patient's cousin had died from an anaphylactic reaction to penicillin and that this incident had led to his refusal.

This is admittedly a difficult case, and difficult cases often lead to bad generalizations. Although it is troubling to allow a patient to die from an easily treatable infection, it is also troubling to override the refusal of a patient when the only evidence of impaired decision-making capacity is the patient's refusal of treatment. Without hindsight, it is problematic to establish a rule that such patients can be considered to have impaired decision-making capacity. Any such rule would give physicians virtually unlimited power to override patients who cannot provide satisfactory reasons for refusing treatment.

In summary, there are cogent ethical and legal reasons to accept refusals of treatment by competent and informed patients. Subsequent chapters discuss how physicians can try to persuade patients to accept beneficial interventions while respecting their right to refuse.

REFERENCES

1. Lo B, Jonsen AR. Clinical decisions to limit treatment. *Ann Intern Med* 1980;93:764–768.
2. President's Commission for the Study of Ethical Problems in Medicine and Biomedical and Behavioral Research. *Making health care decisions*. Washington: U.S. Government Printing Office, 1982.
3. President's Commission for the Study of Ethical Problems in Medicine and Biomedical and Behavioral Research. *Deciding to forego life-sustaining treatment*. Washington: U.S. Government Printing Office, 1983.
4. American College of Physicians. American College of Physicians Ethics Manual. *Ann Intern Med* 1998;128: 576–594.
5. Lo B, Steinbrook R. Beyond the Cruzan case: the U.S. Supreme Court and medical practice. *Ann Intern Med* 1991;114:895–901.
6. Meisel A. *The right to die*, 2nd ed. New York: John Wiley and Sons, 1995.
7. In re Brooks. 32 Ill.2d 361, 205 N.E.2d 435 (1965).
8. Sheldon M. Ethical issues in the forced transfusion of Jehovah's Witness children [see comments]. *J Emerg Med* 1996;14:251–257.
9. Rosengart TK, Helm RE, DeBois WJ, et al. Open heart operations without transfusion using a multimodality blood conservation strategy in 50 Jehovah's Witness patients: implications for a "bloodless" surgical technique. *J Am Coll Surg* 1997;184:618–629.
10. Furrow BR, Johnson SH, Jost TS, et al. *Health law: cases, materials and problems*. St. Paul: West Publishing Co, 1991.
11. Meisel A. *The right to die*, 2nd ed. New York: John Wiley and Sons, 1995:538–542.
12. Fosmire v. Nicoleau, 552 N.E.2d 77 (N.Y. 1990).
13. Norwood Hosp. v. Munoz, 564 N.E.2d 1017 (Mass. 1991).
14. Migden DR, Braen GR. The Jehovah's Witness blood refusal card: ethical and medicolegal considerations for emergency physicians. *Acad Emerg Med* 1998;5:815–824.
15. In re Osborne, 294 A. 2d 372 (D.C. 1972).
16. Prince v. Massachusetts, 321 U.S. 158 (1944).
17. Oscherwitz T, Tulsky JP, Roger S, et al. Detention of persistently nonadherent patients with tuberculosis. *JAMA* 1997;278:843–846.
18. Gasner MR, Maw KL, Feldman GE, et al. The use of legal action in New York City to ensure treatment of tuberculosis. *N Engl J Med* 1999;340:359–366.
19. Curran W. Court-ordered cesarean sections receive judicial defeat. *N Engl J Med* 1990;323:489–492.
20. Levy JK. Jehovah's Witnesses, pregnancy, and blood transfusions: a paradigm for the autonomy of all pregnant women. *J Law Med Ethics* 1999;27:171–189.
21. Goldblatt AD. Commentary: no more jurisdiction over Jehovah. *J Law Med Ethics* 1999;27:190–193.
22. Jonsen A, Siegler M, Winslade W. *Clinical Ethics*, 3rd ed. New York: Macmillan Publishing Company Inc, 1991:61–63.

ANNOTATED BIBLIOGRAPHY

1. President's Commission for the Study of Ethical Problems in Medicine and Biomedical and Behavioral Research. *Deciding to forego life-sustaining treatment*. Washington: US Government Printing Office,1983.
   Lucid and thoughtful exposition of refusal of treatment by patients.
2. Meisel A. *The right to die*, 2nd ed. New York: John Wiley and Sons, 1995.
   Comprehensive legal treatise that describes court rulings permitting competent patients to refuse treatment.

CHAPTER 12

Standards for Decisions When Patients Lack Decision-making Capacity

W hen patients lack decision-making capacity, physicians must address two questions:

- What standards should be used when patients cannot give informed consent or refusal?
- Who should act as surrogate for such patients?

This chapter addresses the first question, discussing advance directives, substituted judgments, and the patient's best interests. These should be viewed as a hierarchy: decisions based on advance directives generally should take priority over those grounded in substituted judgments, which in turn should supersede decisions based on best interests (Table 12-1). Chapter 13 addresses the second question.

ADVANCE DIRECTIVES

Many patients fear that they will lose control over care if their decision-making capacity is impaired. Advance directives are statements by competent patients that indicate *who* should act as surrogate or *what* interventions they would accept or refuse in case they should lose decision-making capacity. Although patients are still competent, they give informed consent or refusal. Advance directives respect patients by allowing their preferences and values to guide care even when they can no longer make informed decisions. In addition, advance directives allow patients to relieve stress on family members who must make decisions for them (1).

Advance directives are most useful when they identify whom the patient trusts to make decisions if he or she loses decision-making capacity. Many patients also want to provide substantive directives about what interventions they would want or not want. In most cases, however, the proxy will need to interpret the patient's previous statements rather than simply implement them. Thus, the patient needs to trust the proxy's judgment and discretion. The following case illustrates the usefulness and limitations of advance directives.

CASE 12.1 Oral advance directives.

Mrs. A, a 76-year-old widow with Alzheimer disease, lives in a nursing home. She often does not recognize relatives and friends or respond when asked questions. She requires assistance with dressing, bathing, and eating. When still lucid, she told her children and her friends many times that she wanted "no heroics" if she became senile. After visiting a neighbor who was in intensive care, unconscious after a severe stroke, she told her son, "That is not living. I don't want to die plugged into a machine, unable to recognize my family and having to depend on others to take care of me. If I'm like that, just let me die in peace."

TABLE 12-1
Standards for Making Decisions When Patients Lack Decision-making Capacity

Advance directives.
   Oral statements to family members or friends
   Oral statements to physicians
   Written documents
Substituted judgments.
Best interests of the patient.

    Mrs. A develops pneumonia and sepsis. Her son and daughter remind the physician of these conversations and ask him not to administer antibiotics for the infection or transfer her to an acute care hospital. However, her brother strongly believes that life-sustaining treatment should be provided regardless of her previous statements or expected quality of life. He asserts, "Life is sacred; you can't just let her die." The brother adds, "She's a totally different person. She was so afraid of being senile. But look at her now. She's not suffering. Even though she usually doesn't recognize us, she smiles when I hold her hand or when I play music on the radio."

TYPES OF ADVANCE DIRECTIVES

Oral Statements to Family Members or Friends

Conversations with relatives or friends about what interventions they would want or not want in future situations are the most common advance directives (2,3). Such discussions are frequently used in everyday clinical practice to guide decisions for patients who have lost decision-making capacity.

    Limitations of oral directives. People might comment about the care of other people without intending to direct their own future care. They might also state preferences without thinking deeply about them. In addition, observers might not accurately recall a patient's statements or might disagree over what the patient said.

    Legal status of oral directives. Although oral directives are commonly used in decisions to provide or forego an intervention, a few states severely restrict their use (4). Courts have ruled that advance directives must be "clear and convincing," which requires stronger evidence than a "preponderance of the evidence" but less evidence than "beyond a reasonable doubt." Applying this standard strictly, several states have rejected typical oral advance directives unless they mention the specific intervention and clinical situation at hand—for example, a feeding tube in severe dementia (5). Although most court rulings have concerned cases of severe cognitive impairment, New York requires such clear and convincing evidence even for patients with incurable cancer. Courts in other states, however, have accepted oral statements similar to those by Mrs. A in Case 12.1 as clear and convincing (5).

    Evaluating the trustworthiness of oral directives. Certain characteristics make oral advance directives more trustworthy guides to whether the patient wanted an intervention.

- The patient's preferences are *informed*. Patients who have experienced serious illness or who have had relatives or friends with serious illness are more likely to be informed.
- The directive indicates what *specific treatments* the patient would want or not want *in various clinical situations* rather than simply expressing general preference or values.
- The directive is *repeated* over time, in different situations, to various individuals. Such consistency makes it more likely that the choices are carefully considered and based on deeply held values.

Oral Statements to Physicians

Discussions with physicians are more common than written advance directives (2–4,6). Unlike some oral statements to relatives or friends, directives to physicians are not casual comments. Moreover, physicians can check whether directives are informed. For instance, a physician could have discussed with Mrs. A how most patients with moderate dementia appear to enjoy many activities.

Written Documents

All states have enacted laws authorizing living wills or the appointment of health care proxies (4,7,8). Patients complete a formal legal document that must be witnessed or notarized. A lawyer is not needed to complete these documents. Many states honor forms from other states. Caregivers who follow written directives that meet state requirements are given immunity from civil and criminal liability and professional disciplinary actions. Because statutes vary from state to state, caregivers and patients need to be familiar with their state's laws.

The courts consider written advance directives more reliable evidence of patient choices than oral statements. Courts presume that patients are more likely to think about the issues and to appreciate the consequences of their actions if they complete a formal legal document. However, only about 25% of patients have given written advance directives (9–13).

Living wills. In living wills, patients direct their physicians to withhold or withdraw life-sustaining treatment if they develop a terminal condition or, in some states, enter a persistent vegetative state (PVS). Various states define "terminal condition" differently, usually only in general terms. In most states living wills would not cover conditions such as Alzheimer disease. Patients typically may refuse only interventions that "merely prolong the process of dying." People may disagree on whether this phrase includes antibiotics for pneumonia in Case 12.1. Some states do not allow patients to decline artificial nutrition and hydration through living wills. Because of these limitations, living wills are less flexible and comprehensive than the health care proxy (14–16).

Health care proxy. Competent patients might appoint a health care proxy or agent to make medical decisions if they were to lose decision-making capacity. In some states this process is called *executing* a durable power of attorney for health care. As long as patients remain competent, they continue to make their own health care decisions. This proxy, typically a relative or close friend, has decision-making priority over other potential surrogates. In Case 12.1, if Mrs. A had appointed one of her children as health care proxy, her brother would have no authority to make health decisions. Certain people might not serve as surrogates because of potential conflicts of interest. In California the surrogate may not be the treating physician or employees of the treating physician or institution unless they are relatives of the patient. The health care proxy applies to all situations in which the patient is incapable of making decisions, not just terminal illness. Proxy decisions must be consistent with the patient's previously expressed choices or best interests. However, no additional evidence of the patient's wishes is required if the proxy has been designated in accordance with state requirements. Appointing a health care proxy, supplemented with statements of what life-sustaining treatment the patient would want or refuse in various scenarios, is the best way to provide advance directives.

LIMITATIONS OF ADVANCE DIRECTIVES (4)

Advance Directives Might Not Be Informed

Even after discussions with physicians, only 33% of patients know that patients on a ventilator cannot talk and about one half believe that ventilators are oxygen tanks or that ventilated people are always comatose (17). Similarly, patients have serious misunderstandings about cardiopulmonary resuscitation (CPR). Over one fourth cannot identify any basic characteristics of CPR, such as chest compressions or assisted breathing (17). Only one third know that even if CPR succeeds in restarting the heart a breathing machine is usually needed. Thus, "patients expressed strong preferences about treatments that they did not understand (17)."

Patients also overestimate their prognosis (17,18). In a cohort of patients with metastatic lung or colon cancer, who had a 6-month survival of 45%, most patients were decidedly overoptimistic: 59% believed that their chance of surviving 6 months was greater than 90% (19).

Interpretations of Advance Directives Might Be Problematical

Vague terms. Advance directives often use vague terms such as "heroic" or "extraordinary" care. Physicians are commonly directed to refuse interventions when "the burdens outweigh the benefits of care." As Chapter 15 discusses, these terms are ambiguous and misleading. In Case 12.1 such vague terms provide little guidance. Did Mrs. A want to decline antibiotics for infection or did she want to decline only more invasive interventions such as CPR and mechanical ventilation? Mrs. A said that she did not want life-sustaining treatment if she became "senile," but when does "senility" commence? When she can no longer pursue favorite activities? When she sometimes does not recognize family members? Or only when she no longer responds at all? Studies show that patients' choices in specific scenarios cannot be accurately predicted from their general preferences and goals (20,21).

Application to similar situations. A patient might give advance directives about one situation but develop a different condition. For example, a patient might give directives about dementia but develop a major stroke. Patients differ in how much leeway they want surrogates to take to apply their directive to other circumstances or interventions. In one study 39% of patients wanted their directives to be followed literally, but 31% of patients wanted their surrogates to override their advance directives if their surrogates believed it was best for them (22).

Unrealistic expectations. Physicians sometimes insist on life-sustaining interventions because it is not certain that the patient would not want them. Undue requirements of the patient's wishes might impose burdensome interventions on patients and make them "prisoners of technology (23)." Even if treatments cannot be foregone on the basis of advance directives, they might be withheld or withdrawn on the basis of substituted judgments or best interests.

Advance Directives Might Conflict with the Patient's Best Interests

Following the patient's advance directives might not be in his or her current best interests. For example, surrogates and physicians might wish to override prior refusal of care if a brief intervention is virtually certain to restore the patient to previous health (24).

When providing advance directives, patients make implicit assumptions about their prognosis or situation. However, promising new therapies might become available, other serious medical conditions might develop, a treatment might prove unsuccessful, or a spouse might die. Such developments would make prior directives less pertinent to the current situation.

More fundamentally, the incompetent person might have changed so much since giving advance directives that he or she is essentially a different person from when he or she gave the directives (25,26). In this view, advance directives are not binding. Mrs. A's brother questions whether her previous statements are still relevant because she has changed so dramatically. On the other hand, many people believe that although Mrs. A is not as alert as she once was, she is in essence still the same person and that her directives should be respected.

Patients Might Change Their Minds

After patients indicate that they would decline interventions, in 21% to 28% of cases they subsequently decide that they would accept the interventions, or at least try them (27,28). Acceptance of life-sustaining interventions is less stable. After patients indicate that they would accept life-sustaining interventions, from 43% to 50% indicate in later interviews that they would decline the intervention. Furthermore, 68% of patients who say they would accept a trial of treatment subsequently say they would decline the intervention (27).

Despite these limitations, advance directives should be encouraged. They promote respect for patients as individuals with unique characters and values. They also encourage discussions of life-sustaining interventions among patients, family members, and physicians.

RATIONALE FOR DISCUSSING ADVANCE DIRECTIVES WITH PATIENTS

Most patients—between 59% and 85% of outpatients—want to talk with their physicians about life-sustaining interventions before a clinical crisis occurs (2,3,6), yet few have done so. When thinking or talking about life-sustaining interventions, most patients feel in control, relieved, or cared for (2). Even patients who feel sad or anxious when thinking about life-sustaining treatment still want to have such conversations (2,6). Among hospitalized patients, between 42% and 81% want to discuss end-of-life decisions with their physicians (29,30). Most patients want physicians to take the initiative in discussing advance directives (2,31). The physician can also help patients understand the usefulness and limitations of advance directives. The federal Patient Self Determination Act is intended to promote discussions about advance directives (32). Hospitals, nursing homes, and health maintenance organizations that participate in Medicaid and Medicare must inform patients about their rights to provide advance directives at the time of admission or enrollment. Institutions must also carry out advance directives and educate their staffs about them. Patients are not required to complete an advance directive.

PROBLEMS WITH DISCUSSIONS ABOUT ADVANCE DIRECTIVES

Currently, discussions between patients and physicians about advance directives are problematic. In one study only 11% of patients who had executed advance directives had discussed them with their physicians (33). Almost all discussions concerned general attitudes and feelings rather than specific interventions (33).

Even when discussions occur, they rarely give patients enough information to make informed decisions (34). Physicians usually pose hypothetical scenarios to patients, but they generally discuss extreme scenarios in which there was little variation in patient preferences. Almost all physicians discuss dire scenarios in which patients are permanently unconscious, will not survive outside an intensive care unit, or are about to die. Virtually no patients want interventions in such dire scenarios. Moreover, physicians often discuss reversible scenarios in which patients are expected to regain their previous health. Almost all patients accept even "heroic" interventions in such reversible scenarios. Thus, discussions of these extreme scenarios provide little guidance. Physicians seldom discuss more difficult—and more common—situations, such as when recovery is unpredictable or the patient has chronic disability after treatment.

Typically, physicians use vague language, asking patients what they would want if they were "very, very sick" or "had something that was very serious." Doctors rarely define such terms or ascertain how patients interpreted them. Physicians commonly discuss specific interventions, usually CPR or mechanical ventilation. However, rarely do physicians attempt to learn what patients know about these interventions. In discussing outcomes, physicians seldom give numerical probabilities of success or mention outcomes other than death and complete recovery.

Physicians rarely elicit patients' values, goals for care, and reasons for choices. Most commonly, physicians determine whether patients wanted specific interventions in scenarios without exploring the reasons for those preferences. Even when reasons are discussed, physicians rarely ask patients to define a poor quality of life or being a burden to their family, which are frequent reasons for refusing interventions.

IMPROVING DISCUSSIONS ABOUT ADVANCE DIRECTIVES

When Should Discussions about Advance Directives Be Initiated?

Physicians should discuss advance directives when it would not be surprising if the patient were to lose decision-making capacity or to die (35). Hence, physicians should target not only patients who are "terminal" or in a downhill course, but also those with serious chronic illness such as congestive heart failure, whose course is not so predictable. Patients usually want discussions to occur earlier than physicians do: earlier in the natural history of disease as well as earlier in the patient–physician relationship (31). If the physician waits until clinical deterioration has already occurred, the patient is often too sick to make informed decisions (36).

In some cultures advance directives might be inappropriate. For example, many traditional Chinese patients believe that giving explicit directives implies that they do not trust their family to make decisions for them (37). Moreover, they might believe that designating a single person to make decisions violates their desire for family decision making. Furthermore, some patients believe that talking about future illness will anger ghosts or spirits, who will then bring about the illness or cause bad luck. Such reluctance to discuss future plans needs to be respected.

TABLE 12-2

Topics to Discuss Regarding Advance Directives

Who should serve as proxy?
What are the patient's general preferences and values?
What are the patient's preferences in specific clinical situations?
How should advance directives be interpreted?
How do patients want to be treated near the end of life?

Physicians can resolve many problems with advance directives by explicitly addressing the following issues (Table 12-2):

Who Should Serve as Proxy?

Most patients find it easier to discuss the choice of proxy than to discuss preferences regarding care. Straightforward questions might broach the topic: "I ask all my patients with heart disease how they want decisions to be made. Who would you want to make decisions for you in case you are too sick to talk with me directly?" Those who do not wish to discuss these topics can easily demur.

Patients need to select someone whom they trust to make decisions in unforeseen situations. Although patients should provide guidance to their proxies, it is likely that proxies will have to exercise judgment about what patients would want or what is best for them. Patients cannot anticipate what specific decisions and conditions.

What Are the Patient's General Preferences and Values?

Many physicians focus discussions on specific medical decisions, such as Do Not Attempt Resuscitation (DNAR) orders. However, it is premature to discuss particular decisions before understanding patient's concerns and expectations. Often, specific decisions are easier to make after the patient discusses his or her general values and preferences. Open-ended questions help elicit the patient's perspective (38):

- "When you think of serious illness, what concerns you the most?" Alternatively, "When you think of serious illness, what is most important to you?"
- "Sometimes your family might need to make decisions about your medical care. What things would you want them to take into account?" These questions elicit how the patient defines his or her best interests or an acceptable quality of life.
- "Are there conditions under which you would not want life-prolonging interventions?"

What Are the Patient's Preferences in Specific Clinical Situations?

It is unrealistic to try to discuss all future medical situations. The goal of discussions is not to be exhaustive but to elicit informed choices about likely scenarios and to understand what considerations are important to the patient.

Discuss scenarios that are likely to occur (39). Although the PVS has captured public attention, it is very rare. Rather than discussing dire or completely reversible situations, physicians should discuss common scenarios in which the outcome is uncertain and the interventions are burdensome (17).

Physicians need to describe interventions and their likely outcomes. For CPR, patients need to know about chest compressions, artificial respirations, electroshock, the low likelihood of survival after CPR, and the possibility of neurological compromise (*see* Chapter 17). For mechanical ventilation, patients need to understand that they will have a tube in their throat, will not be able to speak, and will probably need sedation.

For patients with coronary artery disease, cardiopulmonary arrest, cardiogenic shock, and respiratory failure from pulmonary edema should be discussed. What limits would the patient place on life-prolonging interventions if prolonged ventilatory or multisystem failure develops?

For patients with cancer, the physician should discuss altered mental status and sepsis in advanced disease. What types of intervention would the patient be willing to accept? For what likelihood, magnitude, and duration of improvement?

With elderly patients, physicians should discuss severe dementia and stroke. In these situations, would the patient want infections treated with antibiotics or intensive care? Would the patient want a feeding tube if he or she could not swallow food? How would the patient define severe dementia or severe stroke?

Correct unrealistic expectations. Patients might have unrealistic expectations. For example, a woman with lung cancer metastatic to liver and bone might indicate that she wants everything done. In such cases physicians should elicit expectations, concerns, and emotions, using open-ended questions. The physician could say, "What do you think happens to patients whose cancer spreads like that?" "Wish statements" might help physicians explain that the patient's goals are impossible (40). "I wish that were the case. Unfortunately when cancer has spread that much, even breathing machines don't help patients live much longer."

Use of specific checklists. The Medical Directive is a checklist of 12 interventions in each of four clinical scenarios: terminal illness, dementia, PVS, and coma (41). Such specific directives are useful when the patient and physician have discussed these situations and the patient has made truly informed decisions, but they might be misleading if the patient expresses choices without fully appreciating the issues and deliberating about them.

How Should Advance Directives Be Interpreted?

Because advance directives cannot cover all contingencies, it is important to understand how the patient would want the surrogate and physician to interpret his or her preferences.

Physicians need to ask patients to clarify ambiguous statements: "Can you tell me what you mean by 'no heroic treatment'?"

Physicians should also ask patients how much leeway they would allow surrogates to interpret their directives, extrapolate them to unforeseen situations, or override their directives if it seemed in their best interests (22).

How Do Patients Want to Be Treated near the End of Life?

A recent advance directive form enables patients to indicate that they want their families to know that "I love them," "I wish to be forgiven for the times I might have hurt them," and "I forgive them for what they have done to me (42)." In addition, patients can fill out what they would like their family to say if anyone asks how they want to be remembered. This directive shifts the focus to finding closure at the end of life.

CONTINUE DISCUSSIONS OVER TIME

Physicians should not expect to understand the patient's preferences after a single conversation. In addition, patients' choices and values might change as their illness, their life situation, or their appraisal of their situation changes. If patients change their mind, they should tell both the surrogate and the physician, destroy all copies of written advance directives, and complete a new advance directive.

Recommend Written Directives

Physicians should tell patients about the advantages of written advance directives and encourage patients to complete them. This is particularly important in states such as New York and Missouri, whose courts have rejected most oral directives.

Document Discussions in the Medical Record

The physician's note should describe the patient's decision-making capacity, appreciation of the consequences of the patient's choices, and his or her specific preferences about interventions in various situations. It is not necessary for the patient to sign the record.

SUBSTITUTED JUDGMENT

Clear and specific advance directives should be respected, but often patients have given only general directives or no indication of their preferences, as in the following case.

CASE 12.2 Disagreements over substituted judgment.

Mr. S, a 76-year-old widower, suffers a massive stroke and aphasia. Two weeks later he still has paralysis of his right arm and leg. He does not respond consistently to simple requests or questions but sometimes smiles when his hand is held. He develops pneumonia.

Throughout his life he had been reluctant to see physicians and did not regularly take prescribed medications to lower his cholesterol. He loved to take walks and work in his garden. When his wife died of a sudden heart attack, he said, "Death isn't the enemy. She wanted to be active and healthy to the end, and the good Lord granted her wish." He was a proud and independent man who was reluctant to accept help from others. He has given no oral or written advance directives. His son and daughter believe Mr. S would refuse antibiotics. "He disliked being dependent on others and would hate being in a nursing home. In his condition he can't do any of the things he loved in life."

In the absence of clear and specific advance directives, surrogates should try to construct the decision that the patient would make under the circumstances, taking into account all that is known about the patient. The surrogate might imagine that the patient miraculously regains decision-making capacity. What care would the patient choose under the circumstances?

Reconstructing patients' choices is ethically justified because it respects their individuality to the extent that this is possible (26). Patients usually trust a family member or other surrogate to make the best decision possible under circumstances that were not foreseen (1).

PROBLEMS WITH SUBSTITUTED JUDGMENT

Inconsistency

Reasonable people acting in good faith may disagree over what the patient would want. For example, his sister might believe that Mr. S would want antibiotics. "He's been a fighter all his life and never gave up." She recalled that as a young man, Mr. S had overcome tremendous odds to come to America and get a college education.

Inaccuracy

Neither family members nor physicians can accurately state a competent patient's choices regarding future life-sustaining treatment (43–46). In one study only 68% of family members correctly stated a competent patient's preferences for CPR if he or she developed dementia and only 59% of physicians were able to do so (43). This level of agreement between proxies and patients would be expected by chance alone. Surrogates' statements about patients' preferences are closer to what *they* would want in the situation than to what the patient actually wants (47). Even an intensive intervention that facilitated discussions between the patient and proxy about the patient's wishes for end-of-life care failed to increase the level of agreement (48).

Questionable Considerations

Competent patients might not want to be a burden or might want to spare the family the expenses and stress of terminal care (1). It seems reasonable for surrogates to consider these factors when the patient himself has already done so, but it might be self-serving for surrogates to consider such factors when patients have not stated their importance (49). Family members might confound what they would want with what the patient would want.

Unavoidable Speculation

Substituted judgments are inherently less certain than advance directives (50–52). Mr. S's comments about his wife do not necessarily express his own desires for medical care. Even though he could no longer take walks and read, he might adapt to his illness and find life worthwhile. Many independent people learn to accept disabilities and assistance from others. In Case 12.2

the children's reasoning is unconvincing when applied to the converse situation. If a patient had seen physicians regularly, taken medications faithfully, and pursued no hobbies, it would be illogic to infer that he wanted all life-sustaining interventions in this situation.

Conflicts with the Patient's Best Interests

In unusual cases substituted judgments might lead to decisions that contradict the patient's current best interests. For example, family members might say that a mildly demented patient would not want life-prolonging interventions, even though that patient still enjoys activities such as listening to music or playing with grandchildren. Although it would be appropriate to withhold treatment in this situation on the basis of a clear and specific advance directive, it is problematic to do so as a substituted judgment.

Despite the potential pitfalls of substituted judgments, they are desirable because they respect the patient's individuality as a person with unique values and preferences (26).

BEST INTERESTS

For some patients who have not given advance directives, a substituted judgment would be so speculative that it is more honest for the surrogate and physician to base decisions on what they believe is best for the patient (53). A consensus of medical ethicists and clinicians supports decisions based on the patient's best interests (50,54,55). Such decisions are justified by the ethical guideline of beneficence: Physicians must act for the patient's well-being and must weigh the benefits and burdens of interventions for the patient.

Some scholars advocate a best-interests standard because statements previously made by an incapacitated patient in a vastly different situation might not be relevant (25,50,53). For example, these writers believe that preferences expressed by a young, healthy person should not carry much weight years later when that person is severely demented. Indeed, some writers have suggested that the patient with severe dementia should be considered a different person from the one who provided the advance directives, with different values and preferences. In this view previous directives are irrelevant to current decisions.

PROBLEMS WITH BEST INTERESTS

Different people might disagree over what is best for a patient. Disagreements might involve the goals of care, the assessment of the benefits and burdens of an intervention, or the evaluation of the patient's quality of life. Judgments about quality of life are particularly controversial if they are made by a surrogate rather than by the patient because other people underestimate patients' quality of life. Chapter 4 discusses these issues in more detail.

Some surrogates request painful interventions that will only prolong the patient's life a few days. Surrogates might believe that suffering serves a spiritual purpose or that biological life should be prolonged even if the interventions required are very burdensome. Decisions based on such beliefs need to be scrutinized carefully (56). Did the patient hold such views, as opposed to the surrogate? Did the patient say explicitly that he or she would accept painful interventions or decline palliative relief? Many patients who believe their illness serves a spiritual purpose will still decline burdensome interventions. Caregivers might believe that they are causing the patient to suffer if they do not provide standard palliative care (56,57). The ethical guideline of nonmaleficence allows health care workers to refrain from interventions that cause significant suffering and prolong the patient's life for only a few hours or days (*see* Chapter 14) (56).

Incompetent patients who have not given advance directives and have no surrogates often pose difficult cases. Some doctors mistakenly believe all life-sustaining interventions that are technically feasible should be provided to such patients unless they are futile. However, insisting on life-sustaining interventions because it is not certain that the patient would not want them might impose burdensome interventions on patients and make them "prisoners of technology (23)." To safeguard against bias, procedures such as consultation with another physician or with the hospital ethics committee often are useful. Despite problems with best interests, it is an acceptable reason to forego such interventions in such situations.

In summary, advance directives are the preferred way to make decisions for patients who lack decision-making capacity. Advance directives might be oral statements or documents such as living wills or durable powers of attorney for health care. The most comprehensive and flexible advance directives both appoint a proxy and express choices about treatments. In discussions with patients, physicians can ensure that advance directives are informed. In the absence of clear advance directives, surrogates should try to make substituted judgments. If the patient's values and preferences are not known, decisions need to be based on the patient's best interests. In making these decisions, physicians need to guard against two types of errors: withholding treatments that might be beneficial or continuing treatments that the patient would not want.

REFERENCES

1. Singer PA, Martin DK, Lavery JV, et al. Reconceptualizing advance care planning from the patient's perspective. *Arch Intern Med* 1998;158(8), 879–884.
2. Lo B, Mc Leod G, Saika G. Patient attitudes towards discussing life-sustaining treatment. *Arch Intern Med* 1986;146:1613–1615.
3. Emanuel LL, Barry MJ, Stoeckle JD, et al. Advance directives for medical care—a case for greater use. *N Engl J Med* 1991;324:889–895.
4. Lo B, Steinbrook RL. Resuscitating advance directives. *Arch Intern Med* 2004;164:1501–1506.
5. Lo B, Rouse F, Dornbrand L. Family decision-making on trial: who decides for incompetent patients? *N Engl J Med* 1990;322:1228–1231.
6. Steinbrook R, Lo B, Moulton J, et al. Preferences of homosexual men with AIDS for life-sustaining treatment. *N Engl J Med* 1986;314:457–460.
7. Meisel A. *The right to die*, 2nd ed. New York: John Wiley and Sons, 1995.
8. Sabatino CS. The legal and functional status of the medical proxy: suggestions for statutory reform. *J Law Med Ethics* 1999;27(1):46–51.
9. Rubin SM, Strull WM, Fialkow MF, et al. Increasing completion of the durable power of attorney for health care: a randomized controlled trial. *JAMA* 1994;271:209–212.
10. Sulmasy DP, Song KY, Marx ES, et al. Strategies to promote the use of advance directives in a residency outpatient practice. *J Gen Intern Med* 1996;11:657–663.
11. Meier DE, Fuss BR, O'Rourke D, et al. Marked improvement in recognition and completion of health care proxies. *Arch Intern Med* 1996;156:1227–1232.
12. Teno J, Lynn J, Wenger N, et al. Advance directives for seriously ill hospitalized patients: effectiveness with the patient self-determination act and the SUPPORT intervention. *J Am Geriatr Soc* 1997;45(4):500–507.
13. Bradley EH, Wetle T, Horwitz SM. The patient self-determination act and advance directive completion in nursing homes. *Arch Fam Med* 1998;7(5):417–423.
14. Orentlicher D. Advance medical directives. *JAMA* 1991;263:2365–2367.
15. Annas GJ. The health care proxy and the living will. *N Engl J Med* 1991;324:1210–1213.
16. Steinbrook R, Lo B. Decision making for incompetent patients by designated proxy. *N Engl J Med* 1984;310: 1598–1601.
17. Fischer GS, Tulsky JA, Rose MR, et al. Patient knowledge and physician predications of treatment preferences after discussions of advance directives. *J Gen Intern Med* 1998;13:447–454.
18. Murphy DJ, Burrows D, Santilli S, et al. The influence of the probability of survival on patients' preferences regarding cardiopulmonary resuscitation. *N Engl J Med* 1994;330:545–549.
19. Weeks JC, Cook EF, O'Day SJ, et al. Relationship between cancer patients' predictions of prognosis and their treatment preferences. *JAMA* 1998;279:1709–1714.
20. Schneiderman LJ, Kronick R, Kaplan RM, et al. Effects of offering advance directives on medical treatments and costs. *Ann Intern Med* 1992;117:599–606.
21. Fischer GS, Alpert HR, Stoeckle JD, et al. Can goals of care be used to predict intervention preferences in an advance directive? *Arch Intern Med* 1997;157:810–807.
22. Sehgal A, Galbraith A, Chesney M, et al. How strictly do dialysis patients want their advance directives followed? *JAMA* 1992;267:59–63.
23. Angell M. Prisoners of technology: the case of Nancy Cruzan. *N Engl J Med* 1990;322:1226–1228.
24. Danis M, Southerland LI, Garrett JM, et al. A prospective study of advance directives for life-sustaining care. *N Engl J Med* 1991;324:882–888.
25. Dresser RS, Robertson JA. Quality of life and non-treatment decisions for incompetent patients: a critique of the orthodox approach. *Law, Med Health Care* 1989;17:234–244.
26. Blustein J. Choosing for others as continuing a life story: the problem of personal identity revisited. *J Law Med Ethics* 1999;27(1):13–19.
27. Emanuel LL, Emanuel EJ, Stoeckle JD, et al. Advance directives. Stability of patients' treatment choices. *Arch Intern Med* 1994;154(2):209–217.
28. Danis M, Garrett J, Harris R, et al. Stability of choices about life-sustaining treatments. *Ann Intern Med* 1994; 120:567–573.
29. Reilly BM, Magnussen CR, Ross J, et al. Can we talk? Inpatient discussions about advance directives in a community hospital. Attending physicians' attitudes, their inpatients' wishes, and reported experience. *Arch Intern Med* 1994;154(20):2299–2308.

30. Hoffman JC, Wenger NS, Davis RH, et al. Patient preferences for communication with physicians about end-of-life decisions. *Ann Intern Med* 1997;127:1–12.
31. Johnston SC, Pfeifer MP, McNutt R, End of Life Study Group. The discussion about advance directives. Patient and physician opinions regarding when and how it should be conducted. *Arch Intern Med* 1995;155(10):1025–1030.
32. Omnibus Budget Reconciliation Act of 1990. Pub. L. No. 101-508 §§4206,4751.
33. Virmani J, Schneiderman LJ, Kaplan RM. Relationship of advance directives to physician-patient communication. *Arch Intern Med* 1994;154:909–913.
34. Tulsky JA, Fischer GS, Rose MR, et al. Opening the black box: how do physicians communicate about advance directives. *Ann Intern Med* 1998;129:441–449.
35. Lynn J, Schuster JL. *Improving care for the end of life: a sourcebook for health care managers and clinicians*. New York: Oxford University Press, 1999.
36. Council on Ethical and Judicial Affairs AMA. Guidelines for the appropriate use of do-not-resuscitate orders. *JAMA* 1991;265:1868–1871.
37. Bowman KW, Singer PA. Chinese seniors' perspective on end-of-life decisions. *Soc Sci Med* 2001;53:455–464.
38. Lo B, Snyder L, Sox H. Care at the end of life: guiding practice where there are no easy answers. *Ann Intern Med* 1999;130:772–774.
39. Singer PA. Disease-specific advance directives. *Lancet* 1994;344(8922):594–596.
40. Back AL, Arnold RM, Quill TE. Hope for the best, and prepare for the worst. *Ann Intern Med* 2003;138(5):439–443.
41. Emanuel LL, Emanuel EJ. The medical directive. *JAMA* 1989;261(22):3288–3293.
42. Five Wishes. Available at: www.agingwithdignity.org. Accessed November 13, 2002.
43. Seckler AB, Meier DB, Mulvihill M, et al. Substituted judgment: how accurate are proxy predictions? *Ann Intern Med* 1991;115:92–98.
44. Emanuel EJ, Emanuel LL. Proxy decision making for incompetent patients: an ethical and empirical analysis. *JAMA* 1992;267:2067–2071.
45. Suhl J, Simons P, Reedy T, et al. Myth of substituted judgment: surrogate decision making regarding life support is unreliable. *Arch Intern Med* 1994;154:90–96.
46. Sulmasy DP, Terry PB, Weisman CS, et al. The accuracy of substituted judgments in patients with terminal diagnoses. *Ann Intern Med* 1998;128:621–629.
47. Fagerlin A, Ditto PH, Danks JH, et al. Projection in surrogate decisions about life-sustaining medical treatments. *Health Psychol* 2001;20(3):166–175.
48. Ditto PH, Danks JH, Smucker WD, et al. Advance directives as acts of communication: a randomized controlled trial. *Arch Intern Med* 2001;161:421–430.
49. Lo B. Caring for the incompetent patient: is there a doctor in the house? *Law Med Health Care* 1990;17:214–220.
50. Buchanan AE, Brock DW. *Deciding for others*. Cambridge: Cambridge University Press, 1989.
51. Annas GJ. Quality of life in the courts: Earle Spring in fantasyland. *Hastings Cent Rep* 1980;10:9–10.
52. Annas GJ. The case of Mary Hier: when substituted judgment becomes sleight of hand. *Hastings Cent Rep* 1984;14:23–25.
53. Rhoden N. How should we view the incompetent? *Law Med Health Care* 1989;17:264–268.
54. President's Commission for the Study of Ethical Problems in Medicine and Biomedical and Behavioral Research. *Deciding to forego life-sustaining treatment*. Washington: U.S. Government Printing Office, 1983.
55. Meisel A. *The right to die*. New York: John Wiley and Sons, 1989.
56. Alpers A, Lo B. Avoiding family feuds: responding to surrogates' demands for life-sustaining treatment. *J Law Med Ethics* 1999;27:74–80.
57. Braithwaite S, Thomasma DC. New guidelines on foregoing life-sustaining treatment in incompetent patients: an anti-cruelty policy. *Ann Intern Med* 1986;104:711–715.

ANNOTATED BIBLIOGRAPHY

1. Lo B, Steinbrook RL. Resuscitating advance directives. *Arch Intern Med* 2004;164:1501–1506.
   Analyzes limitations of advance directives and argues that emphasis should be on appointing a proxy whom the patient trusts to make decisions.
2. Arnold RM, Kellum J. Moral justifications for surrogate decision making in the intensive care unit: implications and limitations. *Crit Care Med* 2003;31:S347–S353.
   Practical analysis of different standards for decisions regarding incompetent patients.
3. Buchanan AE, Brock DW. *Deciding for others*. Cambridge: Cambridge University Press, 1989.
   Thoughtful book on making decisions for patients who lack the capacity to make informed decisions.
4. Tulsky JA, Fischer GS, Rose MR. Opening the black box: how do physicians communicate about advance directives? *Ann Intern Med* 1998;129:441–449.
   Well-designed study elucidating problems that occur when physicians discuss advance directives with patients.
5. Emanuel EJ, Emanuel LL. Proxy decision making for incompetent patients: an ethical and empirical analysis. *JAMA* 1992;267:2067–2071.
   Summarizes data showing how families and physicians might not be able to state patients' preferences accurately.
6. http://www.partnershipforcaring.org/HomePage Website to download state advance directive forms from the Internet.

CHAPTER 13

Surrogate Decision Making

When patients lack decision-making capacity, physicians turn to surrogates to make decisions on their behalf. Traditionally, family members serve as surrogate decision-makers for such patients. Note that this book uses the term "surrogate" for anyone who makes decisions for a patient who lacks decision-making capacity and reserves the term "proxy" for a surrogate appointed by the patient. This distinction is most helpful when there is disagreement over who should make decisions for the patient. Proxies designated by the patient have a stronger ethical claim to make decisions for such patients than relatives. Also, in some states proxies designated by the patient have better legal standing, particularly if the patient has completed a formal legal document designating them. Chapter 12 discusses the related issue of what standards should be used in making decisions for patients who lack decision-making capacity.

CASE 13.1 Disagreement between family members.

Mrs. R is a 72-year-old widow with severe Alzheimer disease. She does not recognize her family but often smiles when someone holds her hand or gives her a hug. She lives with her sister, who provides help with all activities of daily living together with an attendant. Mrs. R develops pneumonia. She had never indicated what she would want in such a situation or whom she would want to make decisions for her. Her sister believes that Mrs. R would not want her life prolonged in this condition because she prized her independence and asks the physician to withhold antibiotics. Mrs. R's only child is a son who visits once or twice a year. He is outraged at this request. He asserts, "Life is sacred; it's God's gift. We can't just snuff it out."

Because Mrs. R had given no advance directives, a surrogate needs to make decisions on care. Both the sister and the son desire to act as Mrs. R's surrogate. The sister asserts priority because she cared for Mrs. R and has been close to her sister most of her life, yet the son has closer ties of kinship. What justifies selecting one surrogate over the other?

WHO SHOULD SERVE AS SURROGATE?

Among potential surrogates there is a hierarchy that physicians should keep in mind. However, decisions are often best made by consensus rather than by giving one potential surrogate unilateral power.

COURT-APPOINTED GUARDIANS

The courts have legal authority to declare a patient incompetent and to appoint a guardian to make medical decisions for the patient. The legal system offers procedural safeguards, such as notice to all parties, the right to call and cross-examine witnesses, impartial judges, explicit justification for decisions, and an appeals process. However, involving the courts routinely in decisions has serious drawbacks (1,2). First, the courts intrude on highly personal and private issues. The adversarial judicial system might polarize families and physicians rather than foster a mutually acceptable decision. Second, guardianship hearings are usually superficial, and courts do not monitor guardians' decisions (3). Finally, intolerable delays would occur if the courts were frequently involved in decisions on life-sustaining treatment. As one court decision declared, "Courts are not the proper place to resolve the agonizing personal problems that underlie these cases. Our legal system cannot replace the more intimate struggle that must be borne by the patient, those caring for the patient, and those who care about the patient (4)." Court-appointed guardians have legal priority over other potential surrogates. However, physicians and hospitals should involve the courts only as a last resort, when disputes cannot be resolved in a clinical setting.

SURROGATES SELECTED BY PATIENTS

As Chapter 12 discusses, all states have legal procedures for competent patients to appoint a health care proxy (5,6). Generally, the patient must complete a form and have it witnessed or notarized. Many patients find it easier to select who should act as proxy rather than anticipate what they would want in future scenarios. Appointing a proxy might prevent disputes.

In some cases the patient indicates the selection of a surrogate informally but does not complete a legal document appointing the person. If the surrogate and close relatives disagree over plans for care, the physician might then face a conflict between what is ethically appropriate and what is legally protected. Ethically speaking, the person whom the patient wanted to serve as surrogate should have priority. Legally, however, persons might have no standing to make decisions. The physician should try to persuade the family to respect the patient's choice of proxy.

FAMILY MEMBERS

Decisions by families of patients who lack decision-making capacity are standard medical practice (7,8). There are compelling ethical justifications for family decision making (9).

Most People Want Family Members to Serve as Surrogates

A public opinion poll found that 30% of respondents wanted their families to make medical decisions for them if they became incapacitated. An additional 53% wanted their family to make decisions together with their physicians (10). Only 3% of respondents wanted the courts to decide. Patients trust family members to do their best under circumstances that might not be foreseen (11).

Family Members Often Know What the Patient Would Want

Because family members generally have close relationships with patients, they are more likely than other people to have discussed life-sustaining interventions with patients.

Family Members Are Presumed to Act in the Patient's Best Interests

Ties of kinship and affection generally lead family members to care about the patient, deliberate carefully, and do what is best for the patient rather than what is best for themselves (9). Strong social, cultural, and religious norms encourage family members to subordinate their own interests for the sake of relatives in need.

The term "family" should be interpreted in light of demographic facts, such as the large number of unmarried couples living together. Ethically, the crucial issue is not the relationship's legal status but whether it is reasonable to presume that the partner will act in the patient's best interests.

Decision Making by the Family as a Group

For many families the idea of singling out one person as a surrogate might seem to disrespect the family as a whole. Family connections have both ethical and practical significance. Proponents of an ethics of care (*see* Chapter 1) have argued that more attention should be paid to how decisions affect various relationships and that families should have a stronger voice in health care decisions (12,13). In this view relationships among family members will survive after the patient's death.

These relationships deserve respect, and physicians should support attempts to maintain family harmony. From a pragmatic viewpoint, many proxies are reluctant to contradict the views of close relatives. They might feel torn between what they think is best for the patient and what other family members want to do (14).

NO FAMILY MEMBERS AVAILABLE

Decisions are most difficult when patients with impaired decision-making capacity have no advance directives and no family members. In some cases a friend might be an appropriate surrogate. If the friend has an emotional bond with the patient, it is plausible to presume that the friend will act in the patient's best interests (15).

If no one is available as surrogate, it is appropriate for physicians to make decisions on the basis of what they believe is in the patient's best interests. Physicians do not need to administer burdensome interventions that offer little prospect of benefit simply because there is no surrogate to decline them on behalf of the patient. In this situation physicians may forego interventions that they do not consider to be in the patient's best interests. When there is no surrogate, it is advisable for physicians to consult with the hospital ethics committee or another physician. Simply explaining one's reasoning to another person can clarify thinking, identify unwarranted assumptions and unconvincing arguments, and suggest new options for care.

LEGAL ISSUES REGARDING SURROGATE DECISION MAKING

Many states allow relatives to refuse interventions on behalf of such patients, even in the absence of advance directives (5,6,8).

In 31 states legislation specifies which relatives have priority to act as surrogates for incapacitated patients who have not appointed a proxy (6,16,17). Generally, the patient's spouse takes priority over adult children, followed by parents and more distant relatives. Such laws, however, might lead to ethically troubling results, such as favoring the distant son in Case 13.1 over the sister who is closer to the patient. These laws might also be problematic when a spouse is estranged but not legally divorced.

PROBLEMS WITH SURROGATE DECISION MAKING

The physician should serve as the patient's advocate if the surrogate's decision conflicts with the patient's previous statements or best interests.

EMOTIONAL BARRIERS TO DECISIONS

Surrogates commonly find it difficult to make decisions because of emotional stress, such as sadness or denial. Surrogates might also feel guilty over not doing everything for the patient or over "pulling the plug."

DECISIONS INCONSISTENT WITH THE PATIENT'S PREFERENCES OR VALUES

Some surrogates might impose their own values on the patient rather than respect the patient's choices and values. In Case 13.1 the son is basing decisions on religious beliefs about the sanctity of life. When patients themselves hold such views, they are followed out of respect for patient autonomy (*see* Chapter 4). Thus, the physician needs to inquire whether the patient herself held such religious views.

CONFLICTS OF INTEREST

In some cases relatives might promote their own interests, not the patient's. Unscrupulous family members might try to gain control of an inheritance or a pension. When it comes to the basis for their decisions, surrogates are given less leeway than competent patients. For example, patients may forego interventions in order to spare family members emotional distress or to preserve an inheritance for children. Such refusals are heeded in order to respect patient autonomy. However, as Chapter 12 discusses, claims by surrogates that the patient would refuse beneficial interventions for these reasons might be self-serving and need to be scrutinized (18).

Family members cannot be expected to ignore their own needs and interests. Caring for a relative with serious chronic illness can cause emotional distress, fatigue, financial burdens, or conflicts with other responsibilities (19). Most family members subordinate their interests to those of the patient and make considerable sacrifices (20). Physicians should not be overly suspicious about surrogates. Respecting close family relationships is an important social value, and physicians should support families who are trying to deal with difficult situations as best as they can. Simply making sacrifices to care for a relative or being mentioned in a will is not a conflict of interests.

DISAGREEMENTS AMONG POTENTIAL SURROGATES

Case 13.1 illustrates how family members might disagree over decisions. Some physicians withhold interventions only when all family members agree. However, giving every relative a veto might impose interventions that are not in the patient's best interests. Furthermore, it is problematic to give distant or estranged relatives a voice equal to that of those closest to the patient. Realistically, physicians often make decisions with family consensus rather than unanimity. Relatives are often willing to accept a decision made by the rest of the family, even though they would have decided differently themselves.

IMPROVING SURROGATE DECISION MAKING

After sufficient discussions, physicians and surrogates agree on decisions about life-sustaining interventions in almost all cases (21). Chapter 15 gives detailed suggestions for reaching agreement. The following additional recommendations refer specifically to surrogate decision making (Table 13-1).

DISCUSS THE DECISION-MAKING PROCESS

A family meeting can help relatives understand and accept the medical situation (22). The hospital ethics committee might be able to facilitate such discussions. Physicians should acknowledge that decisions are difficult and that people with good intentions might disagree. Doctors can help families clarify their role and can accommodate their grief (23). Physicians should remind everybody that decisions should be based on the patient's preferences and values, not on what surrogates or doctors would choose for themselves.

GIVE A RECOMMENDATION

Physicians should not merely list options and leave it to family members to decide. Doctors should make a recommendation on the basis of what is known about the patient's preferences and values. Recommendations are particularly important when family members disagree or are overwhelmed by guilt or grief.

TABLE 13-1

Suggestions for Improving Surrogate Decision Making

Discuss the decision-making process.
Give a recommendation.
Get help from other health care workers.

GET HELP FROM OTHER HEALTH CARE WORKERS

A nurse, social worker, or chaplain can often help the family accept the medical situation and work through past antagonisms with the patient or among themselves. Furthermore, such persons might provide valuable emotional support to family members.

In summary, surrogates should know the incapacitated patient's preferences, be willing to respect them, and act in the patient's best interests. The patient's own choice of surrogate should be respected. In most cases the standard clinical practice of family decision making is ethically appropriate. When family members disagree, physicians should make efforts to resolve conflicts and achieve consensus.

REFERENCES

1. Meisel A *The right to die*. New York: John Wiley and Sons, 1989:145–169.
2. Lo B, Rouse F, Dornbrand L. Family decision-making on trial: who decides for incompetent patients? *N Engl J Med* 1990;322:1228–1231.
3. Bulcroft K, Kielkopf MR, Tripp K. Elderly wards and their legal guardians: analysis of county probate records in Ohio and Washington. *Gerontologist* 1991;31:156–164.
4. In re Jobes. 529 A. 2d 434 (N.J. 1987).
5. Sabatino CS. The legal and functional status of the medical proxy: suggestions for statutory reform. *J Law Med Ethics* 1999;27(1):46–51.
6. Lo B, Steinbrook RL. Resuscitating advance directives. *Arch Intern Med* 2004;164:1501–1506.
7. *President's Commission for the Study of Ethical Problems in Medicine and Biomedical and Behavioral Research. Deciding to forego life-sustaining treatment.* Washington: U.S. Government Printing Office, 1983.
8. Meisel A. *The right to die*, 2nd ed. New York: John Wiley and Sons, 1995.
9. Arnold RM, Kellum J. Moral justifications for surrogate decision making in the intensive care unit: implications and limitations. *Crit Care Med* 2003;31(5 Suppl):S347–S353.
10. Blendon RJ, Szalay US, Knox RA. Should physicians aid their patients in dying? The public perspective. *JAMA* 1992;267:2658–2662.
11. Singer PA, Martin DK, Lavery JV, et al. Reconceptualizing advance care planning from the patient's perspective. *Arch Intern Med* 1998;158(8):879–884.
12. Jecker N. The role of intimate others in medical decision making. *Gerontologist* 1990;30(1):65–71.
13. Hardwig J. What about the family? *Hastings Cent Rep* 1990;20(2):5–10.
14. Alpers A, Lo B. Avoiding family feuds: responding to surrogates' demands for life-sustaining treatment. *J Law Med Ethics* 1999;27:74–80.
15. Veatch RM. An ethical framework for terminal care decisions. *J Am Geriatr Soc* 1984;32:665–669.
16. Menikoff JA, Sachs GA, Siegler M. Beyond advance directives: health care surrogate laws. *N Engl J Med* 1992;322:1165–1169.
17. American Bar Association. Surrogate consent in the absence of an advance directive, July 1, 2001. http://www.abanet.org/elderly/update.html. Accessed May 20, 2002.
18. Lo B. Caring for the incompetent patient: is there a doctor in the house? *Law Med Health Care* 1989;17:214–220.
19. Covinsky KE, Landefeld CS, Teno J, et al. Is economic hardship on the families of the seriously ill associated with patient and surrogate care preferences? *Arch Intern Med* 1996;156(15):1737–1741.
20. Covinsky KE, Goldman L, Cook FS, et al. The impact of serious illness on patients' families. *JAMA* 1994;272:1839–1844.
21. Prendergast TJ, Luce JM. Increasing incidence of withholding and withdrawal of life support from the critically ill. *Am Rev Resp Dis Crit Care Med* 1997;155:15–20.
22. Way J, Back AL, Curtis JR. Withdrawing life support and resolution of conflict with families. *Br Med J* 2002;325(7376):1342–1345.
23. Tilden VP, Tolle SW, Garland MJ, et al. Decisions about life-sustaining treatment: impact of physicians' behaviors on the family. *Arch Intern Med* 1995;155:633–638.

ANNOTATED BIBLIOGRAPHY

1. Lo B, Rouse F, Dornbrand L. Family decision making on trial: who decides for incompetent patients? *N Engl J Med* 1990;322:1228–1231.
   Argues that families should be presumed to be appropriate decision-makers for patients who lack decision-making capacity.
2. Buchanan AE, Brock DW. *Deciding for others*. Cambridge: Cambridge University Press, 1989.
   Detailed ethical analysis of surrogate decision making.
3. Sabatino CS. The legal and functional status of the medical proxy: suggestions for statutory reform. *J Law Med Ethics* 1999;27:46–51.
   Recent analysis of state laws regarding surrogate decision making.
4. Arnold RM, Kellum J. Moral justifications for surrogate decision making in the intensive care unit: implications and limitations. *Crit Care Med* 2003;31:S347–S353.
   Clear and thoughtful review of surrogate decision making.

CHAPTER 14

Persistent Disagreements over Care

D isagreements over life-sustaining interventions are common. According to one study, staff and family disagreed in 48% of intensive care unit (ICU) cases (1). Although disagreements are resolved in almost all cases (2,3), in a few cases sharp disagreements persist. This chapter discusses cases in which either physicians or patients or their surrogates insist on interventions that the other party considers inappropriate.

Other chapters discuss related issues. Chapter 4 analyzes patient refusals that are not in their best interests. Chapter 13 covers decisions by surrogates that are contrary to the patient's wishes or best interests. Chapter 9 discusses demands by patients or surrogates for "futile" interventions.

PATIENT OR SURROGATE INSISTENCE ON LIFE-SUSTAINING INTERVENTIONS

CLINICAL CONSIDERATIONS

Physicians are exhorted to improve palliative care near the end of life and help patients achieve a peaceful death (4–6). In some cases, however, patients or surrogates insist on life-sustaining interventions that physicians believe cause suffering (5,6).

CASE 14.1 Desire for CPR and mechanical ventilation in end-stage lung disease.

Mr. H was a 29-year-old man with end-stage cystic fibrosis who was admitted to the hospital for antibiotics and respiratory therapy. He was emaciated, required home oxygen, and was dyspneic walking around his home. During conversations he often paused to catch his breath or to cough up thick secretions. Lung transplantation was not an option for him because of recurrent aspiration pneumonia. Mr. H understood that his shortness of breath would get worse. He appreciated that physicians believed that cardiopulmonary resuscitation (CPR) or mechanical ventilation had very little chance of success. He further realized that the physicians believed that if he required intubation and mechanical ventilation, he could not be weaned off the ventilator. He responded, "My entire life has been a struggle. No one thought I would live this long. I've always beaten the odds. I've always been a fighter. I'll keep fighting until the man upstairs tells me it's time to stop."

Mr. H rejected a palliative approach and was willing to accept odds that physicians believed were unacceptable. His core values included overcoming situations that others believed were hopeless. Other patients also want life-sustaining interventions that offer a very small hope of success.

The SUPPORT study documented shortcomings in palliative care at the end of life. This study enrolled over 9,000 hospitalized patients with an advanced stage of one of nine illnesses (4). These patients had a hospital mortality of more than 25% and a 6-month mortality of almost 50%. In the latter phase of this project, research nurses gave physicians computer-generated prognoses for each patient and documented patients' and families' preferences for treatment. For many patients who died, their last days included "undesirable states": 38% spent at least 10 days in an ICU, 46% received mechanical ventilation within 3 days of death, and 45% were unconscious during their last 3 days of life (4,7). Relatives reported that 50% of conscious dying patients experienced moderate or severe pain during their last 3 days of life. These findings were widely interpreted as evidence of inappropriately aggressive use of technology and failure to relieve suffering near the end of life (4–6).

The SUPPORT study also showed that many seriously ill patients desire interventions that have a low likelihood of success. One paper analyzed patients with metastatic cancer whose physicians predicted a 6-month survival of 10%. Thirty-six percent of such patients preferred life-extending therapy rather than relief from pain and discomfort as the primary goal of care (8). Among those patients who believed that they had a 90% chance or better of surviving for 6 months, 61% wanted life-extending therapy, compared to only 15% of patients who estimated their chance for surviving 6 months to be less than 90%.

ETHICAL CONSIDERATIONS

The ethical guideline of beneficence requires physicians to oppose requests for interventions that would not improve outcomes but would cause serious suffering. In this section we analyze three particularly difficult situations: requests that "everything" be done, requests for interventions based on religious beliefs, and requests for interventions that cause suffering with little prospect of medical benefit.

CASE 14.2 Family insistence that everything be done (9).

Bishop P is a 60-year-old African-American man with diabetes, quadriplegia, and persistent infections. One year ago he developed Staphylococcus aureus meningitis, epidural abscess, and pneumonia. During his hospitalization Bishop P developed quadriplegia, respiratory failure, renal failure, and persistent fevers.

Ten months later, Bishop P was rehospitalized with urosepsis from Enterobacter cloacae. Hypotension, respiratory failure, renal failure, stroke, and seizures complicated his course. He required mechanical ventilation and dialysis. Despite multiple courses of antibiotics, his blood cultures remained positive for E. cloacae, resistant to all antibiotics. A drug reaction caused a total body rash, and his skin sheared away around his bandages and electrocardiographic leads. The physicians believed that further interventions would be inhumane and disfiguring, that he would not survive the hospitalization, and that attempts at CPR would be futile.

Bishop P's Pentecostalist church emphasizes faith healing. Bishop P was obtunded and could not state his preferences for care. His family insisted that everything be done because he believed that all life was sacred.

Bishop P's family wanted to act in accordance with his lifelong values. Such substituted judgments by surrogates are a legitimate basis for decisions when patients lack decision-making capacity and have not given clear advance directives (*see* Chapter 12).

REQUESTS THAT "EVERYTHING" BE DONE

In Case 14.2 the family requested that "everything" be done. The physicians should first clarify what they mean by "everything." Many patients or surrogates do not want literally everything done and acknowledge that in some situations interventions might be far more likely to cause suffering or harm than benefit. It is also useful to elicit the values and concerns that animate such requests. Some patients or surrogates might be concerned that if they do not insist on interventions, beneficial treatments will be withheld. Such concerns can be addressed directly.

RELIGION-BASED INSISTENCE ON INTERVENTIONS

As in Case 14.2, many patients base decisions about life-sustaining interventions on their religious or spiritual beliefs (10,11). Religion-based reasons deserve special respect because they reflect a person's core values and identity (9). These beliefs might lead some patients to insist on interventions.

Some patients or surrogates might believe that a miraculous recovery will occur if their faith is strong enough; insisting on treatments might be a way of demonstrating their faith. Other patients or surrogates might want any intervention that prolongs life, even for a very short time. They might have vitalist religious views that life is a good in itself, regardless of its quality, and that human beings must preserve and prolong life until God determines its end (12).

Physicians need sufficient information about the patient's religious beliefs to understand their impact on specific clinical decisions. Individual beliefs might differ from official doctrines. Furthermore, people who share general beliefs, such as the sacredness of life, might differ in their preferences about specific medical technologies (13). To inquire how religion shapes decisions, a physician might say to Bishop P's daughter, "I know that religion plays an important part in your father's life. I'd like to understand it better. Please help me learn more." Physicians might also need to understand details about the patient's religious beliefs, such as attitudes toward miracles, prayer, and divine intervention (14).

REQUEST FOR INTERVENTIONS THAT CAUSE THE PATIENT SUFFERING

In Case 14.2 the family's request for CPR troubled caregivers, who believed that further interventions were causing pain and mutilation without improving his prognosis. The ethical guideline of nonmaleficence, as well as professional integrity, allows health care workers to refrain from providing interventions that cause significant suffering but prolong the patient's life only briefly (9,15). This rationale justifies overriding surrogate preferences and withholding interventions in rare cases.

Some surrogates state that the patient believes suffering serves a spiritual purpose. Caregivers should examine carefully surrogates' claims about the redemptive nature of suffering. First, the family's views might differ from the patient's. Many patients who believe their illness serves a spiritual purpose will still accept medications for pain and decline burdensome interventions (9). Furthermore, many patients who believe that suffering caused by terminal illness serves some higher purpose choose to forego medical interventions that cause additional suffering but provide limited benefits.

RECOMMENDATIONS

Physicians can respond to requests for life-sustaining interventions in several constructive ways (Table 14-1). The suggestions in Chapter 5 on informed consent might also be helpful.

UNDERSTAND THE PATIENT'S OR SURROGATE'S PERSPECTIVE

When patients or surrogates continue to request life-sustaining interventions that the physician considers inadvisable, the doctor should first try to understand their perspective, including their understanding of the illness, their concerns, their goals, and their expectations for care (16,17). This approach is generally more effective than immediately trying to persuade them about specific

TABLE 14-1

Recommendations for Responding to Requests for Life-Sustaining Interventions

Understand the patient's or surrogate's perpective.
Respond to the patient's or surrogate's needs and emotions.
Be sensitive to ethnic and cultural issues.
Use time constructively.
Find common ground for ongoing care.

clinical decisions such as a Do Not Attempt Resuscitation (DNAR) order (18). Open-ended questions are helpful, such as (18):

- "What concerns you most about your illness?"
- "How is treatment going for you (your family)?"
- "As you think about your illness, what is the best and the worst that might happen?"
- "What has been most difficult about this illness for you?"
- "What are your hopes (your expectations, your fears) for the future?"
- "As you think about the future, what is most important to you (what matters the most to you)?"

Such open-ended questions help elicit patient concerns and emotions (19,20).

RESPOND TO THE PATIENT'S OR SURROGATE'S NEEDS AND EMOTIONS

Empathic comments, which reflect the speaker's emotions, encourage patients or surrogates to explore emotions and to discuss difficult topics (18,21,22). In Case 14.1, when Mr. H has difficulty completing sentences, the physician might say, "It can be frightening to not get enough air." Similarly, in Case 14.2, the physician might say, "Do you feel sad seeing your father so sick?" Some physicians might fear that exploring emotions might arouse in the patient and family feelings of anger, hopelessness, or sadness that doctors are powerless to alleviate. However, patients and families will have these emotional responses whether or not physicians choose to probe them. After these emotions are discussed openly, the patient and family no longer must face them alone. Talking about emotional reactions to serious illness is frequently therapeutic and helps patients and families accept a grave prognosis. Furthermore, anxiety and depression can be treated once they are identified. Patients and families who feel they are understood might be more willing to listen to the physician's perspective.

The physicians can also respond to unrealistic expectations without destroying hope. One approach is to "Hope for the best, and prepare for the worst (23)." Also, physicians can use "wish statements" to align with hopes of the patient or family, while suggesting that the desired outcome is unlikely (24). In Case 14.1 the physician might say, " I wish I could make the odds be in your favor."

BE SENSITIVE TO ETHNIC AND CULTURAL ISSUES

Bishop P and his family were African-Americans. Ethnic factors can be significant in end-of-life care. For example, African-Americans and Hispanic-Americans complete advance directives and wish to forego life support less frequently than other patients (25–27). African-Americans might mistrust physicians and hospitals because of a history of discrimination and limited access to medical care (28).

Rather than leave concerns and suspicions unspoken, physicians might ask specifically about trust. "Many African-Americans worry that they will not receive the care they need. How do you feel about that?" Physicians should also acknowledge that mistrust is an understandable reaction. "I imagine I would feel the same way if I had experienced that." Physicians should not immediately try to reassure the family that all appropriate care will be provided (29). Premature reassurance might deter patients from disclosing their concerns and emotions in enough detail that they can be understood (20).

USE TIME CONSTRUCTIVELY

Patients or surrogates are frequently given bad news in the context of being asked to limit life-sustaining interventions. If possible, they should be given time to absorb the new information before making a decision. However, the passage of time alone might not persuade patients or surrogates to limit interventions. Physicians might suggest a time-limited trial of interventions, with plans to discontinue unless clinically significant improvement occurs. Physicians can also use time to direct attention to palliative care. Doctors might say, "Your father is so seriously ill that it's possible that he might die in the hospital. What would be left undone if he were to die suddenly?" Social workers, chaplains, or the hospital ethics committee can also help the family reach closure.

FIND COMMON GROUND FOR ONGOING CARE

The process of negotiation requires that both sides are willing to compromise (30,31). When patients insist on life-sustaining interventions, a common compromise involves not only adding or increasing interventions but also not withdrawing them (32). Although law and ethics do not distinguish between withholding life support and withdrawing it, the emotional difference might be significant to families.

In almost all cases, physicians can reach an agreement with patients or surrogates on an acceptable plan of care (2,3). In rare instances physicians might conclude, after repeated discussions with them and an ethics committee consultation, that they cannot agree with the patient's or surrogate's request. If the requested interventions are futile in a strict sense or cause significant net suffering to the patient, it is ethically acceptable for the physician to decline to provide them. The patient or surrogate should be notified of this decision and of their right to seek another provider.

PHYSICIAN INSISTENCE ON LIFE-SUSTAINING INTERVENTIONS

Physicians and hospitals might seek to give life-sustaining interventions to an unwilling patient. This section focuses on insistence based on the physician's conscience or religious beliefs.

CASE 14.3 Withdrawal of mechanical ventilation.

William Bartling was a 70-year-old man with chronic obstructive lung disease (33,34). A needle aspirate of a new pulmonary nodule revealed adenocarcinoma. After the procedure he suffered a pneumothorax and required a chest tube and mechanical ventilation. During the next 2 months he could not be weaned from the respirator. Mr. Bartling requested that the respirator be disconnected and signed a living will, a durable power of attorney for health care, and a declaration of his wishes. His family also signed documents releasing the physicians and hospital from liability.

The hospital and physicians refused Mr. Bartling's request, arguing that they had an ethical duty to preserve life and that withholding life-sustaining treatment was incompatible with their born-again Christian pro-life beliefs. Attempts to transfer the patient to another hospital that would comply with his wishes were unsuccessful.

The Bartling case posed the question of whether the caregivers may insist on providing life-sustaining interventions over a patient's refusal. In one survey 60% of attending physicians said they would not withdraw a ventilator from a patient with severe chronic obstructive lung disease who wished it discontinued (35).

ARGUMENTS FOR INSISTENCE BY CAREGIVERS ON INTERVENTIONS

Health care professionals and institutions offer several reasons why their moral or religious beliefs should allow them to impose life-sustaining interventions on unwilling patients.

RESPECT THE AUTONOMY OF CAREGIVERS

Health care professionals are moral agents with values, rights, and consciences. In this view, just as patients have the right to refuse interventions, physicians should also have the right to refuse to violate their professional ethics or personal morality. Because the United States respects freedom of religion, it would be particularly repugnant to require health care workers to carry out actions that violate their religious beliefs. Also, it would be counterproductive to require physicians to act against their moral views. A grudging or antagonistic doctor–patient relationship would not be therapeutic.

RESPECT THE MISSION OF HEALTH CARE INSTITUTIONS

Health care institutions might have a mission statement that expresses their goals and values. Hospices have an explicit philosophy of palliative care. Catholic hospitals have policies that forbid abortions. Many people believe that a pluralistic society should encourage such statements of mission so that patients can seek care at institutions whose moral and spiritual views match their own (36,37).

TABLE 14-2

Objections to Caregivers' Insistence on Life-Sustaining Interventions

Undermining the right of refusal.
Confusion between negative and positive rights.
Lack of timely and clear notification of patients.

OBJECTIONS TO INSISTENCE BY CAREGIVERS ON INTERVENTIONS

Insistence by caregivers on providing interventions over the informed objections of patients is ethically troubling for several reasons (Table 14-2).

UNDERMINING THE RIGHT OF REFUSAL

If caregivers could insist on treatment, the right of competent patients to refuse medical interventions would in effect be nullified. In Case 14.3 the court ruled that the patient's refusal of treatment must be respected: "If the right of the patient to self-determination as to his own medical treatment is to have any meaning at all, it must be paramount to the interests of the patient's hospital and doctors (34)."

CONFUSION BETWEEN NEGATIVE AND POSITIVE RIGHTS

Philosophers make a distinction between negative and positive rights. *Negative rights* are claims to be left alone, to be free from unwanted interference or intrusions. An example is the constitutional right to be free of unreasonable searches and seizures. Negative rights might require other people to refrain from intervening, exerting control, or thwarting the person holding the rights. Patients claim the negative right to be free of unwanted medical interventions. To be exercised, this negative right requires physicians to refrain from providing the treatment.

Positive or *affirmative rights*, on the other hand, are claims to receive something or act in a certain way. Positive rights might require others to take action or provide means or resources, not simply to refrain from interfering (38). In Case 14.3 the physicians claimed the positive right to continue medical interventions, even though Mr. Bartling did not want it.

Negative rights are generally considered to carry more moral weight than positive rights (39). Virtually all Western philosophers agree that people have a strong right to be free of unwanted intrusions. This right to be left alone is regarded as fundamental to the idea of a free society. Usually, negative liberty is limited only by promises or role-specific obligations; for example, parents cannot claim a negative right to be freed from providing their children's basic needs. In contrast, positive rights are more difficult to justify and enforce because they generally require other people to do something and because they interfere with the negative rights of others.

LACK OF TIMELY AND CLEAR NOTIFICATION OF PATIENTS

Physicians and nurses who work in a situation in which this conflict is likely to recur should make their position known before taking over care of a patient. Such notification would enable patients to make informed plans for their care and to seek another provider. Similarly, institutions that have policies insisting on certain interventions should notify patients on admission. The burden should be on health care providers to notify patients because they are in a better position to anticipate future scenarios and potential disagreements.

TRANSFERRING CARE OF THE PATIENT

Health care workers should be permitted to withdraw from a case in which they have deep moral objections to the plan of care to be undertaken. However, they also have professional obligations not to abandon patients. Thus, they should allow (and even facilitate) transfer of the patient to a health care worker or an institution that is willing to comply with withdrawal of the intervention.

Some physicians might not want to inform the surrogate of the option of transfer of care because they believe this would constitute cooperation with an immoral act. However, physicians have an obligation to inform patients (or surrogates) of alternatives to the proposed treatment. Generally, even if a physician personally would not carry out a treatment, the physician still needs to mention it if a respected minority of physicians would do so. The obligation would be even stronger if the intervention were generally considered an acceptable option. If the physician did not want to provide the information personally, he or she could ask another physician or the ethics committee to do so.

Even when transfer of care can be arranged, it might place a heavy burden on patients or their families. Patients might face a tragic choice if they must either accept unwanted interventions or else leave caregivers with whom they have developed a long-term relationship. An example is the Requena case, in which a 57-year-old woman with amyotrophic lateral sclerosis wanted tube feedings withheld if she could no longer swallow. The hospital asserted that her decision conflicted with its pro-life values and asked her to accept transfer to another local hospital that would respect her decision. When she refused to accept the transfer, the hospital went to court to force her to leave. According to the court, because she had lived in the hospital for 17 months transfer would be upsetting and burdensome for her. The trial court judge suggested that "by rethinking their own attitudes" the hospital staff "might find it possible to be more fully accepting and supportive of Ms. Requena's decision." The court continued, "It is fairer to ask the health care workers to bend than to ask Ms. Requena to bend (40)."

In summary, the claims of health care professionals to insist on interventions might negate the rights of competent, informed patients to refuse them. Caregivers should not expect to impose treatment on patients if they did not notify them of their insistence when care was initiated.

REFERENCES

1. Breen CM, Abernethy AP, Abbott KH, et al. Conflict associated with decisions to limit life-sustaining treatment in intensive care units. *J Gen Intern Med* 2001;16(5):283–289.
2. Smedira NG, Evans BH, Grais LS, et al. Withholding and withdrawing of life support from the critically ill. *N Engl J Med* 1990;322:309–315.
3. Prendergast TJ, Luce JM. Increasing incidence of withholding and withdrawal of life support from the critically ill. *Am Rev Resp Dis Crit Care Med* 1997;155:15–20.
4. The SUPPORT Investigators. A controlled trial to improve care for seriously ill hospitalized patients. *JAMA* 1995;274:1591–1598.
5. Lo B. End-of-life care after termination of SUPPORT. *Hastings Cent Rep* 1995;25:S6–S8.
6. Lo B. Improving care near the end of life: why is it so hard? *JAMA* 1995;274:1634–1636.
7. Lynn J, Teno JM, Phillips RS, et al. Perceptions by family members of the dying experience of older and seriously ill patients. *Ann Intern Med* 1997;126:97–106.
8. Weeks JC, Cook EF, O'Day SJ, et al. Relationship between cancer patients' predictions of prognosis and their treatment preferences. *JAMA* 1998;279:1709–1714.
9. Alpers A, Lo B. Avoiding family feuds: responding to surrogates' demands for life-sustaining treatment. *J Law Med Ethics* 1999;27:74–80.
10. Lo B, Ruston D, Kates LW, et al. Discussing religious and spiritual issues at the end of life: a practical guide for physicians. *JAMA* 2002;287:749–754.
11. Lo B, Kates LW, Ruston D, et al. Responding to requests regarding prayer and religious ceremonies by patients near the end of life and their families. *J Palliat Med* 2003;6:417–424.
12. Boozang KM. An intimate passing: restoring the role of family and religion in dying. *U Pitt Law Rev* 1997;58:549–617.
13. Dworkin R. *Life's dominion*. New York: Alfred A. Knopf, 1993:328.
14. Orr RD, Genesen LB. Requests for "inappropriate" treatment based on religious beliefs. *J Med Ethics* 1997;23(3):142–147.
15. Braithwaite S, Thomasma DC. New guidelines on foregoing life-sustaining treatment in incompetent patients: an anti-cruelty policy. *Ann Intern Med* 1986;104:711–715.
16. Kleinman A, Eisenberg L, Good B. Culture, illness and care: clinical lessons from anthropologic and cross cultural research. *Ann Intern Med* 1978;89:251–258.
17. Quill TE. Partnerships in patient care: a contractual approach. *Ann Intern Med* 1983;98:228–234.
18. Lo B, Snyder L, Sox H. Care at the end of life: guiding practice where there are no easy answers. *Ann Intern Med* 1999;130:772–774.
19. Lipkin M, Frankel RM, Beckman HB, et al. Performing the interview. In: Lipkin M, Putnam SM, Lazare A, eds. *The medical interview*. New York: Springer-Verlag, 1995:65–82.
20. Maguire P, Faulkner A, Booth K, et al. Helping cancer patients disclose their concerns. *Eur J Cancer* 1996;32A:78–81.

21. Buckman R. *How to Break Bad News*. Baltimore: The Johns Hopkins University Press, 1992.
22. Suchman AL, Markakis K, Beckman HB, et al. A model of empathic communication in the medical interview. *JAMA* 1997;277:678–682.
23. Back AL, Arnold RM, Quill TE. Hope for the best, and prepare for the worst. *Ann Intern Med* 2003;138(5): 439–443.
24. Quill TE, Arnold RM, Platt FW. "I wish things were different": Expressing wishes in response to loss, futility, and unrealistic hopes. *Ann Intern Med* 2001;135:51–55.
25. Rubin SM, Strull WM, Fialkow MF, et al. Increasing completion of the durable power of attorney for health care: a randomized controlled trial. *JAMA* 1994;271:209–212.
26. Blackhall LJ, Murphy ST, Frank G, et al. Ethnicity and attitudes toward patient autonomy. *JAMA* 1995;274: 820–825.
27. McKinley ED, Garrett JM, Evans AT, et al. Differences in end-of-life decision making among black and white ambulatory care cancer patients. *J Gen Intern Med* 1996;11:651–656.
28. Smedley BS, Stith AY, Nelson AR, eds. *Unequal treatment: confronting racial and ethnic disparities in health care*. Washington, DC: National Academies Press, 2003.
29. Lo B, Quill T, Tulsky J. Discussing palliative care with patients. *Ann Intern Med* 1999;130:744–749.
30. Quill TE. Partnerships in patient care: a contractual approach. *Ann Intern Med* 1983;98:228–234.
31. Fisher R, Ury W. *Getting to yes*, 2nd ed. New York: Penguin, 1991.
32. Christakis NA, Asch DA. Biases in how physicians choose to withdraw life support. *Lancet* 1993;342:642–646.
33. Lo B. The Bartling case: protecting patients from harm while respecting their wishes. *J Am Geriatr Soc* 1986;34: 44–48.
34. Bartling v. Superior Court. 209 Cal Rptr. 220 163 Cal. App. 3d 186 (1984).
35. Caralis PV, Hammond JS. Attitudes of medical students, housestaff, and faculty physicians toward euthanasia and termination of life-sustaining treatment. *Crit Care Med* 1992;20:683–690.
36. Miles SH, Singer PA, Siegler M. Conflicts between patients' wishes to forgo treatment and the policies of health care facilities. *N Engl J Med* 1989;321:48–50.
37. Engelhardt HT. *The Foundations of Bioethics*. New York: Oxford University Press, 1986.
38. Collopy BJ. Autonomy in long term care: some crucial distinctions. *Gerontologist* 1988;28(Suppl.):10–17.
39. Beauchamp TL, Childress JF. *Principles of Biomedical Ethics*, 3rd ed. New York: Oxford University Press, 1989.
40. In re Requena. 517 A. 2d 869 (N.J. 1986).

ANNOTATED BIBLIOGRAPHY

1. Alpers A, Lo B. Avoiding family feuds: responding to surrogates' demands for life-sustaining treatment. *J Law Med Ethics* 1999;27:74–80.

   Analyzes cases in which surrogates insisted on interventions that physicians believed were not indicated.
2. Lo B, Quill T, Tulsky J. Discussing palliative care with patients. *Ann Intern Med* 1999;130:744–749.

   Explains that in response to patient and family requests for interventions that are unlikely to be successful, the physician can use empathic comments and open-ended questions to understand their perceptions of illness, concerns, and emotions.
3. Lo B, Ruston D, Kates LW, et al. Discussing religious and spiritual issues at the end of life: a practical guide for physicians. *JAMA* 2002;287:749–754.

   Lo B, Kates LW, Ruston D, et al. Responding to requests regarding prayer and religious ceremonies by patients near the end of life and their families. *J Palliat Med* 2003;6:417–424.

   Two articles that discuss how physicians might respond in disagreements in which the patient's religious concerns or beliefs are salient.
4. Miles SH, Singer PA, Siegler M. Conflicts between patients' wishes to forgo treatment and the policies of health care facilities. *N Engl J Med* 1989;321:48–50.

   Emphasizes the importance of respecting the mission of health care institutions and physicians' moral beliefs. Ideally, patients would seek care from physicians and institutions that share their values.

Decisions about Life-Sustaining Interventions

CHAPTER 15

Confusing Ethical Distinctions

In discussions about life-sustaining interventions, physicians often draw distinctions that seem intuitively plausible but prove problematic on closer analysis. Examples are distinctions between withdrawing and withholding interventions and between extraordinary (or heroic) and ordinary care. On the other hand, some ethical distinctions, although less intuitive, are nonetheless ethically valid. In particular, physicians might not understand the important distinction between providing very high doses of opioids to relieve symptoms and intentionally administering opioids to kill the patient (1). Physicians need to appreciate which distinctions are ethically meaningful and which are not because failure to do so often leads to confusion and poor care.

CASE 15.1 Withdrawal of mechanical ventilation.

Mr. C, a 68-year-old man with severe chronic obstructive lung disease, developed respiratory failure after an episode of bronchitis. He had told his outpatient physician repeatedly that he was willing to be on a ventilator in the intensive care unit, but only for a brief period. If he did not recover, he wanted the physicians to let him die in peace. After 2 weeks on antibiotics, bronchodilators, and mechanical venti- lation, Mr. C showed little improvement and was still in respiratory failure. He asked his physicians to discontinue the ventilator and to keep him comfortable while he died. His family and primary physician believed that his decision was informed.

Some health care workers objected to discontinuing the ventilator. They argued that although the patient may refuse life-sustaining interventions, removing them would be tanta- mount to murder. Other health care workers believed that it would be appropriate to discon- tinue heroic treatments such as the mechanical ventilation but that ordinary treatments such as antibiotics and intravenous fluids needed to be continued. Still others objected to the use of sedating doses of opioids for the relief of dyspnea after the ventilator was withdrawn because they would hasten death.

WITHDRAWING AND WITHHOLDING INTERVENTIONS

Many physicians and nurses are willing to withhold interventions but reluctant to withdraw them once they have been started. In one survey 82% of attending physicians were willing to withhold mechanical ventilation from a patient with severe chronic obstructive lung disease who refused it but only 59% were willing to withdraw the ventilator in such a situation (2). In a more recent study only 78% of physicians and 57% of pediatric intensive care unit (PICU) nurses agreed that with- holding and withdrawing are ethically the same (3).

This distinction seems plausible because discontinuing the ventilator is frequently characterized as a positive action, but not starting the ventilator might seem more passive and therefore less reprehensible. In everyday life, people generally are held more responsible for their actions than for their omissions. This distinction between acting and refraining from action, however, is not tenable in clinical medicine. Philosophers have devised ingenious examples to illustrate how the distinction between acting and refraining from acting cannot, by itself, be decisive (4). Suppose that the ventilator is accidentally disconnected from the patient. It is problematic to argue that it was permissible to refrain from reconnecting the ventilator but not to take action to disconnect it. In either situation the physician has an ethical obligation to respect the patient's preferences and to act in the patient's best interests. If the patient wishes the ventilator continued and the physician does not reconnect it, it is morally wrong, even though the physician might be said to withhold the ventilator or refrain from acting. Conversely, if a patient wishes to discontinue mechanical ventilation, as in Case 15.1, respecting the patient's wishes requires the physician to withdraw it. The distinction between withdrawing and withholding is not decisive; the patient's preferences are. The considerations that justify not initiating a treatment—in Case 15.1 informed refusal by a competent patient—also justify discontinuing it.

In many cases justifications for withdrawing treatment are more powerful than reasons to not initiate it. Additional information might become known after treatment has started—for example, that the patient did not want treatment or has end-stage disease. Furthermore, a hoped-for benefit might not materialize, as shown in Case 15.1 (5). Typically decisions on life-sustaining treatment must be made when the patient's prognosis is still uncertain. A time-limited trial of intensive therapy might be appropriate in this situation (6). If a treatment proves ineffective, there is no point in continuing it. However, if people were unable to discontinue a treatment once it was started, they might not even try interventions that might prove beneficial (7).

The courts have consistently ruled that there is no distinction between discontinuing medical interventions and not initiating them (8,9). In this book we use the term "forego" to include both withholding and withdrawing interventions (5).

EXTRAORDINARY OR HEROIC CARE

People might intuitively distinguish between extraordinary and ordinary care. Interventions that are highly technological, invasive, complicated, expensive, or unusual are sometimes regarded as "heroic" or "extraordinary." Examples are mechanical ventilation and renal dialysis. In contrast, antibiotics, intravenous fluids, and tube feedings are typically considered "ordinary" care. Some ordinary measures are commonly considered basic care or a standard nursing measure, such as a warm, dry bed. Often, it is argued that extraordinary treatments may be withheld or withdrawn, but not ordinary ones. In one survey 74% of doctors and nurses found this distinction helpful in making decisions (10).

This distinction, however, is not logical and is not a reliable guide to decisions (5). It is indeed appropriate to withdraw mechanical ventilation from Mr. C in Case 15.1. However, the reason is not that the ventilator can be characterized as extraordinary or heroic but rather that it provides little benefit and the patient does not want it. Instead of trying to determine whether the technology should be considered extraordinary or ordinary, physicians should examine the benefits and burdens of the intervention in the particular case, as well as the patient's preferences. In other clinical settings, such as during general anesthesia for surgery, mechanical ventilation is highly effective, desired by patients, and universally used. More important, the benefits of the intervention far outweigh the burdens in Case 15.1. Similarly, physicians need to encourage patients or their surrogates to assess the benefits and burdens of interventions rather than try to classify the interventions as heroic or ordinary.

The courts have rejected distinctions between ordinary and extraordinary interventions (8,9). Numerous rulings have declared that interventions ranging from ventilators to tube feedings may be withheld or withdrawn in appropriate circumstances. Chapter 20 discusses tube feedings in more detail.

RELIEVING SYMPTOMS WITH HIGH DOSES OF OPIOIDS AND SEDATIVES

Relief of pain and other symptoms in terminal illness, such as shortness of breath, is often inadequate. In the SUPPORT study of seriously ill patients, 50% of patients who died experienced moderate to severe pain in their last 3 days of life (11). Doctors might be reluctant to prescribe opioids in sufficient doses to relieve symptoms, or nurses might be reluctant to administer them (12). Some health care workers withhold opioids because they fear patients will become addicted. However, addiction rarely develops in terminal illness and should not be a primary consideration under these circumstances. Another concern is that the dose of opioids required to relieve symptoms might hasten the patient's death by suppressing respiration or causing hypotension. The doctrine of double effect, long-standing in moral philosophy, addresses this concern.

THE DOCTRINE OF DOUBLE EFFECT

Like all interventions, opioids and sedatives have both intended effects and unintended side effects. The doctrine of double effect distinguishes effects that are intended from those that are foreseen but unintended (13–16). In this view intentionally causing death is wrong. However, physicians may provide high doses of opioids and sedatives to relieve suffering, provided that they do not intend the patient's death. Such high doses are permitted even if the risk of hastening death is foreseen. The double effect doctrine also requires that the bad effect (the patient's death) not be the means to accomplish the good effect (relief of suffering). In addition, the unintended but foreseen bad effect must be proportional to the intended good effect. For example, it would be inappropriate to begin treatment of mild pain with very large doses of opioids. However, if the patient's suffering is greater, the physician can justify a greater risk of potentially contributing to the patient's death.

PROBLEMS WITH THE DOUBLE EFFECT DOCTRINE

The doctrine of double effect is widely accepted in this context of high doses of opioids and sedatives to relieve pain. One survey found that almost 90% of physicians and nurses agreed that it is appropriate to administer medication to relieve pain even if the medication hastens a patient's death (10). The Supreme Court has accepted the doctrine (*see* Chapter 22).

However, the doctrine presents several problems (13,17). First, it presents a questionable account of intention (13,18). Physicians might have multiple intentions (19). In one study physicians who ordered sedatives and analgesics while withholding life-sustaining interventions said they intended both to decrease pain and to hasten death in about a third of cases (20). Second, the doctrine of double effect seems to focus on how physicians articulate their intentions. The doctrine of double effect seems to imply that physicians are more justified in administering large doses of opioids if they can put out of mind the possibility that death might be hastened. Third, people generally are held accountable for consequences they foresee or should have foreseen, not merely for those consequences that they intended (5). Thus, the doctrine of double effect might be inconsistent with widely held ideas about responsibility for actions.

The issue of intention is further clouded because refusal of medical interventions by a competent patient might involve the intention to hasten death in some cases. Many competent patients who forego life-sustaining interventions do not want to continue a particular treatment but hope nevertheless that they can live without it. However, some patients who refuse life support intend to bring about their death. There is broad agreement that physicians should respect patient refusals of interventions, even when the patient's intention is to die. Thus, although intention is central to the doctrine of double effect, it should not be the only criterion for judging an action right or wrong.

Despite problems with the doctrine of double effect, it is well established that it is acceptable to use opioids to relieve pain and other symptoms, even if it hastens the patient's death. Because of controversies surrounding the doctrine of double effect, it might be helpful to give an alternative justification for high doses of opioids and sedatives to relieve refractory symptoms. When terminally ill patients experience refractory symptoms, the physician is caught between two duties: to relieve suffering and not to cause the patient's death. In balancing these conflicting duties, proportionality is important. The risk of hastening death is warranted if lower doses have failed to relieve the symptoms (5). In this situation it is more important to relieve refractory symptoms than to prolong a painful existence for a few hours or days.

PRACTICAL ASPECTS OF RELIEVING REFRACTORY SYMPTOMS

Intention is judged by a person's actions, as well as by his or her statements. Physicians cannot simply say that they intended to relieve pain; their actions must also be consistent with their statements (1). What approach to the use of opioids and sedatives is consistent with an intent to relieve pain but not to hasten death?

If the physician's intent is to palliate symptoms, his or her actions must allow the possibility for symptoms to be relieved without hastening death. The initial dose should not be expected to suppress respiration or cause hypotension. A lethal dose allows no possibility that the patient would survive and would constitute active euthanasia.

If the physician intends only to palliate suffering, there is no warrant for increasing the morphine dose when the patient is comfortable. In conscious patients the dose can be increased if the patient reports unacceptable symptoms. If patients are unconscious or otherwise unable to report pain, physicians and nurses must assess whether patients are comfortable. The dosage should be increased if the patient is restless or grimaces, withdraws from stimuli, or has hypertension, tachycardia, tachypnea, or any other findings that could reasonably be interpreted as suffering. Increasing sedation in the absence of such signs of distress would imply that the physician intended to hasten death and would cross the line from palliative care to active euthanasia (1).

RESPONSES TO REFRACTORY SUFFERING

Some terminally ill patients might experience suffering that even excellent palliative care and high-dose opioids do not relieve. Examples are uncontrollable pain, dyspnea, bleeding, and inability to swallow oral secretions. How should physicians respond in such dire situations? They have other options such as terminal sedation and voluntarily stopping of eating and drinking (13). Unlike physician-assisted suicide and active euthanasia, these practices are legal in all states.

TERMINAL SEDATION

Terminal sedation goes beyond high-dose opioids in several ways. The patient is sedated to unconsciousness in order to control symptoms, usually through administration of barbiturates or benzodiazepines. In addition, all life-sustaining interventions are withheld. The patient then dies of dehydration, starvation, or some other intervening complication. Although death is inevitable, it is delayed for a few hours to over 7 days, depending on clinical circumstances.

Although widely accepted, terminal sedation is not free of controversy (13). Terminal sedation is sometimes done without the express agreement of patients or surrogates or without explicit discussion that other interventions will be withheld (21). Such cases are problematic. In withholding life-sustaining interventions while a patient is terminally sedated, doctors claim that they are not killing the patient but simply respecting the patient's or surrogate's refusal of interventions. This claim is ethically acceptable only if the patient or surrogate has consented to foregoing these interventions. In addition, there might be confusion about the physician's intention and responsibility. It seems implausible to claim that death is unintended when a patient who wants to die is sedated to unconsciousness, life-sustaining interventions and artificial nutrition are withheld, and death is certain. Although sedation is intended to relieve the patient's suffering, the additional step of withholding fluids and nutrition is needed not to relieve pain but to hasten the patient's wished-for death. Furthermore, the notion that terminal sedation is merely "letting nature take its course" is unconvincing because often the patient dies from the withholding of nutrition and fluids, not of the underlying disease. Some writers argue that terminal sedation cannot be meaningfully distinguished from active euthanasia (22).

Terminal sedation also has limitations as a response to refractory suffering. First, some patients find terminal sedation unacceptable because prolonged unconsciousness before death violates their dignity or causes their families to suffer. Patients who wish to die in their own homes might not be able to arrange terminal sedation at home. Second, terminal sedation cannot relieve some symptoms, such as uncontrollable bleeding or inability to swallow secretions. Although patients are not conscious of these conditions once they are sedated, their death cannot be considered dignified or peaceful.

Despite these concerns, terminal sedation is both ethically and legally acceptable. Doctors can ensure that terminal sedation is appropriate. Physicians should check that the patient has received excellent palliative care, that the decision to carry out terminal sedation is informed and voluntary, and that the patient does not have major depression.

VOLUNTARY STOPPING OF EATING AND DRINKING

When voluntarily stopping eating and drinking, the patient decides to discontinue oral intake and is "allowed to die," primarily of dehydration or some intervening complication (13). Ethically and legally, the right of competent, informed patients to refuse life-prolonging interventions is firmly established. Forcibly feeding a competent patient who refuses food and fluids would violate the patient's autonomy. Because stopping eating and drinking requires considerable patient resolve, the voluntary nature of the action is clear. Stopping eating and drinking might seem natural because severe anorexia commonly occurs in the final stage of many illnesses.

The main disadvantage is that voluntary stopping of eating and drinking requires considerable resolve. The process might last for up to 2 weeks and therefore might seem inhumane. Initially, the patient might experience thirst and hunger. Ice chips and mouth care usually relieve discomfort, and pain medication might also be needed. Subtle coercion might occur if patients are not regularly offered the opportunity to eat and drink, yet such offers might be viewed as undermining the patient's resolve. Patients are likely to lose mental clarity toward the end of this process, which might raise questions about voluntariness or seem unacceptable to some patients or families.

EMOTIONAL REACTIONS TO THESE DISTINCTIONS

Physicians need to appreciate that these topics raise emotional as well as philosophical issues. To many people stopping a treatment is much more difficult emotionally than not starting it. Health care workers might feel that they are causing the patient's death by withdrawing a ventilator, discontinuing vasopressors, turning off a pacemaker or an automatic implantable cardiac defibrillator, or administering large doses of opioids or sedatives. The shorter the time between the withdrawal of the intervention and the patient's death, the more responsible the health care worker might feel for killing the patient. Such feelings might be particularly strong in nurses who are asked to actually disconnect the ventilator or to turn down the settings (23).

Doctors should routinely elicit the concerns, feelings, and objections of other health care workers as well as patients or surrogates about these issues. Moreover, doctors need to acknowledge the depth and sincerity of such feelings. Team meetings and family meetings are often helpful for this purpose. Similarly, physicians need to ascertain whether the patient or family has reservations about the plan of care.

Strong emotional reactions, such as a pang of conscience, might be a clue that further deliberation and discussion are needed. However, health care workers should try to articulate the reasons for their emotional reactions. The fact that something is emotionally difficult does not necessarily mean that it is unethical. In Case 15.1 the attending physician needs to explain that ethically and legally, the cause of Mr. C's death is considered to be his chronic obstructive pulmonary disease, not the discontinuation of mechanical ventilation. Supporting this ethical position, the law clearly states that discontinuing treatment is not murder or suicide (8,24).

The concerns of nurses and house staff should be accommodated if reasonably possible. Nurses who have strong personal objections to the plan of care should not be required to carry it out if other arrangements can be made to care for the patient. Generally, other nurses will volunteer to care for the patient. The attending physician should closely monitor the administration of opioids and sedatives rather than leave it to the nurses and house staff. Nurses and house officers appreciate it when the attending physician is at the bedside when mechanical ventilation is withdrawn.

In summary, several commonly held distinctions regarding life-sustaining interventions are not logically tenable. Physicians should appreciate that it might be appropriate to withdraw interventions that have been started or that some persons consider ordinary care. In addition, administering high doses of opioids and sedatives is appropriate to relieve symptoms in patients who have terminal illness or who have refused mechanical ventilation.

REFERENCES

1. Alpers A, Lo B. The Supreme Court addresses physician-assisted suicide: can its decisions improve palliative care? *Arch Fam Pract* 1999;8:200–205.
2. Caralis PV, Hammond JS. Attitudes of medical students, housestaff, and faculty physicians toward euthanasia and termination of life-sustaining treatment. *Crit Care Med* 1992;20:683–690.
3. Burns JP, Mitchell C, Griffith JL, et al. End-of-life care in the pediatric intensive care unit: attitudes and practices of pediatric critical care physicians and nurses. *Crit Care Med* 2001;29(3):658–664.
4. Brock D. Forgoing life-sustaining food and water: is it killing? In: Lynn J, ed. *By no extraordinary means*, Expanded ed. Bloomington: Indiana University Press, 1989:117–131.
5. President's Commission for the Study of Ethical Problems in Medicine and Biomedical and Behavioral Research. *Deciding to forego life-sustaining treatment*. Washington: U.S. Government Printing Office; 1983: 73–89.
6. Ruark J, Raffin TA, Stanford University Medical Center Committee on Ethics. Initiating and withdrawing life support. *N Engl J Med* 1988;318:25–30.
7. Lo B, Rouse F, Dornbrand L. Family decision-making on trial: who decides for incompetent patients? *N Engl J Med* 1990;322:1228–1231.
8. Meisel A. Legal myths about terminating life support. *Arch Intern Med* 1991;1551:1497–1502.
9. Meisel A. *The right to die*, 2nd ed. New York: John Wiley and Sons, 1995.
10. Solomon MZ, O'Donnell LO, Jennings B, et al. Decisions near the end of life: professional views on life-sustaining treatments. *Am J Public Health* 1993;83:14–23.
11. The SUPPORT Investigators. A controlled trial to improve care for seriously ill hospitalized patients. *JAMA* 1995; 274:1591–1598.
12. Edwards MJ, Tolle SW. Disconnecting the ventilator at the request of a patient who knows he will then die: the doctor's anguish. *Ann Int Med* 1992;117:254–256.
13. Quill TE, Dresser R, Brock DW. The rule of double effect—a critique of its role in end-of-life decision making. *N Engl J Med* 1997;3337:1768–1771.
14. Quill TE, Lo B, Brock DW. Palliative options of last resort: a comparison of voluntarily stopping eating and drinking, terminal sedation, physician-assisted suicide, and voluntary active euthanasia. *JAMA* 1997;278:2099–2104.
15. Gillon R. Foreseeing is not necessarily the same thing as intending. *Br Med J* 1999;318:1431–1432.
16. Sulmasy DP, Pellegrino ED. The rule of double effect: clearing up the double talk. *Arch Intern Med* 1999;159: 545–550.
17. Warnock M. *An intelligent person's guide to ethics*. London: Duckworth; 1998:27–31.
18. Beauchamp TL, Childress JF. *Principles of biomedical ethics*, 4th ed. New York: Oxford University Press; 1994:206–211.
19. Quill TE. Doctor, I want to die. Will you help me? *JAMA* 1993;270:870–873.
20. Wilson WC, Smedira NG, Fink C, et al. Ordering and administration of sedatives and analgesics during the withholding and withdrawal of life support from critically ill patients. *JAMA* 1992;267:949–953.
21. Billings JA. Slow euthanasia. *J Palliat Care* 1996;12:21–30.
22. Orentlicher D. The Supreme Court and physician-assisted suicide: rejecting physician-assisted suicide but embracing euthanasia. *N Engl J Med* 1997;337:1236–1239.
23. Asch DA. The role of critical care nurses in euthanasia and assisted suicide. *N Engl J Med* 1996;334:1374–1379.
24. Lo B. The death of Clarence Herbert: withdrawing care is not murder. *Ann Intern Med* 1984;101:248–251.

ANNOTATED BIBLIOGRAPHY

1. President's Commission for the Study of Ethical Problems in Medicine and Biomedical and Behavioral Research. *Deciding to forego life-sustaining treatment*. Washington: US Government Printing Office, 1983:60–90.
   Lucid discussion of the distinctions brought up in this chapter, showing how they are confusing and therefore best avoided.
2. Brock D. Forgoing life-sustaining food and water: is it killing? In: Lynn J, ed. *By no extraordinary means*, (expanded ed.). Bloomington: Indiana University Press, 1989:117–131.
   Thoughtful analysis of the distinctions discussed in this chapter.
3. Quill TE, Dresser R, Brock DW. The rule of double effect—a critique of its role in end-of-life decision making. *N Engl J Med* 1997;3337:1768–1771.
   Analysis of the doctrine of double effect and its application to decisions on life-sustaining interventions.
4. Quill TE, Lo B, Brock DW. Palliative options of last resort: a comparison of voluntarily stopping eating and drinking, terminal sedation, physician-assisted suicide, and voluntary active euthanasia. *JAMA* 1997;278:2099–2104.
   Analysis of different approaches to responding to refractory suffering at the end of life.

CHAPTER 16

Ethics Committees and Case Consultations

Ethical dilemmas in clinical practice can lead to deep disagreements and strong emotions. The Joint Commission on Accreditation of Healthcare Organizations requires institutions to have a mechanism to address ethical issues in patient care, such as an ethics committee or a consultation service. Ethics case consultations might be carried out by the full ethics committee, by a smaller team, or by an individual consultant; we thus use the term "ethics consultant" to refer to a group or to an individual. Compared to court proceedings, such consultations are timelier, less adversarial, and more flexible. This chapter reviews the goals, problems, and effective procedures of ethics consultations. Although ethics committees usually have several tasks, such as educational activities and development of institutional policies, this chapter focuses only on their work as consultants.

GOALS OF ETHICS CONSULTATIONS

The goal of ethics consultations is to help resolve uncertainty and disagreements over ethical issues in clinical care. Ethics consultations in intensive care unit (ICU) cases involving value conflicts reduce the length of hospitalization for patients who die during the hospitalization and are viewed as helpful by family members (1,2).

CASE 16.1 Disagreement between family and health care team.

A 76-year-old widower with severe Alzheimer disease is cared for by his two daughters and their families. He does not engage in conversations but usually responds appropriately to simple questions. He often smiles when playing with his grandchildren and when watching television. For the third time in 6 months, he is hospitalized for aspiration pneumonia.

The physicians believe that antibiotics are "futile" in this case and strongly recommend a palliative approach. The patient has not appointed a health care proxy but had indicated to his primary physician that his daughters should make decisions for him. His daughters acknowledge that their father has limited life expectancy but believe that he still has acceptable quality of life. "His family was always the most important thing to him. He always said that nothing made him happier than seeing his grandchildren grow up."

CLARIFY THE FACTS OF THE CASE

The first step in ethics case consultations is to gather information about the medical situation and the ethical issues in the case. Ethics committees or consultants should not uncritically accept second-hand data, which might omit important information or views (3,4). Moreover, important information might be omitted or conclusions and inferences presented rather than primary data. For instance, physicians or nurses might describe interventions as "futile" without explaining in what sense they are using this term. In Case 16.1 several clinical issues also need to be clarified, such as the patient's baseline functioning, the effectiveness of mechanical ventilation for treating respiratory failure in this setting, and the risk of recurrent aspiration if the patient recovers. In addition, the ethics consultants need to gather information relevant to the key ethical issues, such as previous statements by the patient about his wishes for care.

IDENTIFY AND ANALYZE UNCERTAINTY AND CONFLICT OVER ETHICAL ISSUES

Physicians, patients, and families commonly use ethical concepts and terms without analyzing them carefully. In Case 16.1 concepts needing clarification are futility (*see* Chapter 9), quality of life (*see* Chapter 4), surrogate decision-making (*see* Chapter 13), and the distinction between ordinary and heroic interventions (*see* Chapter 14). However, although an analysis of ethical issues is essential, few dilemmas in clinical ethics are resolved solely by philosophical analysis.

BUILD CONSENSUS AMONG STAKEHOLDERS

Ethics case consultants should help the stakeholders arrive at decisions that are acceptable to them and that fall within the bounds of acceptable ethical practice (5). Ethics consultants should not impose their own personal views about the course of action but rather allow the stakeholders to reach a decision that is consistent with ethical guidelines, their own values, and the patient's values. This process usually requires discussion and negotiation (Table 16-1).

Help Stakeholders Express Their Views and Concerns

Patients and family members often feel that physicians are not listening to them. Conversely, physicians often complain that patients and family members do not hear their recommendations.

Ethics consultants need to elicit the concerns and views of the various stakeholders. When patients and relatives feel their voices have been heard, they usually are more willing to listen to the physicians' assessment of the patient's prognosis and to recommendations. Moreover, physicians who hear the patient and family generally appreciate that their positions are based on deeply felt concerns, needs, and values. The ethics consultant can facilitate such communication through active listening skills and summarizing each stakeholder's perspective.

Provide Emotional Support

In situations such as the one discussed in Case 16.1, emotions often are intense. In response to the patient's serious clinical situation, the children might have a variety of feelings, including grief, anxiety, and anger.

The attending physician, house officers, and nurses in Case 16.1 felt frustrated that they could not resolve the conflict. Unless such feelings are explicitly expressed and acknowledged, discussion

---

TABLE 16-1

Goals of Ethics Case Consultations

Clarify the facts of the case.
Identify and analyze uncertainty and conflict over ethical issues.
Build consensus among stakeholders.
    Help stakeholders express their views and concerns.
    Provide emotional support.
    Negotiate an acceptable resolution.

---

of substantive issues is unlikely to be fruitful. Thus, an ethics consultant needs to communicate respect and empathy to all parties.

Negotiate an Acceptable Resolution

Ethics consultants need to know how to lead a discussion, to assure that all views are presented, and to help parties appreciate other points of view (6). Formal bioethics programs rarely teach these interpersonal skills. Parties who originally were in conflict are willing to go along with the final plan, even if it is not the approach they would take personally. Even if their view does not prevail, health care workers, patients, or surrogates might feel that their concerns have been addressed and are therefore more willing to accept the final decision.

POTENTIAL PROBLEMS WITH ETHICS CASE CONSULTATIONS

Although ethics consultations might help resolve disputes, they might also be problematic (Table 16-2) (3,7), as the following continuation of Case 16.1 illustrates.

CASE 16.1 Continued.

At the attending physician's request, two members of the ethics committee review the medical record. They agree that antibiotics are futile in this situation. Family members are outraged. "Who are these people? They never even spoke to us."

LACK OF PARTICIPATION OF PATIENTS OR SURROGATES

Patients or relatives usually feel outraged if ethical issues are resolved "behind closed doors" without their knowledge or participation and by people whom they have never met (3). They might feel that their decision-making responsibility has been usurped. In several well-publicized cases, ethics consultations were criticized for failing to allow surrogates of incompetent patients to participate in discussions (7).

BIAS OR PERCEIVED BIAS

Patients or surrogates who disagree with physicians might regard an ethics consultation as serving the interests of physician or institution. Ethics consultants are generally employees of the hospital and might be colleagues of the health care workers in the case. Hence, families might perceive them as siding with the interests of the doctors, nurses, and hospital.

UNSOUND RECOMMENDATIONS

Agreement among ethics committee members or consultants does not guarantee that their recommendations are sound. In Case 16.1 the ethics committee members adopted a view of "futility" that is highly problematic (*see* Chapter 9). Antibiotics are effective in treating the episode of aspiration pneumonia, but they have no impact on the course of dementia or the risk of further episodes of aspiration. Unsound thinking by the ethics consultation team might result from lack of knowledge,

TABLE 16-2

Potential Problems with Ethics Consultations

Lack of participation of patients or surrogates.

Bias or perceived bias.

Unsound recommendations.

Problems beyond the scope of an ethics consultation.

unrecognized bias, or flawed committee procedures. One empirical study found that most committee members had no formal training in bioethics and no recent continuing education (8).

PROBLEMS BEYOND THE SCOPE OF AN ETHICS CONSULTATION

In some cases the problems concern legal liability, staff conflicts, or discharge planning rather than strictly ethical issues. Nurses or house officers might want the ethics committee or consultant to resolve long-standing grievances. It is unwise for ethics committees and consultants to take on the duties of risk managers, hospital administrators, psychiatrists, or social workers.

PROCEDURES FOR ETHICS CASE CONSULTATIONS

For ethics case consultations to be generally accepted, they must be regarded as accessible and fair (3,7).

WHO CAN REQUEST ETHICS CASE CONSULTATIONS?

Attending physicians, who are responsible for patient management, clearly should have the power to ask for ethics consultations. Beyond that, patients or their surrogates, nurses, and house officers should also be able to request case consultations. Disagreements over the need for a consultation generally indicate serious conflicts over patient care or ethical issues. Restricting access to ethics consultations is likely to exacerbate such disputes; rather, to ensure fairness, both sides should be able to request a consultation. If someone other than the attending physician requests an ethics consultation, it is prudent for the ethics consultant to notify the attending physician.

WHO PARTICIPATES IN CASE CONSULTATIONS?

All persons directly involved in the patient's care should be invited to attend an ethics case consultation, such as the patient or surrogate, attending physicians, consultant, trainees, nurses, social workers, and other health care workers providing care. If the patient agrees, family members should also participate. Their attendance ensures that all pertinent information is presented and all viewpoints are represented. As a practical matter, people are more likely to accept recommendations if they are allowed to express their views and to hear the reasoning behind a decision. In some cases health care workers need to think through the ethical concerns before making recommendations to the patient or family. In such cases it is acceptable for the ethics consultants to meet with the health care team alone as a first step.

DOCUMENT RECOMMENDATIONS

Most consultants offer specific recommendations for resolving ethical dilemmas. For instance, in Case 16.1 the ethics consultation can recommend that more information about the patient's previous statements should be gathered and that clear and convincing advance directives should be respected.

Recommendations should be written in the medical record, together with their rationale. Unwritten recommendations invite misunderstandings and reduce accountability. Recommendations are more likely to be followed if they are brief and specific. Direct conversations with the team also increase acceptance of the recommendations.

As with any consultation, the attending physician retains the power to follow or not to follow the recommendations. Ethically and legally, that person, after receiving the recommendations, should act as a reasonable physician would.

ETHICS COMMITTEES AND ETHICS CONSULTANTS

Ethics consultations can be carried out in several ways, such as consultations by a full committee, a small team, or an individual consultant (9). These options have advantages and disadvantages, depending on the situation.

ETHICS COMMITTEES

Interdisciplinary ethics committees typically comprise physicians, nurses, house officers, social workers, and clergy. The committee should also include lay members, who often can point out overlooked issues and arguments and help health care workers better understand the patient's perspective.

The committee members' personal qualities are as important as their professional backgrounds. Colleagues should respect committee members for their clinical judgment and interpersonal skills. Committee members should be willing to learn about clinical ethics, receptive to different ideas and points of view, capable of dealing with emotionally charged topics and interpersonal disagreements, and able to tolerate ambiguity.

Advantages of Ethics Committees for Case Consultations

Diverse perspectives within an interdisciplinary committee can lead to thorough and thoughtful discussions (10), particularly in complex, difficult cases (11). An interdisciplinary ethics committee sends an important symbolic message to the hospital (10): Ethical issues are the business of everyone who cares for patients, and clinicians can learn to resolve ethical dilemmas. In addition, ethics committees can give a voice to the practical wisdom of experienced clinicians. Consideration by the full ethics committee might be particularly indicated if the case raises new or unusual issues, if the institution has no policy or an exception to the policy is being considered, or if the case has serious implications for the institution (9).

Disadvantages of Ethics Committees for Case Consultations

It might be difficult to mobilize a large ethics committee for urgent consultations. Also, decision-making power might be so diffused through a committee that no individual takes responsibility for a decision (12). Committee members might lack expertise and formal training in clinical ethics (8).

Ironically, a broadly representative committee might not raise diverse viewpoints because of group dynamics. Ethics committee members might feel pressured to reach consensus, avoid controversial issues, and downplay objections (3). The group might discourage members from considering fresh alternatives and seeking additional information. Such "groupthink" might lead to grave errors in judgment (13). Ethics committees might be especially vulnerable to groupthink because of demands for a timely recommendation despite uncertain information and conflicting values and interests.

INDIVIDUAL CONSULTANTS

Instead of an ethics committee, persons with special training in clinical ethics might conduct case consultations (14,15).

Advantages of Individual Consultants

Ethics consultants with special training might be more skilled at case consultation than committee members who have variable training in ethics and dispute resolution. Individual consultants might provide more timely consultation than committee members, obtain primary data, and provide follow-up.

Disadvantages of Individual Consultants

Undue deference to ethics experts. It might be difficult for others to challenge the recommendations of ethics "experts." As a result, discussion might be stifled and divergent viewpoints might not be considered.

Potential for individual bias. Practice standards and quality control are far less developed in clinical ethics than in medical subspecialties (16,17). Many persons carrying out ethics consultations might lack formal training in clinical ethics (8). Furthermore, ethics "experts" might disagree over recommendations in a specific case (18). An individual ethics consultant might provide idiosyncratic recommendations that most other recognized ethics consultants would reject. It would be misleading to represent a private belief or an opinion as the consensus of the field.

CONSULTATION TEAM

Ethics consultation might also be carried out by a small group of consultants, typically a subgroup of the full ethics committee. Such a team might be selected for their expertise and availability to provide ethics consultations.

In summary, ethics case consultations might help resolve ethical dilemmas. No single approach to ethics consultations is appropriate for all hospitals and situations (10,11). In some institutions there might be several individuals who are highly skilled at ethics consultations and are willing to carry them out. In other institutions no single person with special training or experience is available; in this situation a committee would be more sensible. Persons who conduct ethics case consultations need to be aware of the potential pitfalls and the steps that can be taken to avoid them.

REFERENCES

1. Schneiderman LJ, Gilmer T, Teetzel HD, et al. Effect of ethics consultations on nonbeneficial life-sustaining treatments in the intensive care setting: a randomized controlled trial. *JAMA* 2003;290(9):1166–1172.
2. Lo B. Answers and questions about ethics consultations. *JAMA* 2003;290(9):1208–1210.
3. Lo B. Behind closed doors: promises and pitfalls of ethics committees. *N Engl J Med* 1987;317:46–50.
4. Purtilo RB. A comment on the concept of consultation. In: Fletcher JC, Quist N, Jonsen AR, eds. *Ethics consultation in health care*. Ann Arbor: Health Administration Press, 1989:99–108.
5. Aulisio MP, Arnold RM, Youngner SJ, eds. *Ethics consultation: from theory to practice*. Baltimore: The John Hopkins University Press, 2003.
6. Arnold RM, Silver MHW. Techniques for training ethics consultants: why traditional classroom methods are not enough. In: Aulisio MP, Arnold RM, Youngner SJ, eds. *Ethics consultation: from theory to practice*. Baltimore: The John Hopkins University Press, 2003:70–87.
7. Fletcher JC, Moseley KL. The structure and process of ethics consultation services. In: Aulisio MP, Arnold RM, Youngner SJ, eds. *Ethics consultation: from theory to practice*. Baltimore: The John Hopkins University Press, 2003:96–120.
8. Hoffman DE. Are ethics committee members competent to consult? *J Law Med Ethics* 2000;28:30–40.
9. Rushton C, Youngner SJ, Skeel J. Models for ethics consultation: individual, team, or committee? In: Aulisio MP, Arnold RM, Youngner SJ, eds. *Ethics consultation: from theory to practice*. Baltimore: The John Hopkins University Press, 2003:88–95.
10. Swenson MD, Miller RB. Ethics case review in health care institutions. *Arch Intern Med* 1991;152:694–697.
11. Cohen CB. Avoiding "Cloudcuckooland" in ethics committee case review: matching models to issues and concerns. *Law Med Health Care* 1992;20:294–299.
12. Siegler M. Ethics committees: decisions by bureaucracy. *Hastings Cent Rep* 1986;16(3):22–24.
13. Janis IL, Mann L. *Decision-making: a psychological analysis of conflict, choice, and commitment*. New York: Free Press, 1977.
14. LaPuma J, Schiedermayer DL. Ethics consultation: skills, roles, and training. *Ann Intern Med* 1991;114:155–160.
15. Purtilo RB. Ethics consultations in the hospital. *N Engl J Med* 1984;311:983–986.
16. Drane JF. Hiring a hospital ethicist. In: Fletcher JC, Quist N, Jonsen AR, eds. *Ethics consultation in health care*. Ann Arbor: Health Administration Press, 1989:117–134.
17. Fletcher JC, Hoffmann DE. Ethics committees: time to experiment with standards. *Ann Intern Med* 1994;120:335–338.
18. Fox E, Stocking C. Ethics consultants' recommendations for life-prolonging treatment in a persistent vegetative state. *JAMA* 1993;270:2578–2582.

ANNOTATED BIBLIOGRAPHY

1. Lo B. Behind closed doors: promises and pitfalls of ethics committees. *N Engl J Med* 1987;317:46–49.
   Discusses potential problems with ethics committees, such as exclusion of patients and nurses, reliance on second-hand data, and groupthink.
2. Aulisio MP, Arnold RM, Youngner SJ. Health care ethics consultation: nature, goals and competencies. *Ann Intern Med* 2000;133:59–69.
   Report of an interdisciplinary task force to set standards for ethics consultations by ethics committees and individual consultants.
3. Schneiderman LJ, Gilmer T, Teetzel HD, et al. Effect of ethics consultations on non-beneficial life-sustaining treatments in the intensive care setting: a multi-center, prospective, randomized, controlled trial. *JAMA* 2003;290:1166–1172.
   Lo B. Answers and questions about ethics consultations. *JAMA* 2003;290:298–299.
   Randomized clinical trial of ethics consultations in cases of value disagreements and accompanying editorial.

CHAPTER 17

Do Not Attempt Resuscitation Orders

Everyone who dies suffers a cardiopulmonary arrest. Although cardiopulmonary resuscitation (CPR) might revive some patients after cardiopulmonary arrests, in severe illness CPR is much more likely to prolong dying than to reverse death. This chapter discusses the effectiveness of CPR, appropriate reasons for Do Not Attempt Resuscitation (DNAR) orders, the interpretation of such orders, and discussions with patients or surrogates about CPR.

CPR differs from other medical interventions in several ways. When a cardiopulmonary arrest occurs, physicians or nurses who might not know the patient must decide immediately whether to initiate CPR. Otherwise the patient will certainly die. Thus, CPR is attempted in every patient who suffers a cardiopulmonary arrest unless a prior decision has been made not to do so. Unlike other medical interventions, CPR is initiated without a physician's order. Instead, a physician's order is required to withhold CPR—the DNAR order or the No CPR order.

THE EFFECTIVENESS OF CPR

To make informed decisions about CPR, patients (or their surrogates) need to understand the limited effectiveness of CPR in many clinical situations. When CPR is attempted on general wards of an acute care hospital, circulation and breathing are restored in about 40% of cases (1). Of those initially resuscitated, about one third survive to discharge from the hospital. Thus, about 14% of patients on whom CPR is attempted are discharged alive from the hospital (1,2). In other words, even when CPR is attempted, about 86% of patients die. CPR is more effective when patients suffer cardiopulmonary arrests in the operating room, the cardiac catheterization laboratory, and intensive care units (ICUs).

In certain patient groups CPR is even less beneficial. Survival to discharge is significantly lower in patients with metastatic cancer, sepsis, and elevated serum creatinine (1). For patients with metastatic cancer, several older series reported zero survival after CPR (3), although two more recent series report about 10% survival rates in such patients (4,5). In the most recent series, there were no survivors if the arrest was anticipated and occurred after the patient gradually deteriorated, but 22% of patients with unexpected cardiopulmonary arrest were successfully resuscitated and survived to discharge (6).

For patients with sepsis, survival is also highly unlikely. In one series only 1 of 73 patients survived, whereas in another study 0 of 42 patients survived (7,8). CPR is usually ineffective in the elderly, but it is not clear whether this is due to age *per se* or comorbid diseases in the elderly (1,7,9). Outcomes for nursing home residents who receive CPR are also poor. In two series, 0% and 1.7% of nursing home residents on whom paramedics attempted CPR survived (10,11).

Complications might occur in patients who are revived by CPR. A dreaded outcome of CPR is severe neurological impairment. Even though circulation is restored, the brain might suffer severe anoxic damage. In one series only 1 patient survived to discharge among 52 patients who remained unconscious 24 hours after successful initial resuscitation (12). Other medical complications might also occur during CPR. For example, fractured ribs or sternum or flail chest occur in 30% of cases (13).

JUSTIFICATIONS FOR DNAR ORDERS

As with other medical interventions, there are several acceptable justifications for withholding CPR.

PATIENT REFUSES CPR

Competent, informed patients might not want CPR. Many patients wish to die peacefully rather than have physicians and nurses attempt to revive them. Such informed refusals should be respected (14). However, in a large study, when patients wanted CPR withheld, a DNAR order was written in only about 50% of cases (15).

SURROGATE REFUSES CPR

Surrogates might decline CPR for patients who lack decision-making capacity (14). Surrogate decisions should be based on the patient's preferences or best interests.

CPR IS FUTILE IN A STRICT SENSE

As Chapter 10 discusses, physicians may decide unilaterally to withhold interventions that are futile in a strict sense.

CPR Has No Pathophysiological Rationale

A patient might be obviously dead for a length of time incompatible with successful resuscitation. For example, a patient might have rigor mortis or dependent lividity.

Cardiac Arrest Occurs Despite Maximal Treatment

For example, a patient might have progressive hypotension despite maximal therapy.

CPR Has Already Failed in a Patient

When a patient remains pulseless after resuscitative efforts by paramedics in the field, continued CPR would be futile (14).

In these strictly defined situations, physicians appropriately make the decision to stop or withhold resuscitation and CPR should not be offered to patients or surrogates (14,16,17). Instead, physicians should inform them of the DNAR order or the termination of CPR and explain the reasons.

Problematic Appeals to Futility

Physicians often use futility in a looser sense to justify unilateral decisions by physicians to withhold CPR.

Survival after CPR is highly unlikely. Some physicians assert that CPR is "futile" when patients are highly likely to die even if CPR is attempted.

CASE 17.1 Family wants CPR even though survival would be highly unlikely.

A 54-year-old man, bedridden with squamous cell carcinoma of the lung metastatic to liver and bone, is hospitalized for pneumonia. He has never indicated his preferences about CPR. The family insists that he be a "full code," saying that even if he does not regain consciousness or survive the hospitalization, it is worth prolonging life for even a few hours or days. The physicians, however, consider CPR futile because the medical literature reports that very few such patients are discharged alive after cardiopulmonary arrest (3). Furthermore, the doctors consider his quality of life extremely poor.

In Case 17.1 the family regards the goal of CPR as prolonging life, even if it would be unprecedented for the patient to be discharged alive from the hospital. Most physicians, however, consider the goal of CPR to be patient survival to hospital discharge, not merely temporary restoration of circulation and breathing. They point out that society and the medical profession are not obligated to do everything that a patient requests (18,19). Prolonging the patient's life for a few hours or days is not an appropriate goal for care (17).

However, unilateral DNAR orders based on low likelihood of success are problematic (*see* Chapter 9) (20). First, rigorous data outcomes exist for very few clinical conditions (21). Second, physicians are inaccurate and unreliable in predicting outcomes of CPR. One study found that physicians were no better at identifying patients who would survive resuscitation than would be expected by chance alone (1). Third, physicians often define futility far more broadly than recommended in the literature. In a study of DNAR orders based on a quantitative definition of futility, in 32% of cases residents estimated the patient's probability of survival after CPR to be 5% or higher (22). This definition is far looser than the criteria for futility proposed in the literature—namely zero successes in the previous 100 cases (18,19).

The patient's quality of life is unacceptable. Some physicians and ethicists claim that CPR may be withheld from patients who are in a persistent vegetative state or who cannot survive outside an ICU (18,19). As discussed in Chapter 9, it is problematic for physicians to judge that the patient's quality of life is so poor that interventions are futile. DNAR decisions based on such a qualitative notion of futility are also suspect because physicians who make such judgments about competent patients commonly do not talk to them about their quality of life (22).

DISCUSSING DNAR ORDERS WITH PATIENTS

Patients or surrogates need to discuss CPR with physicians if they are to make informed decisions about it. Physicians cannot accurately determine patients' preferences about CPR without asking them directly. In the large multicenter SUPPORT study, physicians misunderstood patients' preferences about CPR in about 50% of cases (23).

BARRIERS TO DISCUSSIONS

Some physicians believe that patients do not want to discuss DNAR decisions. In fact, most ambulatory patients—between 67% and 85%—want to discuss life-sustaining treatment with physicians (24,25). Among hospitalized patients, between 42% and 81% want to discuss end-of-life decisions with their physicians (26,27).

Physicians sometimes hesitate to discuss DNAR orders with patients, fearing that they will lose hope, become depressed, refuse highly beneficial treatments, or even attempt suicide. Such adverse outcomes, however, almost never occur.

TARGETING DISCUSSIONS

Physicians typically discuss CPR only with patients whom they believe are at high risk for cardiopulmonary arrest. The prospect of cardiopulmonary arrest becomes more salient as a patient's condition worsens. However, if discussions are deferred, patients might become so sick that they are no longer capable of making medical decisions on discussing CPR with their physicians (28). Additionally, targeting sicker patients for discussions about CPR reinforces the belief that DNAR discussions signify a bleak prognosis. Selective discussions might also be inequitable. Physicians discuss DNAR orders more frequently with patients with acquired immunodeficiency syndrome or cancer than with patients with cirrhosis, who have similarly poor prognoses (29).

For these reasons physicians should routinely discuss CPR with all adult inpatients with serious illness. Ideally, such discussions would be initiated in the ambulatory setting. When patients lack decision-making capacity, physicians should conduct discussions about CPR with appropriate surrogates.

PATIENT MISUNDERSTANDINGS ABOUT CPR

Many patients misunderstand basic information about the nature of CPR. Few patients understand that mechanical ventilation is usually required after CPR and that patients on a ventilator are usually conscious but cannot talk (30). Patients substantially overestimate favorable outcomes after

CPR (31). Many patients who initially accept CPR change their minds after they are informed about the nature and outcomes of CPR (31,32).

IMPROVING DISCUSSIONS ABOUT DNAR ORDERS

Better discussions with physicians will help patients make informed decisions. Table 17-1 summarizes the following suggestions.

Place Discussions in Context

It is often better to start with a discussion of the patient's concerns and goals for care rather than the specific decision about CPR (33).

Routinely Invite Patients to Discuss CPR

Physicians can raise the issue of CPR in a straightforward manner. "I try to discuss with all patients what to do if they become too sick to talk with me directly. How would you feel about discussing this?" If the patient agrees, the physician can continue, "One important issue is CPR. Let me explain what CPR is . . . " Some physicians try to dissuade patients from CPR by describing it in graphic detail, such as "pounding on your chest." Such biased information, however, undermines the goal of informed patient decision-making.

Provide Information so that Patients Can Make Informed Decisions

Often, doctors shroud DNAR discussions in euphemisms or technical jargon (34). Physicians sometimes ask patients, "If your heart or lungs stop, would you like us to start them up again?" Such phrasing suggests that CPR is as simple and effective as jump-starting an automobile battery or changing an electrical fuse. The question is whether patients want doctors to *try* to revive them, even though the likelihood of death is 86% or more. Physicians can be explicit without being blunt or offensive. To avoid bias due to framing effects, physicians should explain that if CPR is attempted, overall 14% of patients will survive the hospitalization and 86% will die. Doctors can describe CPR (including chest compressions, electroshock, and intubation) and the possible outcomes (including survival, persistent unconsciousness, and death). Even after discussions with physicians, patients often have serious misunderstandings about CPR. For example, patients often do not realize that after resuscitation, mechanical ventilation is usually needed (30).

Make Explicit Recommendations About CPR

Physicians can offer recommendations while still allowing patients ultimate decision-making power. If CPR would be futile in a strict sense, physicians should not offer patients or surrogates a choice but instead inform them of the DNAR order and its rationale.

Reassure Patients About Ongoing Care

Some patients fear that after a DNAR order, physicians will give up on them. Physicians need to emphasize plans for treating other problems, seeing the patient regularly, and providing palliative care.

TABLE 17-1

Improving Discussions with Patients or Surrogates about DNAR Orders

Routinely invite patients to discuss CPR.
Provide information so that patients can make informed decisions.
Make explicit recommendations about CPR.
Reassure patients about ongoing care.
Repeat discussions at subsequent visits.

Repeat discussions at subsequent visits

Patients or surrogates often need time to think about issues and deal with their emotions. Thus, repeating discussions helps them make informed choices about CPR.

Physicians can improve their skills at DNAR discussions. Currently, doctors seldom observe more experienced physicians carry out such discussions or have colleagues watch them (35). Asking the advice of colleagues about a particular situation, role playing, and reviewing videotapes of simulated discussions might be helpful.

IMPLEMENTING DNAR ORDERS

WRITING A DNAR ORDER

DNAR orders are common in critically and terminally ill patients. CPR is not attempted for 89% of seriously ill patients who die in acute care hospitals (36). To prevent misunderstandings, physicians should write DNAR orders in the medical record. In addition, the physician should explain in a progress note the rationale for the DNAR order, document the agreement of the patient or surrogate, and describe plans for further care. In an urgent situation, nurses may accept a DNAR order over the telephone, with the understanding that the physician will sign the order promptly. DNAR orders should be reviewed periodically, particularly if the patient's condition changes.

Oral DNAR orders might lead to mistakes, misunderstandings, and confusion. They create ethical quandaries and legal jeopardy for nurses who respond to cardiopulmonary arrests. Generally, the use of oral rather than written DNAR orders indicates serious disagreements and a need for further discussions.

INTERPRETATION OF DNAR ORDERS

Implications for Other Treatments

Strictly speaking, a DNAR order means only to withhold CPR. Other treatments, such as antibiotics, transfusions, and even intensive care, might still be appropriate. However, the same reasons that make CPR inappropriate might also render other interventions unsuitable. Many hospitals now require more detailed orders than simply "no CPR." For example, the physician might have to specify on a checklist whether to provide mechanical ventilation (37,38). Such detailed orders are useful because nurses need to know whether abnormalities such as hypotension or ventricular arrhythmia should be treated or allowed to progress and lead to cardiopulmonary arrest.

"Limited" or "Partial" DNAR Orders

In some cases physicians may wish to restrict resuscitative efforts to a fixed period or withhold aspects of advanced life support, such as defibrillation or intubation (7). One rationale for physician-limited DNAR orders is that patients who do not respond to basic CPR might have suffered irreversible brain damage. The fear is that resuscitation might restore breathing and circulation in a patient who will never regain consciousness. However, this rationale is problematic. During an attempted resuscitation, there are virtually no reliable signs of irreversible brain damage or brain death (14). Furthermore, stopping resuscitation after basic CPR will reduce the chances for patient recovery. Even if basic CPR is ineffective, advanced life support might restore circulation, breathing, and consciousness.

"Limited" DNAR orders are appropriate, however, when an informed patient (or surrogate) consents to them or requests them. For instance, patients with chronic obstructive lung disease may decline mechanical ventilation but agree to other resuscitative measures.

Preventing Misunderstandings

Some physicians are reluctant to write DNAR orders because they fear that other health care workers—consultants, house staff, nurses, or respiratory therapists—might cease to provide needed care to the patient. Conversely, some nurses believe that once a DNAR order is made, physicians will stop rounding on patients or stop talking to them. Concerns that DNAR orders might lead to suboptimal care need to be addressed openly. Everyone needs to appreciate that DNAR orders do not mean "provide no care."

Slow or Show Codes

"Slow codes" or "show codes" appear to provide CPR but actually do not—or do so in a way that is known to be ineffective (39,40). For example, the code team is not paged immediately, a medical student is allowed to make repeated attempts to intubate the patient, or drugs are injected into the bed rather than into the patient. Such orders are usually given orally and not written down. Slow or show codes are commonly considered when the patient has a grim prognosis but an attending physician insists that CPR be attempted or the patient or surrogate insists that "everything" be done. Show codes are unacceptable because they deceive patients or families, compromise the ethical integrity of health care professionals, and cause confusion and cynicism among health care workers.

SPECIAL SETTINGS

Anesthesia for Surgery and Invasive Procedures

Patients with DNAR orders might undergo surgery for palliation or conditions unrelated to their primary diagnosis (41). Many physicians want to "suspend" DNAR orders in the operating room, when the patient's vital functions are deliberately depressed by anesthesia and maintained using techniques similar to those of advanced cardiac life support (42–44). If resuscitation were not permitted, medications might be titrated to ensure greater hemodynamic stability but lighter anesthesia, less analgesia, and less amnesia. CPR is much more successful in the operating room than elsewhere in the hospital. In one study, 65% of patients who had a cardiopulmonary arrest in the operating room survived to discharge and 92% of those whose arrest was caused by anesthesia survived (45). Another reason for suspending DNAR orders during surgery is the physician's sense of responsibility for intraoperative deaths (*see* Chapter 38).

If patients with DNAR orders undergo surgery or invasive procedures, physicians should discuss how the DNAR orders will be interpreted perioperatively (41). Plans should be documented clearly in the medical record. Similar considerations apply to DNAR orders in radiology departments, where medications might lead to cardiopulmonary arrest that is easily reversed (46–48).

Emergency Medical Services

When emergency medical personnel are called to the home of a patient with serious illness, CPR might not be appropriate. Paramedic policies and protocols should include provisions for DNAR orders (14). DNAR orders can be documented with an identification card or bracelet, a sticker on the telephone or refrigerator, a formal order sheet, or a computerized registry. A DNAR order should not preclude other appropriate care, such as oxygen or transport to the hospital. Similarly, emergency departments need to establish DNAR policies and procedures.

Nursing Homes

Few nursing home residents who suffer cardiopulmonary arrest are successfully resuscitated (10,11). Extended care facilities should establish institutional policies about the provision of CPR and procedures for designating residents as not to be resuscitated. Residents with DNAR orders should have access to appropriate emergency services.

Family Presence During Resuscitation Efforts

Many family members would like to be present during resuscitation efforts (14,49). Studies show that the overwhelming majority of relatives who observe resuscitation attempts view it as important and helpful. Being present might also help them adjust to the patient's death and reduce the likelihood of prolonged grief. In contrast, many physicians and nurses object to relatives being present during resuscitation, fearing that it will prove traumatic for laypeople, cause stress in caregivers, or even interfere with resuscitative attempts. Because family members apparently find that the benefits of their presence outweigh the risks, hospitals should offer relatives the opportunity to be present at resuscitation efforts (14). Hospitals should prepare the family for what they will see and provide emotional support.

In conclusion, CPR is not appropriate for many patients. Physicians should elicit patients' preferences about CPR and write DNAR orders in the medical record. For physicians the question is no longer whether they should discuss DNAR orders with their patients but how to do so with compassion and caring.

REFERENCES

1. Ebell MH, Becker LA, Barry HC, et al. Survival analysis after in-hospital cardiopulmonary resuscitation. *J Gen Intern Med* 1998;13:805–816.
2. Saklayen M, Liss H, Markert R. In-hospital cardiopulmonary resuscitation. *Medicine* 1995;74:163–175.
3. Faber-Langendorf K. Resuscitation of patients with metastatic cancer: is transient benefit still futile? *Arch Intern Med* 1991;151:235–239.
4. Vitelli CE, Cooper J, Ragatko A, et al. Cardiopulmonary resuscitation and the patient with cancer. *J Clin Oncol* 1991;9:111–115.
5. Rosenberg M, Wang C, Hoffman-Wilde S, et al. Results of cardiopulmonary resuscitation: failure to predict survival in two community hospitals. *Arch Intern Med* 1993;153:1370–1375.
6. Ewer MS, Kish SK, Martin CG, et al. Characteristics of cardiopulmonary arrest in cancer patients as a predictor of survival after cardiopulmonary resuscitation. *Cancer* 2001;92(7):1905–1912.
7. Evans AL, Brody BA. The do-not-resuscitate order in teaching hospitals. *JAMA* 1985;253:2236–2239.
8. Bedell SE, Delbanco TL, Cook EF, et al. Survival after cardiopulmonary resuscitation in the hospital. *N Engl J Med* 1983;309:579–586.
9. Murphy DJ, Murray AM, Robinson BE, et al. Outcomes of cardiopulmonary resuscitation in the elderly. *Ann Intern Med* 1989;111:199–205.
10. Applebaum GE, King JE, Finucane TE. The outcome of CPR initiated in nursing homes. *J Am Geriatr Soc* 1990;38:197–200.
11. Awoke S, Mouton CP, Parrott M. Outcomes of skilled cardiopulmonary resuscitation in a long-term care facility: futile therapy? *J Am Geriatr Soc* 1992;40:593–595.
12. Longstreth WT, Inui TS, Cobb LA, et al. Neurologic recovery after out-of-hospital cardiopulmonary arrest. *Ann Intern Med* 1983;98:588–592.
13. Moss AH. Informing patients about cardiopulmonary resuscitation when the risks outweigh the benefits. *J Gen Intern Med* 1989;4:349–355.
14. Guidelines 2000 for Cardiopulmonary Resuscitation and Emergency Cardiovascular Care. Part 2: Ethical Aspects of CPR and ECC. *Circulation* 2000;102:I12–21.
15. The SUPPORT Investigators. A controlled trial to improve care for seriously ill hospitalized patients. *JAMA* 1995;274:1591–1598.
16. Blackhall LJ. Must we always use CPR? *N Engl J Med* 1988;317:1281–1285.
17. Tomlinson T, Brody H. Futility and the ethics of resuscitation. *JAMA* 1990;264:1276–1280.
18. Schneiderman LJ, Jecker NS, Jonsen AR. Medical futility: its meaning and ethical implications. *Ann Intern Med* 1990;112:949–954.
19. Schneiderman LJ, Jecker NS, Jonsen AR. Medical futility: response to critiques. *Ann Intern Med* 1996;125:669–674.
20. Alpers A, Lo B. When is CPR futile? *JAMA* 1995;273:156–158.
21. Rubenfeld GD, Crawford SW. Withdrawing life support from mechanically ventilated recipients of bone marrow transplants: a case for evidence-based guidelines. *Ann Intern Med* 1996;125:625–633.
22. Curtis JR, Park DR, Krone MR, et al. The use of the medical futility rationale in do not attempt resuscitation orders. *JAMA* 1995;273:124–128.
23. Teno JM, Hakim RB, Knaus WA, et al. Preferences for cardiopulmonary resuscitation: physician-patient agreement and hospital resource use. *J Gen Intern Med* 1995;10:179–186.
24. Shmerling RH, Bedell SA, Lilienfeld A, et al. Discussing cardiopulmonary resuscitation: a study of elderly outpatients. *J Gen Intern Med* 1988;3:317–321.
25. Lo B, McLeod G, Saika G. Patient attitudes towards discussing life-sustaining treatment. *Arch Intern Med* 1986;146:1613–1615.
26. Reilly BM, Magnussen CR, Ross J, et al. Can we talk? Inpatient discussions about advance directives in a community hospital. Attending physicians' attitudes, their inpatients' wishes, and reported experience. *Arch Intern Med* 1994;154(20):2299–2308.
27. Hoffman JC, Wenger NS, Davis RH, et al. Patient preferences for communication with physicians about end-of-life decisions. *Ann Intern Med* 1997;127:1–12.
28. Council on Ethical and Judicial Affairs AMA. Guidelines for the appropriate use of do-not-resuscitate orders. *JAMA* 1991;265:1868–1871.
29. Wachter RM, Luce JM, Hearst N, et al. Decisions about resuscitation: inequities among patients with different diseases but similar prognoses. *Ann Intern Med* 1989;111:525–532.
30. Fischer GS, Tulsky JA, Rose MR, et al. Patient knowledge and physician predications of treatment preferences after discussions of advance directives. *J Gen Intern Med* 1998;13:447–454.
31. Murphy DJ, Burrows D, Santilli S, et al. The influence of the probability of survival on patients' preferences regarding cardiopulmonary resuscitation. *N Engl J Med* 1994;330:545–549.
32. O'Brien LA, Grisso JA, Maislin G, et al. Nursing home residents' preferences for life-sustaining treatments. *JAMA* 1995;254:1175–1179.
33. Lo B, Quill T, Tulsky J. Discussing palliative care with patients. *Ann Intern Med* 1999;130:744–749.
34. Tulsky JA, Chesney MA, Lo B. How do medical residents discuss resuscitation with patients? *J Gen Intern Med* 1995;10:436–442.
35. Tulsky JA, Chesney MA, Lo B. "See one, do one, teach one?" Housestaff experience discussing do-not-resuscitate orders. *Arch Intern Med* 1996;156:1285–1289.
36. Lynn J, Teno J, Phillips RS, et al. Perceptions by family members of the dying experience of older and seriously ill patients. *Ann Intern Med* 1997;126:97–106.

37. Mittelberger JA, Lo B, Martin D, et al. Impact of a procedure-specific do not resuscitate order form on documentation of do not resuscitate orders. *Arch Intern Med* 1993;153:228–232.
38. O'Toole EE, Youngner SJ, Juknialis BW, et al. Evaluation of a treatment limitation policy with a specific treatment-limiting order page. *Arch Intern Med* 1994;154(4):425–432.
39. Muller JH. Shades of blue: the negotiation of limited codes by medical residents. *Soc Sci Med* 1992;34:885–898.
40. Gazelle G. The slow code—should anyone rush to its defense? *N Engl J Med* 1998;338:467–469.
41. Clemency MV, Thompson NJ. Do not resuscitate orders in the perioperative period: patient perspectives. *Anesth Analg* 1997;84(4):859–864.
42. Cohen CB, Cohen PJ. Do-not-resuscitate orders in the operating room. *N Engl J Med* 1991;325:1879–1882.
43. Truog RD. "Do not resuscitate" orders during anesthesia and surgery. *Anesthesiology* 1991;74:606–608.
44. Walker RM. DNR in the OR: resuscitation as an operative risk. *JAMA* 1991;266:2407–2412.
45. Olsson GL, Hall B. Cardiac arrest during anesthesia: a computer-aided study in 250,543 anaesthetics. *Acta Anaesthesiol Scand* 1988;32:653–664.
46. Jacobson JA, Gully JE, Mann H. "Do not resuscitate" orders in the radiology department: an interpretation. *Radiology* 1996;198:21–24.
47. McDermott VG. Resuscitation and the radiologist. *Ann Intern Med* 1998;129:831–833.
48. Heffner JE, Barbieri C. Compliance with do-not-resuscitate orders for hospitalized patients transported to radiology departments. *Ann Intern Med* 1998;129:801–805.
49. Tsai E. Should family members be present during cardiopulmonary resuscitation? *N Engl J Med* 2002;346(13):1019–1021.

ANNOTATED BIBLIOGRAPHY

1. Tulsky JA, Chesney MA, Lo B. How do medical residents discuss resuscitation with patients? *J Gen Intern Med* 1995;10:436–442.
   Shows how, in discussions with patients regarding CPR, residents failed to provide key information about CPR and missed opportunities to discuss the patient's values and goals.
2. Murphy DJ, Burrows D, Santilli S. The influence of the probability of survival on patients' preferences regarding cardiopulmonary resuscitation. *N Engl J Med* 1994;330:545–549.
   Concludes that patients overestimate survival after CPR and that when such misunderstandings are corrected, patients are less likely to accept CPR.
3. Curtis JR, Park DR, Krone MR. The use of the medical futility rationale in do not attempt resuscitation orders. *JAMA* 1995;273:124–128.
   Empirical study documenting problems and mistakes that occur when physicians claim that CPR would be futile.
4. Guidelines 2000 for Cardiopulmonary Resuscitation and Emergency Cardiovascular Care. Part 2: Ethical Aspects of CPR and ECC. *Circulation* 2000;102:I12–21.
   Consensus ethical guidelines presented in CPR certification courses.

CHAPTER 18

Tube and Intravenous Feedings

Tube and intravenous feedings can prolong life in patients who cannot take adequate nutrition by mouth. In conditions such as short bowel syndrome, parenteral hyperalimentation can allow patients to lead active lives for many years. However, in severe, progressive illness such as advanced dementia or metastatic cancer, tube and intravenous feedings might merely prolong death and subject patients to indignity. Nationwide, 34% of nursing home residents with severe cognitive impairment have feeding tubes (1).

CASE 18.1 Tube feedings in a patient with severe dementia (2).

A patient's daughter leaves a phone message. "My mother, Mrs. F, has eaten nothing all weekend. What should we do?" A 70-year-old woman with severe dementia, Mrs. F rarely speaks, is confined to a wheelchair, and requires diapers for incontinence. She has been kept out of a nursing home by the efforts of a devoted family and a geriatric day care center. During the past year her social actions have decreased and her food intake has become increasingly erratic. First she stopped feeding herself. Now, although her family feeds her by hand, her intake continues to decline. Once she required overnight hospitalization for dehydration. During the past week she has been clamping her mouth shut, pushing the spoon away with her hand, and spitting out food. Over the weekend even coaxing with her favorite foods was unsuccessful. Those who care for her must now face a dreaded question: If hand feedings continue to fail, should she be fed through a feeding tube? The situation evokes strong and conflicting reactions. The patient's sister says, "We can't let her starve to death!" The daughter, however, says, "She's telling us to stop. We're just torturing her."

REASONS TO PROVIDE TUBE AND INTRAVENOUS FEEDINGS

ALLOWING PHYSICIANS TO TREAT REVERSIBLE CAUSES OF FEEDING PROBLEMS

Decreased oral intake might result from reversible medical problems, such as intercurrent illness, mouth lesions, or side effects of medications. Psychosocial problems, such as a desire for more control, depression, or a change of caregivers, might also cause feeding problems. Sometimes making hand feedings more acceptable to the patient can address refusals to eat. The caregiver can slow the pace of feeding, offer smaller bites, alter the taste or consistency, remind the demented patient to swallow, or gently touch the patient (2,3). Temporary use of tube or intravenous feedings might resolve the crisis and allow the underlying problem to be identified and treated.

WITHHOLDING TUBE AND INTRAVENOUS FEEDING WOULD STARVE PEOPLE TO DEATH

Everyone has temporarily experienced thirst or hunger and can imagine how agonizing it must be to starve to death. Similarly, everyone appreciates how upset infants become when they are not fed. By analogy, some people believe that adult patients with terminal illness or advanced dementia suffer when feeding tubes are withheld. In addition, tube feedings clearly prolong life for years in persons in persistent vegetative state (PVS). Finally, some physicians believe that discontinuing tube or intravenous feedings makes them the direct cause of the patient's death.

TUBE AND INTRAVENOUS FEEDINGS ARE ORDINARY CARE

Many people regard tube feedings as basic humane care. In one survey, 16% of physicians agreed with this position (4). In this view, feeding is an essential part of caring for the helpless, just like providing a warm, clean bed (5). Tube feedings are also a means of expressing compassion, caring, and love.

WITHHOLDING TUBE AND INTRAVENOUS FEEDINGS WOULD LEAD TO ABUSES

Fears of abuses and slippery slopes cause some people to insist on providing artificial feedings. Suppose artificial feedings are withheld in a case in which the reasons seem compelling. This precedent might make it easier to withhold artificial feedings or other life-sustaining interventions in other cases, even if the reasons are not as convincing. The next patient's family might not be so loving, or the next physician might not be so careful about searching for treatable feeding problems. Eventually, life-prolonging interventions might be withheld in cases that would previously have been regarded as inappropriate. According to this line of argument, the only way to prevent such a loosening of standards is to prohibit the action under all circumstances.

REASONS TO WITHHOLD TUBE AND INTRAVENOUS FEEDINGS

Those who would allow artificial feedings to be withheld from patients with severe, progressive illness frame the issues differently. They agree that it is morally obligatory to give bottles to infants, provide groceries to homebound persons, and place spoonfuls of food in the mouth of a person with dementia. However, opponents offer several reasons for withholding tube feedings when patients such as Mrs. F refuse oral intake.

TUBE AND INTRAVENOUS FEEDINGS MERELY PROLONG DYING

Many people believe that tube and intravenous feedings only prolong death for terminally ill patients. They consider it inhumane to force-feed people with severe dementia or metastatic cancer only to have them succumb to pneumonia or some other complication. Furthermore, it is problematic to say that withholding artificial feedings causes the patient's death. Determining *a single* cause of death when many factors are contributing to the patient's death is a controversial philosophical topic (6). Nonetheless, in such cases death is usually attributed to the underlying dementia or cancer and not to the act of forgoing medical interventions—provided that the reasons for withholding treatment are ethically acceptable. Chapter 14 discusses these distinctions in detail.

SUCH PATIENTS SELDOM SUFFER IF TUBE AND INTRAVENOUS FEEDINGS ARE WITHHELD

Patients with severe dementia or metastatic cancer seldom experience thirst or hunger if they continue to refuse oral intake. In a study from a comfort care unit, almost all lucid, terminally ill patients reduced intake of food and fluids to less than their nutritional needs. About two thirds never experienced hunger, and about one third experienced hunger only initially. Symptoms of thirst or dry mouth were more common, with 36% experiencing them until death. In all patients small intake of food and fluids, ice chips, and meticulous mouth care relieved symptoms of hunger and dry mouth (7). In another study hospice nurses rated quality of death of patients who refused food and water as 8 on a 9-point scale, where 9 was a very good death (8). With reduced oral intake, symptoms such as nausea, vomiting, edema, cough, and incontinence are reduced (3). Furthermore, pain medications should be given if needed, just as they are provided to patients with respiratory failure who decline mechanical ventilation.

TUBE AND INTRAVENOUS FEEDINGS CANNOT BE CONSIDERED ORDINARY CARE

Labeling artificial feedings as "ordinary" care is questionable. Cessation of the desire for food and drink is part of the natural history of severe illnesses such as severe dementia or metastatic cancer. In other Western societies, such as the United Kingdom and Sweden, tube feedings are rarely administered to patients with severe dementia (9). In addition, long-term intravenous or nasogastric tube feedings have become technically possible only in the past 30 years. The Food and Drug Administration regulates artificial feedings as drugs and medical devices, not as foods. Furthermore, feeding gastrostomy or jejunostomy tubes require a surgical or endoscopic procedure for insertion.

More fundamentally, most writers on medical ethics and virtually all court decisions reject the distinction between "extraordinary" and "ordinary" care (*see* Chapter 14) (10–12). The issue is not whether an intervention can be considered "extraordinary" or "ordinary" but whether its benefits outweigh its burdens for the individual patient (11). As with other interventions, tube and intravenous feedings should not be provided simply because they are technically feasible.

TUBE AND INTRAVENOUS FEEDINGS HAVE BURDENS AND BENEFITS

Like all interventions, tube and intravenous feedings have burdens as well as benefits. For patients with severe dementia or metastatic cancer, the benefits of tube feedings are limited. Treatable conditions are identified and corrected in few such patients (13). One cohort study found that 50% of patients with severe dementia who receive tube feedings died within 6 months (14).

Recent articles argue that tube feedings do not prolong life in patients with severe dementia. This simple claim is misleading unless it is carefully qualified. First, such patients often die from infection or other comorbidities, which tube feedings do not address. Second, patients with advanced dementia might survive for extended periods while taking only small amounts of food and fluids offered by mouth. However, if they have no oral intake whatever, tube feedings prolong life in the sense that without them, patients die in 1 or 2 weeks.

The burden of tube feedings might be substantial. Complications of tube feedings in elderly patients include aspiration pneumonia in 46% of cases and agitation leading to self-extubation in 61% (15). Tube feedings might not reduce the risk of aspiration pneumonia compared with oral intake (15). Aspiration pneumonia appears to be as common with gastrostomy tubes as with nasogastric tubes (16). In one study of tube feedings in a nursing home, restraints were applied in over 50% of patients to prevent them from pulling out their feeding tubes. (13). Patients who pull out feeding tubes might be communicating refusal, expressing discomfort or anger, seeking attention or control, or acting in a purely reflexive manner.

Restraining demented patients to prevent them from pulling out tubes compromises their independence and dignity, particularly because they cannot appreciate how the feeding tube will help them (2). Restraints also increase patient agitation. Sedation or "chemical restraint," which might appear to be more acceptable, also compromises patient dignity. Many patients do not want to be restrained. In a study of nursing home residents, 33% said they wanted tube feedings if they were unable to eat because of permanent brain damage that also left them unable to recognize people. However, after learning that physical restraints are sometimes applied to patients receiving tube feedings, 25% of residents who initially wanted tube feedings or were not sure changed their minds and preferred not to have them (17).

CARE SHOULD BE PROVIDED DIRECTLY, NOT THROUGH SYMBOLS

If the goal of care is to provide comfort and compassion, caregivers should do so directly rather than through symbolic actions (2). This can be done by offering patients food and water by hand, moistening their mouth and lips, holding their hand, or giving a backrub.

Ironically, artificial feedings might be impersonal. With tube feedings the caregiver might focus more attention on technical issues, such as positioning the feeding tube and checking the residual volume, than on the patient. If tube feedings proceed without complication, social interaction between the caregiver and patient can be minimal. Moreover, the patient has no control over tube feedings except to pull out the tube. In contrast, with hand feedings patients determine the timing, pace, and even the content of feedings. Patients are in control if they turn away or clamp their mouths shut. Thus, hand feedings that provide inadequate nutrition might meet more of the patient's human needs than tube feedings that deliver adequate calories impersonally.

SLIPPERY SLOPE ARGUMENTS ARE UNPERSUASIVE

Slippery slope arguments shift attention away from the individual patient to future patients or to society as a whole. The patient's family and physicians might assert that the proper focus should be on what is best for the individual patient, not on what precedent is set. Under the guideline of beneficence, physicians should act for the individual patient's benefit, not for the benefit of third parties, such as future patients. It seems cruel to impose interventions that are not in the patient's best interests in order to protect other people from harm. A better approach would be to develop adequate safeguards to protect others.

Another rebuttal to slippery slope arguments is empirical: There is little evidence that withholding tube feedings from severely demented patients has led to inappropriate withholding of care in other situations.

Finally, slippery slope objections also apply to withholding any form of life-sustaining intervention. Singling out artificial feedings as leading to a slippery slope implicitly assumes that they differ in significant ways from other interventions. This distinction is untenable.

LEGAL ISSUES

According to court decisions, artificial feedings are similar to other medical interventions, which have benefits and burdens for the patient (12,18). The predominant judicial opinion is that artificial feedings are medical interventions that may be withheld under appropriate circumstances, not comfort measures that must always be given. In several states courts have ruled that tube feedings may be withheld from a patient's PVS or minimally conscious state only if there is clear and convincing evidence that the patient would refuse.

CLINICAL RECOMMENDATIONS

When patients with conditions such as severe dementia stop eating and cannot be fed by hand, physicians and surrogates need to discuss the goals of care as well as the benefits and burdens of tube feedings. Decisions are difficult when patients have not provided advance directives. If there are reversible problems that impair oral intake, temporary intravenous or tube feedings are appropriate. Long-term tube feedings are appropriate if patients have no irreversible life-threatening problems and would consider their quality of life acceptable. However, tube feedings are not indicated if the patient has serious, progressive illness and a poor quality of life and if a caring surrogate agrees that the goal should be to provide comfort.

Many cases will fall into a gray area. A trial of tube feedings might then be helpful. If they are well tolerated, the benefits probably outweigh the burdens. If the patient repeatedly pulls out a nasogastric tube, the goals need to be reconsidered. If prolonging life is still deemed the goal, a feeding gastrostomy or jejunostomy would be appropriate. Such tubes are less obtrusive than nasogastric tubes and more difficult to remove. Tying the patient down or sedating the patient to keep the tube in place is difficult to reconcile with the goal of providing humane care (2). Instead, it might be appropriate to withhold tube feedings. Food and water should still be offered by hand. However, compassion and comfort are better expressed through direct attention and affection than by forced feedings.

REFERENCES

1. Mitchell SL, Teno JM, Roy J, et al. Clinical and organizational factors associated with feeding tube use among nursing home residents with advanced cognitive impairment. *JAMA* 2003;290(1):73–80.
2. Lo B, Dornbrand L. Guiding the hand that feeds: caring for the demented elderly. *N Engl J Med* 1984;311:402–404.
3. Billings JA. Comfort measures for the terminally ill: is dehydration painful? *J Am Geriat Soc* 1985;33:808–810.
4. Hodges MO, Tolle SW, Stocking C, et al. Tube feedings: internists' attitudes regarding ethical obligations. *Arch Intern Med* 1994;154:1013–1020.
5. John Paul II. Address of John Paul II to the participants in the International Congress on "Life-Sustaining Treatments and Vegetative State: Scientific Advances and Ethical Dilemmas." The Holy See. http://www.vatican.va/holy_father/john_paul_ii/speeches/2004/march/documents/hf_jp-ii_spe_20040320_congress-fiamc_en.html 2004. Access date: January 12, 2005.
6. Brock D. Forgoing life-sustaining food and water: is it killing? In: Lynn J, ed. *By no extraordinary means*, Expanded ed. Bloomington: Indiana University Press, 1989:117–131.
7. McCann RM, Hall WJ, Groth-Juncker A. Comfort care for terminally ill patients: the appropriate use of nutrition and hydration. *JAMA* 1994;272:1263–11266.
8. Ganzini L, Goy ER, Miller LL, et al. Nurses' experiences with hospice patients who refuse food and fluids to hasten death. *N Engl J Med* 2003;349(4):359–365.
9. Norberg A, Norberg B, Gippert H, et al. Ethical conflicts in long-term care of the aged: nutritional problems and the patient-care worker relationship. *Br Med J* 1980;1:377–378.
10. Steinbrook R, Lo B. Artificial feedings: solid ground, not slippery slope. *N Engl J Med* 1988;318:286–290.
11. *President's Commission for the Study of Ethical Problems in Medicine and Biomedical and Behavioral Research. Deciding to forego life-sustaining treatment.* Washington: U.S. Government Printing Office, 1983:82–89.
12. Meisel A. A retrospective on Cruzan. *Law Med Health Care* 1992;20:340–353.
13. Quill TE. Utilization of nasogastric feeding tubes in a group of chronically ill, elderly patients in a community hospital. *Arch Intern Med* 1989;149:1937–1941.
14. Meier DE, Ahronheim JC, Morris J, et al. High short-term mortality in hospitalized patients with advanced dementia: lack of benefit of tube feeding. *Arch Intern Med* 2001;161(4):594–599.
15. Ciocon JO, Sliverstone FA, Graver LM, et al. Tube feedings in elderly patients. *Arch Intern Med* 1988;148:429–443.
16. Finucane TE, Christmas C, Travis K. Tube feeding in patients with advanced dementia. *JAMA* 1999;282:1365–1370.
17. O'Brien LA, Siegert EA, Grisso JA, et al. Tube feeding preferences among nursing home residents. *J Gen Intern Med* 1997;12:364–371.
18. Meisel A. *The right to die*, 2nd ed. New York: John Wiley and Sons, 1995:592–608.

ANNOTATED BIBLIOGRAPHY

1. Lo B, Dornbrand L. Guiding the hand that feeds: caring for the demented elderly. *N Engl J Med* 1984;311:402–404. Argues that tube feedings might not be appropriate for severely demented patients who refuse feedings by hand, particularly if patients are tied down to prevent them from pulling out the tubes.
2. Gillick MM. Rethinking the role of tube feeding in patients with advanced dementia. *N Engl J Med* 2000;342:206–210.
   Finucane TE, Christmas C, Travis K. Tube feeding in patients with advanced dementia. *JAMA* 1999;282:1365–1370.
   Two articles that argue that tube feedings should be discouraged in patients with advanced dementia.

CHAPTER 19

Physician-Assisted Suicide and Active Euthanasia

Although traditional medical ethics prohibit assisted suicide and active euthanasia, public opinion and policies in the United States are divided. In 1994, Oregon legalized physician-assisted suicide. However, several states recently passed laws criminalizing physician-assisted suicide. In 1996 the Supreme Court ruled that there is no constitutional right to physician-assisted suicide and that states may prohibit it (1). Studies document that physician-assisted suicide and active euthanasia are carried out despite legal prohibitions (2). Two juries acquitted Jack Kevorkian, a nonpracticing pathologist who publicized numerous cases in which he assisted in a patient's suicide, before he was convicted of murder for administering a lethal dose to a patient.

DEFINING TERMS CLEARLY

Imprecise terminology and rhetorical slogans mar the debate on assisted suicide and euthanasia. Several actions should be distinguished.

ACTIVE VOLUNTARY EUTHANASIA

In active euthanasia the physician administers a lethal dose of medication, such as potassium chloride. The physician both supplies the means of death and is the final human agent in the events leading to the patient's death. Active euthanasia is sometimes called *mercy killing*. Euthanasia is called *voluntary* when the patient requests it, *involuntary* when the patient opposes it, and *nonvoluntary* when the patient lacks decision-making capacity and cannot express a preference. There is general agreement that involuntary euthanasia is wrong because it violates a patient's right not to be killed. Nonvoluntary euthanasia is also generally considered unacceptable because it might be applied selectively to the disadvantaged and the vulnerable.

ASSISTED SUICIDE

In assisted suicide the patient swallows a lethal dose of drugs or activates a device to administer the drugs. Physicians might assist in a variety of ways. They might provide the means for suicide, provide information on it, or refer the patient to the Hemlock Society for information.

Many people consider assisted suicide less ethically problematic than active euthanasia. Although the physician provides the means of death, the patient must carry out an independent act. This fact might have several important ethical implications. First, subsequent intervening action by the patient might lessen the physician's moral responsibility. In this view, patients who have free will are morally responsible for their acts. Although other people might influence the patient, they are not regarded as causing the patient's actions unless there is coercion. Second, the justification might be stronger because taking an action to commit suicide is a more direct expression of the patient's autonomy than is a request for active euthanasia. Third, there might be less danger of abuse. If the patient changes his or her mind on suicide, he or she simply does not take the relevant pills. In contrast, a patient might feel pressure to go through with arrangements for active euthanasia.

Physicians, however, must not underestimate their moral responsibility if they assist a patient in committing suicide. The motive, intent, justification, and outcome are the same as in active euthanasia. In other situations people might be held morally responsible for assisting or encouraging another person to commit an immoral act.

Some physicians who prescribe a lethal dose of medications might claim that they did not know that the patient planned commit suicide. For example, some doctors might prescribe secobarbital upon a patient's request without discussing suicide. It would be disingenuous to abjure responsibility in this situation, however. Doctors almost never prescribe secobarbital except as a means for suicide. Most important, by not broaching suicide, physicians forego an opportunity to provide better palliative care, which often leads patients to change their minds on suicide.

WITHHOLDING OR WITHDRAWING MEDICAL INTERVENTIONS

Active euthanasia and assisted suicide are usually distinguished from withholding or withdrawing interventions, which are also termed *allowing to die* or *passive euthanasia*. Ethically and legally, medical interventions may be withheld or withdrawn if a competent patient or an appropriate surrogate refuses them (*see* Chapter 14). A patient's refusal of life-sustaining treatment is honored because patients have a right to be free of unwanted bodily invasions. Under such circumstances the underlying *illness*, not the *physician's* action or inaction, is considered the cause of death. Therefore, concern that assisted suicide or active euthanasia is improper should not lead physicians to impose interventions that the patient or surrogate does not want.

This distinction between killing and allowing to die provides practical guidance, but it is problematic for several reasons (3,4). First, some patients who refuse life-prolonging interventions want to hasten their death, not just to be free of unwanted medical interventions (5). Second, many philosophers have rejected the distinction between acting and refraining from action, pointing out that withholding effective treatment would be condemned if done against the patient's wishes or for malicious motives. However, even though *some* cases of foregoing life-sustaining interventions are hard to distinguish from physician-assisted suicide, it does not follow that *all* cases of foregoing life-sustaining interventions are equivalent to physician-assisted suicide.

ADMINISTERING APPROPRIATE DOSES OF OPIOIDS OR SEDATIVES

Active euthanasia and assisted suicide can be distinguished from providing high doses of opioids or sedatives to relieve severe pain in patients with terminal illness or to relieve dyspnea when patients forego mechanical ventilation (1). As Chapter 14 discusses, the appropriate goal of care in these situations is to relieve suffering. In rare cases the dose required to relieve distress might hasten death. Concerns about active euthanasia and assisted suicide should not deter physicians from providing aggressive palliative care (6). Indeed, fears that terminal distress will not be adequately relieved impel some patients to seek active euthanasia and assisted suicide (7,8).

REASONS IN FAVOR OF ASSISTED SUICIDE AND ACTIVE EUTHANASIA

Proponents of these acts offer several justifications for their position (9,10).

RESPECT FOR PATIENT AUTONOMY

The prospect of a long, debilitating illness that would destroy their sense of identity and dignity horrifies many persons. People might fear loss of privacy and increased dependence on others for basic needs such as feeding, bathing, and toilet use. They also might not want their family and friends to remember them as progressively debilitated. Proponents contend that competent patients with terminal illness should have control over the time and manner of their death. In this view it is inconsistent to permit patients to end their lives by refusing medical interventions after a complication occurs but not to end it more directly beforehand.

COMPASSION FOR PATIENTS WHO ARE SUFFERING

Some argue that assisted suicide and active euthanasia show compassion for patients in the final stages of a terminal illness. Many people regard it as inhumane to require such patients to suffer a downhill course while waiting to die of complications. As one author put it, "People who want an early peaceful death for themselves or their relatives are not rejecting or denigrating the sanctity of life; on the contrary, they believe that a quicker death shows more respect for life than a protracted one (11)." Some terminally ill patients have refractory symptoms despite optimal palliative care. For example, some patients with cancer of the esophagus or head and neck cannot swallow their secretions, some patients with acquired immunodeficiency syndrome suffer refractory diarrhea, and some cancer patients experience intractable bleeding. Such patients can be sedated so that they are no longer conscious of their symptoms, but they will not have dignified or peaceful deaths.

Proponents of assisted suicide also argue that physicians cannot prevent people from killing themselves; they can only alter the means by which patients end their lives. If lethal drugs are not available, patients might resort to hanging or guns. Such means of death are gruesome and distress family members and friends. Advocates contend that terminally ill patients should have a more humane means of ending their lives.

REASONS AGAINST ASSISTED SUICIDE AND ACTIVE EUTHANASIA

Traditional codes of medical ethics prohibit physician participation in assisted suicide or active euthanasia (12–14). Active euthanasia is illegal in all states, and most states explicitly prohibit assisted suicide.

THE SANCTITY OF LIFE

Many people assert that assisted suicide and active euthanasia demean the sacredness of human life and violate fundamental moral prohibitions against killing human beings.

SUFFERING CAN ALMOST ALWAYS BE RELIEVED

Palliative care is often inadequate in terminally ill patients. Opponents fear that assisted suicide and active euthanasia will allow physicians to avoid the difficult task of providing physical and spiritual comfort to dying patients. Some people suggest that suffering can be redemptive and that patients have a duty to endure it or cope courageously (13).

REQUESTS FOR ASSISTED SUICIDE ARE NOT AUTONOMOUS

Most terminally ill patients change their minds on suicide after receiving better palliative care or treatment for depression. Thus, their initial requests may not be truly autonomous. Physicians have an ethical obligation to prevent suicide because the vast majority of patients who attempt suicide have a psychiatric illness, such as major depression, that can be treated (*see* Chapter 40). Even among patients with cancer, most suicidal individuals are clinically depressed, and major depression can be treated (15,16).

FEARS OF ABUSE

A slippery slope might occur: If physician-assisted suicide is permitted for competent terminally ill patients, it is logically inconsistent to prohibit it for patients who are not competent or not terminally ill or to prohibit active euthanasia. For example, if competent patients have a right to physician-assisted suicide, it would be inconsistent to deny it to patients who have previously requested it but have lost decision-making capacity. A patient with mild Alzheimer disease might not want to live if he or she could no longer recognize his or her family. At that stage, however, the patient would no longer be capable of making an informed request. Thus, if the patient is not permitted to request physician-assisted suicide or active euthanasia through an advance directive, the patient would face a cruel dilemma: to end life when it is still meaningful or to live in an unacceptably dehumanized condition. Furthermore, some patients with severe amyotrophic lateral sclerosis (ALS) might want to hasten their death to avoid further dependency and to relieve their suffering. However, such patients are not terminally ill and might lack the physical ability to ingest medication without assistance. Thus, respecting their wishes to hasten death might require active euthanasia.

A second type of slippery slope might also occur. At first, physicians who participate in assisted suicide might carefully ensure that every case is appropriate, but over time they might become less diligent in providing palliative care or checking that the patient's request is voluntary. Eventually, assisted suicide might occur when palliative care was grossly inadequate or major depression was unaddressed.

Active euthanasia raises particular fears about abuse. Euthanasia for competent patients logically leads to euthanasia of patients who lack decision-making capacity. Furthermore, relief of unbearable suffering might be used to justify active euthanasia in mentally incapacitated patients who had never requested it. Another fear is that pressures to control health care costs will result in nonvoluntary euthanasia of persons whose care is regarded as too burdensome or too expensive (17). Patients with chronic illness or disability might feel pressured by family members or physicians into terminating their lives.

THE PHYSICIAN'S ROLE

Opponents argue that active euthanasia and assisted suicide are incompatible with the physician's role as healer. In this view patients would lose trust in physicians if these practices were permitted. In one study, 19% of oncology patients said they would change physicians if their physician told them they had provided active euthanasia or physician-assisted suicide for other patients (18).

LEGALIZATION OF PHYSICIAN-ASSISTED SUICIDE IN OREGON

In Oregon, terminally ill, competent adults may request medication to end their lives (19,20). The patient must make a written request that is witnessed by two people who attest that the patient is competent, acting voluntarily, and not coerced. Fifteen days after this written request, the patient must repeat the request orally. An additional 48 hours must elapse before the prescription can be filled. The patient may rescind the request at any time. Physicians must ensure that patients are informed about their diagnosis, prognosis, and therapeutic alternatives, such as palliative care. A consultant must confirm that the patient has a terminal disease, is capable of making health care decisions, is informed, and is acting voluntarily. Patients with a psychiatric disorder that impairs judgment must be referred for counseling. Physicians who comply with the provisions of the law are granted legal immunity from criminal, civil, and professional disciplinary actions. Physicians and other health care workers may refuse to participate. If a patient ingests a lethal dose of medication under this law, life insurance policies are not voided. Several groups of patients fall outside this law's coverage. The law specifically prohibits active euthanasia, mercy killing, and lethal injection. Physicians are not allowed to provide assistance to patients who are too incapacitated to take lethal medication themselves. Patients are excluded if they suffer from nonterminal illnesses, lack decision-making capacity, or are too sick to survive the waiting periods. Patients may not request suicide assistance through advance directives or surrogate decision-makers.

In Oregon, 9 deaths per 10,000 are cases of physician-assisted suicide reported to the state (21,22). Compared to other terminal patients, these patients were more concerned about loss of autonomy and loss of control over bodily functions because of their illness (22). Poverty, lack of education or health insurance, or poor quality of care did not play a major role in the patient's decision (23). Over two thirds of these patients did not receive the requested prescription from the first doctor they asked (23). Some physicians who participated in physician-assisted suicide reported a large emotional toll (22).

THE PRACTICE OF PHYSICIAN-ASSISTED SUICIDE AND ACTIVE EUTHANASIA

Despite legal prohibitions, physician-assisted suicide and active euthanasia are practiced in the United States.

REQUESTS FOR PHYSICIAN-ASSISTED SUICIDE AND ACTIVE EUTHANASIA ARE COMMON

In a national sample, 18% of physicians said that in their careers they had received a request for physician-assisted suicide and 11% said they had received a request for active euthanasia. In another study over 50% of oncologists had received a request for physician-assisted suicide and 38% had received a request for active euthanasia (24). Twelve percent of cancer patients said they had serious discussions about active euthanasia or physician-assisted suicide with their family or physician, and 3.4% said they hoarded drugs (24).

REQUESTS ARE MORE COMMON IN DEPRESSED PATIENTS

Nineteen percent of patients who received physician-assisted suicide and 39% of patients who received active euthanasia were depressed (2). In another study cancer patients who were depressed were 4.6 times more likely to have discussed euthanasia (24).

PHYSICIANS PROVIDE REQUESTED ASSISTANCE EVEN WHEN IT IS ILLEGAL

Among physicians, 3.3% had written a prescription to be used to hasten death and 4.7% had administered a lethal injection (2). Among oncologists, 13% had assisted suicide and 1.8% had performed active euthanasia.

PHYSICIANS ARE CONFUSED ABOUT WHAT CONSTITUTES PHYSICIAN-ASSISTED SUICIDE AND ACTIVE EUTHANASIA

In some cases that physicians characterized as physician-assisted suicide or active euthanasia, it would be accurate to describe the situation differently. For example, in 13% of cases physicians actually provided high doses of opioids for pain relief; such palliation of symptoms is ethically distinct from assisted suicide or active euthanasia. In another 9% of cases, patients overdosed without asking the physician for a prescription for a lethal dose; this cannot be described as physician-assisted suicide or active euthanasia (18). Furthermore, 12% of physicians who said that they had assisted suicide actually ordered a nurse to inject medications to end the patient's life; it would be accurate to characterize this action as active euthanasia (18).

PROPOSED SAFEGUARDS ARE OFTEN VIOLATED

When physicians prescribe a prescription for physician-assisted suicide, suggested safeguards, such as persistent requests and second opinions, are often not followed. In two studies patients repeated their request in only 51% and 60% of cases and doctors obtained a second opinion in only 1% and 40% of cases (2,18).

In 54% of cases of active euthanasia, a family member or partner rather than the patient made the request (2). A second opinion was obtained in only 32% of cases. In 94% of cases immediate assistance was requested.

PATIENTS FREQUENTLY DO NOT USE PRESCRIPTIONS FOR LETHAL DOSES OF MEDICATION

Approximately 40% of patients who receive prescriptions for lethal doses of medication do not use them (2,25). Presumably the prescription provided reassurance that the patient was in control of the final days.

PHYSICIAN-ASSISTED SUICIDE HAS AN EMOTIONAL IMPACT ON THE PHYSICIAN

In one study, 18% of physicians who had assisted suicide were uncomfortable doing it (2). In another study, although 53% of respondents were comfortable assisting suicide or performing active euthanasia, 24% regretted performing them (18).

LEGALIZATION OF ASSISTED SUICIDE AND
ACTIVE EUTHANASIA IN THE NETHERLANDS

In the Netherlands active euthanasia and assisted suicide are legal in certain situations (26). A competent patient with a terminal illness must make a voluntary and persistent request for active euthanasia or assisted suicide, and two physicians must certify that the patient is terminally ill. In the Netherlands active euthanasia occurs in between 2.3% and 2.4% of deaths and assisted suicide occurs in between 0.2% and 0.4% (27).

MOST PATIENTS WITHDRAW THEIR REQUESTS FOR EUTHANASIA OR ASSISTED SUICIDE

Patients' requests for active euthanasia or assisted suicide usually do not last. When patients ask physicians to help them die, only one third of requests are serious and persistent. Of these, only one third actually receive active euthanasia or assisted suicide; most change their minds after obtaining better palliative care. Thus, only 11% of patients who initially request active euthanasia or assisted suicide accept it later (28).

PROCEDURAL SAFEGUARDS ARE VIOLATED

In 0.7% of deaths physicians ended the patient's life without the patient's explicit, concurrent request (27). In about one half of these cases, the patient had discussed these decisions previously with the physician. In a few cases, however, the physician did not discuss these actions with anyone, including relatives or colleagues.

CONSEQUENCES FOR SURVIVORS

Family and friends of cancer patients who died by euthanasia had fewer symptoms of traumatic grief and fewer posttraumatic stress reactions than family and friends of patients who died of natural causes (29).

UNINTENDED CONSEQUENCES

When patients attempted physician-assisted suicide, technical problems occurred in 10% of cases, most commonly difficulty swallowing the pills. Complications occurred in 7%, most commonly nausea and vomiting. In 18% of cases a physician administered a lethal drug, most commonly because the patient did not die or did not die as soon as expected. When physicians attempted active euthanasia, technical problems occurred in 5% of cases, most commonly difficulty finding a vein. Complications occurred in 3% of cases, most commonly spasm and myoclonus. In 5% of cases death did not occur or took longer than expected (30).

POLICY OPTIONS

Several public policies are possible about physician-assisted suicide and active euthanasia. One option is to continue traditional prohibitions. However, these practices occur even though they are illegal. Abuses might be more likely to occur if decisions remain secret than if they are discussed openly. Furthermore, prosecutors are reluctant to bring charges against physicians who convincingly assert that they were relieving the patient's suffering, and juries are reluctant to convict such doctors. This discrepancy between the law in the books and the law in practice is problematic because enforcement might be inconsistent or biased (6). A second option is to legalize these practices under certain conditions, such as in Oregon. The challenge is whether effective safeguards against abuses can be developed. A third option is to keep active euthanasia and assisted suicide illegal but to acknowledge that in exceptional cases, such practices might be ethically justified and legally condoned (31). The risk of legal sanctions would help deter these actions in questionable or inappropriate cases.

HOW SHOULD PHYSICIANS RESPOND TO REQUESTS
FOR ASSISTED SUICIDE OR ACTIVE EUTHANASIA?

Physicians must be prepared for questions from patients on assisted suicide or active euthanasia. Like the general public, doctors disagree over the morality of these controversial actions (2). Regardless of their personal views, physicians can respond in certain ways (Table 19-1) (32–35).

FIND OUT THE REASONS FOR THE REQUEST

Why is the patient asking a question or making a request at this time? A request or question might represent a response to unrelieved suffering, a demand for more control, emerging psychosocial problems, a spiritual crisis, or a fear of abandonment (33,36). Requests might be triggered by loss of dignity, pain, and dependence on others (28). Only rarely is pain the sole reason for a patient's request. Physicians also need to screen patients for major depression, which can be treated even in terminally ill patients (16).

Some physicians fear that talking about assisted suicide or active euthanasia will encourage patients to carry out these acts. Such fears are unfounded. Most terminally ill patients have already thought about these issues and feel relieved that physicians are willing to discuss them. Suicidal patients with terminal illness deserve the same careful evaluation and mobilization of resources as patients who are not terminally ill (37).

PROVIDE MORE INTENSIVE PALLIATIVE CARE

If their suffering or concerns are addressed, most patients find life worth living. Pain relief can be improved through using higher and more frequent doses of opioids, administering them on a regular schedule rather than as needed, and giving patients more control over dosage. In addition to alleviating physical suffering, physicians can help patients come to terms with their mortality and to find meaning in the final stage of their lives. Instead of immediately trying to resolve problems or reassure patients, doctors can explore the patient's suffering using open-ended questions and empathic

TABLE 19-1

Responding to Requests for Assisted Suicide or Active Euthanasia

Find out the reasons for the request.
Provide more intensive palliative care.
Reaffirm patient control over treatment decisions.
Do not impose your values on patients.
Consult a trusted and wise colleague.

comments: "That sounds very distressing. Can you tell me more? (38)." Attentive listening validates the patient's emotions and shows the patient that he or she has been understood. The physician should consult with palliative care specialists, psychiatrists or psychologists, social workers, chaplains, and hospice workers as needed. Physicians also can arrange hospice-type home care, mobilize family members and friends, and be available during patients' final weeks and days.

REAFFIRM PATIENT CONTROL OVER TREATMENT DECISIONS

Some patients might seek to hasten death because they fear they will be subjected to unwanted life-prolonging interventions. Physicians need to reassure patients that their decisions to forego life-sustaining interventions will be respected.

DO NOT IMPOSE YOUR OWN VALUES ON PATIENTS

Proponents of assisted suicide should not write a lethal prescription on request without evaluating the patient for depression and inadequate palliative care. Conversely, opponents of these actions should not denigrate the patient's request but rather communicate empathy and compassion for the patient's plight.

CONSULT A TRUSTED AND WISE COLLEAGUE

Most physicians find patient requests for assisted suicide or active euthanasia to be highly stressful. As with any other difficult case, a second opinion or discussion with a colleague is generally helpful. Often, a colleague can suggest how to improve palliative care or how to talk with the patient.

DECLINING TO GIVE ASSISTANCE

Physicians should not participate in assisted suicide or active euthanasia against their conscience or religious beliefs. When communicating their refusal, physicians need to elicit and address the patient's concerns and show empathy for the patient's plight. The physician might say, "I hear that you are deeply distressed by your illness. I'll try my best to relieve your suffering. But I can't help you kill yourself. My conscience won't allow me to do that." Such physicians need to emphasize their commitment to provide ongoing palliative care.

SITUATIONS IN WHICH ASSISTED SUICIDE MIGHT BE JUSTIFIED

Many physicians can conceive of a case in which they would consider assisted suicide morally permissible (39). The following circumstances would constitute the strongest case for agreeing to a patient's request (9,10).

- *The patient has a terminal illness* or a progressive, incurable condition causing unrelenting suffering, such as ALS.
- *The patient is experiencing intractable symptoms* despite optimal palliative care. Even the best palliative care cannot relieve intractable bleeding or inability to swallow secretions. Actual distress is more compelling than anticipated future symptoms. Many physicians are more sympathetic to patients with physical distress than to patients with mental distress. The distinction between physical and mental suffering might be philosophically untenable, but it is helpful for pragmatic reasons because mistakes and abuse are less likely with physical distress.
- *The patient's request is voluntary, informed, and repeated.* Ideally, the patient raises the issue and is willing to discuss it with family members, friends, or clergy.
- *The physician has a long-term relationship with the patient* that started before the patient requested assistance with suicide.
- *The physician has obtained second opinions* about the adequacy of palliative care and the absence of depression.

In the rare cases in which these conditions are present, it is ethical for physicians to assist in suicide.

Active euthanasia is more problematic because it presents greater potential for abuse. Although requests by surrogates for active euthanasia are usually motivated by compassion, surrogates might confound their own values and desires with those of the patient. They might interpret a gesture or a look as an unspoken request to hasten death, saying, for example, "I looked into his eyes and I just knew what he was asking me to do." The risk of projection, misinterpretation, and abuse are great in this situation. Prohibiting active euthanasia for patients who lack decision-making capacity is sound public policy.

In conclusion, it should never be easy for a physician to respond to the request of a patient who is dying in great suffering despite good palliative care. Even in the most compelling case, decisions will be difficult and conscientious and reasonable persons will disagree. Ultimately, physicians will find answers in their own conscience, personal morality, and religious beliefs. Regardless of the physician's decision, however, patients deserve an honest answer to their questions or request. More important, physicians must demonstrate their dedication to relieving suffering and their willingness to be with patients during the process of dying.

REFERENCES

1. Alpers A, Lo B. The Supreme Court addresses physician-assisted suicide: can its decisions improve palliative care. *Arch Fam Pract* 1999;8:200–205.
2. Meier DE, Emmons CA, Wallenstein S, et al. Physician-assisted death in the United States: a national prevalence survey. *N Engl J Med* 1998;338:1193–1201.
3. Brock D. Forgoing life-sustaining food and water: is it killing? In: Lynn J, ed. *By no extraordinary means*, Expanded ed. Bloomington: Indiana University Press, 1989:117–131.
4. Alpers A, Lo B. Does it make clinical sense to equate terminally ill patients who require life-sustaining interventions with those who do not? *J Am Med Assoc* 1997;277:1705–1708.
5. Kadish SH. Letting patients die: legal and moral reflections. *Calif Law Rev* 1992;80:857–888.
6. Alpers A. Criminal act or palliative care: prosecutions involving the care of the dying. *J Law Med Ethics* 1998; 26:308–331.
7. Angell M. Euthanasia. *N Engl J Med* 1988;319:1348–1350.
8. Foley KM. The relationship of pain and symptom management to patient requests for physician-assisted suicide. *J Pain Symptom Manage* 1991;6:289–297.
9. Quill TE, Cassel CK, Meier DE. Care of the terminally ill: proposed clinical criteria for physician-assisted suicide. *N Engl J Med* 1992;327:1380–1384.
10. Miller FG, Quill TE, Brody H, et al. Regulating physician-assisted death. *N Engl J Med* 1994;331:119–123.
11. Dworkin R. *Life's dominion*. New York: Alfred A. Knopf, 1993:328.
12. Singer PA, Siegler M. Euthanasia—a critique. *N Engl J Med* 1990;322(26):1881–1883.
13. Pellegrino ED. Doctors must not kill. *J Clin Ethics* 1992;3:95–102.
14. Foley K. Competent care for the dying instead of physician-assisted suicide. *N Engl J Med* 1997;336:54–58.
15. Conwell Y, Caine ED. Rational suicide and the right to die: reality and myth. *N Engl J Med* 1991;325:1100–1102.
16. Block SD. Assessing and managing depression in the terminally ill patient. *Ann Intern Med* 1999;132:209–218.
17. Sulmasy DP. Managed care and managed death. *Arch Intern Med* 1995;155:133–136.
18. Emanuel EJ, Daniels ER, Fairclough DL, et al. The practice of euthanasia and physician-assisted suicide in the United States: adherence to proposed safeguards and effects on physicians. *JAMA* 1998;280:507–513.
19. Oregon Death with Dignity Act. Ballot Measure 16 (November 8, 1994 general election).
20. Alpers A, Lo B. Physician-assisted suicide in Oregon: a bold experiment. *JAMA* 1995;274:483–487.
21. Hedberg K, Hopkins D, Kohn M. Five years of legal physician-assisted suicide in Oregon. *N Engl J Med* 2003;348(10):961–964.
22. Chin AE, Hedberg K, Higginson GK, et al. Legalized physician-assisted suicide in Oregon—the first year's experience. *N Engl J Med* 1999;340:577–583.
23. Sullivan AD, Hedberg K, Hopkins D. Legalized physician-assisted suicide in Oregon, 1998-2000. *N Engl J Med* 2001;344(8):605–607.
24. Emanuel EJ, Fairclough DL, Daniels ER, et al. Euthanasia and physician-assisted suicide: attitudes and experiences among oncology patients, oncologists, and the general public. *Lancet* 1996;347:1805–1810.
25. Back AL, Wallace JI, Starks HE, et al. Physician-assisted suicide and euthanasia in Washington state: patient requests and physician responses. *JAMA* 1996;275:919–925.
26. Sheldon T. Holland decriminalises voluntary euthanasia. *Br Med J* 2001;322:947.
27. van der Maas PJ, van der Wal G, Haverkate I, et al. Euthanasia, physician-assisted suicide, and other medical practices involving the end of life in the Netherlands, 1990-1995. *N Engl J Med* 1996;335:1699–1705.
28. van der Maas PJ, van Delden JJM, Pijnenborg L, et al. Euthanasia and other medical decisions concerning the end of life. *Lancet* 1991;338:669–674.
29. Swarte NB, van der Lee ML, van der Bom JG, et al. Effects of euthanasia on the bereaved family and friends: a cross sectional study. *Br Med J* 2003;327(7408):189.
30. Groenewoud JH, van der Heide A, Onwuteaka-Philipsen BD, et al. Clinical problems with the performance of euthanasia and physician-assisted suicide in The Netherlands. *N Engl J Med* 2000;342(8):551–556.

31. Tulsky JA, Alpers A, Lo B. A middle ground on physician-assisted suicide. *Camb Q Healthc Ethic* 1996;5:33–43.
32. Emanuel LL. Facing requests for physician-assisted suicide: toward a practical and principled clinical skill set. *JAMA* 1998;280:643–647.
33. Quill TE. Doctor, I want to die. Will you help me? *JAMA* 1993;270:870–873.
34. Block SD, Billings JA. Patient requests to hasten death: evaluation and management in terminal care. *Arch Intern Med* 1994;154:2039–2047.
35. Bascom PB, Tolle SW. Responding to requests for physician-assisted suicide: "These are uncharted waters for both of us...." *JAMA* 2002;288(1):91–98.
36. Muskin PR. The request to die: role for a psychodynamic perspective on physician-assisted suicide. *JAMA* 1998;279:323–328.
37. Hirschfeld RMA, Russell JM. Assessment and treatment of suicidal patients. *N Engl J Med* 1997;337:910–915.
38. Lo B, Quill T, Tulsky J. Discussing palliative care with patients. *Ann Intern Med* 1999;130:744–749.
39. Bachman JG, Alcser KH, Doukas DJ, et al. Attitudes of Michigan physicians and the public toward legalizing physician-assisted suicide and voluntary euthanasia. *N Engl J Med* 1996;334:303–309.

ANNOTATED BIBLIOGRAPHY

1. Quill TE, Cassel CK, Meier DE. Care of the terminally ill: proposed clinical criteria for physician-assisted suicide. *N Engl J Med* 1992;327:1380–1384.
   Proposes circumstances in which assisted suicide would be ethically permissible.
2. Pellegrino ED. Doctors must not kill. *J Clin Ethics* 1992;3:95–102.
   Eloquent summary of reasons for opposing assisted suicide and active euthanasia.
3. Alpers A, Lo B. Physician-assisted suicide in Oregon: a bold experiment. *JAMA* 1995;274:483–487.
   Describes the Oregon law legalizing physician-assisted suicide and analyzes the ethical and practical problems in implementing the law.
4. Quill TE. Doctor, I want to die. Will you help me? *JAMA* 1993;270:870–873.
   Emanuel LL. Facing requests for physician-assisted suicide: toward a practical and principled clinical skill set. *JAMA* 1998;280:643–647.
   Bascom PB, Tolle SW. Responding to requests for physician-assisted suicide: "These arc uncharted waters for both of us...." *JAMA* 2002;288:91–98.
   Suggestions on how doctors can respond when terminally ill patients request physicians to hasten their death. The first two papers are by a proponent and a opponent of physician-assisted suicide, respectively.
5. Meier DE, Emmons CA, Wallenstein S, et al. Physician-assisted death in the United States: a national prevalence survey. *N Engl J Med* 1998;338:1193–1201.
   Emanuel EJ, Daniels ER, Fairclough DL, ct al. The practice of euthanasia and physician-assisted suicide in the United States: adherence to proposed safeguards and effects on physicians. *JAMA* 1998;280:507–513.
   Two well-designed empirical studies elucidating the practice of physician-assisted suicide and active euthanasia in the United States despite legal prohibitions.

CHAPTER 20

The Persistent Vegetative State

Because they are breathing and their hearts are beating, patients in the persistent vegetative state (PVS) are alive. However, they are not aware of their environment and cannot respond to other people or communicate with them. Although PVS is uncommon, the cases of Karen Ann Quinlan, Nancy Cruzan, and Theresa Schiavo, patients in PVS, dramatized fundamental questions about the goals of medicine and the definition of being a person.

This chapter describes the clinical features of PVS, discusses some of the philosophical quandaries it presents, and analyzes appropriate justifications for limiting life-prolonging interventions for patients in this condition.

CLINICAL FEATURES

DEFINITION OF VEGETATIVE STATE

Patients in a vegetative state have no cortical function but have preserved brainstem function. As far as can be determined, they are unconscious, with no awareness of their environment (1,2). They show no purposeful activity and cannot obey verbal commands. Because their cortical structures have been destroyed, they cannot experience pain. However, it is important for physicians and family members to appreciate that some neurologic functions are maintained. "Vegetative" functions, such as breathing and circulation, remain intact. Thus, patients in a vegetative state usually do not require mechanical ventilation. In addition, these patients are not comatose because they have cycles of sleeping and waking. While they are awake, their eyes might be open. Roving eye movements are present, and tracking might occasionally occur. Reflexes such as sucking, chewing, and swallowing might also be present. Pupillary, oculocephalic, and deep tendon reflexes are sometimes preserved. Patients might withdraw or posture in response to noxious stimuli and startle and turn in the direction of sudden loud noises. Such patients might grunt, grimace, smile, and produce tears. Because of these preserved neurologic functions, some observers believe that patients in a vegetative state are aware of their surroundings or have responded to them. Some observers might claim that the patient watched them cross the room or cried when they talked to them. Other observers at other times, however, cannot replicate these "responses" in any consistent manner.

The diagnosis of a vegetative state requires repeated examinations by an experienced neurologist. The diagnosis is clinical, and diagnostic tests are not essential. Positron-emission tomography scans in patients in a PVS show low brain metabolism, similar to what is seen in patients under general anesthesia.

DEFINITION OF PERSISTENT VEGETATIVE STATE

A PVS is defined as a vegetative state that has lasted 1 month (1). In the United States about 10,000 to 25,000 adults and 4,000 to 10,000 children currently are in a PVS (1,2). A crucial issue is determining when a PVS has become permanent.

Prognosis for recovery of consciousness can be accurately established only after the patient has been in a vegetative state for some time (1). The required time of observation will depend on the etiology. After nontraumatic injury, such as anoxic brain damage during a cardiac arrest, very few patients awaken after 3 months. After trauma, patients rarely awaken after 12 months in a vegetative state.

No intervention has been shown to be effective in restoring consciousness. In a few well-documented cases, patients in true PVS have recovered consciousness more than 3 months after anoxic injury or more than 12 months after traumatic injury (1,3). Patients who recover consciousness have moderate or severe residual neurologic impairments.

The mean survival of patients in a PVS is 2 to 5 years. A few patients have been reported to survive longer than 15 years. Patients in a PVS require tube feedings because they are unable to swallow and protect their airway. They are incontinent and require total nursing care. Common complications are decubitus ulcers, aspiration pneumonia, and urosepsis.

PVS needs to be distinguished from other catastrophic neurological conditions. In *brain death* there is neither cortical nor brainstem function (*see* Chapter 21). Thus, the electroencephalogram (EEG) shows no activity. In the *locked-in syndrome* patients are conscious but have no motor function. Such patients might be able to communicate by blinking their eyes. Patients with *severe dementia* might be virtually unresponsive, but they are conscious and might have some motor function. The term *minimally conscious state* has been used to describe patients who are conscious but have severe neurologic impairments. The term is best avoided because it cannot be defined precisely (4).

Misunderstandings about PVS are common. Despite extensive clinical evidence that patients in a PVS lack the cortical capacity to be conscious of pain (1), 25% of neurologists believed that patients in a vegetative state experience feelings of pain and 22% believed that such patients are more comfortable with tube feedings (5).

WHAT TREATMENT IS APPROPRIATE?

Many persons would be horrified to be kept alive if there were virtually no likelihood of regaining consciousness. To them, life as a "vegetable" is a fate worse than death. They would reject tube feedings and other interventions.

A more radical and controversial position is that all medical interventions should be withheld or withdrawn from patients in a PVS because they have lost the essential characteristics of being a person, which include consciousness and the ability to have social interactions and to respond. In this view it is not merely *permissible* to withdraw tube feedings from patients in a PVS but *mandatory* to do so (6,7).

In contrast, other people believe strongly that persons in a PVS should receive life-prolonging interventions. Some family members do not believe that the patient is unconscious, claiming that the patient responds to them. Others reject the prognosis, believing that the patient will recover despite unfavorable odds. Still others believe a life without consciousness remains sacred. In their view it would violate human dignity to forego basic care such as feeding tubes and antibiotics, which allow patients to survive for years and have few adverse effects (8).

MEDICAL INTERVENTIONS MAY BE WITHHELD OR WITHDRAWN

As Chapter 13 discussed, when patients lack decision-making capacity, interventions ranging from cardiopulmonary resuscitation (CPR) to antibiotics for infection may be withheld on the basis of advance directives or decisions by appropriate surrogates (1,2).

It is worth noting how a consensus has developed since the 1976 Karen Ann Quinlan case (*see* Chapter 22). In that case the issue was whether to discontinue a ventilator (at the time, doctors did not know that patients in a PVS do not require ventilatory assistance). In recent cases decisions to withhold CPR from patients in a PVS were not challenged. More recent controversies have focused on whether feeding tubes should be regarded differently from other medical interventions.

TUBE FEEDINGS ARE A MEDICAL INTERVENTION, WHICH MAY BE WITHHELD OR WITHDRAWN

Some people consider feeding tubes "ordinary" nursing care that must always be provided. However, feeding tubes have benefits and burdens that must be assessed for the individual patient. As Chapter 18 discussed, it is permissible to withhold or withdraw tube feedings from persons in a PVS, in accordance with the patient's prior directives or best interests (1,9,10). In practice, many people are ambivalent about tube feedings in PVS. In a survey of neurologists, 88% believed that it is ethical to forego artificial nutrition in PVS; however, 47% also believed that artificial nutrition should generally be provided.

Controversies over interventions in a PVS are not technical issues to be decided solely by physicians. Value judgments on the definition of a human being are unavoidable. Ultimately these issues are not susceptible to logical proof or refutation. They can be resolved only by appealing to deeply personal or religious beliefs. These beliefs might lead people to strikingly different conclusions about appropriate care of patients in a PVS.

In summary, physicians need to understand the clinical features of PVS and the criteria for diagnosing it. Many ethical dilemmas regarding PVS can be resolved by applying guidelines for decisions in patients who lack decision-making capacity. It is permissible to withdraw feeding tubes and other interventions in accordance with advance directives or decisions by appropriate surrogates.

REFERENCES

1. The Multi-Society Task Force on PVS. Medical aspects of the persistent vegetative state. *N Engl J Med* 1994; 330:1499–1508, 1572–1579.
2. Wade DT. Ethical issues in diagnosis and management of patients in the permanent vegetative state. *Br Med J* 2001;322(7282):352–354.
3. Childs NL, Mercer WN. Late improvement in consciousness after post-traumatic vegetative state. *N Engl J Med* 1996;334:24–25.
4. Bernat JL. Questions remaining about the minimally conscious state. *Neurology* 2002;58:337–338.
5. Payne K, Taylor RM, Stocking C, et al. Physicians' attitudes about the care of patients in the persistent vegetative state: a national survey. *Ann Intern Med* 1996;125:104–110.
6. Schneiderman LJ, Jecker NS, Jonsen AR. Medical futility: its meaning and ethical implications. *Ann Intern Med* 1990;112:949–954.
7. Schneiderman LJ, Jecker NS, Jonsen AR. Medical futility: response to critiques. *Ann Intern Med* 1996;125:669–674.
8. John Paul II. Address of John Paul II to the participants in the International Congress on "Life-sustaining treatments and vegetative state: scientific advances and ethical dilemmas." Available at: http://www.vatican.va/holy_father/john_paul_ii/speeches/2004/march/documents/hf_jp-ii_spe_20040320_congress-fiamc_en.html. Accessed May 12, 2004.
9. President's Commission for the Study of Ethical Problems in Medicine and Biomedical and Behavioral Research. *Deciding to forego life-sustaining treatment.* Washington: U.S. Government Printing Office, 1983.
10. Council on Scientific Affairs and Council on Ethical and Judicial Affairs. Persistent vegetative state and the decision to withdraw or withhold life support. *JAMA* 1990;263:426–430.

ANNOTATED BIBLIOGRAPHY

1. The Multi-Society Task Force on PVS. Medical aspects of the persistent vegetative state. *N Engl J Med* 1994; 330:1572–1579.
   Wade DT. Ethical issues in diagnosis and management of patients in the permanent vegetative state. *Br Med J* 2001;322:352–354.
   Two articles that are comprehensive reviews of clinical features and prognosis.
2. American Neurological Association Committee on Ethical Affairs. Persistent vegetative state: report of the American Neurological Association Committee on Ethical Affairs. *Ann Neurol* 1993;33:386–390.
   Excellent review of clinical and ethical issues.
3. Payne K, Taylor RM, Stocking C, et al. Physicians' attitudes about the care of patients in the persistent vegetative state: a national survey. *Ann Intern Med* 1996;125:104–110.
   Documents widespread misconceptions about PVS among physicians.

CHAPTER 21

Determination of Death

Before the development of intensive care, patients were declared dead when breathing and circulation stopped. However, such traditional concepts of death are now problematic because a patient's breathing and circulation can be sustained on life support after all cerebral functions have been permanently lost. Thus, criteria for brain death have been developed and are widely accepted. Accurate and consistent determinations of death are essential because declaring a patient dead has profound emotional and practical consequences (1–3). Mourning commences and funeral services are held. Dead persons are buried or cremated. Their organs might be removed for transplantation. Their spouses might remarry, pensions and health insurance coverage are terminated, their properties pass on to heirs, and their life insurance policies are paid. Defining death is controversial because it involves cultural, social, and religious values, as well as scientific judgment. Furthermore, discussions are complicated by frequent misunderstandings about brain death.

This chapter discusses ethical issues regarding traditional, whole-brain, and higher brain criteria for death.

PROBLEMS WITH CARDIOPULMONARY CRITERIA FOR DEATH

In the absence of artificial life support, brain function ceases minutes after cessation of heartbeat and breathing. With the development of intensive care units (ICUs), however, circulation and breathing can be sustained for months even though the brain has irreversibly ceased to function and the patient will never recover. Most people believe it would be pointless to sustain vital functions in such a situation.

Organ transplantation has also raised ethical issues about the declaration of death. Transplantation of vital organs, which is potentially life-saving to recipients, cannot be performed without clear agreement that the organ donor has died. Transplant teams want to retrieve organs as soon as possible. On the other hand, relatives and the public want assurance that organs are not harvested prematurely from persons who are not truly dead.

Disputes about the determination of death might also arise with persons on whom criminal acts were committed. Some defendants in murder trials have contended that the person's death was caused by discontinuation of life-sustaining treatment, not by their actions (4).

Because of these problems with traditional cardiopulmonary criteria for death, the definition of death was revised to include absence of brain function, also known as brain death.

THE CONCEPT OF BRAIN DEATH

Patients who have permanently lost all brain function are considered dead, even though medical technology supported their circulation and breathing. Brain death is defined as irreversible loss of functioning in the entire brain, both cortex and brainstem. This is also called *whole-brain death*.

Brain death is tantamount to "permanent cessation of the functioning of the organism as a whole" (5). Because the brain is the coordinating and integrating center of the body, death of the brain ensures that the organism as a whole can no longer function. Destruction of the brain generally leads to cessation of spontaneous cardiac function within a week (6).

Currently, the clinical tests for brain death include coma, absence of brainstem function, and apnea (7). Potentially reversible, confounding causes of coma, such as drug overdose or hypothermia, must be ruled out. Circulation and spinal cord reflexes might be intact in brain death. Confirmatory testing with an electroencephalogram (EEG) or angiography might be helpful but is not required. In children the determination of brain death is more complicated because prognosis is more difficult to establish (8,9).

In recent years these criteria for brain death have been questioned. In some brain-dead patients, there might be persistence of some cerebral blood flow, oxygen and glucose metabolism, EEG activity, brainstem-evoked potentials, and secretion of antidiuretic hormone (10). Moreover, spontaneous body movements generated by the spine might be present (7). In exceptional cases there might be a substantial discrepancy between determinations of death using brain death criteria and traditional cardiopulmonary criteria. Several pregnant women meeting brain death criteria had their vital functions sustained for months until the fetus could be delivered (11).

CONTROVERSIES OVER BRAIN DEATH

There is widespread confusion over brain death (12). Only 35% of physicians who were responsible for declaring death were able to identify irreversible loss of all brain function as the criterion for determining death and apply it to simple case vignettes. Among other health care workers involved in the care of persons declared brain dead, over 70% were unable to identify the legal and medical criteria for brain death. When asked to explain their personal opinions about two case vignettes, 58% of all respondents did not consistently use a coherent concept of death. Thirty-six percent believed that it is appropriate to retrieve organs from a patient in a vegetative state who does not meet criteria for whole-brain death. Moreover, hospital policies on criteria for brain death vary considerably and might not be consistent with expert guidelines (13,14).

Whole-brain death criteria have been criticized for being both too narrow and too inclusive. These controversies illustrate the impact of cultural, social, and religious values on the definition of death.

HIGHER BRAIN DEATH

Some writers argue that a person should be considered dead if there is irreversible loss of higher brain function in the cerebral cortex rather than loss of whole-brain function (15). These writers argue that consciousness, self-awareness, the potential for thought, and interactions with others are essential for being a person (16). However, most writers reject a "higher brain" or neocortical definition of death (17). Reliable clinical tests for higher brain death are not available. The concept of higher brain death seems to confuse what it means to be a person with what it means to be alive. It might be appropriate to say that individuals without cortical function are no longer persons in the philosophic sense of having rights and interests. However, it does not follow logically that they should be considered dead. Finally, higher brain criteria contradict deeply held beliefs about death. Burying or cremating individuals in a persistent vegetative state or with severe dementia, who have no cortical function but who are still breathing and have a pulse, seems intuitively wrong.

DISAGREEMENT ON THE CONCEPT OF BRAIN DEATH

Some persons reject the concept of brain death for religious or philosophic reasons (18,19). For example, some orthodox Jews, Native Americans, and Japanese believe that a person is alive until he or she literally stops breathing (20). No distinction is made between mechanical ventilation and spontaneous breathing. In this view a person on a ventilator who meets the standards for brain death is not dead.

LEGAL STATUS OF BRAIN DEATH

Most states have adopted the Uniform Determination of Death Act, which declares, "Any individual who has sustained either (1) irreversible cessation of circulatory and respiratory functions, or (2) irreversible cessation of all functions of the entire brain, including the brain stem, is dead. A determination of death must be made in accordance with accepted medical standards (4)." Thus, a person may be declared dead if he or she meets either cardiopulmonary criteria (absence of breathing and pulse) or brain death criteria. For most patients who are not on life support, these two criteria are equivalent.

Two states defer to patient beliefs about the definition of death. New Jersey authorizes the declaration of brain death, except in cases in which the physician has "reason to believe" that "such a declaration would violate the personal religious beliefs of the individual (21)." For such individuals death must be declared according to traditional cardiorespiratory criteria. Similarly, New York requires "reasonable accommodation of the individual's religious or moral objection" to brain death criteria (22).

PRACTICAL SUGGESTIONS ON BRAIN DEATH

An experienced neurologist should be consulted before a patient is declared brain dead. Once brain death has been determined, relatives need to be told. Such discussions require sensitivity and patience. Some family members might believe the patient will regain consciousness, particularly if the death was sudden or unexpected. In almost all cases compassionate explanations and emotional support from health care workers help the family accept the situation.

If organ transplantation is feasible, a physician not associated with the transplantation team should declare death, so as to avoid even the appearance of conflict of interest (23,24). Discussion of the possibility of organ donation with the survivors should wait until after the declaration of death, unless the family first raises the issue.

After a patient has been declared dead by brain death criteria, all life-sustaining interventions should be discontinued, with certain exceptions. Maintaining life support might be appropriate until family members can come to the hospital, until organs for transplantation can be harvested or, under exceptional circumstances, until a fetus can be delivered.

In summary, the development of intensive care and organ transplantation has made traditional definitions of death untenable in some cases. Physicians need to understand the clinical criteria for brain death and controversies over the concept. Ultimately the definition of life and death depends on cultural, social, and religious beliefs as well as medical expertise.

REFERENCES

1. Charo RA. Dusk, dawn, and defining death: legal classifications and biological categories. In: Youngner SJ, Arnold RM, Schapiro R, eds. *The definition of death*, Baltimore: The Johns Hopkins University Press, 1999:277–292.
2. Veatch RM. An ethical framework for terminal care decisions. *J Am Geriatr Soc* 1984;32:665–669.
3. Burt RA. Where do we go from here? In: Youngner SJ, Arnold RM, Schapiro R, eds. *The definition of death*. Baltimore: The Johns Hopkins University Press, 1999:332–339.
4. Furrow BR, Johnson SH, Jost TS, Schwartz RL, eds. *Defining death*. St. Paul: West Publishing Co, 1991.
5. Bernat JL. How much of the brain must die in brain death? *J Clin Ethics* 1992;3:21–26.
6. Plum F, Posner JB. *The diagnosis of stupor and coma*, 3rd ed. Philadelphia: FA Davis Co, 1980.
7. Wijdicks EFM. The diagnosis of brain death. *N Engl J Med* 2001;344:1215–1221.
8. Task Force for the Determination of Brain Death in Children. Guidelines for the determination of brain death in children. *Pediatrics* 1987;80:298–300.
9. Mejia RE, Pollack MM. Variability in brain death determination practices in children. *JAMA* 1995;274:550–553.
10. Halevy A, Brody B. Brain death: reconciling definitions, criteria, and tests. *Ann Intern Med* 1993;119:519–525.
11. Field DR, Gates EA, Creasy RK, et al. Maternal brain death during pregnancy: medical and ethical issues. *JAMA* 1988;260:816–822.
12. Youngner SJ, Landefeld CS, Coulton CJ, et al. "Brain death" and organ retrieval: a cross-sectional survey of knowledge and concepts among health professionals. *JAMA* 1989;261:2205–2210.
13. Powner DJ, Hernandez M, Rives TE. Variability among hospital policies for determining brain death in adults. *Crit Care Med* 2004;32:1284–1288.
14. Oropello JM. Determination of brain death: theme, variations, and preventable errors. *Crit Care Med* 2004;32: 1417–1418.

15. Capron AM. Brain death—well settled yet still unresolved. *N Engl J Med* 2001;344:1244–1246.
16. Youngner SJ, Bartlett ET. Human death and high technology: the failure of whole-brain formulations. *Ann Intern Med* 1983;99:252–258.
17. Lynn J. The determination of death. *Ann Intern Med* 1983;99:264–266.
18. Olick RS. Brain death, religious freedom, and public policy: New Jersey's landmark legislative initiative. *Kennedy Inst Ethic J* 1991;1:275–288.
19. Kimura R. Japan's dilemma with the definition of death. *Kennedy Inst Ethics J* 1991;1:123–131.
20. Youngner SJ, Arnold RA, DeVita M. When is "death"? *Hast Cent Rep* 1999;14(6):14–21.
21. The New Jersey Declaration of Death Act. Revised statutes 1991 Title 26, Chapter 6A.
22. New York Codes 1987. §400.16(e)(3).
23. Youngner SJ, Allen M, Bartlett ET, et al. Psychosocial and ethical implications of organ retrieval. *N Engl J Med* 1985;313:321–324.
24. Tolle SW, Bennett WM, Hickam DH, et al. Responsibilities of primary physicians in organ donation. *Ann Intern Med* 1987;106:740–744.

ANNOTATED BIBLIOGRAPHY

1. Wijdicks EFM. The diagnosis of brain death. *N Engl J Med* 2001;344:1215–1221.
   Clinical review of the diagnosis of death using brain-based criteria.
2. Capron AM. Brain death—well settled yet still unresolved. *N Engl J Med* 2001;344:1244–1246.
   Lucid analysis of philosophic confusion over the cardiopulmonary and whole-brain criteria for determining death.
3. Youngner SJ, Arnold RM, Schapiro R. *The definition of death*. Baltimore: The Johns Hopkins University Press, 1999.
   Collection of essays on current controversies on defining death.
4. Halevy A, Brody B. Brain death: reconciling definitions, criteria, and tests. *Ann Intern Med* 1993;119:519–525.
   Discusses whole-brain and higher brain formulations of death, emphasizing that patients who satisfy clinical tests for brain death might still have some brain function.
5. Youngner SJ, Landefeld CS, Coulton CJ. "Brain death" and organ retrieval: a cross-sectional survey of knowledge and concepts among health professionals. *JAMA* 1989;261:2205–2210.
   Survey showing that many health care workers are confused about brain death.

CHAPTER 22

Legal Rulings on Life-Sustaining Interventions

Dramatic legal cases regarding life-sustaining interventions have received prominent news coverage. These landmark court rulings have shaped clinical practice and have motivated people to discuss their preferences for such interventions.

THE QUINLAN CASE

In 1976 the Karen Ann Quinlan case dramatized the dilemma of whether it might be more humane to withdraw life support rather than to prolong life when there is no hope of regaining consciousness (1).

THE CASE

Karen Ann Quinlan was a 22-year-old woman in a persistent vegetative state (PVS) because of an unknown illness. Her physicians agreed that she would never regain consciousness. She was on mechanical ventilation, and her physicians believed that she would die if the ventilator were withdrawn. Her father, after consulting with his priest and the hospital chaplain, asked that the ventilator be withdrawn. When the physicians refused, he asked the courts to appoint him Karen's legal guardian with the authority to terminate the ventilator. The Catholic bishops of New Jersey supported his request.

THE COURT RULING

The New Jersey Supreme Court ruled that Karen Ann Quinlan's right to privacy included a right to decline medical treatment and that her father as guardian could exercise this right on her behalf. Her guardian and family should be permitted "to render their best judgment" as to whether she would have chosen herself to decline treatment.

The court held unanimously that if Karen's guardian and family, her attending physician, and a hospital "ethics committee" agreed that "there is no reasonable possibility" of recovering a "cognitive and sapient state," the ventilator may be withdrawn. In advocating hospital ethics committees, the court wrote, "In the real world and in relationship to the momentous decision contemplated, the value of additional views and diverse knowledge is apparent (1)." No party would face any civil or criminal liability for discontinuing the ventilator. The court also declared that generally such decisions need not be brought to court "not only because that would be a gratuitous encroachment upon the medical profession's field of competence, but because it would be impossibly cumbersome."

IMPLICATIONS OF THE CASE

As the first "right to die" case to gain widespread publicity, the Quinlan case profoundly affected medical ethics. It stimulated discussion about ethical dilemmas regarding life-sustaining interventions. The ruling legitimized the idea that life-sustaining interventions might be inappropriate in some situations. The Quinlan court gave judicial support to decision-making by patients, families, and physicians without routine involvement of the courts in cases about life-sustaining treatment. The Quinlan decision also motivated the development of hospital ethics committees. Strictly speaking, the court intended such committees to review prognoses to ensure that patients such as Ms. Quinlan are truly in a PVS. However, the ruling also encouraged physicians and families to use committees to facilitate discussion of the ethical issues raised by such cases. In hindsight, the Quinlan case makes clear that medical judgments about prognosis are fallible. Although Ms. Quinlan's physicians expected her to die after the ventilator was discontinued, she survived for 10 years in a PVS without ventilatory support. Physicians now realize that most patients in a PVS, having intact brainstem function, breathe without assistance.

THE CRUZAN CASE

In the Cruzan case the U.S. Supreme Court issued its first decision on the "right to die (2–5)." The ruling sparked state and federal legislation to encourage the use of advance directives.

THE CASE

Nancy Cruzan was a 33-year-old woman who was in a PVS following an automobile accident in 1983. A month after the accident, a feeding gastrostomy tube was inserted. In 1986, realizing that her condition would not improve, her parents asked that the tube feedings be discontinued. Because the state hospital caring for Cruzan insisted on a court order, the case entered the legal system.

A year before her accident, Cruzan told her housemate that she "didn't want to live" as a "vegetable." If she "couldn't do for herself things alone even halfway, or not at all, she wouldn't want to live that way and she hoped that her family would know that (6)." Cruzan's parents asked that tube feedings be discontinued because they knew "in our hearts" that she would not want to continue living in her condition (6).

THE MISSOURI RULING

The 1988 Missouri Supreme Court ruling in the case severely restricted family decision-making on behalf of incompetent patients (7). Life-sustaining interventions could be withheld only with "the most rigid of formalities," such as a living will or a clear and convincing statement that the patient *would not want the specific intervention in that situation*. The court found no reliable evidence that Nancy Cruzan would have specifically refused artificial feedings. It asserted that Missouri's "unqualified" interest in preserving life, regardless of the patient's prognosis, outweighed any rights an incompetent patient might have to refuse treatment.

THE U.S. SUPREME COURT RULING

By a 5 to 4 vote, the U.S. Supreme Court affirmed the Missouri ruling in 1990 (8). Although competent patients might have a "constitutionally protected liberty interest in refusing unwanted medical treatment," the Court declared that incompetent patients do not have the same right because they cannot exercise it directly. Thus, states may establish "procedural safeguards" governing medical decisions for incompetent patients that are more stringent than requirements for competent patients.

The majority opinion declared that the individual's right to refuse treatment must be balanced against relevant state interests. The Court held that the Constitution allows states to assert an unqualified interest in "the protection and preservation of human life." It ruled that the Constitution also allows states to establish procedures to prevent abuses, to exclude quality of life as a consideration in treatment decisions, and to err on the side of continuing life-sustaining treatment. In short, states may require life-sustaining interventions when there is no clear and convincing evidence that the incompetent patient would refuse it. Although the Constitution permits states to rely on family decision-making for incompetent patients, it does not mandate that they do so.

In dissent, Justice William Brennan, joined by Justices Thurgood Marshall and Harry Blackmun, declared that being free of unwanted medical treatment is a fundamental constitutional right that extends to incompetent as well as competent patients and includes refusal of artificial fluid and nutrition. Families or patient-designated surrogates should generally make decisions for incompetent patients. In a separate dissent, Justice John Paul Stevens went further, declaring that the Constitution requires that the best interests of the incompetent patient be followed.

THE DEATH OF NANCY CRUZAN

After the Supreme Court ruling, the Cruzans petitioned the trial court in Missouri to rehear the case because new witnesses had come forward. One woman who worked with Cruzan testified that Cruzan had said that if she were a "vegetable," she would not want to be fed by force or kept alive by machines. Cruzan's attending physician changed his mind and was now in favor of stopping her feedings. The state of Missouri withdrew from further court proceedings, and in December 1990 the judge authorized removal of Cruzan's tube feedings (9).

IMPLICATIONS OF THE CRUZAN CASE

The Cruzan ruling spurred legislation to facilitate the use of advance directives. Many states adopted or revised laws specifically allowing patients to appoint health care proxies. The federal Patient Self Determination Act was enacted and took effect in December 1991. Under this law virtually all hospitals, nursing homes, and health maintenance organizations must at the time of admission give patients written information about their right to provide advance directives.

THE PHYSICIAN ASSISTED SUICIDE CASES

THE CASES

Competent, terminally ill patients who wanted to end their lives by taking a lethal dose of medications, along with physicians who were willing to write such a prescription, brought court cases in New York and Washington State. These patients had various terminal illnesses, such as cancer, the acquired immunodeficiency syndrome, and emphysema. The plaintiffs asserted that New York and Washington's prohibitions on physician-assisted suicide were unconstitutional.

THE LOWER COURT RULINGS

Two federal appellate courts declared a constitutional right to physician-assisted suicide. The Second Circuit federal court of appeals ruled that New York State violated the Fourteenth Amendment's guarantee of equal protection by allowing terminally ill patients to hasten death by foregoing life-sustaining treatments while forbidding other terminally ill patients to hasten death using a prescription for a lethal dose of medication (10). In the Washington case the Ninth Circuit appeals court declared that physician-assisted suicide was part of a fundamental right, protected by the Fourteenth Amendment's guarantee of liberty, to determine the time and manner of one's death (11).

THE U.S. SUPREME COURT RULINGS

In 1997 the Supreme Court issued a pair of unanimous rulings that held that there is no constitutional right to physician-assisted suicide (12,13). Thus, the Washington and New York laws prohibiting physician-assisted suicide did not violate the Constitution.

The Supreme Court rejected the conclusion that terminally ill patients had a "fundamental liberty interest" in obtaining physician-assisted suicide. According to the Court, states have legitimate reasons for prohibiting assisted suicide (12). These reasons are preserving human life, preventing suicide, protecting vulnerable groups, protecting the integrity of the medical profession, and avoiding a slippery slope to euthanasia. The Court also ruled that under the Constitution states may permit patients to forego life-sustaining treatment while prohibiting physician-assisted suicide (13). The court declared that the distinction between physician-assisted suicide and withdrawal of life-sustaining treatment is important and logical. When physicians withdraw treatment, they intend only to respect the patient's wishes, not to end the patient's life. Moreover, the cause of death is the underlying fatal disease, not the physician's action.

The Court further declared that the Constitution allows states to prohibit physician-assisted suicide, which intentionally hastens death, while permitting palliative care that might hasten death but is intended to relieve pain (14). According to the Court, the rationale of double effect distinguished the use of high-dose narcotics from euthanasia or assisted suicide. The Court noted that "painkilling drugs may hasten a patient's death, but the physician's purpose and intent is, or may be, only to ease his patient's pain…. The law has long used actors' intent or purpose to distinguish between two acts that may have the same result (14)."

IMPLICATIONS OF THE CASES

The majority opinion concluded that the double effect doctrine provides a rational and constitutional basis for states to allow high-dose narcotics for pain relief in terminally ill patients while prohibiting assisted suicide (15–17). Thus, the majority opinion offers a justification for aggressive palliative care. Three concurring justices went further, suggesting that the Constitution obligates states to permit physicians to provide adequate pain relief at the end of life, even if such care leads to unconsciousness or hastens death. The opinions might help lift legal barriers to palliative care. The Court strongly supported the doctrine of double effect and emphasized the importance of the physician's intention in evaluating the appropriateness of end-of-life care. As Chapter 15 discusses, the Court's reasoning can provide support for the practice of terminal sedation.

THE SCHIAVO CASE

THE CASE

Theresa Schiavo, a 27-year-old woman, suffered a cardiac arrest in 1990 because of potassium abnormalities and lapsed into a PVS. Her husband then won a malpractice suit against the physicians who were caring for her at the time of her cardiac arrest. In 1998, as the legally appointed guardian, her husband asked the court to discontinue tube feedings. Her parents opposed the withdrawal of tube feedings.

THE COURT RULINGS AND THE FLORIDA LAW

The trial court ruled that there was clear and convincing evidence that she would want the feedings discontinued. A long and complicated series of legal disputes ensued. The parents filed various appeals, contending that there was new evidence about her wishes and that her medical condition was misrepresented to the trial court. In 2002 the trial court held a new hearing on her current condition and on whether any new treatments might be effective. That court ruled "the credible evidence overwhelming supports that Terri Schiavo remains in a persistent vegetative state (18)." The court also held that the preponderance of the evidence was that no treatment would significantly improve her quality of life. The parents also claimed that new witnesses would testify that the husband lied about conversations with the patient about her wishes. The court ruled that this new evidence, even if it were accepted as credible, would not meet the legal requirement that the original decision was "no longer equitable (18)."

The state appellate court denied the parents' appeals in four separate rulings. In the fourth ruling the court stated, "It may be unfortunate that when families cannot agree, the best forum we can offer for this private, personal decision is a public courtroom and the best decision-maker is a judge with no prior knowledge of the ward, but the law currently provides no better solution that adequately protects the interests of promoting the value of life (19)." The Florida Supreme Court declined to hear the case.

Pro-life advocates, the Florida legislature, and Governor Jeb Bush then became involved in the case. In 2003 a law called "Terri's law" was enacted authorizing the governor to issue a stay to prevent the withholding of nutrition and hydration from a patient in a PVS who has no written advance directive when a member of the patient's family challenged the withholding of nutrition and hydration. In October 2003, Bush issued such a stay for Ms. Schiavo. In 2004, a Florida court ruled the law was unconstitutional, and the Florida Supreme Court affirmed that decision.

IMPLICATIONS OF THE CASE

Disagreements Among Family Members

The Schiavo case illustrates how intractable and bitter disputes might arise among family members of patients who lack decision-making capacity. Both the husband and the parents accuse each other of acting in bad faith. The courts emphasized the desirability of having a final decision that closed the case. They urged the family to end the dispute and to move forward. However, this case shows how the legal system might not be able to resolve disputes when families are so sharply divided.

Involvement of Third Parties and the Courts

The The Schiavo case is unique because of the involvement of pro-life advocacy groups, the Florida legislature, and the governor. Also, the Internet has allowed considerable information about the case to be widely disseminated. However, such involvement of third parties raises several concerns. One is intrusion into the patient's privacy. Ordinarily, decisions about end-of-life care are delegated to families without interference by third parties who have no direct connection with the patient. In polls the overwhelming majority of persons say that they would want decisions to be made by their families rather than by government officials. However, patients might not anticipate that their family might disagree over their care. Second, the public discussion of the case includes many assertions that contradict the court record. For instance, allegations continue to be made that Terri Schiavo is not in a PVS and that new therapies might significantly improve her condition. Both a trial court and an appellate court have determined, however, that she is in a PVS and that the preponderance of credible evidence indicates that no treatment would significantly improve her condition. In addition, allegations have been made that the patient's husband lied about statements she had allegedly made about her wishes for care.

Although society has designated the courts to resolve such difficult disputes, courts might not be able to provide a definitive answer or to resolve ongoing disagreements. The court challenges to "Terri's law" raise fundamental questions about the appropriate role of the legislative and executive branches of government in disputes that cannot be worked out among the family and physicians.

Importance of Advance Directives

Terri Schiavo did not complete an advance directive designating a proxy to make decisions for her; had she done so, the disputes between the parents and husband would likely have been resolved sooner. It is unrealistic to expect a young healthy woman to anticipate the situation Terri Schiavo is now in and to have informed judgments about what she would want done in a catastrophic illness. However, it is not asking too much for a healthy person to appoint a proxy whom she trusts to make decisions for her.

In summary, landmark court cases have helped shape public policy regarding life-sustaining interventions. Physicians need to know enough about these court rulings to correct misunderstandings by patients and colleagues.

REFERENCES

1. In the matter of Karen Quinlan. 70 N.J. 10, 335 A. 2d 647 (1976).
2. Angell M. Prisoners of technology: the case of Nancy Cruzan. *N Engl J Med* 1990;322:1226–1228.
3. Annas G. Nancy Cruzan and the right to die. *N Engl J Med* 1990;323:670–673.
4. Orentlicher D. The right to die after Cruzan. *JAMA* 1990;264:2444–2447.
5. Lo B, Steinbrook R. Beyond the Cruzan case: the U.S. Supreme Court and medical practice. *Ann Intern Med* 1991;114:895–901.

 6. Brief for petitioners. Cruzan v. Missouri Department of Health; No. 89–1503.
 7. Cruzan v. Harmon. 760 S.W.2d 408.
 8. Cruzan v. Missouri Department of Health. 497 U.S. 261, 110 S.Ct. 2841 (1990).
 9. Cruzan v. Harmon. No. CV384-9P, Circuit court of Missouri (Mo. Cir. Ct. Jasper County Dec 14, 1990) (Teel, J.).
10. Quill v. Vacco. 830 F3d 716 (2nd Cir 1966).
11. Compassion in Dying v. Washington. 79 F3d 790 (9th Cir 1966) (en banc).
12. Washington v. Glucksberg. 117 S.Ct. 2258 (1997).
13. Vacco v. Quill. 117 S.Ct. 2293 (1997).
14. Quill v. Vacco. 117 S.Ct. 2293 (1997).
15. Alpers A, Lo B. The Supreme Court addresses physician-assisted suicide: can its decisions improve palliative care? *Arch Fam Pract* 1999;8:200–205.
16. Burt RA. The Supreme Court speaks: not assisted suicide but a constitutional right to palliative care. *N Engl J Med* 1997;337:1234–1236.
17. Gostin LO. Deciding life and death in the courtroom. *JAMA* 1997;278:1523–1528.
18. In re Guardianship of Theresa Marie Schiavo. No. 90-2908-GB-003 (Fla. Cir. Ct. 2002).
19. In re Guardianship of Theresa Marie Schiavo. 851 So. 2d 182 (Fla. 2003).

ANNOTATED BIBLIOGRAPHY

 1. Meisel A. *The right to die*, 2nd ed. New York: John Wiley and Sons, 1995.
    Comprehensive and lucid treatise on legal rulings on decisions about life-sustaining interventions.
 2. Meisel A. A retrospective on Cruzan. *Law Med Health Care* 1992;20:340–353.
    Reviews legal developments after the 1990 Cruzan decision.
 3. Burt RA. The Supreme Court speaks: not assisted suicide but a constitutional right to palliative care. *N Engl J Med* 1997;337:1234–1236.
    Alpers A, Lo B. The Supreme Court addresses physician-assisted suicide: can its decisions improve palliative care? *Arch Fam Pract* 1999;8:200–205.
    Two articles that discuss the important Supreme Court rulings in the two 1997 physician-assisted suicide cases.

The Doctor–Patient Relationship

CHAPTER 23

Overview of the Doctor–Patient Relationship

$\mathbf{A}$ strong doctor–patient relationship has many dimensions. Physicians have a fiduciary obligation to act in their patients' best interests. To this end, technical expertise and sound clinical judgment are essential. Physicians also should help patients make informed decisions about their care by providing clear information and helping them weigh the pros and cons of alternatives. Physicians should also maintain confidentiality, avoid misrepresentation, and keep promises. Beyond that, patients also want caregivers who have compassion and empathy and who make them feel listened to and cared for. In addition, patients want a primary care physician to guide them through the complicated health care system and coordinate care from specialists, and they also want access to care and continuity of care. They want to be able to see their physician when they need to, and they want a single physician to help them make crucial decisions over the course of an illness.

In modern medicine many incentives encourage physicians to adopt an entrepreneurial approach to their work. The danger of regarding medicine as a business is that many standard business practices might conflict with the goals and ideals of medicine (1). Businesspeople can greatly increase their net income through targeting profitable markets, dropping unprofitable services, and using advertising to increase demand for their product (2). These practices are considered acceptable for people who are selling computers or running a restaurant. However, should physicians or health care organizations offer services only to well-insured patients, drop unprofitable services such as primary care, or increase demand for profitable services that offer little or no benefit to patients? To the extent that health care is considered a need or a right rather than a commodity, such a commercial approach is ethically disturbing. Moreover, medicine as a profession defines itself as putting the patient's interests first (3).

The chapters in this section discuss specific situations in which the doctor–patient relationship is problematic or difficult. Chapter 24 discusses situations in which physicians refuse to care for patients. Doctors might fear that their own health or safety is jeopardized or consider a patient difficult or obnoxious. Chapter 25 discusses the ethical issues that might arise when patients give gifts to their physicians. Chapter 26 analyzes sexual relationships between physicians and patients and discusses how such contact might harm patients. Chapter 27 suggests how physicians should respond when family members or friends provide unsolicited information about a patient and ask that it be kept secret. Chapter 28 analyzes how clinical research, which is essential for medical progress, presents risks to patients who participate in studies. The physician who also is a clinical investigator has additional responsibilities to ensure that the potential benefits of research are proportionate to the risks, to inform patients about the study, and to avoid conflicts of interest.

REFERENCES

1. Kassirer JP. Managed care and the morality of the marketplace. *N Engl J Med* 1995;333:50–52.
2. Jonsen AR. Ethics remain at the heart of medicine: physicians and entrepreneurship. *West J Med* 1986;144:480–483.
3. Medical Professionalism Project. Medical professionalism in the new millennium: a physician charter. *Ann Intern Med* 2002;136(3):243–246.

CHAPTER 24

Refusal to Care for Patients

Physicians may refuse to care for persons because of an unacceptable threat to their personal safety. In other situations physicians may seek to terminate a counterproductive or an adversarial doctor–patient relationship. The following case illustrates such a refusal to care for a patient.

CASE 24.1 Surgery in an HIV-infected patient.

A 43-year-old man with asymptomatic human immunodeficiency virus (HIV) infection, while crossing a street, is struck by a car running a red light. He suffers a comminuted fracture of the proximal femoral shaft. The surgeons decline to operate because the patient's viral titer has not been checked recently, saying that this fracture can be managed without surgery. Moreover, the surgeons say that in orthopedics operations sharp bone fragments from seropositive patients subject health care workers to an unacceptable risk of lethal illness.

In Case 24.1 standard treatment for this fracture is operative fixation with an intramedullary rod (1). Closed treatment requires several months of traction and has poorer outcomes. Similarly, during the severe acute respiratory syndrome (SARS) epidemic of 2002–2003, some health care workers refused to work with infected patients (2). Although the law generally permits physicians to decide which individuals to accept as patients, it seems inhumane for physicians to refuse crucial medical care to sick persons. This chapter analyzes whether physicians have an ethical obligation to care for patients who are contagious, violent, or uncooperative.

THE CONTEXT OF THE DOCTOR–PATIENT RELATIONSHIP

ETHICAL OBLIGATIONS TO CARE FOR PATIENTS

Physicians present themselves to the public as helpers of the sick and needy, using their expertise for the benefit of patients. The ethical ideal is that patients will receive needed care, even in cases in which the physician might find it risky, difficult, or inconvenient. At the beginning of the HIV epidemic the Surgeon General declared, "Health care in this country has always been predicated on the assumption that somehow, everyone will be cared for, and no one will be turned away. As a physician and an American, I'm proud to be part of a tradition of care that will not abandon the sick or disabled, whoever they are (3)."

In the doctor–patient relationship, the patient's best interests should take priority over the doctor's self-interest (*see* Chapter 4). The guideline of beneficence has several important implications for refusals to care for patients. Physicians should not refuse care to patients whom they dislike or find unpleasant or whose actions, such as smoking, alcohol and substance abuse, or not adhering to medications, make treatment more difficult. It would also be ethically objectionable for physicians to refuse care to patients on the basis of social class, ethnic background, lifestyle, or political or religious beliefs. Even in war physicians are expected to attend to the sick and injured, regardless of which side they are on. Furthermore, physicians are exhorted to provide needed medical care even to patients whose actions or beliefs they find morally objectionable. Doctors are expected to provide care to the perpetrator of a violent assault as well as to the victim.

This ethical ideal of providing needed care, regardless of the patient's characteristics, has limits. In providing care, physicians are not expected to compromise their own moral or religious beliefs. For example, Catholic physicians are not required to perform abortions. Although physicians are urged to tolerate patient behavior they personally consider immoral, they are not obligated to carry out what they regard as an immoral action. One philosopher has cautioned physicians to distinguish deeply held moral objections from "personal distaste or prejudice (4)." Another acceptable limit is the physician's health and safety. In Case 24.1 the physicians claim that serious personal risks override their ethical obligation to provide care.

LEGAL DEFINITION OF THE DOCTOR–PATIENT RELATIONSHIP

Society as a whole and individual physicians have a moral obligation to care for sick persons, yet doctors generally have no legal duty to provide care. The law generally characterizes the doctor–patient relationship as a contract between autonomous individuals who are free to enter into or break off the relationship, provided that the patient is not abandoned (5). Courts have ruled that physicians have no legal duty to treat new patients who seek care in the absence of an agreement to provide medical care, such as a contract with a health maintenance organization (HMO). For example, it is legal for physicians to have their receptionist schedule new patient appointments only for people with adequate health insurance. Similarly, physicians may restrict the scope of their practice to a particular specialty or range of problems. Thus, an internist would not be expected to perform surgery, just as a psychiatrist would not be expected to treat meningitis.

The legal right to decline to care for patients, however, is limited in many important ways. Employment contracts, as with hospitals or HMOs, may oblige physicians to care for all qualified persons who seek treatment. Similarly, physicians who are on call for a hospital may be required as a condition of staff privileges to provide care to persons who present there. As discussed later in this chapter, emergency departments are required to provide indicated emergency care to patients who seek it.

The Americans with Disabilities Act also forbids physicians from declining to care for patients on the basis of race, sex, national origin, religion, or disability (6). However, physicians and hospitals are not required to provide care when an "individual poses a direct threat to the health or safety of others that cannot be eliminated or reduced by reasonable accommodation (7)." Direct threat refers to "a significant risk of substantial harm," not merely to a "slightly increased risk" or a "speculative or remote risk (8)." The determination of risk must be made according to objective, scientific evidence, not according to the health care worker's subjective judgment. Caring for HIV-infected persons is not considered a "direct threat" to health care workers (8).

OCCUPATIONAL RISKS TO PHYSICIANS

Health care workers might contract serious or fatal contagious diseases on the job. During the SARS epidemic of 2002–2003, a disproportionate percentage of cases and deaths occurred among physicians and nurses caring for hospitalized patients with SARS. Physicians and nurses also feared that their families might become secondarily infected. However, most doctors and nurses cared for patients with SARS despite knowing they were at risk for a potentially fatal disease for which there was no effective treatment and for which preventive measures might be inadequate.

Early in the HIV epidemic fears of occupational HIV infection were widespread. The risk of seroconversion after a percutaneous exposure to the blood of a seropositive patient is 0.3% (9). After mucocutaneous exposure the risk is 0.09% (10). Surgeons and operating room staff are at higher risk for occupational HIV infection than office-based physicians. Later, this risk was reduced through the availability of highly active antiretroviral regiments that could suppress HIV titers in the patient's blood. Moreover, postexposure prophylaxis with antiretrovirals was shown to reduce transmission by 81% (11). In addition, the development of laparoscopic techniques for many operations further reduced risks to surgeons and operating room staff. However, the magnitude of a risk is only one component of a person's perception of the risk. The risk of occupational HIV infection and SARS seems especially ominous because these diseases can be fatal, can be transmitted to loved ones, and can be acquired on the job despite precautions.

Other serious infections that can be acquired through occupational exposure are hepatitis C and multidrug-resistant tuberculosis. In addition, angry or psychotic patients might physically threaten or harm health care workers. In one survey, 20% of residents said that they had been physically assaulted during their training (12). Fearful of these serious occupational risks, physicians might be reluctant to provide care to patients they regard as contagious or violent. Avoiding such patients, however, might conflict with their needs for medical care.

RESPONDING TO OCCUPATIONAL RISKS

Acknowledge and Address Fears

Physicians must acknowledge their human fears and limitations; only then are reflection, discussion, and constructive action possible. Fears about safety need to be acknowledged as an understandable human reaction rather than condemned as hysteria (13). In previous epidemics many physicians, including Galen and Sydenham, fled from patients with fatal contagious diseases (14). Health care workers will benefit from having their concerns addressed in a nonjudgmental way.

Some common techniques for encouraging health care workers to accept occupational risks are usually ineffective. Moral exhortations to provide care in risky situations might go unheeded. Indeed, health care workers might be outraged at the suggestion that it is unethical to worry about their personal safety. Reassurance that a risk is low or comparable to other risks frequently proves to be counterproductive (15 17). People reject the suggestion that because they accept risks of greater magnitude, such as the risk of automobile accidents, they should also accept the risk in question (17).

Reduce the Occupational Risks

Hospitals and clinics must provide a safe working environment, which includes protective equipment and instruments such as masks, gowns, and gloves. However, at the onset of an epidemic the best protective measures might not be known. New equipment might need to be developed and made available, such as retractable needles to prevent bloodborne infections. Health care institutions also need policies to protect health care workers, such as having security guards readily available when care is provided to violent patients.

Balance Risks to Health Care Workers and Benefits to Patients

Health care workers should provide care if the medical benefit to the patient is clearly established, substantial, and highly probable, provided that appropriate precautions have been taken to reduce risk. On the other hand, severe risks to health care workers might justify delaying or denying interventions whose benefits are unproved, uncertain, or marginal.

Judgments about the benefits and risks of treatment need to be scientifically sound. In Case 24.1 it would be misleading for physicians to say that operative reduction for this condition is not indicated in seropositive persons. Such surgery is routinely performed for this indication in patients who have other diseases, such as cancer, with poor prognoses. If physicians bias their medical judgments in order to avoid caring for seropositive persons, patients and the public will justifiably question their recommendations on other issues.

DIFFICULT DOCTOR–PATIENT RELATIONSHIPS

Ideally, the doctor–patient relationship is a partnership whose goal is the patient's well-being. In some cases, however, the relationship might be unproductive or adversarial and the physician might consider the patient a "problem" or "difficult" patient (18–20).

CASE 24.2 Disruptive and uncooperative patient.

Ms. W is a 35-year-old woman with end-stage renal disease who repeatedly misses dialysis appointments and requires emergency dialysis. She also does not take her medications regularly or follow her diet, is frequently intoxicated, and disrupts the dialysis unit with her obscene language and attempts to strike health care workers. Her nephrologist negotiates a contract with her; he agrees to continue to provide dialysis while she agrees keep scheduled appointments, enter substance abuse treatment, follow her diet, take her medications, and seek psychological counseling. When Ms. W does not change her behavior, he notifies her that he will no longer provide chronic dialysis and gives her a list of other nephrologists in the area. When she presents to the emergency department with hyperkalemia and congestive heart failure, the nephrologist considers refusing dialysis (21).

In Case 24.2, Ms. W repeatedly misses appointments, fails to take her medications, and requires emergency care after missing scheduled appointments. Furthermore, she is disruptive, angry, and violent. Physicians commonly view such patients as "bad" patients who have broken the implicit rules of the doctor–patient relationship (20). When providing care, health care workers should not have to suffer verbal or physical abuse and neither should other patients (22). Moreover, health care workers are understandably frustrated when the patient's own actions bring about or exacerbate medical problems. In addition, such a patient is often considered difficult because he or she provokes such strong negative reactions in health care workers that a therapeutic relationship no longer exists (20). Doctors resent spending so much time and energy on such a patient that they provide insufficient attention to other patients. In less dramatic cases physicians might feel insulted or denigrated by a patient's racist, sexist, or homophobic comments.

IMPROVING DIFFICULT DOCTOR–PATIENT RELATIONSHIPS

In most cases physicians can find ways to improve a difficult doctor–patient relationship (Table 24-1).

Acknowledge That Problems Exist

The first step is for physicians and patients alike to acknowledge problems. The physician might say, "I sense that both of us are disappointed with how your care is turning out."

Try to Understand the Patient's Perspective

Physicians might feel that some patients intentionally vex them, making medical care more difficult. From the patient's perspective, however, there might be sound reasons for missing appointments, such as difficulties with insurance coverage, transportation, or childcare. Illness might cause patients to feel angry, frustrated, helpless, or out of control. Also, patients might not have control over some behaviors because of substance abuse or psychiatric conditions.

Physicians can elicit patients' perspectives through open-ended questions about the impact of their illness, competing demands in their life, and barriers to care. Acknowledging a patient's emotions also encourages further discussion. Once their problems and frustration are acknowledged, patients might be better able to appreciate how their behavior is disrupting their care or the care of other patients. The physician might say, "We're trying our best to help you, but it's hard for us if you shout and don't keep appointments."

Try to Understand Your Own Responses

Physicians need to understand how their own actions might exacerbate the patient's behavior. Physicians and nurses who are frustrated and angry at having to provide emergency dialysis might vent their anger on the patient or treat her curtly. Differences in ethnic background, social class, and lifestyle often exacerbate tensions.

TABLE 24-1

Improving Difficult Doctor–Patient Relationships

Acknowledge that problems exist.
Try to understand the patient's perspective.
Try to understand your own responses.
Try to negotiate mutually acceptable grounds for continued care.

Try to Negotiate Mutually Acceptable Plans for Continued Care

Physicians can try to set limits on disruptive behaviors and find mutually acceptable conditions for the doctor–patient relationship (23). A psychiatric or social work consultation can often be helpful. For example, patients might be given more control over some aspects of their care. As in Case 24.2, physicians can warn patients that certain behaviors will lead to termination of the doctor–patient relationship. Doctors can negotiate a formal "contract" that explicitly sets conditions under which the patient and physician will continue the relationship—for example, requiring a family member to accompany the patient to dialysis sessions or having the patient accept treatment for substance abuse and mental illness (21).

In the case of patients who make prejudiced or insulting comments, physicians might need to set limits. If the physician is the brunt of the insult, he or she might say, "It sounds like you're not comfortable with me as your doctor, and I must say that it's hard for me to focus on being a doctor when people make comments like that. I'm willing to try to find a way that we can work together. However, if you want to get care in the clinic here, we ask you not to say things like that." If the doctor is on call and there is no realistic option of getting another doctor, the patient should be told, "I'm the doctor on call tonight. It sounds like you're not comfortable with me as your doctor, and I must say that it's hard for me to focus on being a doctor when you make comments like that. You and I need to work together so that you can get the care you need overnight. How do you think we can do that?"

TERMINATING THE DOCTOR–PATIENT RELATIONSHIP

The patient and physician may agree to transfer the care of the patient to another physician. Physicians may also unilaterally terminate the doctor–patient relationship in certain situations—for example, when Ms. W in Case 24.2 broke her agreement about subsequent behavior and continued to be disruptive and violent. Because termination is a drastic measure, it should be used only as a last resort after attempts to find common ground for ongoing care have failed.

Patient Abandonment

Legally and ethically, physicians may not abandon patients with whom they have established a doctor–patient relationship (21). When terminating a relationship, physicians need to give patients reasonable written notice, so that patients have time to find a new physician and obtain needed care for ongoing medical problems in a timely manner. To help patients find another physician, doctors can give patients a list of other qualified physicians in the area or refer them to the county medical society.

Obligation to Provide Emergency Care

An emergency department is required to provide emergency care to patients who seek it. The public relies on emergency departments and physicians to provide proper emergency treatment and expects them to do so. Delays in emergency care might seriously harm patients. Furthermore, once emergency departments begin a medical evaluation, patients justifiably rely on them to provide proper care.

The federal Emergency Medical Treatment and Labor Act (EMTLA) prohibits emergency departments from transferring patients in unstable condition who need emergency care as well as pregnant women in active labor (24). Every person seeking treatment in an emergency department must receive a screening examination. If the patient is found to have an emergency condition, the hospital must provide treatment to stabilize the patient's condition, within the constraints of the available staff and facilities.

Thus, if Ms. W in Case 24.2 presents to the emergency department with life-threatening hyperkalemia and congestive heart failure, emergency dialysis must be provided (22). This requires a nephrologist and dialysis nurse. Therefore, the health care workers who refuse to provide chronic dialysis might still have to perform emergency dialysis. Sometimes different individuals or institutions can share the emergency care of such patients.

In summary, physicians have an ethical obligation to care for patients even at some annoyance or personal risk. Before unilaterally terminating a difficult doctor–patient relationship, physicians should try both to understand the patient's perspective and to find some mutually acceptable arrangement for continuing care.

REFERENCES

1. Skinner HB, ed. *Current diagnosis and treatment in orthopedics*, 3rd ed. New York: Lange Medical Books/McGraw-Hill, 2003.
2. Sibbald B. Right to refuse work becomes another SARS issue. *CMAJ* 2003;169:141.
3. Koop CE. Testimony before Presidential Commission on AIDS. 1987 September 8.
4. Jonsen A, Siegler M, Winslade W. *Clinical ethics*, 3rd ed. New York: Macmillan, 1991:73–74.
5. Annas GJ. Not saints, but healers: the legal duties of health care professionals in the AIDS epidemic. *Am J Public Health* 1988;78:844–849.
6. Americans with Disabilities Act of 1990. 42 USC §§12181,12182.
7. Americans with Disabilities Act Public Accommodation Regulations. 28 CFR § 36.201.
8. Gostin LO, Feldbaum C, Webber DW. Disability discrimination in America: HIV/AIDS and other health conditions. *JAMA* 1999;281:745–752.
9. CDC. Updated public health service guidelines for management of health care worker exposures to HBV, HCV, and HIV and recommendations for postexposure prophylaxis. *MMWR* 2001;50:1–52.
10. Gerberding JL. Clinical practice. Occupational exposure to HIV in health care settings. *N Engl J Med* 2003;348(9): 826–833.
11. CDC. Case-control study of HIV seroconversion in health-care workers after exposures to HIV-infected blood—France, United Kingdom and United States, January 1988–August 1994. *MMWR* 1995;44(50):929–933.
12. Cook DJ, Liutkus JF, Risdon CL, et al. Residents' experiences of abuse, discrimination and sexual harassment during residency training. McMaster University Residency Training Programs. *CMAJ* 1996;154:1657–1665.
13. Gerbert B, Maguire B, Badmer V, et al. Why fear persists: health care professionals and AIDS. *JAMA* 1988;260: 3481–3483.
14. Zuger A, Miles SH. Physicians, AIDS, and occupational risk. Historic traditions and ethical obligations. *JAMA* 1987;258:1924–1928.
15. Nelkin D. Communicating technological risk: the social construction of risk perception. *Ann Rev Public Health* 1989;10:95–113.
16. Slovic P. Perception of risk. *Science* 1987;236:280–285.
17. National Research Council. *Improving risk communication*. Washington: National Academy Press, 1989.
18. Groves JE. Taking care of the hateful patient. *N Engl J Med* 1978;298:883–887.
19. Drossman DR. The problem patient: evaluation and care of medical patients with psychosocial disturbances. *Ann Intern Med* 1978;88:366–372.
20. Stokes T, Dixon-Woods M, McKinley RK. Breaking up is never easy: GPs' accounts of removing patients from their lists. *Fam Pract* 2003;20(6):628–634.
21. Orentlicher D. Denying treatment to the noncompliant patient. *JAMA* 1991;265:1579–1582.
22. Friedman EA. Must we treat noncompliant ESRD patients? *Semin Dial* 2001;14(1):23–27.
23. Quill TE. Partnerships in patient care: a contractual approach. *Ann Intern Med* 1983;98:228–234.
24. 42 U.S.C. § 1395dd.

ANNOTATED BIBLIOGRAPHY

1. Annas GJ. Not saints, but healers: the legal duties of health care professionals in the AIDS epidemic. *Am J Public Health* 1988;78:844–849.
   Discusses how physicians have no legal duty to treat patients in most situations despite a strong moral duty to do so.
2. Cantor J, Baum K. The limits of conscientious objection–may pharmacists refuse to fill prescriptions for emergency contraception? *N Engl J Med* 2004;351:2008–12.
   Argues that institutions should make reasonable attempts to accommodate health care workers' refusals to provide care based on conscience but that patients should be referred to other facilities that will provide care.
3. Friedman EA. Must we treat noncompliant ESRD patients? *Semin Dial* 2001;14:23–27.
   Discusses legal, ethical, and clinical aspects of denying treatment to noncompliant, abusive, violent dialysis patients.
4. Gostin LO, Feldbaum C, Webber DW. Disability discrimination in America: HIV/AIDS and other health conditions. *JAMA* 1999;281:745–752.
   Summary of disability law that explains that physicians may decline to care for infectious patients only if there is a significant risk of substantial harm.

CHAPTER 25

Gifts from Patients to Physicians

Modest gifts from patients, such as holiday cards, cookies or candy, flowers, and toys for children, gratify physicians and allow patients to express their appreciation. Other gifts, however, can cause problems. Expensive gifts might compromise the physician's judgment. Very personal gifts imply more than a professional relationship. Physicians might find that a gift from a patient makes them uncomfortable, and they might be uncertain how to respond.

Gifts from patients are often considered simply matters of social convention and etiquette, not ethics. This chapter points out how gifts from patients might raise ethical issues because they might change the doctor–patient relationship, impair clinical judgment, or erode public trust. Because physicians often find it embarrassing to discuss gifts, this chapter also suggests how to respond to problematic gifts from patients.

REASONS FOR PATIENTS TO GIVE GIFTS TO PHYSICIANS

TO THANK PHYSICIANS

Patients commonly send gifts to express appreciation to physicians for their care. Patients who have recovered from serious illness are understandably grateful to their physicians, particularly if the diagnosis was difficult, the treatment was complicated, or the physician was particularly supportive or involved.

TO SATISFY THEIR OWN NEEDS

Gifts might also reflect the patient's psychological needs.

CASE 25.1 Cookies from a lonely elderly patient.

A 74-year-old widow has hypertension, osteoarthritis, and mild depression. She has no surviving relatives, few friends, and few social activities. A new resident takes over her care. She talks about her sadness and emptiness, and he encourages her to attend a senior center. On the next visit she brings him a box of home-baked cookies.

For lonely patients, their physician might be one of the few people who listen or pay attention to them. Bringing a gift might give them a sense of purpose or alleviate their loneliness. Taking initiative and showing concern for other people might be therapeutic for them. For other patients, giving physicians small gifts allows them to make a personal connection to an otherwise impersonal medical care system.

TO ENHANCE FUTURE CARE

In a few cases gifts might represent expectations for future care rather than thanks for past efforts. Patients might feel that bestowing a gift will gain them special consideration. For instance, some patients might want to have the last appointment of the day because of difficulties getting off from work. Other patients might hope that gifts will gain them timely appointments or faster responses to phone calls. In rare cases patients who give gifts might subsequently ask physicians to do something that is ethically questionable.

CASE 25.2 Request for disability certification.

A patient with mild asthma gives his physician a toy for his son at Christmas. The next month he asks the physician to complete a form for a disability parking sticker. The patient does not meet the objective criteria for hypoxemia or dyspnea listed on the form.

In Case 25.2 the timing of the gift and the request are disturbing. The physician might feel manipulated because an apparently thoughtful gift might have had strings attached. Deceiving third parties about a patient's condition is ethically problematic (*see* Chapter 6). To do so after receiving a gift would appear like accepting a bribe.

TO MEET CULTURAL EXPECTATIONS

In some cultures gifts to physicians or other healers are routinely expected. Such gifts might show respect or be considered an essential aspect of the healing process. In some societies bribery might be necessary to ensure access to care. Physicians need to consider whether gifts might have special cultural significance for patients and correct any misconceptions about the U.S. medical care system.

PROBLEMS WITH GIFTS

It is human nature for patients who have given gifts to expect some consideration in return, either consciously or unconsciously (1). However, some gifts might create ethical problems because of patients' inappropriate expectations.

EXPECTATIONS FOR PERSONAL TREATMENT

Some patients might believe that gifts entitle them to special treatment, such as more convenient or prompter appointments. Other patients might expect freedom to call the physician at home or to have medications refilled over the telephone without an office visit. Even apparently small gifts might be problematic if such expectations become burdensome to physicians. For example, physicians understandably want to limit add-on appointments and after-hours phone calls in order to reduce personal stress and to protect their family life, yet they might find it difficult to refuse a request from a patient who has given a gift.

CHANGES IN THE DOCTOR–PATIENT RELATIONSHIP

Some gifts might change the doctor–patient relationship inappropriately.

CASE 25.1 continued. Focus on the physician's problems rather than the patient's.

The lonely, elderly patient starts to bring cookies or other gifts of food at every visit. Moreover, visits now focus on the physician rather than on the patient. The patient inquires about what foods the physician likes so that she can plan her next gift. She also expresses concern about whether he is getting enough sleep and has enough time off.

In Case 25.1 an overworked and underappreciated house officer might be delighted that someone takes a personal interest in him, but it is problematic if the physician assumes the role of a surrogate grandchild. Patient visits should focus on the patient's problems, not the physician's. The physician might miss opportunities to encourage and reinforce the patient's efforts to become more socially active in the community. In the long run it is counterproductive and unrealistic for lonely patients to depend totally on the medical system for their emotional and social needs.

In other circumstances gifts violate the boundaries of the professional relationship. An extreme example might be the gift of lingerie or other intimate apparel. Such gifts imply a personal relationship, not a professional one. Patients who overstep the boundaries of a professional relationship are acting out their own needs or fantasies. Not only should such gifts be refused but also appropriate boundaries need to be promptly and firmly reestablished. After such a gift, a physician who feels uncomfortable continuing the doctor–patient relationship might need to arrange to transfer care to another physician.

IMPAIRMENT OF CLINICAL JUDGMENT

Gifts can create or strengthen personal ties, but too close a relationship might be undesirable. It is difficult to provide care to a close relative because emotional ties might cloud clinical judgment (2). In a similar way, gifts that establish or imply a very close personal relationship might compromise the physician's judgment. Expectations of special treatment might compromise care, as when a patient expects the physician to diagnose and treat a complicated problem on the basis of a telephone call rather than an office visit. Psychologically, it is difficult to say no to patients who have given gifts, even if they request interventions that are unsound medical practice or not in their best interests. Similarly, a gift from a seriously ill patient might be problematic if it leads the physician to misrepresent bad news or causes the patient to develop unrealistic expectations.

EROSION OF PUBLIC TRUST

The doctor–patient relationship might be weakened if other patients believe that they will receive second-class care unless they offer gifts. Physicians serve as gatekeepers, allocating appointments, their time and attention, and, in managed care systems, health care resources. Generally, phone calls or appointments are allocated primarily on the basis of patient need. It would damage both the individual physician and the profession as a whole if patients believed that the best way to get the physician's attention is through a gift. Even a perception that physicians are allocating their efforts on the basis of favoritism would erode public trust.

SOLICITING GIFTS

Although this chapter has focused on gifts that patients offer to physicians, solicitation of gifts by physicians also merits attention. It is unethical for physicians to solicit personal gifts in return for services rendered because physicians' fees should be adequate compensation for their services. It might also be problematic for physicians to solicit contributions for some cause, such as a hospital or a political movement. Such solicitations might seem a natural way for physicians to work for causes they believe in, but patients might not feel free to decline the solicitation if their physician solicits it personally and therefore knows whether they have responded. They might fear that the physician will not render prompt or meticulous care in the future if they refuse.

HOW TO RESPOND TO GIFTS FROM PATIENTS

In responding to gifts physicians need to take into account the nature of the gift and the circumstances.

ACCEPT APPROPRIATE GIFTS GRACIOUSLY

In most cases gifts from patients are well intentioned and appropriate and should be accepted graciously. Indeed, many patients would feel insulted if physicians did not accept homemade cookies, toys for Christmas, or clothes for a new baby. Similarly, it would be unfeeling not to accept a small gift after the physician has devoted a great deal of effort in helping a patient recover from a difficult illness.

DO NOT LET GIFTS GO TO YOUR HEAD

Physicians should not allow gifts from patients to give them an exaggerated sense of their importance or their skill. Many patients, because they are sick and dependent, are extremely grateful for competent, humane care. It is gratifying that such qualities in physicians are recognized and reinforced, but physicians should appreciate that they might not have done anything extraordinary, just provided standard care.

APPRECIATE THAT SOME GIFTS ARE PROBLEMATIC

Some gifts might seem disproportionate to the services rendered (3).

CASE 25.3 Tickets to an opera.

A 52-year-old businessman establishes care with a new physician. At the first visit they discuss preventive measures such as exercise and diet. The next week the businessman offers the physician opera tickets to the opening night gala.

Intuitively, some gifts seem out of proportion to what the physician has done. Most physicians would feel comfortable accepting gifts worth less than $20, but many would feel uncomfortable accepting $1,000 tickets to the opening night of an opera after a routine new patient visit. Even if a wealthy patient considers this a small gift, it might give the wrong impression to other patients. Furthermore, the physician might wonder whether such a lavish gift reflects unrealistic expectations for care. Finally, many physicians feel uncomfortable accepting cash gifts because they seem associated with commerce and profits.

GET ADVICE ABOUT THE GIFT

Most physicians, even if they are uncomfortable about gifts, hesitate to discuss them with colleagues. Physicians might not appreciate that many colleagues also feel awkward and uncertain about gifts. Other people, however, can help the physician interpret the significance of gifts and understand the patient's possible expectations. In judging a gift's appropriateness, physicians can apply a practical rule of thumb: How would colleagues and other patients react if they knew about the gift? If other patients would question the gift, it is best not to accept it.

CONSIDER SHARING THE GIFT WITH OTHERS

Concerns about gifts can often be prevented or resolved by sharing the gift with others and letting the patient know. For example, the physician might donate the gift to charity or share it with other staff who care for the patient. Homemade cookies and cakes can be shared with office staff. Monetary gifts can be given to a house staff fund for refreshments or books, to the hospital volunteer fund, or to a medical charity. The physician should let the patient know how the gift was distributed and explain why this was done. Such sharing acknowledges the patient's thoughtfulness while making it less likely that the patient will feel entitled to special care from the physician.

DECLINE GIFTS WITHOUT REJECTING THE PATIENT

Even when physicians believe that declining a gift is appropriate, they might find it awkward to do so. Several strategies might allow the physician to decline the gift while respecting the patient's feelings. In each approach physicians should start by saying that they are grateful and touched. One approach is to explain that accepting such a gift might compromise the physician's ability to give high-quality care in the future. Although this approach is straightforward, patients often protest that they would never ask for special consideration. A second approach is to decline the gift politely but firmly without giving more specific reasons. Physicians might simply say that they could not possibly accept the gift and that their policy is not to accept such gifts, even though they are touched by the thoughtfulness. This strategy often works in conjunction with telling the patient that the gift will be shared with others.

If the physician suspects that gifts reflect the patient's social isolation or other needs, as in Case 25.1, these issues should be addressed separately during patient visits.

WHAT IF THE PATIENT LATER REQUESTS SPECIAL TREATMENT?

After a gift the patient might later request special treatment. A practical guideline is for physicians to do what they would have done if the same request had come from a patient who had not given a gift (3).

In conclusion, gifts from patients strengthen social relationships and expectations. Usually, gifts are thoughtful gestures of appreciation that should be accepted graciously. Some gifts, however, can be problematic. Discussing gifts with colleagues and considering how other patients would react might help physicians respond to them appropriately.

REFERENCES

1. Murray TH. Gifts of the body and the needs of strangers. *Hastings Cent Rep* 1987;17:30–38.
2. LaPuma J, Priest ER. Is there a doctor in the house? An analysis of the practice of physicians treating their own families. *JAMA* 1992;267:1810–1812.
3. Lyckholm LJ. Should physicians accept gifts from patients? *JAMA* 1998;280:1944–1946.

ANNOTATED BIBLIOGRAPHY

1. Lyckholm LJ. Should physicians accept gifts from patients? *JAMA* 1998;280:1944–1946.
   Brief, thoughtful review of the topic.

CHAPTER 26

Sexual Contact between Physicians and Patients

The Hippocratic Oath forbids sexual relationships between physicians and patients. Some people, however, believe that this prohibition is no longer appropriate: Sexual mores have changed, and sexual relationships between consenting adults should be considered private. This chapter argues that sexual contacts between physicians and patients are unethical if they take advantage of patients' trust, dependency, and vulnerability.

PREVALENCE OF SEXUAL CONTACT BETWEEN PHYSICIANS AND PATIENTS

In a national survey 9% of physicians reported at least one sexual contact with a patient or former patient (1). Most cases involved male physicians and female patients. This study excluded cases in which the sexual relationship preceded the medical care, such as the provision of medical care to a spouse. Twenty-three percent of respondents said that one or more of their patients had revealed sexual contact with a previous physician. In other studies between 5% and 10% of psychiatrists and other mental health professionals admitted to sexual contact with patients (2).

JUSTIFICATIONS FOR SEXUAL CONTACT BETWEEN PHYSICIANS AND PATIENTS

Several justifications are commonly offered for relaxing the traditional prohibition on sexual contacts between physicians and patients (3).

RESPECT FOR PRIVACY

Generally, sexual relationships between consenting adults are considered private matters with which other people and society have no right to interfere. To many it makes no difference that the partners are physician and patient. In this view it is demeaning and unrealistic to view patients as so vulnerable that they cannot make their own decisions about their private lives. Accordingly, restricting freedom to enter into sexual relationships would be paternalistic and intrusive.

LACK OF HARM TO PATIENTS

Many people believe that patients are no more likely to be harmed in sexual relationships with their physicians than they are in other sexual relationships. In the United States short-term relationships and divorces are common. Anecdotally, many people know of happy marriages between physicians and former patients. In this view, even if some sexual relationships with physicians harm patients, there is no reason to prohibit all such relationships.

LACK OF SOCIAL OPPORTUNITIES FOR PHYSICIANS

In small towns and rural areas a physician might care for a large proportion of the community. Social opportunities for physicians would be very limited if romantic and sexual relationships with patients were barred.

OBJECTIONS TO SEXUAL RELATIONSHIPS WITH CURRENT PATIENTS

Professional codes of ethics consider sexual relationships with current patients unethical. The American Medical Association (AMA) recently declared, "Sexual conduct or a romantic relationship with a patient concurrent with the physician–patient relationship is unethical (2)." Patients might feel "angry, abandoned, humiliated, mistreated, or exploited by their physicians. Victims have been reported to experience guilt, severe mistrust of their own judgment, and mistrust of both men and physicians (2)." There are several reasons for such role-specific restrictions on physicians (Table 26-1).

PHYSICIANS SHOULD NOT TAKE ADVANTAGE OF THE DOCTOR–PATIENT RELATIONSHIP

It might be difficult for patients to make truly autonomous decisions on sexual relationships with physicians. The physician–patient relationship arises from the patient's illness, which can cause patients to be vulnerable and dependent (4). Patients usually place great weight on their physicians' advice and judgment and naturally develop feelings of trust, gratitude, and admiration toward physicians. Unconsciously, the patient might mistake such feelings for romantic or sexual attraction. Patients as well as physicians might not appreciate how such positive feelings result from the doctor's role as well as the doctor's personal attributes. Although such transference has been most clearly described in patients undergoing psychotherapy, similar feelings might occur in all physicians–patient relationships. Physicians might also misinterpret their own feelings of caring and concern for patients, which are a natural part of the doctor–patient relationship, as romantic or sexual attraction.

In the course of a professional relationship, patients make intimate revelations to physicians, as in the following case.

CASE 26.1 Current patient receiving active therapy.

A 45-year-old male physician is treating a 32-year-old woman for depression and peptic ulcer disease. The woman reveals that she was sexually abused as a child. The physician, who is going through a divorce, finds her attractive and considers initiating a romantic and sexual relationship with her.

TABLE 26-1

Objections to Sexual Relationships with Current Patients

Physicians should not take advantage of the doctor–patient relationship.

Physicians have power over patients.

Trust in the profession will be undermined.

Some patients are particularly vulnerable.

In Case 26.1 a depressed patient discloses private information, which she might not have told anyone else. In their professional role, physicians are privy to intimate personal information. During the medical history physicians may take a detailed sexual history. Patients may reveal their innermost fantasies and fears. Patients undress for examinations and allow physicians to touch them and even invade their bodies during medical or surgical procedures. Such intimacy within the doctor–patient relationship is one-sided. Physicians do not ordinarily reveal their personal feelings, thoughts, or bodies to patients. Thus, physicians know much more personal information about patients than patients know about them. Physicians might betray the patient's trust if they take advantage of such intimate information, either consciously or unconsciously, in pursuing sexual relationships with patients.

PHYSICIANS HAVE POWER OVER PATIENTS

Physicians have power over patients that they can use to their advantage in sexual relationships. Inequalities in power might make it more difficult for patients to decline sexual relationships with them than with other people. In Case 26.1 the very framing of the issues implies unequal power: The physician considers initiating a sexual liaison, as if it were inconceivable that the patient would refuse. Because physicians order tests and treatments and schedule appointments, they control patients' access to medical care. There might be an implied or inferred threat that if the patient does not agree to sexual contact, the doctor–patient relationship will be terminated (5). Physicians might also provide false reassurance to patients that an effective therapeutic relationship can continue even if a sexual liaison is initiated (5). In egregious cases the physician might portray a sexual liaison as part of medical therapy.

TRUST IN THE PROFESSION WILL BE UNDERMINED

If the profession were to condone sexual relationships with patients, the public might begin to believe that physicians are motivated by self-interest and are willing to take advantage of patients. Patients might be reluctant to visit physicians or discuss intimate matters. Patients with psychiatric or gynecological problems might be particularly deterred from seeking care.

SOME PATIENTS ARE PARTICULARLY VULNERABLE

Some patients might be especially harmed in sexual relationships with physicians. In Case 26.1 the patient's depression might compromise her ability to consent freely to a sexual relationship. Furthermore, patients who have suffered incest or rape might find it difficult to refuse sexual relationships with authority figures and might feel particularly betrayed if the current relationship repeats previous traumatic experiences. Such persons might not even be aware that they are repeating a previous pattern of behavior.

THE PATIENT'S MEDICAL CARE MIGHT BE COMPROMISED

When physicians provide care to a spouse, they might not be thorough in taking a history, conducting an examination, or ordering diagnostic tests (6). Similarly, providing medical care to a sexual partner might lead to suboptimal care. When physicians are having a sexual relationship with patients, their clinical judgment is likely to be compromised (7). They might not be thorough in taking a history, conducting an examination, considering certain diagnoses, or ordering diagnostic tests.

LEGAL ISSUES

Sexual relationships between physicians and current patients might lead to criminal charges or to disciplinary action by licensing boards (8–10). Physicians might also face civil suits for malpractice. Malpractice insurers might exclude coverage for civil claims relating to sexual misconduct, asserting that such behavior is not part of providing medical care.

COMPARISONS WITH OTHER PROFESSIONS

In other professions sexual relationships with clients are also condemned. Churches are strongly criticized for covering up sexual relationships between clergy and parishioners and transferring offending priests or ministers without appropriate disciplinary action. Similarly, lawyers have been criticized for sexual relationships with clients, particularly clients in divorce cases. As in medicine, the charge is that these professionals abuse their trust and power in sexual relationships with clients.

SEXUAL RELATIONSHIPS WITH FORMER PATIENTS

Although sexual relationships with current patients are generally considered inappropriate, there is less agreement about relationships with previous patients. In the previously cited survey, although 94% of physicians considered it unethical to have sexual relationships with current patients, only 36% of physicians considered it unethical to have sexual relationships with former patients (1).

CASE 26.2 Former patient, with no ongoing relationship.

A female emergency physician treats a 28-year-old man who requires a tetanus shot for a foot injury. Several years later they meet again as single parents whose children are in the same school. They discover that they share many interests. The physician wonders if a romantic relationship would be unacceptable because of their previous professional relationship.

In Case 26.2 it is unlikely that the former patient feels dependent on the physician. Furthermore, the patient revealed little personal information during the doctor–patient relationship and is not particularly vulnerable on that basis. A relationship between equals seems as possible for them as for any other couple.

Feelings of dependency, however, might persist after care is terminated, as in the following case.

CASE 26.3 Recent surgical patient.

A male surgeon performs an emergency laparotomy on a woman with appendicitis. During postoperative visits he finds himself spending much more time with her than he usually does with patients. She is appreciative of his attention and solicitous about his long hours and fatigue. A month after her final postoperative visit, he invites her to dinner.

In Case 26.3 the patient might have strong feelings of gratitude and dependency soon after emergency surgery. Unlike Case 26.2, it might be more difficult for the patient to make an independent judgment about a relationship or to decline invitations from the surgeon, compared with other men she knows.

About former patients, the AMA states, "Sexual or romantic relationships with former patients are also unethical if the physician uses or exploits trust, knowledge, emotions, or influence derived from the previous professional relationship (2)." Thus, it is important to identify situations in which dependency in doctor–patient relationship continues (11). Several factors should be considered.

TERMINATION OF MEDICAL CARE

Termination of care and absence of contact should be complete, including cessation of office visits, telephone consultations, prescriptions, and reminder postcards about appointments or screening tests. In addition, a new physician should be identified so that the patient no longer regards the partner as his or her physician. The purpose of terminating care should not be the initiation of a sexual relationship.

NATURE OF THE DOCTOR–PATIENT RELATIONSHIP

Some types of medical care are so intimate that the doctor–patient relationship might never be completely ended. Counseling and therapy might evoke powerful feelings of transference that last for years. Patients might have intense feelings of dependency and gratitude toward physicians years after therapy has been terminated. The American Psychiatric Association considers any sexual contact with a former psychiatric patient as unethical. Some patients might be particularly vulnerable because of past victimization (12). In specialties such as surgery or gynecology, which involve unique and intimate physical contact, the patient might still regard the physician as being in that role years later. In contrast, in Case 26.2 tetanus immunization is so routine that any feelings of dependency in the patient are likely to be transient and weak. In that situation the patient's dependence on the physician might be similar to dependence on a librarian.

TIME SINCE LAST MEDICAL CARE

In Case 26.3, during the immediate postoperative period the patient's feelings of vulnerability and dependency undoubtedly continue. Amorous advances by the physician might take advantage of these feelings in the patient. The passage of time helps extinguish feelings of dependency toward physicians and reduces the risk that physicians will abuse their power in initiating sexual relationships with patients (5). To prevent abuse, the Ontario College of Physicians and Surgeons Task Force recommends a waiting period of 2 years since the last episode of patient care, with no contact in the interim (13). The crucial issue, however, is not simply the amount of time but rather the lack of a continuous relationship and the "potential for misuse of emotions derived from the former professional relationship (2)."

CIRCUMSTANCES OF RENEWAL OF CONTACT

If the doctor and former patient renew their acquaintance in a medical context, the patient might resume his or her previous role as dependent patient. On the other hand, the physician and former patient might meet again in a nonmedical context, as in Case 26.2. Being reacquainted in a nonmedical setting makes it more likely that the relationship is not colored by the previous doctor–patient relationship.

SUGGESTIONS

Physicians who are considering sexual relationships with current or former patients might consider the following suggestions.

RECOGNIZE EARLY SIGNS OF ROMANTIC INTEREST

Rarely are sexual or romantic feelings so overwhelming that the physician is swept away by uncontrollable passion. Physicians should be alert to early signs of romantic feelings for a patient. For example, they might look forward to the next visit or pay particular attention to their appearance on the day of the patient's visit. Sexual misconduct often begins with seemingly minor violations of the boundaries of the doctor–patient relationship, such as talking about the physician's problems rather than the patient's or scheduling appointments outside office hours (7). Recognizing these early symptoms gives physicians time to act thoughtfully and to consider the potential problems (9).

SEEK ADVICE

It is hard to think critically about romantic or sexual interests. The AMA recommends that "it would be advisable for a physician to seek consultation with a colleague before initiating a relationship with a former patient (2)." Confidential advice can provide an honest appraisal of the potential harm to the patient, the physician, and the medical profession. Such counsel might be a safeguard for physicians who might otherwise act impulsively. Although discussing such an intimate decision with other people might seem intrusive, such sexual relationships are not completely private if they harm patients or undermine public trust in the medical profession.

RESPONDING TO ADVANCES BY PATIENTS

In some cases the patient, not the physician, takes the initiative in pursuing a romantic or sexual liaison. However, physicians might still be considered responsible because they are in a better position than patients to recognize the potential harms of such relationships. In medical decisions physicians do not simply accede to a patient's requests or demands. Physicians have an ethical duty to act in patients' best interests, even if it clashes with their own self-interest.

In summary, patients naturally feel trust, dependency, and gratitude toward their physicians. Sexual relationships with current patients exploit such feelings and are unethical. Sexual relationships with former patients are also unethical to the extent that the physician takes advantage of emotions and influence deriving from the doctor–patient relationship.

REFERENCES

1. Gartrell NG, Milliken N, Goodson WH, et al. Physician-patient sexual contact: prevalence and problems. *West J Med* 1992;157:139–143.
2. Council on Ethical and Judicial Affairs of the American Medical Association. Sexual misconduct and the practice of medicine. *JAMA* 1991;266:2741–2745.
3. Appelbaum PS, Jorgenson LM, Sutherland PK. Sexual contact between physicians and patients. *Arch Intern Med* 1994;154:2561–2565.
4. Pellegrino ED, Thomasma DG. *For the patient's good: the restoration of beneficence in health care.* New York: Oxford University Press, 1988.
5. Appelbaum PS, Jorgenson L. Psychotherapist-patient sexual contact after termination of treatment: an analysis and proposal. *Am J Psychiatry* 1991;148:1466–1473.
6. LaPuma J, Priest ER. Is there a doctor in the house? An analysis of the practice of physicians' treating their own families. *JAMA* 1992;267:1810–1812.
7. Gabbard GO, Nadelson C. Professional boundaries in the physician-patient relationship. *JAMA* 1995;273:1445–1449
8. Johnson SH. Judicial review of disciplinary action for sexual misconduct in the practice of medicine. *JAMA* 1993;270:1596–1600.
9. Gutheil TG, Gabbard GO. Misuses and misunderstandings of boundary theory in clinical and regulatory settings. *Am J Psychiatry* 1998;155(3):409–414.
10. Dehlendorf CE, Wolfe SM. Physicians disciplined for sex-related offenses. *JAMA* 1998;279(23):1883–1888.
11. Malmquist CP, Notman MT. Psychiatrist-patient boundary issues following treatment termination. *Am J Psychiatry* 2001;158(7):1010–1018.
12. Schoener G. Psychotherapist–patient sexual contact after termination of treatment [Letter]. *Am J Psychiatry* 1992;149:981.
13. An Independent Task Force Commissioned by the College of Physicians and Surgeons of Ontario. The Preliminary Report of the Task Force on Sexual Abuse of Patients; 1991 May 27.

ANNOTATED BIBLIOGRAPHY

1. Council on Ethical and Judicial Affairs of the American Medical Association. Sexual misconduct and the practice of medicine. *JAMA* 1991;266:2741–2745.
   Thoughtful discussion of the topic, proposing that all sexual contact during the physician–patient relationship is unethical.
2. Gabbard GO, Nadelson C. Professional boundaries in the physician-patient relationship. *JAMA* 1995;273:1445–1449.
   Discusses how sexual misconduct with patients usually begins with apparently minor violations of the therapeutic relationship.

CHAPTER 27

Secret Information about Patients

Physicians might receive information about a patient from family members or friends who ask that their role be kept secret (1). Doctors find such unsolicited information disconcerting. Telling the patient the secret might pass on inaccurate or unhelpful information, while keeping the secret might involve the physician in deception. This chapter discusses the ethical issues posed by such secret information and how physicians can respond.

TYPES OF SECRETS

Most commonly, a family member tells the doctor about the patient's deleterious personal habits, such as alcohol use or smoking (1). The family member often tells a member of the physician's staff rather than the physician directly. The informer hopes that the physician will make the patient stop these unhealthy behaviors. Another type of secret involves mental or physical incapacity. The family member might tell the physician that the patient is demented, depressed, or psychotic. Similarly, the family might be concerned that an elderly patient can no longer drive safely or live independently. The confider also might seek to draw the physician into family disputes over money, marital problems, or the lifestyles of grown children. Finally, family members might alert the physician to hidden physical symptoms, such as chest pain, that the patient might choose not to discuss.

PROBLEMS WITH SUCH INFORMATION

Secret information can be problematic in many ways. The information might be inaccurate. The informer might have ulterior motives, such as gaining an advantage in a family dispute. Secrets are disrespectful to the patient because they involve deception rather than open discussions. Finally, such secret disclosures trap the physician in a bind because both disclosing and keeping the secret are objectionable.

APPROACHES TO SECRETS

When presented with such a secret, the physician has several options, some of which involve deception or undermine patient trust.

REVEAL THE SECRET TO THE PATIENT

There are several ethical objections to keeping such a secret. Patients might consider it a violation of trust if physicians talk to other people about them behind their backs (2). Patients might question the physician's allegiance. It is also deceptive for physicians to base their recommendations and plans on secret information from third parties rather than on the history obtained from the patient. Chapter 6 discusses why deception is ethically problematic for physicians.

Keeping secrets from patients is also impractical. Like all forms of deception, it might require additional, increasingly elaborate deception. Patients might ask why the physician is posing a particular question or ordering a particular test. In that case physicians will have to either reveal the secret information or deceive the patient.

DO NOT DISCLOSE TO THE PATIENT

One physician who was philosophically opposed to keeping such secrets found that in about one half of cases he did not tell the patient (1). First, there may be no point in doing so because the information is obvious or trivial. For example, a family member's report that the patient was a heavy smoker provides no new information if the patient smells of cigarettes. Second, the physician does not disclose the information because it is not relevant to the patient's medical care. For example, few physicians want to get involved in a parent's concerns about a patient's marriage. Third, disclosure might do more harm than good in the short run. Revealing the mother's objections to the patient's marriage might well precipitate or intensify a family argument. Fourth, the physician might intend to tell the patient but find no opportunity to bring it up naturally in the conversation. Physicians must appreciate that the right moment to disclose the secret may never occur.

In some cases the physician promised to keep the secret. The physician was then caught between conflicting obligations to be forthright with patients and to keep promises. Physicians can avoid this dilemma and maintain their primary obligation to the patient by rejecting the informer's initial request to keep the information secret. Family members often preface their revelations with phrases such as, "I don't want my husband to know I told you, but. . . ." It would be prudent for physicians to interrupt at this point, before the information is revealed, and explain their policy of disclosing such information and its source to patients.

ASK INFORMERS TO DISCLOSE THEIR ROLE

Ethically, the best approach is for the physician to convince the informer to tell the patient about the information presented to the physician or to allow the physician to disclose the source of the information. If this is done, the physician can discuss the issue freely with the patient.

In summary, physicians face dilemmas when family members or friends give information about patients that they ask to be kept secret. Acquiescence with such secrets, even if well intentioned, might undermine the patient's trust. Telling the family member or friend that the information needs to be shared with the patient is the most effective way to prevent such an outcome.

REFERENCES

1. Burnham JF. Secrets about patients. *N Engl J Med* 1991;324:1130–1133.
2. Bok S. *Secrets*. New York: Pantheon Books, 1982.

ANNOTATED BIBLIOGRAPHY

1. Burnham JF. Secrets about patients. *N Engl J Med* 1991;324:1130–1133.
   Thoughtful discussion of the topic based on the author's clinical experience.

CHAPTER 28

Clinical Research

Clinical research is essential for medical progress. Physicians can be involved in research in various roles, from referring patients to a clinical study to serving as an investigator. In these roles physicians need to understand the ethical issues raised by each stage of clinical research.

ETHICAL ISSUES AT VARIOUS STAGES OF RESEARCH

When patients consider entering a research project, their personal physicians should make a recommendation about participation. Even if an institutional review board (IRB) or a funding agency has approved the project, the treating physician needs to assess independently whether the research study is appropriate for that particular patient. Moreover, when studies target persons with a particular medical condition, many IRBs do not allow researchers to contact participants directly without the treating physician's permission. Among the relevant considerations are the importance of the research question, the rigor of the study design, the selection of participants, and the risks and benefits of the study. Because of the social utility of clinical research, physicians generally should encourage their patients to participate in well-designed studies, but treating physicians also need to protect their patients' interests.

Traditionally, clinical research has been regarded as risky and potential participants were considered guinea pigs who might be subjected to dangerous interventions that would confer little or no benefit and who therefore needed to be protected. Increasingly, however, clinical research is regarded as beneficial rather than risky because it provides access to potentially life-saving new therapies in such conditions as cancer, human immunodeficiency virus (HIV) infection, and organ transplantation. Patients who are eager to obtain promising new drugs for fatal conditions want increased access to clinical research, not greater protection (1).

Clinical research should be distinguished from innovative clinical practice, in which a physician goes beyond the usual standards of practice to try to benefit a particular patient. For example, a surgeon might modify a technique or an internist might use a drug for an indication not approved by the Food and Drug Administration (FDA).

DESIGN OF THE RESEARCH PROTOCOL

According to the ethical guideline of beneficence, research protocols should aim to provide valid and generalizable knowledge and the research's prospective benefits should be proportional to the risks to participants. Thus, if the research question has already been settled or is trivial, or if the design of the study is so weak that valid conclusions are impossible, even slight risk to participants cannot be justified.

Randomized Controlled Trials

Although randomized controlled trials are the most rigorous design for evaluating interventions, they might present special ethical concerns because treatment is determined by chance. The ethical basis for assigning treatment by randomization is the judgment that both arms of the protocol are in clinical equipoise. Current evidence does not prove that either arm is superior. Some experts believe that one arm offers more effective treatment, but others believe the opposite (2). Furthermore, individual patients and their physicians must find randomization acceptable. If physicians believe strongly that one arm of the trial is superior for a particular patient and can provide treatment offered in that arm outside the study, they cannot in good faith recommend that patients enter the trial. Similarly, a particular patient might not consider the alternatives equivalent, as when medical and surgical interventions are compared.

SELECTION OF PARTICIPANTS IN RESEARCH

CASE 28.1 Research on patients with dementia.

A new urinary catheter has been devised. A clinical trial is proposed to evaluate whether the new catheter is clinically more effective than the conventional catheter. Nursing home residents with Alzheimer disease and incontinence will be recruited as participants because enrollment and follow-up will be easier than in ambulatory patients.

Participants in research assume risks in order to gain potential benefits for themselves and for society as a whole. The potential benefits and harms of participation in research should be distributed equitably among groups eligible for the study. Vulnerable, disadvantaged, or minority groups should be neither overrepresented in dangerous studies nor underrepresented in trials of promising new therapies.

Patients Who Lack Decision-making Capacity

As in Case 28.1, patients who lack decision-making capacity cannot give informed consent to research studies, yet research is essential to improve therapies for their conditions. It seems reasonable to allow surrogates to consent to research that presents minimal risks and offers the prospect of direct therapeutic benefits to participants (3). One study cautions, however, that surrogate decisions regarding research for mentally incapacitated persons often are not based on the patients' wishes or best interests (4). In that study 31% of surrogates who believed that the patient would refuse to participate nonetheless gave consent, apparently contradicting the patient's preferences. Furthermore, 20% of surrogates who would not themselves agree to the study nevertheless allowed the patient to participate in the research, perhaps acting in a manner contrary to what they consider the patient's best interests.

Patients Whose Consent Might Not Be Free

Potential participants in research might be vulnerable because their consent might be constrained. Participants might depend on physician-researchers for ongoing medical care, as in nursing homes, Veterans Affairs hospitals, or public hospitals and clinics. As in Case 28.1, such dependent populations are sometimes recruited as research participants because access for recruitment is easier and follow-up more complete than with more autonomous individuals. However, such patients might not feel free to refuse to participate. They or their surrogates might fear that their physicians will be upset if they do not enroll in research studies, in which case they could not readily transfer their care to another physician or institution.

Fairness requires that vulnerable populations not be used as a source of research participants primarily for the convenience of investigators, if other populations would also be suitable participants for the study. The use of vulnerable participants for research is more justifiable if the research addresses the condition that makes the participants vulnerable, if it offers the prospect of direct therapeutic benefit, or if advocates for the vulnerable population have approved the project.

INFORMED CONSENT

The guideline of respect for persons and their autonomy requires that adult participants give informed consent to participate in research. Participants in research should be regarded not as sources of data but as individuals whose welfare and rights must be respected. The primary physician plays an important ethical and clinical role in helping the patient make an informed decision, as in the following case.

CASE 28.2 Invasive hemodynamic monitoring.

A 70-year-old woman develops congestive heart failure after a myocardial infarction. She is eligible to participate in a study of the dose–response properties of a new angiotensin-coverting enzyme inhibitor in patients with congestive heart failure. The study involves Swan–Ganz catheterization and hemodynamic monitoring in the coronary care unit when the drug is started and again 6 months later. The patient has always been reluctant to be hospitalized and to undergo invasive cardiac procedures.

In this case participation in the study offers little direct benefit to the patient. Numerous effective standard therapies exist. Although patients generally should be encouraged to enter well-designed clinical studies for altruistic motives, this patient might well react adversely to a prolonged stay in intensive care or to invasive procedures. The primary physician should raise these concerns with the patient and try to ensure that the patient is informed about the research study. Table 28-1 lists pertinent issues that the prospective subject needs to understand (5).

The Nature of the Research Project

The prospective subject should be told explicitly that research is being conducted, what its purpose is, and how the participants are being recruited. Any financial interest of the investigators in the drug or device being studied needs to be disclosed (6).

The Procedures of the Study

Participants need to know what they will be asked to do in the research project. On a practical level, they should be told how much time will be required and how often. That blood will be drawn might mean more to participants than the names of the tests that will be conducted. Procedures that are not standard care should be identified as such. Alternative procedures or treatments that might be available outside the study should be discussed. If the study involves blinding or randomization, these concepts should be explained in terms that the patient can understand.

The Potential Harms and Benefits of the Study

Medical, psychosocial, and economic harms and benefits should be described in lay terms. These include physical harm from complications of tests or treatments, as well as psychosocial harm such as loss of privacy and inconvenience.

Economic risks might also be important. Participants should appreciate that insurance companies may deny reimbursement for procedures that are not standard clinical care. In Case 28.2, for example, the patient needs to understand that she might need to pay for the costs of hemodynamic monitoring in the cardiac care unit, which would not ordinarily be carried out.

Assurances That Participation in the Research Is Voluntary

Participants must be told that declining to participate in the study will not compromise their medical care and that they may withdraw from the project at any time.

TABLE 28-1

Informed Consent in Research Projects

The nature of the research project.
The procedures of the study.
The potential harms and benefits of the study.
Assurances that participation in the research is voluntary.
Misconceptions about research.

Misconceptions About Research

A common misconception is that research will provide direct therapeutic benefits to the participants. This has been termed the *therapeutic misconception* (7,8). Most promising new interventions, despite encouraging preliminary results, fail to show significant advantages over standard therapy. Patients might downplay the risks and be unrealistically optimistic about the benefits.

The primary physician plays a crucial role in helping the patient make an informed decision. After talking with an enthusiastic clinical investigator, patients might have an unrealistic impression of the study. The primary physician can elicit and correct any misunderstandings and encourage the patient to ask questions. Finally, the primary doctor should make a recommendation on the basis of the patient's values. In Case 28.2, given the patient's reluctance about invasive procedures, the physician should recommend against participating in the protocol.

PROTECTION OF CONFIDENTIALITY

Confidentiality is important for its own sake (*see* Chapter 5) and also promotes participation in research. For example, concerns about breaches of confidentiality might deter potential participants from participating in research regarding HIV infection, mental illness, or genetics. Investigators need to take appropriate steps to protect the confidentiality of research data. During the informed consent process, potential participants need to be told about possible risks to confidentiality and the steps that will be taken to avoid them.

In some studies identification of child abuse, elder abuse, or contagious diseases can be anticipated. In clinical practice such cases must be reported to appropriate officials. Investigators need to determine in advance whether cases identified during the research project will be reported and, if so, inform patients during the informed consent process.

REVIEW BY AN INSTITUTIONAL REVIEW BOARD

Approval from an IRB is required for most federally funded research, for research that will be submitted to the FDA to gain approval for new therapies, and for all researchers at many universities. The function of IRB review is to protect research participants. The best-intentioned researchers, in their eagerness to conduct important research, might not pay sufficient attention to potential ethical problems.

COMPETING AND CONFLICTING INTERESTS

The researchers and the treating physicians might have competing and conflicting interests because the goal of carrying out important and valid research might conflict with the goal of acting in the best interests of the individual patient.

COMPETING AND CONFLICTING INTERESTS FOR TREATING PHYSICIANS

Finder's Fees for Research Participants

In some situations physicians might receive a finder's fee for referring patients to a research project.

CASE 28.3 Finder's fees.

To encourage enrollment in a clinical trial of a new antibiotic, physicians are offered $350 for referring patients who subsequently enroll in the study. The referring physician needs to make a phone call to the coordinating research nurse, who will explain the study to the patient.

Enrollment is often the rate-limiting step in clinical trials, and finder's fees facilitate their completion. However, finder's fees also give the appearance that physicians refer patients to clinical trials for their own interest rather than the patient's (9). Critics of finder's fees also point out that the analogous situation of kickbacks for referring patients to another physician for clinical care is considered unethical. Furthermore, the physician's reward might seem excessive for the services rendered.

Dual Roles for Clinician-Investigators

The investigator might also be an eligible research subject's primary physician. Such patients might fear that their future care will be jeopardized if they decline to participate in research. Furthermore, what is best for a particular patient's medical care might not be what is best for the research project. In some situations it might be better for the patient to drop out of the study and receive individualized care that differs from the research protocol. As an investigator, however, the physician wants study participants to continue to the end of the trial. If many participants drop out, the study's capacity to answer the research question will be compromised.

Such role conflicts should be explained to participants in advance. Whenever possible, the patient should have the opportunity to receive care from a personal physician who is not associated with the study. Because the welfare of the patient should be paramount, the role of personal physician should take priority over the role of clinical researcher.

COMPETING AND CONFLICTING INTERESTS FOR RESEARCHERS

Physician-researchers might have competing or conflicting interests that might compromise their research's integrity. These other interests might impair researchers' objectivity and undermine public trust in research (10). Even the most scrupulous and well-intentioned investigators might subconsciously introduce bias into the research design, data collection, or analysis (10,11).

Academic Rewards

Research publications lead to academic prestige, grants, and promotions.

Research Funded by Drug Manufacturers

Clinical investigators are increasingly turning to drug companies for funding (12). The company manufacturing the drug has an interest in having the drug proved effective. Thus, the bias against publishing negative studies might be particularly strong in studies sponsored by drug companies (13). Another problem is that reimbursement from the drug company to investigators might greatly exceed the research's actual costs. Such excess reimbursement might offer researchers perverse incentives both to suggest experimental therapy for a patient when conventional therapy is in the patient's best interests and to interpret findings in the most favorable light (14).

Financial Interest in the Drug Manufacturer

Investigators might hold stock or stock options in the company making the drug under study, thus making their compensation affected by the study's results. Clinical researchers who hold options might reap huge financial rewards if the treatment were shown to be effective, in addition to any compensation for time and effort. However, if the drug proves ineffective, investigators face an inevitable conflict of interest: Fostering scientific progress will unavoidably harm their personal financial interests.

RESPONDING TO COMPETING AND CONFLICTING INTERESTS

Treating physicians must respond to competing and conflicting interests regarding research they conduct or refer patients to. This chapter will not discuss how researchers should address conflicts of interest in their role (5,15).

Disclose Competing and Conflicting Interests

Treating physicians need to disclose to patients if they are also investigators in any research projects that they discuss with the patient or to which they refer the patient. In a landmark court case a patient sued a physician-researcher who had patented a cell line derived from the patient's cells without his knowledge or permission (6). The patient alleged that the physician-researcher had failed to disclose his personal financial stake in the research and had recommended several procedures without disclosing that they were for research, not clinical care. The California Supreme Court declared that physicians need to "disclose personal interests unrelated to the patient's health, whether research or economic, that may affect the physician's professional judgment (6)." This ruling implies that patients must be told if referring physicians receive a finder's fee for referring patients to a study.

Manage Competing or Conflicting Interests

Although disclosure is necessary to protect patients, in some situations treating physicians need to go further and manage or eliminate conflicts of interest. Problems with finder's fees can be eliminated if the amount of the fee is commensurate with the services performed. If a physician is simply making a phone call to refer the patient, $350, as in Case 28.3, seems excessive.

If the treating physician is also an investigator in a clinical trial the patient enrolls in, whenever possible the patient should be offered the opportunity to receive care from a personal physician who is not associated with the study. Because the patient's welfare should be paramount, the personal physician's role should take priority over the clinical researcher's role.

Ban Certain Situations That Give Rise to Conflicts of Interest

Clinical investigators should avoid direct financial stakes in the therapies under evaluation. As one writer has noted, "It is difficult enough for the most conscientious researchers to be totally unbiased about their own work, but when an investigator has an economic interest in the outcome of the work, objectivity is even more difficult (10)." Many productive investigators support such prohibitions (16,17).

In conclusion, rigorous clinical research is essential to evaluate promising new therapies. Physicians should encourage patients to participate in appropriate clinical research. Investigators should ensure that the potential benefits of research are proportionate to the risks and that participants give informed consent. Conflicts of interest, which might impair objectivity and erode public trust in research, should be avoided.

REFERENCES

1. Levine C, Dubler NN, Levine RJ. Building a new consensus: ethical principles and policies for clinical research on HIV/AIDS. *IRB* 1991;13:1–17.
2. Freedman B. Equipoise and the ethics of clinical research. *N Engl J Med* 1987;317:141–145.
3. National Bioethics Advisory Commission. *Research involving persons with mental disorders that may affect decision making capacity.* Rockville, MD: National Bioethics Advisory Commission, 1998.
4. Warren JW, Sobal J, Denney JH, et al. Informed consent by proxy: an issue in research with elderly patients. *N Engl J Med* 1986;315:1125–1128.
5. Lo B. Addressing ethical issues. In: Hulley S, Cummings SB, Browner WS, Grady D, Hearst N, Newman TB, eds. *Designing clinical research*, 2nd ed. Philadelphia: Lippincott Williams & Wilkins, 2001:215–230.
6. Moore v. Regents of University of California. 51 Cal.3d 120; Cal. Rptr. 146, 793 P.2d 479 (1990).
7. Lidz CW, Appelbaum PS. The therapeutic misconception: problems and solutions. *Med Care* 2002;40(9 Suppl): V55–V63.
8. Joffe S, Cook EF, Cleary PD, et al. Quality of informed consent in cancer clinical trials: a cross-sectional survey. *Lancet* 2001;358(9295):1772–1777.
9. Lind S. Finder's fees for research subjects. *N Engl J Med* 1990;323(3):192–194.
10. Relman AS. Economic incentives in clinical investigation. *N Engl J Med* 1989;320:933–934.
11. Hillman AL, Eisenberg JM, Pauly MV, et al. Avoiding bias in the conduct and reporting of cost-effectiveness research sponsored by pharmaceutical companies. *N Engl J Med* 1991;324:1362–1365.
12. American Federation for Clinical Research guidelines for avoiding conflict of interest. *Clin Res* 1990;38:239–240.
13. Davidson DA. Source of funding and outcome of clinical trials. *J Gen Intern Med* 1986;1:155–158.
14. Shimm DS, Spece RG. Industry reimbursement for entering patients into clinical trials: ethical issues. *Ann Intern Med* 1991;115:148–151.
15. Lo B, Wolf LE, Berkeley A. Conflict-of-interest policies for investigators in clinical trials. *N Engl J Med* 2000; 343:1616–1620.
16. Healy B, Campeau L, Gray R, et al. Conflict-of-interest guidelines for a multicenter clinical trial of treatment after coronary-artery bypass-graft surgery. *N Engl J Med* 1989;320(14):949–951.
17. Topol EJ, Armstrong P, Van de Werf F, et al. Confronting the issues of patient safety and investigator conflict of interest in an international trial of myocardial reperfusion. *J Am Coll Cardiol* 1992;19:1123–1128.

ANNOTATED BIBLIOGRAPHY

1. Levine RJ. *Ethics and regulation of clinical research.* Baltimore, MD: Urban & Schwarzenberg, 1986.
   Comprehensive and thoughtful book on all aspects of designing and conducting clinical research.
2. National Bioethics Advisory Commission. *Research involving persons with mental disorders that may affect decisionmaking capacity.* Rockville, MD: National Bioethics Advisory Commission, 1998.
   Analyzes ethical dilemmas that occur when research participants lack the capacity to make informed decisions.
3. Federman DD, Hanna KE, Rodriguez LL, eds. *Responsible research: a systems approach to protecting research participants.* Washington: National Academies Press, 2003.

Comprehensive report from the Institute of Medicine on the oversight of research with human participants, discussing how to improve the IRB system.

4. Field MJ, Behrman RE, eds. *The ethical conduct of clinical research involving children.* Washington: National Academies Press, 2004.

Report from the Institute of Medicine on the special ethical issues concerning research with children.

5. Lidz CW, Appelbaum PS. The therapeutic misconception: problems and solutions. *Med Care* 2002;40(9 Suppl): V55–V63.

Explains that research subjects commonly believe that research is designed to provide them therapeutic benefits, when in fact the goal of research is to advance scientific knowledge.

Conflicts of Interest

CHAPTER 29

Overview of Conflicts of Interest

In *The Doctor's Dilemma,* George Bernard Shaw questioned whether people can be "impartial where they have a strong pecuniary interest on one side (1)." He wrote, "Nobody supposes that doctors are less virtuous than judges; but a judge whose salary and reputation depended on whether the verdict was for plaintiff or defendant, prosecutor or prisoner, should be as little trusted as a general in the pay of the enemy. To offer me a doctor as my judge, and then weight his decision with a bribe of a large sum of money . . . is to go wildly beyond . . . [what] human nature will bear (1)." Shaw's words have particular relevance to contemporary U.S. medicine because of increasing concerns over conflicts of interest.

A conflict of interest exists when a person entrusted with the interests of a client, dependent, or the public violates that trust. Rather than acting in the patient's best interests, physicians might promote their own self-interest or the interests of a third party, such as a hospital, physician group, or insurance plan. Some conflicts of interest are financial, such as those resulting from reimbursement incentives or personal investments in medical facilities. Other conflicts of interest involve personal or professional roles, as when physicians respond to mistakes, deal with impaired colleagues, or need to learn invasive procedures.

Conflicts of interest might be ethically problematic for physicians for several reasons. First, patients might suffer physical harm. Second, even though the patient suffers no clinical harm, the integrity of medical judgment might be compromised. Third, conflicts of interest undercut patients' trust that physicians are acting on their behalf.

Chapters 30 to 36 analyze specific conflicts of interest. This chapter discusses how to define conflicts of interest, who should decide what constitutes an unacceptable conflict of interest, and how physicians can manage conflicts of interest.

CONFLICTS OF INTEREST IN NONMEDICAL SITUATIONS

Conflicts of interest occur in all professions and in public service (2). For example, a trustee might use the trust fund of an elderly person or child for his own profit. A public official might accept expensive gifts or trips from a company whose business he or she oversees.

Consider a judge who presides over a case involving a relative or a former law partner or in which the judge has a personal financial stake in the outcome (3). In such a situation the judge's decisions might favor the relative, the former partner, or self-interest. Even if the outcome of the legal proceedings is fair, the process by which the decision was reached might be biased. For instance, the judge might take into account inappropriate factors or make rulings about motions and objections that no impartial decision-maker would make. These procedural errors would be disturbing even if the outcome seemed fair. Public trust in the judicial system might be undermined. Simply the appearance of a conflict of interest might be unacceptable.

The judge might honestly believe that he or she will be impartial and might even consciously try to compensate for having ties to a litigant. Nonetheless, the opposing party and the public might still suspect that another judge would have decided the case differently. People naturally tend to believe that they are acting with integrity, even when this might not be the case. Thus, even if the individual judge believes that he or she can be impartial, that judge might be required to withdraw from the case. Society decides when judges or officials must recuse themselves, through legislation, regulation, and case law (3). There is no implication that the judge is immoral or unprofessional. Instead, the idea is that it would be untenable to place anyone in such a situation.

HOW ARE CONFLICTS OF INTEREST DEFINED?

People often use the term "conflict of interest" without defining it clearly.

DETRIMENTAL PATIENT OUTCOMES

In medicine, the narrowest definition of conflict of interest is that the patient's outcome is worse because the physician has subordinated the patient's best interests (4,5). The physician might do so either intentionally or subconsciously.

COMPROMISE OF PHYSICIANS' JUDGMENT OR THE DECISION-MAKING PROCESS

More broadly, the physician's judgment or decision-making process might be compromised, even though clinical outcomes are not impaired. Failure to order an indicated test or therapy because of a conflict of interest must be distinguished from an error or incompetence.

POTENTIAL FOR DETRIMENTAL OUTCOMES OR COMPROMISED JUDGMENT

A still broader definition of conflicts of interest includes the *potential* for detrimental outcomes or for compromised judgment without evidence of *actual* harm or compromised judgment (6). For example, personal investments in medical facilities provide physicians financial incentives for ordering more services, even when they are not medically necessary (*see* Chapter 31). In any particular case, however, it might be difficult to show that a physician's decisions are inappropriate or that the patient suffered harm.

PERCEIVED CONFLICTS OF INTEREST

Some situations present only *perceived* conflicts of interest, without actual harm or even significant potential for harm. For example, many physicians believe that accepting small gifts from drug companies, such as pens and writing pads, is harmless (*see* Chapter 33), but the perception of a conflict of interest might be damaging even though the actual or potential harm to patients is small. If the public believes that physicians are serving the interests of drug companies rather than those of their patients, trust in the individual doctor or the profession as a whole might be undermined.

Physicians might be offended because concerns about potential or perceived conflicts of interest seem to impugn their integrity. Doctors need to understand that the public is not singling them out for censure, but simply treating them as human and therefore fallible. The situation is problematic, not the person; it would be untenable to place anyone in such a situation.

COMPETING VERSUS CONFLICTING INTERESTS

The interests of the patient and physician never coincide completely. *Conflicting* interests cannot both be fulfilled. The physician literally cannot advance one interest without setting back the other. *Competing* interests, in contrast, though not congruent with the patient's best interests, can be furthered without harm to the patient. Conversely, the patient's interests can be achieved without gravely setting back the competing interests. For example, time devoted to patient care cannot be spent on continuing medical education, teaching, clinical research, personal hobbies, or family activities. Such competing interests can usually be accommodated.

SITUATIONS THAT ARE NOT CONFLICTS OF INTEREST

The term *conflict of interest* is often used loosely. A conflict of interest, in the senses defined above, needs to be distinguished from conflicts between ethical guidelines, disagreements among health care professionals, or disagreements between patients and physicians.

REIMBURSEMENT INCENTIVES

Medicine is regarded as an altruistic profession because its primary goal is to benefit the patient, not to maximize physicians' income. However, no one expects physicians to work for free or begrudges them a comfortable income. Helping the sick is commendable and difficult work and requires extensive training. This tension between altruism and self-interest is unavoidable in medicine (7). Financial rewards to the doctor should ideally be secondary to fostering patients' well-being.

Any reimbursement system might provide incentives to physicians to act contrary to patients' best interests. Fee-for-service reimbursement provides incentives to increase services and to give services of little or no benefit, thereby raising the cost of health care (*see* Chapter 31). Managed care systems, which use capitation and prospective payment, might provide incentives to decrease health care services and withhold beneficial care (*see* Chapter 32).

The concern about financial incentives is not simply that unscrupulous physicians will deliberately subordinate the patient's interests to their own self-interest or the interests of hospitals or insurance plans (8). Subtle incentives might also exert unconscious influence on physician decisions. When several management options are plausible, "financial incentives may influence even the best, most highly principled doctors to overlook subtle clues that suggest an optimal approach (8)."

MANAGING CONFLICTS OF INTEREST

It is often difficult to draw a clear line between improper conflicts of interest and situations in which the interests of the patient are adequately protected. When conflicting interests are identified, how can sick and vulnerable patients be protected? Physicians should take the following steps (Table 29-1), which are discussed in more detail in subsequent chapters dealing with specific conflicts of interest.

REAFFIRM THAT THE PATIENT'S INTERESTS ARE PARAMOUNT

Individual physicians and the medical profession need to reaffirm their fiduciary responsibility to their patients (9). The doctor's primary responsibility is to foster the well-being of patients, not the doctor's own self-interest or third parties' interests.

To check whether they are acting in the patient's best interest, doctors might ask what they would recommend if they were working under the opposite reimbursement system. Physicians in managed care might ask whether they would recommend the intervention under fee-for-service. Similarly, fee-for-service physicians might ask what they would recommend if they or the hospital would lose money doing the procedure. The answer is simple: Physicians should recommend care that is in the patient's best interests, no more and no less. The goal of economic incentives should be to "prompt the physician to consider costs appropriately—to remind him pointedly that economics really does matter—but not to distort his reasoning. A well-designed incentive should prompt the physician to

TABLE 29-1

Managing Conflicts of Interest

Reaffirm that the patient's interests are paramount.
Disclose conflicts of interest.
Take precautions to protect patients.
Prohibit certain actions and situations.

consider more carefully what he does with clinical uncertainties and borderline options; it should not induce him to forego what he believes is clearly in the patient's interest (10)."

Although reaffirming fiduciary responsibilities to the patient is a necessary first step, other steps might also be needed.

DISCLOSE CONFLICTS OF INTEREST

Disclosure is salutary for several reasons. First, the requirement to disclose incentives might prevent physicians and organizations from making unacceptable arrangements. If the physician would find it hard or awkward to justify a situation, it probably presents an unacceptable conflict of interest. In controversial situations it is prudent for physicians to err on the side of the patient's interests rather than their own self-interest. Second, patients who know about a conflict of interest might be able to make more informed decisions by placing the physician's recommendations in context and compensating for any bias. However, it might be unrealistic to expect patients to assess whether a situation has biased the physician's judgment. Thus, in many situations, disclosure alone might be inadequate to protect patients.

TAKE PRECAUTIONS TO PROTECT PATIENTS

In some circumstances society may determine that additional steps must be taken to safeguard patients or the public. Physicians' actions may be regulated and their discretion limited (11). For example, in clinical research, review by an institutional review board is required (*see* Chapter 28).

PROHIBIT CERTAIN ACTIONS AND SITUATIONS

Although disclosure and precautions are necessary steps, they might still be insufficient to protect patients. Some actions and situations present such strong and direct conflicts of interest that they should be prohibited. Because "it is difficult if not impossible to distinguish cases in which financial gain does have improper influence from those in which it does not," it might be prudent to prohibit certain actions and situations (6). For example, continuing education programs controlled by drug companies might provide biased or incomplete coverage of topics. To avoid this, programs should not accept support from drug companies that attempt to influence the choice of topics or speakers (*see* Chapter 33).

In summary, conflicts of interest are ethically perilous because they might harm patients, impair physician judgment, and undermine trust in physicians. The ethical ideal is that patients' interests should take priority over physicians' self-interest or third parties' interests.

REFERENCES

1. Shaw GB. *The doctor's dilemma*. London: Penguin Books, 1946.
2. Wells P, Jones H, Davis M. *Conflicts of interest in engineering*. Dubuque: Kendall/Hunt Publishing Company, 1986.
3. Gillers S, Dorsen N. *Regulation of lawyers: problems of law and ethics*. Boston: Little, Brown and Company, 1989:790–808.
4. Rothman KJ. Conflicts of interest: the new McCarthyism in science. *JAMA* 1993;269:2782–2784.
5. Rodwin MA. *Medicine, money, and morals: physicians' conflicts of interest*. New York: Oxford University Press, 1993.
6. Thompson DF. Understanding financial conflicts of interest. *N Engl J Med* 1993;329:573–576.
7. Jonsen AR. Watching the doctor. *N Engl J Med* 1983;308:1531–1535.
8. Hillman AL. Health maintenance organizations, financial incentives, and physicians' judgments. *Ann Intern Med* 1990;112:891–893.
9. Medical professionalism in the new millennium: a physician charter. *Ann Intern Med* 2002;136(3):243–246.
10. Morreim EH. *Balancing act: the new medical ethics of medicine's new economics*. Boston: Kluwer Academic Publishers, 1991:124.
11. Rodwin MA. *Medicine, money, and morals: physicians' conflicts of interest*. New York: Oxford University Press, 1993:179–211.

CHAPTER 30

Bedside Rationing of Health Care

Physicians are ethically obligated to act in patients' best interests (*see* Chapter 4). However, acting in the best interests of one patient might sometimes make it impossible for physicians to act on behalf of another patient who is much more likely to benefit from care. Dilemmas arise because resources such as physician time and intensive care beds are in limited supply and people have different priorities for limited resources (1,2).

CASE 30.1 Limited coronary care beds.

Mr. H presents to the emergency department with substernal chest pain. An electrocardiogram (ECG) shows an acute anterior myocardial infarction, multifocal ventricular premature beats, and some couplets. The cardiac care unit (CCU) and intensive care unit (ICU) are full. One of the patients in the CCU is a 73-year-old man who had an emergency operation for a ruptured aortic aneurysm. A week after the operation, he is comatose, septic, in ventilatory and renal failure, and has hypotension despite vasopressors. Another patient in the CCU experienced chest pain after an angioplasty earlier in the day but has no persistent ECG changes and has normal cardiac enzymes. The physicians consider whether to transfer one of these patients out of the CCU to free a bed for Mr. H.

In Case 30.1 the patient with multisystem failure is so sick that he is highly unlikely to survive even if CCU care is continued. The postangioplasty patient is receiving only monitoring, not active treatment, and is highly likely to have a good outcome even if he is transferred out of the unit. In contrast, Mr. H might benefit greatly from thrombolytic and antiarrhythmic therapy, which can be administered only in an ICU. If CCU beds were allocated on a strictly first-come, first-served basis, Mr. H would be denied substantial benefits.

This chapter discusses the ethical considerations that arise when one patient's interests conflict with other patients' interests. In addition, this chapter analyzes whether the scarcity of financial resources justifies limiting the care of an individual patient. Chapter 34 deals with conflicts of interest between the health care provider and patient rather than conflicts of interest between patients.

The terms used to discuss these issues are hard to define precisely, are often used inconsistently, and commonly evoke strong emotions (3–5). In this book "allocation" refers to decisions that set levels of funding for programs rather than determine care for individual patients. For example, funds must be allocated between Medicaid and other social programs such as education and transportation and, within Medicaid, between inpatient services and prenatal care. Sometimes these policy-level choices are termed "macroallocation." In contrast, this book uses the term "rationing" to refer to decisions at the bedside or in the office to limit care for individual patients because of limited resources. The term *rationing* often connotes limiting beneficial care because it is too expensive. The term "microallocation" is also used in this context. The term rationing excludes clinical decisions that are a straightforward implementation of macroallocation policies, such as health plans' decisions not to cover cosmetic surgery. Unlike other countries, such as Great Britain, the United States has not developed coherent societal allocation policies (6,7). The ethical issue is whether, in the absence of a fair social agreement on allocation, physicians can ethically carry out rationing at the bedside.

ARGUMENTS AGAINST BEDSIDE RATIONING

Traditionally, bedside rationing by physicians has been considered unethical (8,9). Opponents of bedside rationing argue that doctors should act as fiduciaries and patient advocates, helping patients receive all the beneficial care that the system allows. One eminent physician wrote, "Physicians are required to do everything that they believe may benefit each patient without regard to costs or other societal considerations. In caring for an individual patient, the doctor must act solely as the patient's advocate, against the apparent interests of society as a whole (10)." This fiduciary role is deemed essential for maintaining patient trust. In their roles as citizens and civic leaders, physicians should help determine how resources should be allocated. At the bedside, however, physicians should not limit care to one patient primarily to benefit other patients or to save money for society. Such arguments have particular relevance in for-profit managed care systems in which savings from rationing may be used for executive salaries and returns to shareholders.

ARGUMENTS IN FAVOR OF BEDSIDE RATIONING

An absolute prohibition against bedside rationing, however, is ethically problematic (Table 30-1).

ACTING IN THE PATIENT'S BEST INTERESTS IS NOT AN ABSOLUTE DUTY

The physician's ethical obligation to act in an individual patient's best interests is not absolute. In several circumstances physicians are ethically or legally required to act against the patient's best interests in order to benefit third parties. For example, although maintaining confidentiality of medical information is in a patient's best interest, it is overridden when infectious diseases, threats of physical violence, or the patient's inability to drive safely might harm third parties (*see* Chapter 5). Furthermore, the guideline of beneficence is limited. The physician is not obliged to do literally everything that might benefit the patient. One philosopher writes that the traditional ethic of advocacy needs to be redefined to "proportional advocacy": the advocate "argues not for 'everything possible' but for everything 'probably beneficial' (11)." Similarly, the American Medical Association declares that "physicians must advocate for any care they believe will materially benefit their patients (12)." Other advocates of the fiduciary role enjoin physicians to practise "parsimonious" or "efficient" medicine, without defining those terms (8,9). These views acknowledge that if physicians ordered all tests and drugs that provided any benefit, costs would soar out of control. All these views allow some forms of rationing, without calling it such. It is more honest to call rationing by name (5) and to proceed to more constructive debates over when it is justified (4).

TABLE 30-1

Arguments in Favor of Bedside Rationing

Acting in the patient's best interests is not an absolute duty.
Leaving physicians out of microallocation decisions will harm patients.
Other patients might be seriously harmed if resources are not rationed.

LEAVING PHYSICIANS OUT OF MICROALLOCATION DECISIONS WOULD HARM PATIENTS

If physicians were not involved in microallocation, clinical decisions would be made according to utilization review guidelines or by health care administrators. Such decisions fail to take into account meaningful differences in individual patient circumstances that are too complex to be captured in simple guidelines or rules (13–16). Physicians can often bring to bear pertinent clinical information to justify an exception to a general rule (17).

OTHER PATIENTS MIGHT BE SERIOUSLY HARMED IF RESOURCES ARE NOT RATIONED

Providing care to one patient might deny care to another patient who would receive much greater medical benefit. Two patients might be competing for such limited resources as physician time or ICU beds. In this situation informal rationing is standard medical practice that has strong ethical justification.

CASE 30.2 Limited physician time.

Mr. M, a 48-year-old man, comes to the physician's office after 40 minutes of crushing substernal chest pain and shortness of breath. At the same time, a 21-year-old woman with asthma comes to the office with worsening shortness of breath for the past day despite increasing use of inhaled bronchodilators. These patients do not have appointments, and the physician's schedule is already full.

Because their time is limited, physicians must decide which patients deserve higher priority. In a life-threatening situation such as a probable myocardial infarction in Case 30.2, the priority of the emergency case over other patients is clear. Mr. M needs to be stabilized and transported to the emergency department. Regularly scheduled patients presumably would agree to wait because they would want similar priority if they should find themselves in such a serious emergency. However, how is an emergency defined? If care is promptly instituted for the woman with a severe asthma attack, her symptoms of shortness of breath will be relieved more rapidly and a hospitalization might be avoided. However, it might be difficult to determine how much benefit or potential harm to the asthma patient justifies asking regularly scheduled patients to wait. Referring the asthma patient to the emergency department would not resolve the dilemma but only push it back a step. Emergency physicians there would need to prioritize patients presenting for care.

Physicians routinely make decisions to allocate their time, and indeed patients and society expect them to do so. It is difficult to imagine that anyone other than the physician or nurse would decide who should wait. General rules can be set—for example, patients with serious emergencies should take priority and patients with minor or self-limited illnesses should wait. However, physicians need to interpret those general rules in a particular case—for example, by deciding whether a patient's asthma attack is severe enough to warrant asking other patients to wait.

In Case 30.1 essential medical resources—CCU beds—are in short supply. Some ethicists assert that physicians have an ethical obligation to ration scarce intensive care beds by transferring out of the CCU patients who are either too sick or too healthy to benefit significantly from intensive care (18). In clinical practice physicians frequently transfer patients in order to allow others to receive intensive care. When the CCU or ICU is full, physicians identify patients who are too sick to benefit from continued intensive care and set more restrictive standards for admission to the unit. Such transfers occur commonly and, under mild resource constraints, physicians can make such transfers without adversely affecting overall patient outcomes (19).

Increasing the supply of CCU beds will not resolve the problem of rationing but only postpone the dilemma of the last bed. Transferring patients to other hospitals with open CCU beds is also not a solution because Mr. H needs immediate treatment.

In Case 30.1 an identified patient would be seriously harmed if care were not rationed. In the following case a future patient will predictably be harmed unless care is rationed.

CASE 30.3 Shortage of blood products.

A 36-year-old man with alcoholic cirrhosis is admitted for severe variceal bleeding and encephalopathy. He is not a candidate for liver transplantation because of his active alcohol and amphetamine use. The surgeons do not believe he will survive a portacaval shunt operation. After 3 days he has consumed 42 units of blood and continues to bleed briskly despite endoscopic sclerotherapy and percutaneous placement of a therapeutic portal-systemic shunt (TIPS). The regional blood bank has only three more units of his type of blood despite appeals for more donations. It is New Year's Eve, when many persons who have met with automobile accidents will need blood transfusions.

In Case 30.3 there is no identified individual who will be harmed if blood products are not rationed, but the existence of such an individual is virtually certain. Many persons with trauma can recover completely with vigorous emergency care. Thus, a future patient might be seriously harmed if all available blood were given to the patient in Case 30.3, who has not improved despite maximal care.

Physicians might be reluctant to ration interventions to patients who are already receiving care because of loyalty or fidelity—that is, doctors might believe that they have implicitly promised to provide ongoing care and not to curtail it to benefit other patients. The position's emotional appeal is clear, and keeping promises is an important ethical guideline. However, maintaining fidelity should refer to appropriate ongoing care, not to unlimited care regardless of the benefits to the patient or the harms to others.

Although limitations on transfusions are justified in Case 30.3, there are problems in implementing such limits in a fair manner. Various physicians might set different limits in practice. Some physicians might stop after 40 units, others after 60 units. More specific practice standards would make such decisions more consistent and therefore fairer.

RATIONING ON THE BASIS OF FINANCIAL RESOURCES

In some situations compelling ethical arguments exist for limiting care to one patient in order to provide much more beneficial clinical services to other patients. However, when rationing is done primarily to save money rather than to benefit other patients directly, the reasons are generally weaker. The following case illustrates these issues.

CASE 30.4 Expensive care for a patient with poor prognosis and quality of life.

Mrs. D is a 76-year-old woman with severe dementia. She recognizes her family only occasionally and does not respond to health care workers' questions or requests. She develops chronic renal failure and symptoms of uremia. While competent, she had never expressed her preferences about renal dialysis. Although her primary physician and the nephrologist strongly recommend that renal dialysis not be performed, her family insists on it. They believe that as long as she recognizes them and smiles, her life should be prolonged. They understand that dialysis would not improve her mental functioning or mobility.

At the time the public hospital in the community is considering closing obstetrical and substance abuse services because of budget deficits. The physicians feel they are accomplices to an unjust health care system if they use resources on this patient when more pressing health needs are unmet. A vascular surgery consultant writes in the medical record, "In the current climate of out-of-control medical costs, it is unconscionable to provide expensive care for this patient."

As discussed in Chapter 14, it would be appropriate to provide renal dialysis to Mrs. D because it would achieve the family's goal of prolonging her life at a quality they consider acceptable. The physicians, however, believe that Mrs. D's quality of life is so poor that the cost of dialysis is not justified.

Physicians should support more enlightened policies regarding allocation, but in most circumstances attempts by physicians to ration care on the basis of costs at the level of the individual patient, although well intentioned, are not justified.

NO PUBLIC POLICY AUTHORIZES PHYSICIANS TO RATION ON THE BASIS OF COSTS

The physicians caring for Mrs. D felt partly responsible for the soaring cost of health care. However, no public policy authorizes physicians to limit the care of patients on renal dialysis to save resources for other patients. On the contrary, U.S. public policy pays for dialysis to all patients with end-stage renal failure. In the 1960s selecting patients for a limited number of renal dialysis machines on the basis of prognosis or quality of life proved so controversial that Congress singled out end-stage renal disease for universal coverage under the Medicare program.

BEDSIDE RATIONING BASED ON COSTS WOULD BE INCONSISTENT AND UNFAIR

Physicians at one hospital might withhold dialysis from Mrs. D, but physicians at another hospital might provide it. Indeed, the public nursing home in the area provided chronic dialysis to numerous patients with severe Alzheimer's disease. It violates the ethical guideline of justice to treat similar patients unequally. Whether or not Mrs. D receives dialysis should not be based on the choice of hospital.

Bedside rationing might also be unfair if certain patients or certain interventions are singled out for review. It makes little sense to limit one health care intervention as not cost-effective without looking at the cost-effectiveness of other interventions as well. Many people would object to limiting dialysis for Mrs. D if other interventions, such as intensive care for patients with extremely poor prognoses, were not similarly scrutinized.

MONEY SAVED BY RATIONING CANNOT BE REALLOCATED

Physicians in the United States who save money on the care of an individual patient generally cannot redirect those resources to patients or projects with higher priority (20). If physicians terminated dialysis on Mrs. D, they could not redirect funds to more pressing medical or social needs, such as prenatal care or childhood immunizations. Furthermore, in managed care organizations savings from limiting care to patients might be directed toward higher salaries for administrators or greater profits for investors (21). In the absence of broader health care reform, attempts to limit health care costs at the bedside are ineffective gestures.

Limiting care for one patient in order to have resources available to patients who would benefit more from them is more strongly justified if several conditions are met (22). First, saved resources would be reallocated to interventions that provide greater benefits for the population of patients receiving care. Second, the physicians would not benefit directly from saving resources. Third, the limitations in care are applied to all similar patients with no exceptions based on privileged social status.

Opponents of bedside rationing would argue that physicians in Case 30.4 fulfilled their ethical obligations to use limited resources prudently by discussing dialysis with Mrs. D's family and making a strong recommendation against it.

AN EXAMPLE OF ETHICALLY ACCEPTABLE BEDSIDE RATIONING: TIERED FORMULARY BENEFITS

In some situations it is ethically acceptable for physicians to limit services to one patient in order to conserve a pool of money that pays for services to a population of patients. Formulary restrictions are one common example. Because drug expenditures are the fastest growing of all health care costs, most managed care plans have established restricted formularies and tiered copayments. For example, patients might have a $10 copayment for preferred drugs on the formulary, a $20 copayment for nonpreferred formulary drugs, and a still higher copayment for nonformulary drugs. Preferred drugs are usually cheaper than other drugs in the same class because a discount from the manufacturer has been negotiated.

In some situations there might be no meaningful clinical differences among drugs in a class but significant differences in cost—for example, different angiotensin converting-enzyme inhibitors for congestive heart failure. It is ethical for the physician to start with the presumption that preferred formulary drugs are appropriate. For instance, the physician can recommend that the patient try a preferred drug. For a stable chronic condition, the risk to the patient of using a preferred medication within the same class of drugs is small, provided the patient receives close follow-up care.

This presumption in favor of a preferred drug may be overridden in some situations. For example, a patient might develop unacceptable side effects, an unsatisfactory clinical outcome, or poor adherence. The physician also might need to provide guidance to patients as to whether a nonpreferred drug is worth the higher out-of-pocket cost. In addition, physicians also need to help patients when their drug coverage does not permit them to afford all the prescriptions they need.

TABLE 30-2

Suggestions for Physicians Considering Bedside Rationing

Try to get more resources for the patient within the system.
Make decisions openly.
Get a second opinion.
Notify patients or surrogates when care is rationed.

SUGGESTIONS FOR PHYSICIANS

Physicians who are considering rationing care at the bedside should take several actions (Table 30-2).

TRY TO GET MORE RESOURCES FOR THE PATIENT WITHIN THE SYSTEM

Physicians should try to obtain more resources within the system. For example, in Case 30.1 beds in the postoperative recovery room might be used as temporary ICU beds. Such efforts, however, might lead to other problems, such as disruption of operating room schedules.

MAKE DECISIONS OPENLY

Discussing rationing dilemmas explicitly might identify unquestioned assumptions and hidden value judgments. When people must make their arguments and values explicit, others can present rebuttals or disagreements.

GET A SECOND OPINION

Eliciting a second opinion from another attending physician or from a hospital ethics committee or consultant might improve decision-making. For example, such a review might clarify the patients' prognosis or point out unwarranted value judgments.

NOTIFY PATIENTS OR SURROGATES WHEN CARE IS RATIONED

Patients or their surrogates should be notified when beneficial care will be rationed. It is disrespectful to transfer patients out of intensive care or stop transfusions without explaining to them or their families what is happening. If possible, it is preferable to make such explanations before a clinical crisis occurs.

In summary, bedside rationing might be ethically appropriate if providing services to one patient would directly deprive another patient of services that will provide much greater medical benefits. However, decisions to ration in order to save money might be problematic. Physicians facing such bedside rationing decisions should take steps to help ensure that these decisions are consistent and fair.

REFERENCES

1. Thurow LC. Learning to say "no". *N Engl J Med* 1984;311:1569–1572.
2. Fuchs VR. The "rationing" of medical care. *N Engl J Med* 1984;311:1572–1573.
3. Eddy DM. Rationing by patient choice. *JAMA* 1991;265:105–108.
4. Asch DA, Ubel PA. Rationing by any other name. *N Engl J Med* 1997;336:1668–1671.
5. Ubel PA, Goold S. Recognizing bedside rationing: clear cases and tough calls. *Ann Intern Med* 1997;126:74–80.
6. Schwartz WB. The inevitable failure of current cost-containment strategies. Why they can provide only temporary relief. *JAMA* 1987;257:220–224.
7. Boren SD. I had a tough day today, Hillary. *N Engl J Med* 1994;330:500–502.

8. Pellegrino ED, Thomasma DG. *For the patient's good: the restoration of beneficence in health care.* New York: Oxford University Press, 1988.
9. Kassirer JP. Managing care—should we adopt a new ethic? *N Engl J Med* 1998;339:397–398.
10. Levinsky NG. The doctor's master. *N Engl J Med* 1984;311:1573–1575.
11. Jonsen AR. *The new medicine and the old ethics.* Cambridge: Harvard University Press, 1990:59.
12. Council on Ethical and Judicial Affairs. *Code of medical ethics: current opinions with annotations.* Chicago: American Medical Association, 1998:143.
13. Hillman AL. Managing the physician: rules versus incentives. *Health Aff (Millwood)* 1991;10:138–146.
14. Hall MA. *Making medical spending decisions.* New York: Oxford University Press, 1997.
15. Morreim EH. Fiscal scarcity and the inevitability of bedside budget balancing. *Arch Intern Med* 1989;149: 1012–1015.
16. Morreim EH. *Balancing act: the new medical ethics of medicine's new economics.* Boston: Kluwer Academic Publishers, 1991.
17. Ellrodt AG, Conner L, Riedinger M, et al. Measuring and improving physician compliance with clinical practice guidelines. *Ann Intern Mec* 1995;122:277–282.
18. Engelhardt HT, Rie MA. Intensive care units, scarce resources, and conflicting principles of justice. *JAMA* 1986; 255:1159–1164.
19. Strauss MJ, LoGerfo JP, Yeltatzie JA, et al. Rationing of intensive care unit services: an everyday occurrence. *JAMA* 1986;255:1143–1146.
20. Daniels N. Why saying no to patients in the United States is so hard. *N Engl J Med* 1986;314:1380–1383.
21. Woolhandler S, Himmelstein DU. Costs of care and administration at for-profit and other hospitals in the United States. *N Engl J Med* 1997;336:769–774.
22. Pearson SD. Caring and cost: the challenge for physician advocacy. *Ann Intern Med* 2000;133(2):148–153.

ANNOTATED BIBLIOGRAPHY

1. Levinsky NG. The doctor's master. *N Engl J Med* 1984;311:1573–1575.
   Argues eloquently that the physician's primary responsibility is to the individual patient, not to society.
2. Daniels N. Why saying no to patients in the United States is so hard. *N Engl J Med* 1986;314:1380–1383.
   Points out that in the U.S. system there is no way to direct money saved on one patient to more cost-effective purposes.
3. Asch DA, Ubel PA. Rationing by any other name. *N Engl J Med* 1997;336:1668–1671.
   Clarifies the range of situations in which physicians limit beneficial services because they are too costly.
4. Boren SD. I had a tough day today, Hillary. *N Engl J Med* 1994;330:500–502,
   First-person account by medical director of a managed care plan, describing the types of expensive interventions that insurers are asked to cover.
5. Pearson SD. Caring and cost: the challenge for physician advocacy. *Ann Intern Med* 2000;133:148–153.
   Suggests criteria for appropriate bedside rationing.

CHAPTER 31

Incentives for Physicians to Increase Services

Under fee-for-service reimbursement, physicians and health care organizations can increase their incomes by providing more services. They can see more patients, see them more frequently, perform more interventions per patient, and raise their charges for services (1).

PROBLEMS WITH FEE-FOR-SERVICE REIMBURSEMENT

Fee-for-service reimbursement offers incentives to increase all services, not only those services that are effective or cost-effective. Under fee-for-service reimbursement, many earlier studies found extensive overuse of expensive interventions such as carotid endarterectomies, coronary artery bypass operations, and pacemakers (2–5). When patients receive interventions that are unnecessary or of only marginal benefit, they are exposed to unwarranted risks.

Fee-for-service reimbursement also encourages physicians to use invasive procedures rather than to spend time talking with patients about decisions or counseling them about preventive care (6). For example, Medicare reimburses a cardiologist a professional fee of $445 for inserting a temporary pacemaker, a procedure that takes about 30 minutes. In contrast, Medicare reimbursement for a 1-hour family meeting about withdrawing life-sustaining procedures is $100. Fee-for-service reimbursement also causes significant conflicts of interest, as discussed next.

SELF-REFERRAL BY PHYSICIANS

Physician self-referral can occur in two ways. First, doctors might invest in freestanding facilities, such as clinical laboratories or radiology services, to which they refer patients. This arrangement is also called a *joint venture*. In the early 1990s, physicians in Florida and several other states owned almost all freestanding radiology centers (7). Second, physicians may carry out radiology imaging or clinical laboratory testing in their own offices. For example, internists commonly carry out and interpret chest x-rays, cardiologists perform echocardiography, and orthopedic surgeons carry out magnetic resonance imaging (MRI) scans. Both types of self-referral raise ethical concerns about overutilization of services and conflicts of interest (8–10).

Empirical studies show that physicians who self-refer in both these ways order significantly more imaging studies and generate higher radiology costs than other physicians (7,8,11). It is believed that many of these additional studies are not warranted. In general, greater use of medical services is not associated with better patient outcomes (12). However, only one study has examined this question directly, finding that the percentage of inappropriate MRI studies was greater when self-referring physicians ordered studies (8).

JUSTIFICATION FOR SELF-REFERRAL

Proponents argue that such physician investment increases access to care because state-of-the-art technology might not be available otherwise (9). The evidence, however, does not support these claims. For example, none of the physician-owned radiation therapy centers in Florida were located in rural areas or inner cities (13).

Advocates argue that if physicians take financial risks when investing in freestanding facilities, they should be able to share in any profits. Physicians might be more willing than other investors to take such risks because they better appreciate the promise of new technologies (9).

PROBLEMS WITH SELF-REFERRAL

A conflict of interest might arise when physicians recommend services from which they profit financially. The American Medical Association (AMA) states that self-referral might "undermine the commitment of physicians to professionalism (9)." Payment to physicians for referring a patient is considered fee-splitting or a kickback. These are considered unethical because those physicians are not being compensated for providing medical services, but only for referring patients to another provider.

Even the appearance that physicians are trying to increase profits might erode trust in the profession. According to the AMA, "There are some activities regarding their patients that physicians should avoid whether or not there is evidence of abuse (9)." Financial reward for physicians is traditionally regarded as a consequence of serving patients, not as a goal to be pursued for its own sake.

Poor quality of care has been documented for radiology studies performed in physicians' offices. Deficiencies have been found in the quality of equipment, images, and interpretations.

PROHIBITIONS ON JOINT VENTURES

Joint ventures have been condemned as a kickback because physicians are profiting from referring a patient for medical services. Federal regulations prohibit physicians from referring Medicare or Medicaid patients to a health care entity in which they or their family members have a financial relationship, such as ownership or investment (14). Moreover, physicians may not bill Medicare for services provided under a prohibited referral, nor may Medicare pay for such services. The prohibition includes clinical laboratory, radiology, prescription drugs, and durable medical equipment. Exceptions are made for ancillary services provided in the physician's office, group medical practices, health maintenance organizations and hospitals, rural areas, and investment in facilities whose stock is publicly traded. Many states have enacted similar prohibitions.

Disclosure of physician ownership of outside facilities is ethically desirable, as with any conflict of interest. However, disclosure does not diminish referrals by physician-investors to outside facilities in which they have a financial interest (15). Even if patients know that the physician has a financial incentive to increase referrals, they might not be able to judge whether recommendations for testing or treatment are sound. In addition, patients might be afraid of offending physicians if they do not go to the facility in question.

DISTINGUISHING SELF-REFERRAL FROM OTHER PRACTICES

Referring patients for tests or treatments carried out by the physician or in the physician's office is distinguished from referral to outside facilities in which the physician has a financial interest (9). First, procedures as endoscopy, bronchoscopy, coronary angiography and angioplasty, and surgery are an integral part of specialist care. It would make little sense for one surgeon to evaluate the patient and then refer the patient to another surgeon for the actual procedure. Also, payment for services that physicians or their staff carry out are distinguished from kickbacks physicians receive for simply referring the patient for a service. Second, obtaining laboratory tests or imaging studies in the physician's office serves the patient's best interests because it is convenient and enhances continuity of care.

RESPONSES TO SELF-REFERRAL TO IN-OFFICE SERVICES

Although there are no legal prohibitions on physicians' referring patients to ancillary services in their office or clinic, there are ethical concerns about overutilization of services and poor quality of care. With regard to quality of care, insurers and professional organizations have set certification standards for training of physicians and staff, quality control procedures and audits, equipment, technical procedures, and interpretation of images (8). Similarly, clinical laboratories in physicians' offices must meet federal standards for certification. In addition, physicians should involve colleagues in decision-making—for example, presenting cases at conferences (16). Moreover, physicians should not set up equipment and services in their offices if there is no demonstrated need, and they should not carry out procedures if they lack appropriate training and experience.

NONFINANCIAL INCENTIVES TO PROVIDE MORE SERVICES

Social and psychological factors reinforce financial incentives in fee-for-service medicine to provide more services. First, both the public and physicians regard high-technology procedures such as MRI, angioplasty, and endoscopy as the epitome of excellent medical care. The prestige that hospitals and physicians gain by providing these services encourages their wider use. Second, the inherent uncertainty in clinical medicine encourages the use of additional interventions. One response to such uncertainty is to perform an additional test or to try a new drug. Faced with an individual patient, physicians might recommend interventions that they would not recommend as a general clinical guideline (17). Finally, the malpractice system encourages "defensive medicine," the ordering of interventions of small marginal benefit to patients in order to prevent potential lawsuits.

In summary, the fee-for-service reimbursement system encourages physicians to provide more services and in some instances to overuse services. Both health care organizations and individuals need to ensure that clinical decisions are based on patients' best interests, not on their own self-interest.

REFERENCES

1. Roe RB. The UCR boondoggle: a death knell for private practice? *N Engl J Med* 1981;305:41–45.
2. Franks P, Clancy CM, Nutting PA. Gatekeeping revisited—protecting patients from overtreatment. *N Engl J Med* 1992;327:424–429.
3. Brook RH, Park RE, Chassin MR, et al. Predicting the appropriate use of carotid endarterectomy, upper gastrointestinal endoscopy, and coronary angiography. *N Engl J Med* 1990;323:1173–1177.
4. Greenspan AM, Kay HR, Berger BC, et al. Incidence of unwarranted implantation of permanent cardiac pacemakers in a large medical population. *N Engl J Med* 1988;318:158–163.
5. Winslow CM, Josecoff JB, Chassin M, et al. The appropriateness of performing coronary artery bypass surgery. *JAMA* 1989;260:505–509.
6. Hsiao WC, Dunn DL, Verrilli DK. Assessing the implementation of physician payment reform. *N Engl J Med* 1993;328:928–933.
7. Mitchell JM, Scott E. New evidence of the prevalence and scope of physician joint ventures. *JAMA* 1992;268: 80–84.
8. Kouri BE, Parsons RG, Alpert HR. Physician self-referral for diagnostic imaging: review of the empiric literature. *Am J Roentgenol* 2002;179(4):843–850.
9. Council on Ethical and Judicial Affairs AMA. Conflicts of interest: physician ownership of medical facilities. *JAMA* 1992;267:2366–2369.
10. Iglehart JK. Efforts to address the problem of physician self-referral. *N Engl J Med* 1991;325:1820–1824.
11. Hillman BJ, Joseph CA, Mabry MR, et al. Frequency and costs of diagnostic imaging in office practice—a comparison of self-referring and radiologist-referring physicians. *N Engl J Med* 1990;323:1604–1608.
12. Wennberg JE, Freeman JL, Shelton RM, et al. Hospital use and mortality among Medicare beneficiaries in Boston and New Haven. *N Engl J Med* 1989;321:1168–1173.
13. Mitchell JM, Sunshine JH. Consequences of physician ownership of health care facilities—joint ventures in radiation therapy. *N Engl J Med* 1992;327:1497–1501.
14. Stout SM, Warner DC. How did physician ownership become a federal case? The Stark Amendments and their prospects. *HEC Forum* 2003;15(2):171–187.

15. *Financial arrangements between physicians and health care businesses.* Washington: Office of the Inspector General, U.S. Dept. of Health and Human Services, 1989.
16. DeMaria AN. Self-referral in cardiology. *J Am Coll Cardiol* 2004;43(8):1500–1501.
17. Redelmeier DA, Tversky A. The discrepancy between medical decisions for individuals and for groups. *N Engl J Med* 1990;322:1162–1164.

ANNOTATED BIBLIOGRAPHY

1. Kouri BE, Parsons RG, Alpert HR. Physician self-referral for diagnostic imaging: review of the empiric literature. *Am J Roentgenol* 2002;179:843–850.
Review of empirical studies of extent and consequences of self-referral for patients.

CHAPTER 32

Incentives for Physicians to Decrease Services

The U.S. is expected to spend over $10,000 per capita on health care in 2013. Total expenditures will be $3.3 trillion dollars, over 18% of the gross domestic product (1). Despite these expenditures, the United States continues to have worse infant mortality and life expectancy than other countries that spend less per capita on health care and provide universal health insurance. Eliminating inefficiency and waste will not solve the problem of rising costs because new medical technologies and an aging population will continue to drive them up (2,3). Although the goal of restraining health care costs is appropriate, the means employed might raise ethical concerns. The ethical guideline of justice requires physicians to be prudent because health care resources are limited. However, this ethical obligation might conflict with the obligation to act in individual patients' best interests. Patients do not want to forego beneficial care in order to save money for society or for insurers (4,5).

Many cost control measures used by managed care in the 1990s created conflicts of interest for physicians and undermined their traditional fiduciary role. Specific practices were

- Allowing patients to see only physicians in the plan
- Requirements that primary care physicians serve as "gatekeepers" to approve referrals to specialists
- Financial incentives to physicians, such as capitation, to provide fewer services
- Administrative measures, such as utilization review, practice guidelines, and restrictions on prescription drugs

Such pressures to control expenditures have been strongly criticized because the savings might be used to pay for salaries of executives and for dividends to shareholders in for-profit plans. A public backlash has led insurers to back away from these managed care tools. Excesses in early managed care have been eliminated, such as steep financial incentives to physicians to limit costs, cumbersome authorization processes, and gag rules to prevent physicians from disclosing options for care that the insurer did not cover.

This chapter analyzes how the self-interest of physicians and health care organizations might conflict with the patient's best interests. Chapter 30 analyzes the related issue of conflicts of interest between different patients.

CASE 32.1 Drugs not on preferred list.

Ms. R, a 64-year-old business executive, has diabetes and hypertension. Urine analysis shows microalbuminuria. Evidence-based practice guidelines recommend that she take an angiotension converting enzyme (ACE) inhibitor, which will lower her risk for renal failure. She sees an advertisement for a new ACE inhibitor that has once-a-day dosage and asks you if she should be on it. Under her insurance plan her copayments are $20 a month for generic drugs, $30 a month for preferred drugs on *the plan's formulary, and $60 a month for nonpreferred drugs. The advertised drug is a nonformulary drug; the patient would need to pay the full price of $200 a month.*

Case 32.1 illustrates the current approach to restraining costs through increased copayments and deductibles so that patients have personal incentives to control costs (6–8). Because out-of-pocket expenses for prescription drugs have increased sharply, insurers have increased copayments and instituted tiered benefits. This approach resolves some conflicts of interests for physicians because both they and their patients have an interest in cost-effective care. However, cost-sharing also raises ethical concerns because it might discourage use of essential drugs and lead to worse outcomes for patients with chronic illness (9,10). Raising copayments deters the use of ACE inhibitors in plans that have multitier formulary systems (11). ACE inhibitors are expensive but prevent renal failure in patients with diabetes and proteinuria (11). Thus, for Ms. R, financial incentives in her insurance plan tend to compromise the quality of diabetes care. Consequently, patients commonly ask physicians whether it is worth paying more out-of-pocket for certain drugs (12). The physician can then play the role of advising the patient. No longer is the physician viewed as an agent of the insurance plan who is unwilling to prescribe newer and more expensive drugs.

ETHICAL CONCERNS ABOUT INCENTIVES TO DECREASE SERVICES

BENEFICIAL CARE MIGHT BE WITHHELD

Ideally, incentives to control costs lead physicians to eliminate services that offer little or no benefit to patients. However, physicians might also be encouraged to withhold interventions that provide substantial benefit, as in Case 32.1 (13–15).

Empirical evidence on how managed care affects the quality of care and health outcomes is inconclusive. Overall, outcomes seem to be similar in managed care and fee-for-service care (16,17).

Both physicians and the public believe that some forms of managed care compromise the quality of care (18–20). In one study 20% of physicians believed that gatekeeping has a negative effect on the overall quality of care, compared to 6% who believe that it has a positive effect (21). More specifically, 40% of physicians believed that gatekeeping has a negative effect on the appropriate use of specialist care. However, physicians also reported that gatekeeping improves coordination of care and preventive care. In another survey nearly 50% of physicians believed that formularies had a negative impact on the quality of care, but only 13% thought they had a positive impact (22). Such concerns might be greater in for-profit managed care plans, where savings might be reallocated to salaries for plan executives or for returns to investors.

Limits on interventions might be carried out unfairly. Patients who are socially privileged, who are more persistent in demanding services, or who are more skilled at gaming the system might be more likely to obtain desired interventions.

THE FIDUCIARY ROLE OF PHYSICIANS MIGHT BE UNDERMINED

Cost-containment measures might lead patients to question whether physicians are acting in their best interests. In one survey 61% of persons in heavily managed plans were worried that if they became sick the plan would be more concerned about saving money than providing the best medical treatment (19). In comparison, 51% of persons in less tightly managed plans and 32% of patients in traditional plans had such worries. In another study capitated patients had lower levels of trust in their physicians than fee-for-service patients (23).

Financial incentives to reduce costs might create conflicts of interest. Physicians might act in their own self-interest or in third parties' interest rather than in patients' best interests. Utilization review and practice guidelines might put physicians in the role of implementing policies set by administrators rather than acting as professionals who exercise independent clinical judgment. Furthermore, an emphasis on cost containment and efficiency leads physicians to become entrepreneurs focused on profits instead of healers focused on patient well-being (24).

RESPONSIBILITY OF HEALTH CARE ORGANIZATIONS FOR INCENTIVES TO DECREASE SERVICES

Health care organizations can eliminate or mitigate conflicts of interest in several ways (25).

USE ACCEPTABLE FINANCIAL INCENTIVES

As a means of reducing costs, incentives to physicians have advantages over guidelines or rules (26,27). Incentives allow physicians to exercise discretion and take into account the circumstances of an individual case. In addition, incentives avoid micromanagement and bureaucratic requirements for documentation. However, very direct and strong incentives to decrease services that involve a large percentage of the physician's income create an unacceptable risk that physicians will act contrary to patients' interests (28–31).

Increasingly, managed care organizations are using a blend of incentives. Physicians might receive a base salary, with adjustments for productivity, utilization, patient satisfaction, and quality of care (32,33). For instance, physicians might receive a bonus for ensuring that patients receive indicated preventive measures, such as screening mammography. Such balanced reimbursement systems encourage a strong doctor–patient relationship and quality of care as well as cost containment.

DISCLOSE ECONOMIC INCENTIVES TO PATIENTS

Managed care systems should disclose to enrollees their financial arrangements with physicians (34). Federal Medicare and Medicaid regulations require such disclosure, as do some state laws (29,35,36). Such disclosure need not reduce patient trust in physicians or insurers (37). Disclosure might benefit patients in several ways. It might help patients choose a physician, physician group, or plan. Knowing how physicians are reimbursed might help patients put physicians' recommendations into context and decide whether to appeal or pay out of pocket if coverage is denied. Most important, disclosure might deter problematic financial arrangements that would be difficult to defend in public.

ALLOW JUSTIFIED EXCEPTIONS TO GUIDELINES AND FORMULARY RESTRICTIONS

Even the best clinical guidelines or utilization review system cannot cover all cases appropriately. There might be circumstances that the guidelines did not anticipate or capture, or a case might have particular features that justify an exception (38). The physician is in a unique position to identify justified exceptions to general guidelines. Organizations need to allow legitimate exceptions. For example, insurance plans may limit the number of prescription drugs per patient that are covered. For patients with multiple chronic illnesses, these limits can lead to exacerbations of illness and increased use of emergency services (9). Hence, liberal exception policies are needed for patients at high risk for adverse outcomes. Health insurers also need to institute appeals procedures that are not unduly burdensome for physicians and patients. The ethical justification for practice guidelines and formulary restrictions assumes that physicians can identify patients for whom an exception is justified and that neither patients nor physicians are deterred from obtaining approvals for exceptions by a complicated authorization or appeals process.

In short, health care organizations can create an ethical climate in which incentives to limit services have a stronger ethical justification (39). First, there should be a means of reallocating saved resources to interventions that would provider greater benefits for the population of patients receiving care. Second, the physicians would not profit directly from saving resources. Third, the limitations in care are applied equitably to all similar patients, regardless of social status.

RESPONSES BY PHYSICIANS TO INCENTIVES TO DECREASE SERVICES

When an effective test or treatment is not covered by the insurance plan, the physician faces issues of disclosing the intervention, recommending it, and helping the patient obtain it (25) (see Table 32-1).

DISCLOSE OPTIONS TO PATIENTS

In Case 32.1 the patient asks the physician about a nonformulary drug. In other cases the physician must decide whether to tell the patient about services that are available outside the system, even if the plan will not cover them. On the one hand, physicians might fear that such disclosure will only make the patient angry and that they will be the target of that anger. On the other hand, the ethical guidelines of autonomy and beneficence require physicians to discuss alternatives that might offer significant clinical benefits to patients. If patients are not informed of alternatives outside the managed care system, they cannot try to obtain them or make informed decisions about their care. Patients might try to convince the plan to pay for care outside the system, pay out of pocket for care, or postpone care until they can change insurance plans.

RECOMMEND OPTIONS THAT PROVIDE SIGNIFICANT CLINICAL BENEFITS

The physician should recommend out-of-plan options that provide clinically significant benefits over care available in the plan. Recommendations should take into account published evidence, clinical judgment about the individual case, and the patient's values.

Physicians also might be legally liable if, against their medical judgment, they withhold beneficial care at the insurer's behest. In a case involving premature hospital discharge, one court declared, "the physician who complies without protest with the limitations imposed by a third-party payer, when his medical judgment dictates otherwise, cannot avoid his ultimate responsibility for his patient's care (40)."

Acting in the patient's best interests is not an absolute duty. Physicians have no ethical obligation to order or provide interventions against their medical judgment. Moreover, physicians should not recommend or order an intervention when another option has a more favorable balance of benefit to risk. The term "benefit" needs to be interpreted broadly in order to include psychosocial variables as well as biomedical outcomes. For some patients convenience in taking medications, reassurance about not missing a serious diagnosis, or rapid recovery to full function are extremely important.

It is ethical for physicians to take into account the cost of care when several approaches have similar outcomes for patients. When the ethical guideline of beneficence provides no strong reason to recommend one option over another, the guideline of justice might then be decisive. The prudent use of limited health care resources might be an acceptable reason to choose one of the options. In Case 32.1 it is appropriate to use preferred drugs that require multiple daily doses rather than more expensive, equivalent drugs in the same pharmaceutical class. Physicians and patients need to acknowledge that such decisions are a form of bedside rationing (41) but recognize that they can be ethically appropriate. Physicians should be willing to discuss these issues openly and honestly with patients (39).

It might subsequently become apparent that the preferred drug fails to benefit a particular patient. The patient might have an unsatisfactory outcome, unacceptable side effects, or find it impossible to take several doses a day. These adverse outcomes justify trying the more expensive drug.

ACT AS PATIENT ADVOCATE

The guideline of beneficence urges physicians to act as advocates to intercede for or speak on behalf of patients (25,42). Advocacy should be based on sound clinical judgment and evidence. It is not doing whatever the patient requests. Advocating for a patient is fair only if it would also be appropriate for other physicians to advocate for patients in similar situations. In Case 32.1 the physician would not be justified in requesting coverage for the nonformulary drug if the patient is doing well on the current drug. Physicians need to make reasonable efforts to help patients obtain authorizations or make appeals to obtain care. Such efforts might include filling out forms and making phone calls.

AVOID DECEPTION

Physicians sometimes use deception to obtain insurance coverage for a patient. In one survey 39% of physicians reported that during the past year they had exaggerated the severity of a patient's condition, changed a patient's billing diagnosis, or reported signs and symptoms the patient did not have in order to help the patient get needed care (43). Such deception is more common when physicians believe that it is unfair for the plan not to cover the intervention, when they believe that the insurer's appeals process was unwieldy, and when the patient's condition is more serious (44). However, avoiding deception is a basic ethical guideline that serves to limit obligations to serve as patient advocates (42). Lying and deception undermine social trust because people cannot trust that other statements are truthful. Chapter 6 argues in detail that deception of insurers is not justified, except as a last resort after appeals have failed (25).

PATIENTS' REQUESTS FOR INTERVENTIONS THAT PHYSICIANS
BELIEVE ARE INAPPROPRIATE

Such requests might occur in any system of health care but might be more acrimonious in managed care.

CASE 32.2 Patient requests medically unwarranted diagnostic tests.

A 26-year-old man receiving care in a health maintenance organization (HMO) has mild occipital headaches without any other symptoms for 2 weeks, associated with a period of increased stress at work. Heat or acetaminophen promptly relieves his headaches. His examination is remarkable only for mild trapezius spasm. His neurological examination is normal. He insists on a magnetic resonance imaging (MRI) scan to be sure that he does not have a brain tumor. He also wants a referral to a neurologist. The physician believes that the patient has tension headaches and that further workup would not be indicated. The patient exclaims, "You're just trying to save money for the HMO!"

The key ethical issue in this case is whether the MRI scan or neurology referral would benefit the patient. The likelihood of finding a serious intracranial lesion is so low in this case that an MRI or referral would not be recommended, even under fee-for-service reimbursement. The mere possibility that the headaches might be caused by a serious intracerebral lesion does not justify scanning or referral at this time. Anecdotal reports of patients who had a brain tumor discovered on an MRI for headaches should be regarded simply as anecdotes, not as persuasive evidence of effectiveness. It is ethically appropriate for the physician to follow practice guidelines or utilization review restrictions that disallow the test or referral (Table 32-1). Indeed, it might be less stressful for physicians to say that insurer will not cover the test or referral.

Rarely, a patient might be so worried about having a brain tumor that the patient's everyday activities are compromised. In this situation it might be appropriate to order an imaging study or referral for reassurance and to appeal a utilization review denial. However, the test should be part of a comprehensive plan of care that would also include counseling to address the patient's fears of cancer.

How can the physician respond to the patient's charge that the physician is merely trying to save money for the system (45)? First, the physician should explore the patient's concerns and acknowledge the uncertainty of medical diagnosis. Also, the doctor should explain to the patient why these interventions are not recommended at this time. The physician should arrange to see the patient

TABLE 32-1

Responses by Physicians to Incentives to Decrease Services

Disclose options to patients.

Recommend options that provide significant clinical benefits.

Act as patient advocate.

Avoid deception.

again in case the headaches do not resolve satisfactorily. In addition, the doctor should leave open the possibility of imaging studies or referral in the future if needed.

In summary, within the constraints of health care plans, physicians need to act as patient advocates when the patient could receive significant clinical benefit from a referral, test, or therapy that the plan disallows. In addition, financial incentives that are highly likely to lead physicians to order medically inappropriate care need to be identified and limited.

APPENDIX: COST-CONTAINMENT MEASURES IN MANAGED CARE

The term "managed care" covers a variety of organizational features (46). Managed care systems include HMOs and preferred provider organizations (PPOs) (47). Patients in HMOs select a primary physician or physician group and must obtain covered services through them. HMO physicians contract to provide comprehensive medical care for capitated payments, which are a fixed amount per patient, regardless of the actual costs of care. A few HMOs are staff or group model HMOs, with a closed panel of physicians working primarily for the HMO. Other HMOs are less tightly organized independent practice associations (IPAs), which contract with physicians or physician groups to provide services. A physician or group might belong to several competing IPAs.

In PPOs "preferred" physicians and hospitals accept discounted fee-for-service reimbursement rates and administrative controls in exchange for a flow of patients. PPO patients might also visit nonpreferred providers in the network, but at additional cost.

Point of service (POS) plans allow still greater choice of physicians or hospitals for higher premiums. Out-of-network care is still covered, but less completely and with higher copayments.

We discuss here how managed care systems try to control health care expenditures through gatekeeping, financial incentives, and administrative measures.

THE PHYSICIAN AS GATEKEEPER

In many managed care systems primary care physicians serve as gatekeepers who must approve referrals to subspecialists or hospitalizations for them to be reimbursed. Gatekeepers might be financially at risk for the costs of care for their panel of patients.

Gatekeeping restrictions are unpopular with patients and physicians alike (48). Demands for "freedom of choice" of physicians have led many plans to modify strict gatekeeping. Direct access to some specialists, such as gynecologists, is common and even mandated in some states. Some insurers are offering plans that provide unrestricted access to specialists (48).

FINANCIAL INCENTIVES TO PHYSICIANS

Managed care plans might offer physicians a range of incentives to practice cost-effective medicine (31).

Capitation

Plans may pay primary physicians or physician groups on a capitated basis. The provider receives a fixed amount per patient enrolled, regardless of how often the patient visits.

Salary

Salary is common as a base reimbursement in staff-model HMOs and in large physician groups. Both salary and capitation provide a financial incentive to limit the amount of health care provided and to avoid more complicated patients.

Bonus and Withhold

Primary care physicians might also be financially liable for excessive expenditures (14,28,31). The managed care plan might withhold part of the primary care physician's capitated payments, and, if expenditures are high, the plan might keep the withheld funds. Alternatively, some plans give gatekeepers a bonus if expenditures for specialty care or hospitalizations fall below a target level.

Balanced Incentives

Increasingly, physicians also receive bonuses for patient satisfaction, adherence to prevention and chronic care guidelines, and other measures of quality of care (32,33,47). These quality incentives counterbalance incentives to provide fewer services.

Typical bonuses range from 5% to 10% of net income (32). When more of the physician's income is at stake, concerns about conflicts of interest intensify.

Incentives that a managed care plan presents to a physician group might differ from the incentives the group presents to the individual physician. Physicians also commonly face various incentives from different insurance plans and might not know the details of reimbursement for any particular patient.

ADMINISTRATIVE MEASURES TO CONTROL COSTS

In addition to financial incentives, managed care systems use a variety of administrative measures to control costs. Most fee-for-service plans also use some of these techniques.

Utilization Review

Such programs include prior authorization, concurrent review, discharge planning, and case management for high-cost patients (49). They are intended to discourage physicians from providing unnecessary or marginal services. However, some utilization review procedures might disallow interventions that physicians consider medically necessary and beneficial to patients (18,50).

Practice Guidelines or Protocols

These specify how physicians should act in certain circumstances (26). They may limit inappropriate use of specialists or diagnostic tests, correct underuse of beneficial interventions, and reduce unjustified variations in practice. However, physicians might reject such guidelines as "cookbook medicine" or bureaucratic infringements on physicians' professional judgment.

Direct Limitations on Services

Most insurance plans have formularies that exclude certain expensive drugs and provide financial incentives to patients to use generic drugs and preferred drugs for which plans have negotiated favorable prices.

DESELECTION

Some physicians fear that their contract with an insurance care plan will not be renewed if they are identified as high utilizers of resources or appeal many utilization review decisions (51,52). Such concerns might lead physicians to provide fewer services, independently of any direct financial incentives to do so.

REFERENCES

1. Heffler S, Smith S, Keehan S, et al. Health spending projections through 2013. *Health Aff (Millwood)* 2003; Suppl:W3–54–65.
2. Schwartz WB. The inevitable failure of current cost-containment strategies. Why they can provide only temporary relief. *JAMA* 1987;257:220–224.
3. Eddy DM. Health system reform: will controlling costs require rationing services? *JAMA* 1994;272:324–328.
4. Pauly MV. Medicare drug coverage and moral hazard. *Health Aff (Millwood)* 2004;23(1):113–122.
5. Boren SD. I had a tough day today, Hillary. *N Engl J Med* 1994;330:500–502.
6. Regopoulos LE, Trude S. Employers shift rising health care costs to workers: no long-term solution in sight. *Issue Brief Cent Stud Health Syst Change* 2004(83):1–4.
7. Trude S, Grossman JM. Patient cost-sharing innovations: promises and pitfalls. *Issue Brief Cent Stud Health Syst Change* 2004(75):1–4.
8. Robinson JC. Renewed emphasis on consumer cost sharing in health insurance benefit design. *Health Aff (Millwood)* 2002;Suppl Web Exclusives:W139–W154.
9. Soumerai SB. Benefits and risks of increasing restrictions on access to costly drugs in Medicaid. *Health Aff (Millwood)* 2004;23(1):135–146.
10. Huskamp HA, Deverka PA, Epstein AM, et al. The effect of incentive-based formularies on prescription-drug utilization and spending. *N Engl J Med* 2003;349(23):2224–2232.
11. Kamal-Bahl S, Briesacher B. How do incentive-based formularies influence drug selection and spending for hypertension? *Health Aff (Millwood)* 2004;23(1):227–236.

12. Alexander GC, Casalino LP, Meltzer DO. Patient–physician communication about out-of-pocket costs. *JAMA* 2003;290(7):953–958.
13. Hillman AL, Pauly MV, Kerman K, et al. HMO managers' views on financial incentives and quality. *Health Aff (Millwood)* 1991;10:207–219.
14. Hillman AL. Financial incentives for physicians in HMOs: is there a conflict of interest? *N Engl J Med* 1987;317:1743–1748.
15. Rodwin MA. *Medicine, money, and morals: physicians' conflicts of interest.* New York: Oxford University Press, 1993.
16. Miller RH, Luft HS. Does managed care lead to better or worse quality of care? *Health Aff* 1997;16(5):7–25.
17. Miller RH, Luft HS. HMO plan performance update: an analysis of the literature, 1997-2001. *Health Aff (Millwood)* 2002;21(4):63–86.
18. Borowsky SJ, Davis MK, Goertz C, et al. Are all health plans created equal? The physician's view. *JAMA* 1997;278(11):917–921.
19. Blendon RJ, Brodie M, Benson JM, et al. Understanding the managed care backlash. *Health Aff* 1998;17(4): 80–94.
20. Kerr EA, Hays RD, Mittman BS, et al. Primary care physicians' satisfaction with quality of care in California capitated medical groups. *JAMA* 1997;278:308–312.
21. Halm EA, Causino N, Blumenthal D. Is gatekeeping better than traditional care? *JAMA* 1997;278:1677–1681.
22. Landon BE, Reschovsky JD, Blumenthal D. Physicians' views of formularies: implications for Medicare drug benefit design. *Health Aff (Millwood)* 2004;23(1):218–226.
23. Kao AC, Green DC, Zaslavsky AM, et al. The relationship between method of physician payment and patient trust. *JAMA* 1998;280:1708–1714.
24. Kassirer JP. Managing care—should we adopt a new ethic? *N Engl J Med* 1998;339:397–398.
25. Povar GJ, Blumen H, Daniel J, et al. Ethics in practice: managed care and the changing health care environment: medicine as a profession managed care ethics working group statement. *Ann Intern Med* 2004;141(2): 131–136.
26. Hillman AL. Managing the physician: rules versus incentives. *Health Aff (Millwood)* 1991;10:138–146.
27. Hall MA, Berenson RA. Ethical practice in managed care: a dose of realism. *Ann Intern Med* 1998;128:395–402.
28. Hillman AL. Health maintenance organizations, financial incentives, and physicians' judgments. *Ann Intern Med* 1990;112:891–893.
29. Latham SR. Regulation of managed care incentive payments to physicians. *Am J Law Med* 1996;22:399–432.
30. Orentlicher D. Paying physicians more to do less: financial incentives to limit care. *Univ Richmond Law Rev* 1996;30:155–197.
31. Pearson SD, Daniels N, Emanuel E. Ethical guidelines for physician compensation based on capitation. *N Engl J Med* 1998;339:689–693.
32. Grumbach K, Osmond D, Varanizan K, et al. Primary care physicians' experience of financial incentives in managed care systems. *N Engl J Med* 1998;339:1516–1521.
33. Epstein AM, Lee TH, Hamel MB. Paying physicians for high-quality care. *N Engl J Med* 2004;350(4):406–410.
34. Levinson DF. Toward full disclosure of referral restrictions and financial incentives by prepaid health plans. *N Engl J Med* 1987;317:1729–1731.
35. Gallagher TH, Alpers A, Lo B. HCFA's new regulations for financial incentives in medicare and medicaid managed care. *Am J Med* 1998;105:409–415.
36. Miller TE, Sage WM. Disclosing physician financial incentives. *JAMA* 1999;281:1424–1430.
37. Hall MA, Dugan E, Balkrishnan R, et al. How disclosing HMO physician incentives affects trust. Not all cost-minimizing physician incentives are ethically troubling to patients. *Health Aff (Millwood)* 2002;21(2):197–206.
38. Ellrodt AG, Conner L, Riedinger M, et al. Measuring and improving physician compliance with clinical practice guidelines. *Ann Intern Med* 1995;122:277–282.
39. Pearson SD. Caring and cost: the challenge for physician advocacy. *Ann Intern Med* 2000;133(2):148–153.
40. Wickline v. State of California. 228 Cal.Rptr. 661 (Cal. App. 1986).
41. Ubel PA, Goold S. Recognizing bedside rationing: clear cases and tough calls. *Ann Intern Med* 1997;126: 74–80.
42. Morreim EH. Gaming the system: dodging the rules, ruling the dodgers. *Arch Intern Med* 1991;151:443–447.
43. Wynia MK, Cummins DS, VanGeest JB, et al. Should physicians manipulate reimbursement rules to benefit patients? *JAMA* 2000;284(11):1382–1383.
44. Werner RM, Alexander GC, Fagerlin A, et al. The "Hassle Factor": what motivates physicians to manipulate reimbursement rules? *Arch Intern Med* 2002;162(10):1134–1139.
45. Gallagher TH, Lo B, Chesney M, et al. How do managed care physicians respond to patients' requests for costly, unindicated tests? *J Gen Intern Med* 1997;12:663–668.
46. Tye S, Phillips KA, Liang SY, et al. Moving beyond the typologies of managed care: the example of health plan predictors of screening mammography. *Health Serv Res* 2004;39(1):179–206.
47. Bodenheimer T. Physicians and the changing medical marketplace. *N Engl J Med* 1999;340:584–588.
48. Bodenheimer T, Lo B, Casalino L. Primary care physicians should be coordinators, not gatekeepers. *JAMA* 1999;281:2045–2049.
49. Hoy EW, Curtis RE, Rice T. Change and growth in managed care. *Health Aff (Millwood)* 1991;10:18–36.
50. Kaiser Family Foundation. Survey of physicians and nurses. In: www.kff.org; July, 1999.
51. Blum JD. The evolution of physician credentialing into managed care selective contracting. *Am J Law Med* 1996;22:173–204.
52. Woolhandler S, Himmelstein DU. Extreme risk—the new corporate proposition for physicians. *N Engl J Med* 1995;333:1706–1708.

ANNOTATED BIBLIOGRAPHY

1. Kassirer JP. Managed care and the morality of the marketplace. *N Engl J Med* 1995;333:50–52.
   Eloquent plea that professional ethics is incompatible with a profit-oriented, entrepreneurial approach to medicine.
2. Pearson SD, Daniels N, Emanuel E. Ethical guidelines for physician compensation based on capitation. *N Engl J Med* 1998;339:689–693.
   Suggestions for a just system of incentives in managed care.
3. Hall MA, Berenson RA. Ethical practice in managed care: a dose of realism. *Ann Intern Med* 1998;128:395–402.
4. Hall MA. *Making medical spending decisions*. New York: Oxford University Press, 1997.
   An article and a book that both argue that financial incentives to physicians to limit care can be ethical and in fact are preferable to rules set by administrators.
5. Miller TE, Sage WM. Disclosing physician financial incentives. *JAMA* 1999;281:1424–1430.
   Analyzes the rationale for disclosure of financial incentives to physicians.
6. Epstein AM, Lee TH, Hamel MB. Paying physicians for high-quality care. *N Engl J Med* 2004;350:406–410.
   Thoughtful overview of use of physician incentives to improve quality of care.
7. Povar GJ, Blumen H, Daniel J, et al. Ethics in practice: managed care and the changing health care environment: medicine as a profession managed care ethics working group statement. *Ann Intern Med* 2004;141:131–136.
   Consensus guidelines for ethical practice in managed care.

CHAPTER 33

Gifts from Drug Companies

Gifts from drug companies to physicians are ubiquitous. One study found that 97% of residents were carrying at least one item, such as reference books (90%), pens (79%), and information cards (70%), that had pharmaceutical insignia (1). Although gifts and subsidies from drug companies might foster medical education and provide welcome perks to physicians and students, some gifts might impair the physician's judgment or create the impression of a conflict of interest. This chapter presents arguments for and against accepting gifts from drug companies or manufacturers of medical products and suggests guidelines for such gifts.

TYPES OF GIFTS

In 2003 pharmaceutical manufacturers spent over $13 billion—almost 12% of sales—in advertising and promotions to physicians (2). Gifts and subsidies from drug companies to physicians range from token to lavish.

Small gifts that bear the company or product name include pens and message pads, as well as more expensive items such as umbrellas, flashlights, and clocks. Drug companies might also distribute medical books and equipment, such as reflex hammers.

MEALS AND HOSPITALITY

Drug companies frequently provide lunch or refreshments at hospital conferences or continuing medical education (CME) courses. Conference organizers often solicit these subsidies to increase attendance. Companies also host dinners coupled with a talk for physicians.

CONTINUING MEDICAL EDUCATION AND CONFERENCES

Drug companies might support hospital conferences by paying honoraria and travel expenses for speakers. Over half the support for continuing medical education programs is from commercial entities. In an era of financial constraints, such subsidies might enable hospitals or medical schools to invite nationally prominent experts. Drug companies might also subsidize continuing education courses and professional society meetings in exchange for setting up booths to display their products.

REASONS FOR DRUG COMPANIES TO OFFER GIFTS

One commentator observed, "No drug company gives away its shareholders' money in an act of disinterested generosity (3)." There is substantial evidence that drug companies strengthen recognition of their products through gifts to physicians (4). One study found that doctors who attended a drug company–sponsored CME or who accepted funds for travel or lodging for educational symposia were more likely to prescribe the sponsor's medications. This occurred even if physicians forgot the sponsors' names or believed that they could not be influenced. Doctors who met with pharmaceutical representatives or accepted industry-paid meals were more likely to request formulary additions or to prescribe in nonrational ways. Physicians who received gifts from pharmaceutical manufacturers, even practice-related gifts, were more likely to believe that gifts did not affect prescribing behavior.

REASONS FOR ACCEPTING DRUG-COMPANY GIFTS

Gifts from drug companies might subsidize continuing education courses and thereby enhance medical education and professional society meetings. Even providing lunches for hospital conferences might improve educational programs by increasing attendance. Thus, some argue that all drug-company gifts and subsidies overall have more benefit than harm. If physicians refused all gifts and subsidies from drug companies, patients would pay the same amount for drugs but their physicians would receive less education.

OBJECTIONS TO ACCEPTING DRUG-COMPANY GIFTS

Table 33-1 summarizes objections to accepting gifts from drug companies.

GIFTS CREATE THE EXPECTATION OF RECIPROCITY

Gifts create relationships and obligations in the recipient, such as grateful conduct, good will, and reciprocation (5,6). The problem is not that physicians would immediately change prescribing practices after receiving a free lunch. Rather, as one writer has warned, "The sell is much more subtle. All the advertiser may expect is that, other things being equal, if you subsequently have to make a decision it is more likely to be in the favor of the advertiser (7)."

GIFTS IMPAIR OBJECTIVITY

Objectivity of presentations at conferences and continuing education courses might be compromised if the drug company selects speakers and topics, prepares slides for presentations, writes or edits talks, or trains the presenters (8). A speaker might selectively present or emphasize data favorable to one drug or class of drugs rather than draw from the overall body of available data (9). Research sponsored by pharmaceutical companies is more likely to report results that favor the sponsor's drug than research sponsored by nonprofit organizations (10–12). Studies find bias in the design and publication of results in some industry-sponsored clinical trials (13,14).

When academic institutions sponsor CME programs, physicians expect the institution to select the speakers and topics independently without drug company interference. Because the bias introduced into programs supported by pharmaceutical companies is "almost never obvious (8)," it might have a greater impact than clear-cut advertising by drug companies.

TABLE 33-1

Objections to Accepting Gifts from Drug Companies

Gifts create the expectation of reciprocity.
Gifts impair objectivity.
Gifts increase the cost of health care.
Gifts demean the profession.
Gifts give the appearance of conflict of interest.

GIFTS INCREASE THE COST OF HEALTH CARE

Ultimately patients and their insurers pay for drug-company gifts to physicians. Given the rising cost of drugs, it might be unseemly for physicians to receive even small gifts from drug companies. One physician criticized, "Am I supposed to believe that the members of a clinical department are so impoverished that they cannot buy their own pens or pizza and beer?" (7). Even low-cost gifts, such as pens and notepads, might undermine evidence-based prescribing by reminding physicians of certain drugs, regardless of their actual effectiveness.

GIFTS DEMEAN THE PROFESSION

Dependence on drug-company subsidies to support CME programs demeans physicians (7). If the public realized that physicians attend conferences only if lunch is provided or the registration fee is subsidized, they might infer that physicians place little value on keeping up to date with medical research.

GIFTS GIVE THE APPEARANCE OF CONFLICT OF INTEREST

Even if gifts from pharmaceutical companies do not actually influence a physician's therapeutic decisions, the appearance of bias and conflict of interest might be deleterious. After all, physicians are not choosing medications for their own use and paying the bills themselves; they are prescribing for their patients. According to one survey, patients are more likely than physicians to believe that gifts are not appropriate and that gifts influence physician behavior (15). About 30% of patients believe that even small gifts such as a mug, pen, or lunch would influence physician behavior, compared to about 10% of physicians (15).

Outside of medicine, society has enacted strict rules regarding conflicts of interest that might undermine trust in public officials. Judges are expected to refuse gifts from persons or companies who have a financial stake in their professional decisions. Government officials may not accept gifts of more than nominal value from persons or organizations who would be affected by or gain financially from their decisions. By analogy, it might be inappropriate for physicians to accept drug-company gifts that create even the appearance of a conflict of interest.

RECOMMENDATIONS

FORBID CERTAIN PRACTICES

Certain types of gifts and support from drug companies are so likely to raise questions about bias and impropriety that they should be banned (8,16). For example, the American College of Physicians, the American Medical Association, the Accreditation Council for Continuing Medical Education, and the Pharmaceutical Manufacturers Association agree that it is unethical for physicians to accept direct payments to attend activites that have no educational value (17). Course directors should retain complete control of the scientific program and choice of speakers when drug companies support CME. In addition, the company should not select the physicians who attend the educational program or pay for their expenses or time. In accredited CME, speakers' conflicts of interest must be resolved. Any honoraria or consulting fee from commercial entities is considered a conflict of interest (18). Recently the pharmaceutical industry declared that occasional meals provided in conjunction with informational presentations must be modest. Drug company representatives may not provide items for the personal benefit of healthcare professionals, such as tickets to a sporting or recreational event. Drug company representatives may not provide items, such as tickets to a sporting or recreational event for healthcare professionals' benefit.

ALLOW CERTAIN OTHER PRACTICES

Some types of gifts or support are widely considered acceptable. At professional society meetings, drug companies often underwrite the printing of abstract books. In turn, they set up displays in an exhibition hall. Many physicians accept pens or note pads that bear the names of drug companies or their products. However, even these small items might impair objectivity and give the appearance of conflicts of interest.

DISCLOSE GIFTS TO THE PUBLIC

It might be difficult to distinguish between what is acceptable and what is not. A helpful rule of thumb is, "What would your patients or the public think if they knew you had accepted these gifts?" (17). In borderline cases it would be judicious to err on the side of declining gifts.

In summary, gifts from drug companies might raise at least the appearance of conflicts of interest, increase the cost of health care, and impair objectivity. Physicians need to remember that ultimately their primary concern should be their patients' best interests, not their own personal convenience or well-being.

REFERENCES

1. Sigworth SK, Nettleman MD, Cohen GM. Pharmaceutical branding of resident physicians. *JAMA* 2001;286(9): 1024–1025.
2. Rosenthal MB, Berndt ER, Donohue JM, et al. Promotion of prescription drugs to consumers. *N Engl J Med* 2002;346(7):498–505.
3. Rawlins MD. Doctors and the drug makers. *Lancet* 1984;2:276–278.
4. Wazana A. Physicians and the pharmaceutical industry: is a gift ever just a gift? *JAMA* 2000;283(3):373–380.
5. Dana J, Loewenstein G. A social science perspective on gifts to physicians from industry. *JAMA* 2003;290(2): 252–255.
6. Chren M, Landefeld S, Murray TH. Doctors, drug companies, and gifts. *JAMA* 1989;262:3448–3451.
7. Waud DR. Pharmaceutical promotions: a free lunch? *N Engl J Med* 1992;327:351–353.
8. American College of Physicians. Physicians and the pharmaceutical industry. *Ann Int Med* 1990;112(8):624–626.
9. Kessler DA. Drug promotion and scientific exchange: the role of the physician investigator. *N Engl J Med* 1991; 325:201–203.
10. Lexchin J, Bero LA, Djulbegovic B, et al. Pharmaceutical industry sponsorship and research outcome and quality: systematic review. *Br Med J* 2003;326(7400):1167–1170.
11. Friedman LS, Richter ED. Relationship between conflicts of interest and research results. *J Gen Intern Med* 2004;19:51–56.
12. Bhandari M, Busse JW, Jackowski D, et al. Association between industry funding and statistically significant pro-industry findings in medical and surgical randomized trials. *CMAJ* 2004;170(4):477–480.
13. Lenzer J. Alteplase for stroke: money and optimistic claims buttress the "brain attack" campaign. *Br Med J* 2002; 324(7339):723–729.
14. Krzyzanowska MK, Pintilie M, Tannock IF. Factors associated with failure to publish large randomized trials presented at an oncology meeting. *JAMA* 2003;290(4):495–501.
15. Gibbons RV, Landry FJ, Blouch DL, et al. A comparison of physicians' and patients' attitudes towards pharmaceutical industry gifts. *J Gen Intern Med* 1998;13:151–154.
16. Gifts to physicians from industry. *JAMA* 1991;265:501.
17. Coyle SL. Physician-industry relations. Part 1: individual physicians. *Ann Intern Med* 2002;136(5):396–402.
18. Steinbrook R. Commercial support and continuing medical education. *N Engl J Med* 2005;352:In press.

ANNOTATED BIBLIOGRAPHY

1. Wazana A. Physicians and the pharmaceutical industry: is a gift ever just a gift? *JAMA* 2000;283:373–380. Summary of the empirical evidence of the impact of gifts on physician behavior and attitudes.
2. Coyle SL. Physician–industry relations. Part 1: individual physicians. *Ann Intern Med* 2002;136:396–402. Coyle SL. Physician–industry relations. Part 2: organizational issues. *Ann Intern Med* 2002;136:403–406. Critical analysis of drug-company sponsorship of CME and medical conferences.
3. Chren M, Landefeld S, Murray TH. Doctors, drug companies, and gifts. *JAMA* 1989;262:3448–3451. Argues that gifts from drug companies create expectations of reciprocity that might compromise physicians' responsibility to their patients' interests.
4. Waud DR. Pharmaceutical promotions: a free lunch? *N Engl J Med* 1992;327:351–353. Spirited article arguing that physicians should not accept any gifts from drug companies.
5. Steinbrook R. Commercial support and continuing medical education. *N Engl J Med* 2005;352:In press. Analysis of new standards on conflicts of interests in CME, to assure that presentations are balanced and free of bias.

CHAPTER 34

Disclosing Errors

An estimated 40,000 Americans die every year because of medical errors (1). In one survey 42% of the public and 35% of physicians reported that an error had occurred in their care or a family member's care (2). Disclosure of mistakes to patients and colleagues is difficult for physicians, who might fear recriminations from patients, setbacks to their professional reputation or livelihood, and lawsuits. One study found that house officers who made serious errors reported them to attending physicians in only 54% of cases and to patients or families in only 24% of cases (3). In another survey one third of physicians said they would not tell the family about an error that was fatal to the patient (4). The following case illustrates dilemmas posed by physicians' errors.

CASE 34.1 Overdose of insulin.

A 54-year-old man with diabetes is hospitalized for congestive heart failure. The resident prescribes 100 units of insulin rather than the patient's usual dose of 10 units, and the patient receives the higher dose. He develops hypoglycemia, seizures, and coma. Upon recovery, both the patient and his family ask physicians why the seizures occurred. The health care team wonders how to respond.

The patient and family naturally want to know why his condition changed so dramatically. The team is reluctant to tell them that an error occurred, fearing that they would get angry and perhaps take legal action.

Traditionally, such errors have been viewed as deficits in knowledge, effort, or conscientiousness, and the physician who wrote the wrong dosage would be blamed. However, a different view of error has been accepted, one that makes blaming the physician problematic (5–7). First, errors like the one in Case 34.1 usually are due to a momentary loss of concentration or attention, which are beyond the doctor's voluntary control. Such lapses are unavoidable because human cognition and attention are limited and fallible. A "slip of the pen" could happen to the most expert and careful physician. Second, there are multiple system causes for the error. The pharmacist who dispensed the medication and the nurse who administered it failed to detect the incorrect dosage. The resident or attending physician might have provided inadequate supervision. More training for physicians, nurses, and pharmacists is unlikely to reduce these errors. Instead, the health care delivery system needs to be redesigned (8). For example, computerized ordering of medications would reliably detect such errors in dosage. Furthermore, communication and working relationships among physicians, pharmacists, and nurses might need to be changed.

This chapter discusses the reasons for and against disclosing errors and suggests how physicians can respond to them. *Error* refers to a failure of a plan to be completed as intended or the use of a wrong plan to achieve an aim (1). Errors can be either acts or omissions. Errors might—or might not—result in harm to patients; when no harm is done, the incident is called a *near miss* or a *close call*. Errors can or cannot be avoidable. Adverse events are defined as undesired patient outcomes that result from medical care rather than from the underlying disease; they include situations in which the treatment plan was appropriate and carried out correctly, such as side effects of drugs.

REASONS NOT TO DISCLOSE ERRORS TO PATIENTS OR SURROGATES

Physicians commonly offer several reasons against disclosing serious errors to patients or surrogates.

THE PHYSICIAN IS NOT REALLY RESPONSIBLE FOR THE ERROR

Physicians understandably do not want to take the blame for errors if they are not morally responsible. If systems flaws and limits in human cognition cause errors, they are beyond people's control. Individual physicians should not be held morally responsible for actions and events beyond their control (5). Thus, the traditional response of blaming the individual for errors might not enhance patient safety, except in the case of negligent or intentional violations of a clear standard of care or performance (5). Similarly, remedial education programs can be effective only in situations in which a deficiency in knowledge or skill causes the error. Instead, with most errors, patient safety can be enhanced only by systems-level responses that provide additional defenses against the adverse consequences of errors. Examples of such defenses that might be useful in Case 34.2 are checklists, bar coding, and computerized ordering of medications. This systems approach to errors has proved effective in the field of anesthesia and in other complex fields such as commercial aviation. Determining the cause of a serious error is essential to improving quality of care and preventing recurrences of the error, but uncertainty over cause and responsibility should not deter physicians from informing patients or surrogates about the error.

DISCLOSURE WOULD HARM THE PATIENT OR SURROGATE

Physicians might believe that if errors are disclosed, patients or surrogates might worry unnecessarily about other aspects of care. Such worry might cause stress or deter patients from seeking necessary care or accepting beneficial interventions in the future.

DISCLOSURE WOULD HARM HEALTH CARE PROFESSIONALS

Physicians might fear that patients or families might respond to disclosure of errors by becoming angry, filing a lawsuit, or leaving the physician's practice. In surveys most respondents said they would change physicians if their physician committed a life-threatening error (9,10). The reluctance of physicians to acknowledge errors, however, creates a vicious circle because patients become more upset if they believe physicians are not forthright about an error.

Health care workers might be concerned that their reputations or careers will be damaged if they disclose a serious error to a supervising physician. Colleagues and supervisors who are told of an error might be punitive rather than supportive (3).

REASONS TO DISCLOSE ERRORS TO PATIENTS OR SURROGATES

There are several strong reasons to disclose errors to patients or their surrogates (Table 34-1).

DISCLOSURE RESPECTS THE PATIENT

Almost all patients report that they would want even minor errors disclosed to them (9,10). Patients want to know what happened, why it happened, how adverse consequences will be mitigated, and how recurrences will be prevented (11). In addition, patients seek an apology (11). Disclosure would reassure them that they are receiving complete information about their care and would enhance their trust in physicians. Unless the patient in Case 34.1 is told about the insulin overdose, he cannot understand this episode. He might well fear that seizures and coma will recur or that he

TABLE 34-1
Reasons to Disclose Mistakes to Patients or Surrogates
Disclosure respects the patient.
Disclosure benefits the patient.
Disclosure benefits the physician.
Disclosure maintains public trust.

has a grave problem, such as a brain tumor. Fearing a recurrence, he might change jobs or cut back on activities such as driving or travel. Under the doctrine of informed consent, physicians have an affirmative duty to provide the patient or surrogate with pertinent information about the patient's condition and the options for care. This duty to disclose goes beyond merely responding honestly to questions. In thinking about disclosure, physicians might imagine that the patient is a close relative. How would they feel if a dramatic change occurred in their relative's condition and the health care team was not forthright about what happened?

DISCLOSURE BENEFITS THE PATIENT

Disclosure enables patients or surrogates to take steps to mitigate the harms that the error caused. Patients might need additional tests, treatment, close monitoring, or additional follow-up care. Patients or families are more likely to cooperate with such measures if they understand the reasons for them.

Disclosure might also allow patients to be compensated for harms resulting from errors. In Case 34.1 the patient required intensive care, a prolonged hospitalization, and a computed tomography (CT) scan following the error. It seems unfair and callous to ask the patient or an insurer to pay for this additional care. Moreover, most patients want charges for such care to be waived (9). Furthermore, it is seems reasonable to compensate patients for lost income or serious disability resulting directly from errors (12). Patients cannot negotiate such compensation unless they or their surrogates are aware that an error occurred.

DISCLOSURE BENEFITS THE PHYSICIAN

When a serious error has been made, it seems callous and deceptive not to admit it and to avoid taking responsibility for it. When a person harms another, apologizing is the expected social response and a prerequisite to making amends and being forgiven (13,14).

Disclosure might also mitigate adverse impacts on the physician's livelihood. One study found that patients are less likely to change doctors if they are told of errors and the physician accepts responsibility (9). However, in most scenarios, disclosure and apology did not reduce the respondent's likelihood of seeking legal advice.

Nondisclosure might worsen the situation for the physician. The patient or family will likely learn the cause of a dramatic complication, such as the seizures in Case 34.1. They will probably feel outraged and betrayed if they were not informed promptly. In one survey patients said that they would be more likely to sue if the physician had not informed them of an error and they found out in some other way than if the physician voluntarily admitted the error immediately after committing it (10). Legal liability might also be greater if the physician conceals negligent actions and the patient is harmed by reliance on such misrepresentation (15).

DISCLOSURE MAINTAINS PUBLIC TRUST

Nondisclosure might harm the profession as a whole, not just the individual physician. If the public perceives a pattern of nondisclosure, patients might believe that doctors are more concerned with protecting themselves than with doing what is best for patients. Such mistrust might affect other aspects of care.

WHAT SHOULD PHYSICIANS SAY TO PATIENTS?

The Joint Commission for the Accreditation of Health Care Organizations requires hospitals to tell patients when unanticipated outcomes of care occur (16). However, many hospitals report that they would not disclose preventable harms, primarily because of concerns about malpractice (17).

In Case 34.1 the physician clearly made an error, the patient suffered serious harm, and the error caused a poor outcome. Under these circumstances the physician's responsibility to the patient should prevail over any self-interest in concealing the error. The physician should take the initiative in disclosing relevant information. First, physicians should explicitly acknowledge that an error occurred and offer an apology (12). Second, the physician needs to explain the error and its consequences. Third, the physician should explain what can and will be done to mitigate the resulting harms to the patient and to prevent the error from recurring.

Some physicians might make only limited disclosure of errors—for example, telling the patient and family in Case 34.1 only that the seizures were caused by low blood sugar, without saying that an error occurred. Other physicians might say they regret what happened but take responsibility for the error. However, a partial apology might be worse than none; patients might view them as evasive and mean-spirited. In addition, the patient and family are likely to probe for details—for example, to ask what caused his glucose to be low. The most appropriate ethical response to concerns about a lawsuit in Case 34.1 would be for the risk manager to offer a fair out-of-court settlement.

SITUATIONS IN WHICH DISCLOSURE IS CONTROVERSIAL

In many cases it might not be clear that the physician should disclose an error to patients or take responsibility for it.

THE ERROR CAUSED NO HARM

Sometimes physicians make definite errors but the patient suffers no harm. These errors have been called "near misses."

CASE 34.2 Incorrect prescription.
A physician prescribed a sulfonamide antibiotic to a patient with a history of allergy to those medications. A nurse discovered the error, and the prescription was changed after two doses. No adverse effects occurred.

Such near misses need to be reported to quality improvement programs in order to identify system problems that might lead to similar errors that do harm patients. However, should such near misses be disclosed to the patient? In Case 34.2 some physicians might argue that if the prognosis or future care of the patient is not altered, there is no point in telling the patient of the error. Such physicians might hesitate to burden patients with all the uncertainties and adjustments made in the course of care. In addition, patients might be harmed if they lost confidence in physicians and hospitals.

Even in this case, however, there are strong reasons to disclose the error to patients. Disclosure is likely to strengthen the doctor–patient relationship because patients respect physicians for being honest. Disclosure might also promote patient well-being; because of this error the diagnosis of drug allergy might be reconsidered. Furthermore, patients themselves might call attention to errors—for example, after noticing that the medication has been changed. If this occurs, physicians might find it difficult to explain the situation if the physician did not tell the patient of the error immediately. Finally, there is little risk to physicians in disclosing "near misses" because patients who suffer no harm are unlikely to get angry with the physician and cannot sue if no harm occurred.

OUTCOME WOULD HAVE BEEN POOR EVEN WITHOUT THE ERROR

In other cases the physician makes an error and the patient suffers a poor outcome but the poor outcome would have occurred even if there had been no error. The adverse outcome, for example, might be due to the underlying disease.

CASE 34.3 Failure to administer appropriate treatment.

A 52-year-old man developed vomiting and ataxia, followed by stupor and coma. He was taken to the emergency department, where he had a blood pressure of 200/105, which was not treated while a CT scan was obtained. He was found to have a cerebellar hemorrhage and died in the emergency department.

In this case standard care would be to lower blood pressure before obtaining the CT scan. However, once comatose, he would almost certainly have died even if his blood pressure had been lowered.

In such situations, when telling the family about the patient's death, the physicians should not say that an error was a contributing factor. Physicians must recognize, however, that determining whether an error caused an adverse outcome is very difficult (18) and that their belief that the error caused no harm to the patient might be biased or self-serving. Consultation with an experienced colleague might help physicians evaluate their judgment and actions accurately.

Even if an error is not mentioned, family members might ask physicians whether everything was done to prevent an adverse outcome. This question deserves both a literal and deeper response. On the literal level, it would be deceptive to say that everything was done when the physician knows that this was not the case. On another level, the survivors might be asking whether *they* should have acted differently or whether the patient suffered needlessly. The physician needs to acknowledge and respond to these concerns. For instance, the physician might say, "It's natural when someone dies suddenly to ask if anything more could have been done. In hindsight, we may all wish we had acted differently. When a patient dies in the emergency department, we review the case to see if there are any things we can improve for the next case. However, once patients with this kind of bleeding into the brain lose consciousness, the bleeding is so severe that they don't recover. . . . One thing that is clear is he didn't suffer."

ADVERSE OUTCOME COULD NOT HAVE BEEN AVOIDED

Some adverse events related to a procedure are due to a mishap during the procedure, such as poor technique or a slip of the instrument. System factors, such as inadequate training or supervision, might be contributing factors. In other cases, however, the unintended outcome could not have been avoided.

CASE 34.4 Foreseeable complication of an invasive procedure.

A 43-year-old man with interstitial lung disease undergoes a bronchoscopy and transbronchial biopsy. The procedure is performed following accepted procedures. He suffers a pneumothorax that requires insertion of a chest tube for 2 days. The patient was informed of this risk prior to the procedure.

In this case the patient suffered a known complication of an invasive procedure that was appropriate and skillfully performed. The physician needs to review the case to be certain that the standard of care was followed. The patient agreed to the procedure and accepted the risks. Although the physician must explain the unintended adverse outcome and should express regret over it, the doctor is not to blame for this complication.

DISCLOSING ERRORS BY TRAINEES TO AN ATTENDING PHYSICIAN

In teaching hospitals serious errors by trainees might not be reported to attending physicians (3).

DISCLOSURE OF SERIOUS ERRORS BY TRAINEES TO SUPERVISING PHYSICIANS

Students, house officers, and fellows might be reluctant to tell supervisors about errors because they might fear that grades, recommendations, or future positions might be jeopardized. Supervisors might also be judgmental rather than supportive when told of errors.

Attending physicians, however, are ethically and legally responsible for patient care. They cannot perform this role adequately if significant information about the patient is withheld. Importantly, attending physicians might learn of such errors even if trainees do not disclose them. Most supervising physicians believe that failure to disclose errors is worse than making them in the first place (19). Although trainees are expected to make some errors, covering them up raises doubts about reliability, trustworthiness, and character.

RESPONSES TO ERRORS BY TRAINEES

Once a trainee has disclosed an error, the supervising physicians need to respond on several levels.

Elicit and Acknowledge the Trainee's Emotional Distress

Appropriate emotional support needs to be provided. The supervisor can put the trainee's feelings in context: Although it causes distress to admit an error, it is a sign of responsibility and caring. Moreover, it is essential to do so if the trainee is to learn from the error (3). Understanding this link between emotional distress and learning might offer the resident some solace.

Review the Medical Issues and Decisions

The supervisor can help the trainee learn from the error and make constructive changes in practice to prevent similar errors in the future. Such constructive changes might include seeking more advice in difficult cases, reading more about the medical problem, and confirming key clinical data personally rather than relying on someone else's report (3). Discussing errors explicitly can also help other trainees avoid similar errors (20).

Discuss How to Disclose the Error to the Patient or Surrogate

If disclosure is appropriate, the attending physician should inform the patient together with the trainee. Such joint discussions would provide trainees with emotional support and role modeling.

ERRORS BY OTHER HEALTH CARE WORKERS

A physician might become aware of a definite error by another health care worker that seriously harmed a patient. For example, in Case 34.1 a coworker on the primary team, another clinical service, or a different hospital might have made the overdose of insulin. Even if the current physician did not make the error, the patient still needs to understand what happened and perhaps take action to mitigate the harms caused by the error. Thus, the current physician might question whether he or she should disclose the error to the patient.

ETHICAL ISSUES REGARDING ERRORS BY OTHER HEALTH CARE WORKERS

From the patient's perspective, the reasons for disclosing errors to patients hold for errors by other health care workers as well as one's own errors. However, it is often more difficult for physicians to deal with errors by other health care workers. The facts of the case might be unclear. Even if physicians review the medical record, they might not know what actually happened, particularly at another hospital. In addition, disclosure might conflict with the current physician's self-interest. The other physician or institution might become irate or stop referring patients. Physicians in training who notice a serious error by a senior physician might fear retaliation (*see* Chapter 36). In addition, the patient or family might vent their anger on the current physician, who bears no responsibility for the error.

RESPONSES TO ERRORS BY OTHER HEALTH CARE WORKERS

Faced with a clear and serious error by another health care worker, the current physician might take several approaches.

Wait for the Patient to Ask

Waiting for the patient to ask is ethically problematic because physicians have an affirmative obligation not only to answer patients' questions honestly but also to disclose relevant information to patients.

Ask the Other Physician to Disclose

Although asking the other physician to disclose the error might be easiest for the current physician, it might be problematic for the patient or family. The previous physician might choose not to tell the patient or might provide misleading information about the error.

Arrange a Joint Conference

If the patient is still receiving care at the institution in which the error occurred, a conference might be held with the current physician, the previous physician, and the patient or family. This approach allows the other physician to take the lead in revealing the error while ensuring that the discussion is appropriate.

Tell the Patient

Although telling the patient leads to appropriate disclosure, it might undermine the relationships between the patient and the previous physician and between the two physicians. It is possible that the other doctor wanted to talk to the patient directly and would have carried out the discussion appropriately. If this approach is taken, it would be preferable to give the other physician the opportunity to talk to the patient first.

In summary, the decision to acknowledge an error should be based on ethical guidelines, not on expedience. Disclosure of errors is difficult, but failure to disclose errors that cause serious harm undermines physicians' credibility and compromises their integrity. Anticipating potential adverse consequences of disclosure allows physicians to cope with them. Ultimately the quality of medical care is enhanced if physicians are willing to admit their errors and learn from them.

REFERENCES

1. Kohn LT, Corrigan JM, Donaldson M, eds. *To err is human: building a safer health system.* Washington: National Academy Press, 2000.
2. Blendon RJ, DesRoches CM, Brodie M, et al. Views of practicing physicians and the public on medical errors. *N Engl J Med* 2002;347(24):1933–1940.
3. Wu AW, Folkman S, McPhee SJ, et al. Do house officers learn from their mistakes? *JAMA* 1991;265:2094.
4. Novack DH, Detering BJ, Arnold R, et al. Physicians' attitudes toward using deception to resolve difficult ethical problems. *JAMA* 1989;261:2980–2985.
5. Runciman WB, Merry AF, Tito F. Error, blame, and the law in health care—an antipodean perspective. *Ann Intern Med* 2003;138(12):974–979.
6. Reason JT. Understanding adverse events: the human factor. In: Vincent C, ed. *Clinical risk management: enhancing patient safety*, 2nd ed. London: BMJ Books, 2001:9–30.
7. Reason J. Human error: models and management. *Br Med J (Clin Res Ed)* 2000;320(7237):768–770.
8. Nolan TW. System changes to improve patient safety. *Br Med J* 2000;320(7237):771–773.
9. Mazor KM, Simon SR, Yood RA, et al. Health plan members' views about disclosure of medical errors. *Ann Intern Med* 2004;140(6):409–418.
10. Witman AB, Park DM, Hardin SB. How do patients want physicians to handle mistakes? A survey of internal medicine patients in an academic setting. *Arch Intern Med* 1996;156(22):2565–2569.
11. Gallagher TH, Waterman AD, Ebers AG, et al. Patients' and physicians' perspective regarding the disclosure of medical errors. *JAMA* 2004;289:1001–1007.
12. Wu AW, Cavanaugh TA, McPhee SJ, et al. To tell the truth: ethical and practical issues in disclosing medical mistakes to patients. *J Gen Intern Med* 1997;17:770–775.
13. Hilfiker D. Facing our mistakes. *N Engl J Med* 1984;310:118–122.
14. Frenkel DN, Liebman CB. Words that heal. *Ann Intern Med* 2004;140(6):482–483.
15. Furrow BR, Johnson SH, Jost TS, et al. *Health law: cases, materials, problems*, 3rd ed. St. Paul: West Publishing Co, 1997:385–388.
16. American Society for Healthcare Risk Management. *Disclosure of Unanticipated Events: The Next Step in Better Communication with Patients.* Chicago: American Society for Healthcare Risk Management, 2003.
17. Lamb RM, Studdert DM, Bohmer RM, et al. Hospital disclosure practices: results of a national survey. *Health Aff (Millwood)* 2003;22(2):73–83.
18. Hofer TP, Hayward RA. Are bad outcomes from questionable clinical decisions preventable medical errors? A case of cascade iatrogenesis. *Ann Intern Med* 2002;137(5 Part 1):327–333.
19. Bosk CL. *Forgive and Remember: Managing Medical Failure.* Chicago: University of Chicago Press, 1979.
20. Pierluissi E, Fischer MA, Campbell AR, et al. Discussion of medical errors in morbidity and mortality conferences. *JAMA* 2003;290(21):2838–2842.

ANNOTATED BIBLIOGRAPHY

1. Hilficker D. Facing our mistakes. *N Engl J Med* 1984;310:118–122.
   Eloquent first-person account of a physician's reaction to serious mistakes and the need to acknowledge mistakes.
2. Wu AW, Folkman S, McPhee SJ, et al. Do house officers learn from their mistakes? *JAMA* 1991;265:2089–2094.
   Reports that house officers who accepted responsibility for serious mistakes were more likely to make constructive changes in practice but were also more likely to experience emotional distress. Attending physicians were told of serious mistakes only 54% of the time, and patients or families were told of the mistake in only 24% of cases.
3. Kohn L. Corrigan J, Donaldson M, eds. *To err is human: building a safer health system*. Washington: National Academy Press, 2000.
   Recommends the establishment of a confidential system of reporting medical mistakes in order to prevent future errors.
4. Gallagher TH, Waterman AD, Ebers AG, et al. Patients' and physicians' perspective regarding the disclosure of medical errors. *JAMA* 2004;289:1001–1007.
   Explains that perspectives of physicians and patients differ markedly about disclosure of medical errors.

CHAPTER 35

Impaired Colleagues

Physicians who are impaired or incompetent might harm patients. Society relies on the medical profession to regulate itself (1), yet colleagues of impaired physicians are often reluctant to intervene, even in egregious cases. The following case illustrates common dilemmas regarding impaired colleagues.

CASE 35.1 Drinking alcohol while on call.

Dr. New, a young internist who has recently joined a group practice, is at a party. She overhears a senior colleague, Dr. Elder, answer a page. Dr. Elder has been drinking and has slurred speech. Over the phone he prescribes 1.25 mg of digoxin, an unusually large dose. From what she hears of the conversation, Dr. New suspects that she has previously covered for this patient, an elderly man with mild renal insufficiency, a recent hip fracture repair, and postoperative pneumonia.

Dr. New is in a quandary. Although she suspects that a patient is at risk of a drug overdose, she cannot be sure. Should she intervene to protect the patient from this suspected mistake? If so, should she confront Dr. Elder or talk to the house officer or nursing supervisor covering the service? Even if she protects this patient, what about other patients Dr. Elder might harm? Dr. New wants to prevent harm to patients, but she is reluctant to jeopardize the career of a colleague or her own future.

This chapter discusses intervening with impaired colleagues, reasons to take action, and practical suggestions. Chapter 34, which discusses errors, contains related materials. Errors by impaired or incompetent colleagues are more serious than other errors because they are more likely to be repeated. Although many errors are due to system problems, those discussed in this chapter are due to shortcomings of an individual physician.

CAUSES OF IMPAIRMENT AND INCOMPETENCE

Common causes of impairment are alcoholism, substance abuse, and psychiatric and medical illness, such as depression and Alzheimer's disease (2). Many impaired physicians can be treated effectively in programs that stress confidential rehabilitation rather than punishment (3). Physicians might also be incompetent because of inadequate knowledge and skills or careless behavior—for example, failing to round on patients.

REASONS FOR INTERVENING WITH IMPAIRED COLLEAGUES

Physicians have an ethical obligation to be competent, based on the ethical guidelines of refraining from causing harm and acting in their patients' best interests. There are also compelling ethical reasons for physicians to intervene with seriously impaired colleagues, even though the patients who might be harmed are not their own (Table 35-1).

TABLE 35-1

Reasons for Intervening with Impaired Colleagues

To prevent harm to patients.
To carry out professional self-regulation.
To help the impaired colleague.

PREVENT HARM TO PATIENTS

People have a duty to prevent serious harm to others when it can be done at minimal risk or inconvenience to themselves (4). Modern professional codes of ethics also require physicians to protect patients from impaired colleagues. The American College of Physicians Ethics Manual states, "It is the responsibility of every physician to protect the public from an impaired physician.... All steps must be taken to assure that no patient is harmed because of actions or decisions made by an impaired physician (5)." An impaired physician's colleagues might be in a unique position to prevent harm to patients because they have not only the expertise to evaluate the quality of care rendered by colleagues but also the opportunity to do so.

In other occupations workers whose impairment might endanger the public are aggressively identified. For example, airline pilots and train engineers are required to submit to drug testing before hiring, after accidents, and on a random basis (6). A commercial pilot who is suspected of drinking while on duty may be removed from the cockpit. Critics charge that the treatment of impaired physicians, in comparison, is too lax. It seems inconsistent to forbid pilots to drink while on duty but to allow physicians to drink while on call.

CARRY OUT PROFESSIONAL SELF-REGULATION

Society grants the medical profession considerable autonomy to regulate itself through selecting applicants for medical school and residency, defining standards of practice, certifying physicians, and disciplining members. The rationale for such professional autonomy is that laypeople do not have the expertise to determine whether physicians are impaired or incompetent. Society expects the profession to screen out practitioners who might endanger patients. If people believe that physicians are covering up for impaired or incompetent colleagues, they will lose trust in the medical profession and society might regulate physicians directly.

HELP THE IMPAIRED COLLEAGUE

Impaired physicians might harm themselves and their families as well as their patients through automobile accidents, violent episodes, or lapses in judgment. Furthermore, impaired physicians might destroy their livelihood and their families' economic security. Intervening with impaired colleagues might avert such destructive outcomes.

CONCERNS ABOUT INTERVENING WITH IMPAIRED COLLEAGUES

State licensing boards provide strong evidence that physicians are reluctant to intervene with impaired colleagues. Compared with the estimated prevalence of impairment, state boards receive few reports about impaired physicians (7). There might be several reasons for such reluctance.

UNCERTAINTY WHETHER PATIENTS ARE AT SERIOUS RISK

Physicians might be uncertain whether colleagues suspected of impairment are actually placing patients at risk, as in Case 35.1. Dr. New does not know the complete story. Perhaps the patient needed a high dose because he had uncontrolled atrial fibrillation or intestinal malabsorption.

RELUCTANCE TO CRITICIZE COLLEAGUES

Physicians rely on their colleagues' skills, knowledge, and judgment, and it would be difficult to practice medicine without such reliance. Thus, doctors might hesitate to admit that a colleague is impaired because it calls such trust into question. Physicians might also hesitate to probe matters that are often considered private, such as alcohol consumption. Dr. New, for example, might be reluctant to act on the basis of a personal telephone conversation that she accidentally overheard.

Furthermore, doctors are understandably reluctant to undermine a colleague's reputation and livelihood. On a subconscious level physicians might identify with impaired colleagues. If they question a colleague's competence, might other physicians in turn criticize them harshly after a minor error?

RETALIATION AGAINST WHISTLEBLOWERS

Whistleblowers often face personal retaliation despite their good intentions. If Dr. New confronts Dr. Elder, he might get angry or tell her to mind her own business. If she tells other people, colleagues might label her a snitch or a tattletale. Dr. Elder might accuse her of trying to ruin his reputation or trying to build up her own practice. He might even retaliate by criticizing her work and discouraging other physicians from referring patients to her. Dr. Elder could potentially go so far as to sue her for defamation of character or lost income. Even the threat of a lawsuit, its concomitant cost, and adverse publicity might deter Dr. New from pursuing the matter. Dr. New's natural concern about her own career might conflict with her desire to prevent harm to vulnerable patients.

LEGAL ISSUES REGARDING IMPAIRED COLLEAGUES

Many states have adopted laws concerning reporting of impaired or incompetent colleagues (1,8).

REPORTING LAWS

The specific provisions of reporting laws vary from state to state. In Massachusetts physicians must report to the state licensing board colleagues whom they suspect are practicing medicine while impaired. Other states permit such reporting but do not require it. Most states grant legal immunity from civil suits to physicians who report colleagues in good faith.

DIVERSION PROGRAMS

Most states have set up voluntary physician health programs, which are often run by the state medical society rather than the medical licensing bureau, to treat and rehabilitate impaired physicians (3,9). The goal is to allow rehabilitated physicians to continue to practice or to return to work. Physicians entering such programs may be granted confidentiality and immunity from disciplinary actions. That is, physicians are diverted from disciplinary procedures. Several states have reported success in rehabilitating impaired physicians in such programs (2).

THE HEALTH CARE QUALITY IMPROVEMENT ACT

In 1986, Congress passed legislation regarding reporting of incompetent physicians (10). This law requires hospitals and state licensing agencies to report to a federal agency most disciplinary actions related to professional incompetence or misconduct. In addition, insurance companies must report malpractice payments above $10,000. These reports are entered in the National Practitioner Data Bank. To prevent incompetent or impaired physicians from simply resigning from one hospital staff, relocating, and continuing to practice elsewhere, hospitals are required to obtain information from the National Practitioner Data Bank when physicians apply for hospital privileges and periodically thereafter.

The law also confers legal immunity on persons and hospitals who report impaired colleagues in good faith. Specifically, immunity is given to persons who provide "information to a professional review body regarding the competence or professional conduct of a physician (10)." In addition, peer review bodies and persons who work with or assist them are granted legal immunity. Note, however, that in Case 35.1 these provisions would not protect Dr. New if she were to attempt to deal with Dr. Elder outside the formal peer review process.

DEALING WITH IMPAIRED COLLEAGUES

Physicians can deal with impaired colleagues in several ways (Table 35-2).

PROTECT PATIENTS FROM IMMEDIATE HARM

If Dr. New believes that Dr. Elder's order might seriously harm the patient, she should take immediate action. She might consider saying, "I'm sorry to intrude, but I thought I heard you say 1.25 mg of digoxin. I'm afraid the nurses might have heard the wrong dose as well." If the matter is not resolved satisfactorily, Dr. New could call the hospital and ask the nursing supervisor at the hospital to look into the case. Dr. New should also intervene if Dr. Elder is apparently drunk on call even if she had no direct evidence that he had made a questionable medical decision. If Dr. Elder does not agree to have a colleague take calls for him, it would be prudent to notify another senior physician or the chief of the department and arrange for someone else to take calls, at least until Dr. Elder regains sobriety.

DETERMINE WHETHER FURTHER ACTION IS NEEDED

After preventing immediate harm to patients, Dr. New needs to assess whether additional action is needed. Gathering more information about the impaired colleague can usually be done discreetly.

Because whistle-blowing is emotionally difficult and personally risky, physicians might take smaller steps to prevent harm to patients. Many physicians would not refer patients to such a colleague but would otherwise let the matter drop. Other physicians cover up for impaired colleagues rather than confront them. For example, a physician might review a colleague's work and correct that doctor's errors. Although well-intentioned, such actions are ineffective in the long run. To try to monitor all the clinical activities of an impaired or incompetent colleague is impractical and also counterproductive because it simply allows the physician to deny the impairment.

TALK WITH THE COLLEAGUE DIRECTLY

A physician will often want to talk with an impaired colleague directly, particularly if the colleague is a friend. Although such conversations are uncomfortable, they can be effective. The matter can be resolved if the impaired colleague agrees to seek help—for example, by enrolling in a rehabilitation program. Alternatively, physicians impaired by physical illness might decide to retire or to restrict the scope of their practice.

REPORT THE PROBLEM TO RESPONSIBLE OFFICIALS

Dr. New does not need to solve the problem of the impaired colleague by herself. She needs only to decide whether there is sufficient suspicion of impairment to warrant further investigation. In Case 35.1, Dr. New directly observed a situation of potential harm to a patient. She can discharge

---

TABLE 35-2

Dealing with Impaired Colleagues

Protect patients from immediate harm.
Determine whether further action is needed.
Talk with the colleague directly.
Report the problem to responsible officials.

---

her ethical obligations by reporting impaired colleagues to officials who can investigate and take appropriate action. Such officials are the chief of service, the chief of staff of the hospital, or, if a trainee is involved, the director of a training program or student clerkships. These persons are responsible for ensuring the quality of patient care and the competence of medical staff. Alternatively, Dr. New might refer her colleague to the hospital's employee assistance programs or to the state medical society's physician health program (3). In cases of egregious impairment or incompetence, notifying the state licensing board directly might also be advisable. The case's circumstances often determine how physicians prefer to respond to an impaired or incompetent colleague. In one survey most house officers said they were willing to confront a fellow house officer who was impaired by alcohol but preferred to tell the chief resident or the chief of medicine about an attending physician who was similarly impaired. However, house officers were less comfortable confronting a fellow house officer who was incompetent rather than impaired and preferred to refer such matters to a more senior physician (11).

In summary, there are understandable practical reasons for physicians' hesitation to intervene with impaired colleagues. However, there are cogent ethical reasons for physicians to take action to prevent impaired colleagues from harming patients. Pragmatically, there are ways to do so that are safe for whistle-blowers.

REFERENCES

1. American Medical Association. Reporting impaired, incompetent or unethical colleagues. Report 39. Report of the Council on Ethical and Judicial Affairs of the American Medical Association. Chicago: American Medical Association; 1992.
2. Aach RD, Girard DE, Humphrey H, et al. Alcohol and other substance abuse and impairment among physician in residency training. *Ann Intern Med* 1992;116:245–254.
3. O'Connor PG, Spickard A Jr. Physician impairment by substance abuse. *Med Clin North Am* 1997;81(4):1037–1052.
4. Beauchamp TL, Childress JF. *Principles of Biomedical Ethics*, 3rd ed. New York: Oxford University Press, 1989:120–193.
5. American College of Physicians. American College of Physicians Ethics Manual. *Ann Intern Med* 1992;117: 947–960.
6. Modell JG, Mountz JM. Drinking and flying — the problem of alcohol use by pilots. *N Engl J Med* 1990;323: 455–461.
7. Feinstein RJ. The ethics of professional regulation. *N Engl J Med* 1985;312:801–804.
8. Walzer RS. Impaired physicians: an overview and update of the legal issues. *J Legal Med* 1990;11:131–198.
9. Mansky PA. Physician health programs and the potentially impaired physician with a substance use disorder. *Psychiatr Serv* 1996;47(5):465–467.
10. Health Care Quality Improvement Act. 42 U.S.C.A. §§11101–11151 (1990).
11. Reuben DB, Noble S. House officer responses to impaired physicians. *JAMA* 1990;263:958–960.

ANNOTATED BIBLIOGRAPHY

1. American Medical Association. Reporting impaired, incompetent or unethical colleagues. Report 39. Report of the Council on Ethical and Judicial Affairs of the American Medical Association. Chicago: American Medical Association, 1992.
   Discusses ethical and practical issues regarding impaired physicians.
2. Ethics case study: the dilemma of dealing with an impaired colleague. *ACP Observer* 1991;11:10–11.
   Stresses the goals of protecting patients while helping the impaired colleague.
3. Aach RD, Girard DE, Humphrey H. Alcohol and other substance abuse and impairment among physicians in residency training. *Ann Intern Med* 1992;116:245–254.
   Discusses how to help house officers suffering from substance abuse and other causes of impairment.

CHAPTER 36

Ethical Dilemmas Students and House Staff Face

Every clinician in training has entered a patient's room to perform a procedure knowing that someone else could do it more skillfully.

CASE 36.1 Performing an invasive procedure.

Obviously tired after a 9-hour wait in the emergency room, a woman with an asthma exacerbation is finally admitted to the floor. "Oh no, not another needlestick!" she groans, as a medical student approaches to draw arterial blood gases. The medical student gulps silently, aware that his previous attempts at drawing blood gases have been unsuccessful or required multiple punctures.

Trainees' self-interest in learning might conflict with their patients' best interests. Learning clinical skills and taking responsibility might present inconvenience, discomfort, or even risk to patients. Ethical conflicts also arise when trainees observe unethical or substandard care by other physicians. Both trainees and patients benefit when these issues are addressed openly. Ideally, the patient's welfare should be paramount. However, trainees must also be realistic about the power that more senior physicians have over them.

LEARNING ON PATIENTS

In their training medical students might worry that they are taking unfair advantage of patients but hesitate to voice their concerns to their supervisors (1,2). They fear that their reputation or career might suffer if others believe they are reluctant to accept responsibility or are not competent.

INTRODUCING TRAINEES TO PATIENTS

CASE 36.2 Introducing students as physicians.

The attending physician introduces a medical student beginning a third-year clerkship to the patient as "Doctor." When the student raises concerns about this, the attending physician insists that students have to get over their "hang-ups" about taking responsibility. According to the attending physician, patients who seek care at a teaching hospital know that students will be taking care of them. If they did not agree, they would not come to a teaching hospital.

Introducing students as physicians is common (3). In fact, 27% of medical schools fail to identify students as medical students, student doctors, or student physicians on their name tags (4). Several reasons are offered for not introducing trainees as such (5). Patients might not trust trainees or might worry needlessly about provision of care. As in Case 36.2, some physicians believe that patients in a teaching hospital have given "implied consent" to trainees to care for them.

There are compelling reasons to introduce students truthfully. Patient trust cannot be built on misrepresentation. Patients who are misled about a health care provider's role might feel betrayed if they discover the trainee's status. Informed consent requires physicians to disclose pertinent information to patients (*see* Chapter 3). The identity of trainees who will provide care can be highly relevant to a patient's decisions. State laws and accreditation requirements can also require trainees to disclose their educational status to patients (5). The argument that patients who seek care at teaching hospitals have given implied consent to be "teaching material" is untenable. The concept of "implied consent" applies only to emergency situations in which delaying treatment would seriously harm a patient who is unable to give consent.

Protecting patients from unnecessary worry is also an unconvincing reason to withhold information. Most patients agree that trainees enhance the quality of their care and want to contribute to a trainee's education (6,7). Concerns that patients will worry inappropriately should be addressed with more information about teaching hospitals, not less. Trainees are accessible around the clock, often have more time to answer questions, and are closely supervised. Overall, primary teaching hospitals have a lower rate of adverse patient events due to negligence than nonteaching hospitals (8).

Some trainees resort to unfamiliar titles, such as "clinical clerk," that are literally true and avoid the adverse consequences of explicitly calling oneself a student. However, such titles are unacceptable because they are incomprehensible to patients and intended to mislead. "Student physician" is commonly used and emphasizes the special medical training that the student has received.

LEARNING BASIC CLINICAL SKILLS

To learn to take a history, perform a physical examination, draw blood, and start intravenous lines, medical students need to practice on patients. Although patients are not subjected to any serious medical risks, they might be inconvenienced, lose privacy, or experience some discomfort. Out of respect for patients, the attending physician or resident should ask permission first. When asked, almost all patients agree to have students listen to a heart murmur or perform a history and physical examination. Although it is reasonable to ask patients to spend an hour with a student, it is inappropriate to ask them to spend 3 hours for an exhaustive student examination, to miss their meals, or to lose sleep.

LEARNING INVASIVE PROCEDURES

Invasive procedures performed by trainees might raise ethical concerns. In Case 36.1 medical students need practice in order to learn how to perform arterial punctures skillfully. When trainees learn invasive procedures such as lumbar puncture or insertion of central lines, their first patients might experience increased discomfort or even risk. The trainee's self-interest in learning and long-term goal of benefiting future patients might therefore conflict with the short-term goal of providing the best care to current patients.

Trainees frequently do not discuss their participation in invasive procedures with patients (3). One reason for avoiding the issue is the fear that patients will request more experienced physicians (9). Such requests would be understandable. Physicians might consider whether they would be willing to have a trainee perform the procedure on a close relative or whether they would request a more experienced physician.

In the spirit of informed consent, patients need to understand who will be performing invasive procedures and what additional risk, if any, can be attributed to trainees. Such information might be highly pertinent to the patient's decision to undergo a procedure at that institution. For surgical procedures, almost all patients want the attending surgeon to tell them what the resident will do during the operation (6). In one study all obstetric patients believed that student participation should be requested rather than assigned (10). Another study found that patients considered it very important to know that a medical student is going to make the incision, hold retractors, perform rectal or pelvic examinations under anesthesia, suture incisions, or intubate them (9). Patients consider such disclosure more important than medical students do (9).

Attending physicians should tell patients about the participation of students and residents in their care and introduce trainees (6). Patient concerns about unskilled trainees are best resolved by providing more information, not less. When informed and given a choice, most patients allow trainees to do procedures. In one study 80% of patients said they would want to know the experience of the person performing a lumbar puncture (11), but 52% would allow closely supervised medical students to attempt their first lumbar puncture on them and 66% would allow a resident to do so. Patient requests to have a more experienced physician perform the procedure should be honored if possible.

Trainees should carry out procedures only under adequate supervision, except in dire emergencies. Without supervision, the patient might be placed at unnecessary risk and the trainee will not have a good learning experience. The hospital has a responsibility to provide such supervision, and the trainee also has a responsibility to obtain it before starting the procedure. The senior physician should take over the procedure if needed.

LEARNING ON UNCONSCIOUS OR DEAD PATIENTS

Trainees might face further dilemmas when they are asked to learn on unconscious or newly dead patients without explicit consent to do so (12). For example, an attending physician might tell the medical student and intern that they should perform pelvic examinations on a patient under general anesthesia. He says that such examinations provide important learning opportunities because it is easier to palpate the ovaries when the patient is anesthetized. However, pelvic examinations performed under anesthesia without explicit permission violate patient privacy and autonomy (*see* Chapter 41).

Learning invasive procedures on newly dead patients without the next of kin's consent creates similar ethical dilemmas. For instance, after a patient on an intern and student's service dies, the resident might instruct them to practice intubation and insertion of a central venous catheter. "The patient is dead. You can't hurt her, but you might hurt a live patient if you don't practice." Such practice increases skill and thereby benefits future patients (13). However, invasive procedures might be regarded as disfiguring, offensive, or a violation of the corpse's dignity (14). Dead patients are not "teaching material." They deserve to be treated with respect.

Some physicians suggest that practicing invasive procedures should be permitted unless relatives specifically object. However, unless family members are informed that such a practice occurs, they might not know to raise objections (13). A better policy would be to obtain consent from survivors for practicing invasive procedures on newly dead patients (14–16). When consent is sought candidly and compassionately, most family members give permission (17,18). Permission from survivors also helps trainees resolve their own ambivalence or anguish over learning on patients and to appreciate that their training depends on other people's altruism (17).

TAKING TOO MUCH CLINICAL RESPONSIBILITY

Trainees sometimes assume too much decision-making responsibility without adequate supervision (1,2). For instance, a resident on a busy service might tell a subintern to sign his or her name on the physicians' order sheet, saying "You're a good student, and you can page me if you have a real question." However, it is unrealistic to expect the student to distinguish routine orders from serious management decisions. Errors in judgment or dosage can occur even in "routine" orders. Furthermore, the resident is giving the student a mixed message: "Call me for serious problems, but if you're a good student you won't bother me." Discouraging trainees' questions also reduces opportunities for learning. Students who request adequate supervision implicitly criticize the resident and might experience retaliation in grades and evaluations. They might be labeled as "not a team player," "insecure," "incompetent," or "reluctant to assume responsibility."

The training system might place the student in an untenable situation by exerting pressure to take too much responsibility or failing to set clear expectations or provide sufficient supervision. The institution should clarify expectations for supervision of trainees and establish a mechanism for students as well as residents to ask for help. A satisfactory resolution might require system-wide changes, such as more involvement from the attending physician or transfer of some patients to another team.

Trainees are ultimately accountable for taking too much responsibility and placing patients at increased risk. Ethically, trainees need to know their own limitations and should not exceed them.

LIMITS ON WORK HOURS

Residency accreditation bodies have enacted limits on house staff work hours in order to prevent fatigue and burnout and reduce medical errors. However, strictly observing such limits might raise ethical dilemmas.

CASE 36.3 House staff work hours.

During an on-call night, an intern has admitted only two patients. After rounding, he has finished his 30-hour tour-of-duty and is checking out when he gets paged. A 78-year-old woman that you admitted with pyelonephritis now has a temperature of 39 C, a blood pressure of 100/60, a pulse of 110, and seems confused. The cross-covering intern appears stressed. She exclaims, "Look, I've already had four admissions. How can you dump a patient like this?"

In Case 36.3 the harried cross-cover intern accuses her colleague of "dumping" a patient. This term highlights the way in which stressed physicians might focus their attention on their own well-being rather than the patient's interests. Ironically, restrictions on house staff work hours were intended to reduce stress on physicians. The intern signing out might feel that he should help his colleague by staying longer. After all, he might be overwhelmed some day and need similar help. In this case he does not feel tired. Moreover, the patient in early septic shock needs timely attention. It is commendable to help colleagues during unexpected emergencies. However, the on-call systems should anticipate that house officers on call might be overwhelmed. The interns should be able to call on the resident, the attending physician, or a "float" for help. In the long run, asking busy interns to stay additional hours to help others only leads to more stress and fatigue and ultimately greater risk for patients. In this case the intern at the end of shift might say, "Boy, you are really getting hit. Let me try to help. I can sign her out to the resident, who can start antibiotics and stabilize her. I sure hope it lightens up later for you." In this way the outgoing intern need only spend a few extra minutes, the cross-cover physician will feel less stressed, and, most important, the patient will receive care promptly.

In other cases a resident can provide an irreplaceable benefit to a patient or family by working a little longer than the scheduled hours. For example, a resident might be in the middle of a discussion about withdrawing life-sustaining interventions or comforting a family member over a patient's death. It would be desirable for the resident to stay to finish the conversation before signing out to the covering physician. In this situation the rapport and understanding that the physician has developed with the patient or family is not readily transferred to another doctor. Moreover, such rapport is the essential component of care in these end-of-life situations. Under such circumstances strict adherence to the time clock would undermine the ideals of benefiting patients and acting with compassion. However, such situations should remain exceptions and should not create any expectation that trainees should routinely exceed limits of working hours.

RELATIONSHIPS WITH COLLEAGUES

Case 36.3 illustrates how helping stressed colleagues is altruistic and helps create mutual expectations of reciprocity. Ultimately patient care is also enhanced when physicians support and help each other.

CASE 36.4 Lying or equivocating on rounds.

A 54-year-old man is admitted with severe pancreatitis. Overnight he required large volumes of fluid in order to maintain his blood pressure. While the intern is presenting the patient on rounds, the attending physician asks, "So what happened to his calcium?" The intern remembers that calcium is an important prognostic factor that should be followed in pancreatitis. Although he checked the patient's laboratory tests, the intern cannot remember whether he specifically reviewed the calcium. He thinks he would have noticed if the calcium had not been normal.

In Case 36.4 the intern feels a tension between making a good impression on the attending physician and acting for the patient's good. If the intern says that the calcium was normal when it was not, the subsequent plan of care might be inappropriate. Hence, the ethical analysis is clear: The intern should say exactly what he did and offer to verify the value at the nearest computer terminal.

However, it would be simplistic to view this situation only as a clash between self-interest and beneficence. The hospital and team's culture is important. If the attending physician tends to criticize trainees sharply, the intern will be deterred from telling the truth. Conversely, if a resident and attending physician can reinforce the value of truth-telling by stopping rounds to look up the value and by discussing why the calcium level is important in this case, it will encourage the intern to tell the truth.

Moreover, a teaching style that leads interns to feel stressed might be counterproductive. Slips in which a person forgets something are to be expected. Usually they are due to the limits of human cognition, not carelessness. Exhorting interns to be more careful or by shaming them to teach them a lesson cannot remedy slips; instead, interns need help in developing a routine for keeping track of labs or a checklist to ensure that essential tasks are carried out.

UNETHICAL BEHAVIOR OR SUBSTANDARD CARE BY OTHER PHYSICIANS

Trainees might be involved in cases in which senior physicians appear to violate ethical guidelines (19).

CASE 36.5 Failure to obtain informed consent for sterilization.

An attending obstetrician performs a tubal ligation on a 32-year-old Latina woman on Medicaid who has just delivered her sixth child by cesarean section. According to the chart the patient refused sterilization at her last prenatal visit. The resident who delivered the baby and served as the translator for the patient is outraged. The delivery room nurse confirms that no informed consent was obtained but cautions, "Don't ruin your career over this."

Some disagreements reflect reasonable differences of clinical judgment or misunderstanding by the trainee. In Case 36.5, however, the attending physician is violating the ethical guideline of respecting patient autonomy as well as laws on informed consent. The resident felt outraged at the event, frustrated at being powerless, guilty that she did not intervene, and ashamed that she had become an accomplice in an unethical deed. She believed that the attending physician's action was both sexist and racist.

Trainees who are involved in a patient's case might also observe grossly substandard care by senior physicians, as when they fail to round on patients, write progress notes, or answer pages. In cases of clearly inadequate care, the trainee has an ethical obligation to protect patients and to not mislead them. In addition, there is an ethical obligation to try to prevent harm to future patients if a pattern of impairment exists (*see* Chapter 35). However, there are also strong countervailing pragmatic considerations, as we discuss next.

RISKS TO WHISTLEBLOWERS

Fear of retaliation is a legitimate practical concern for trainees (20). The obstetrics resident in Case 36.5 might receive a bad evaluation or unfavorable treatment during the rest of her training. As in all occupations, whistleblowers might suffer harm even if their accusations prove valid. Ideally, the patient's well-being should take priority over the trainee's self-interest. Individual trainees need to decide how much personal risk as a whistleblower they are willing to accept relative to the harm they might prevent.

SUGGESTIONS FOR TRAINEES

Involve Other Physicians

Trainees often feel that they have to resolve these troubling situations by themselves. However, they should discuss the situation with trusted colleagues and senior physicians. These discussions allow trainees to verify that they have observed unethical misconduct or markedly substandard care and not that they merely have a reasonable difference of clinical judgment. Such reality testing is often crucial for their peace of mind and sense of integrity. In addition, other people might provide emotional support, give advice, and intervene constructively. The chief resident, clerkship or residency director, and chief of service have an obligation to address issues of unethical or incompetent behavior (20). Furthermore, every hospital should have procedures, such as quality assurance programs or a patient ombudsperson, for investigating such cases (20).

Decide What to Tell the Patient

In addition to informing appropriate senior physicians, the trainee needs to consider what to tell patients, if anything. There are strong reasons why patients should have truthful information about events that will affect their future medical care and life plans. The sterilized woman in Case 36.5 cannot make informed decisions about reproduction if she does not know that a tubal ligation was performed.

Trainees do not need to inform the patient personally if they inform some responsible senior physician, such as the chief of service. However, trainees need to answer truthfully if the patient asks the trainee directly what happened.

Protect Their Own Interests

If the harm to patients is serious, the ethical ideal is for trainees to fulfill their obligations to patients, even at some risk to their careers. However, trainees should also minimize risks to themselves. Measures such as writing an angry note in the chart or directly accusing the attending physician of being unethical are likely to inflame the situation. Involving more senior physicians can reduce the risk of reprisals. Trainees who are unwilling to be identified as accusers can still discuss episodes with the quality assurance committee or chief of staff. In this way, if other people are willing to come forward there will be corroborating evidence. In addition, trainees should keep records of how they raised their concerns.

In summary, medical students, house officers, and fellows face unique clinical dilemmas. Trainees' interests in learning clinical medicine and invasive procedures might conflict with patients' interests. In addition, the ethical guideline of preventing harm to patients might conflict with trainees' career advancement. The ethical ideal is for all trainees to act in patients' best interests, even at some personal risk or disadvantage.

REFERENCES

1. Rosenbaum JR, Bradley EH, Holmboe ES, et al. Sources of ethical conflict in medical housestaff training: a qualitative study. *Am J Med* 2004;116:402–407.
2. Christakis DA, Feudtner C. Ethics in a short white coat: the ethical dilemmas that medical students confront. *Acad Med* 1993;68:249–254.
3. Cohen DL, McCullough LB, Kessel RWI, et al. A national survey concerning the ethical aspects of informed consent and the role of medical students. *J Med Educ* 1988;63:821–829.
4. Silver-Isenstadt A, Ubel PA. Medical student name tags: identification or obfuscation. *J Gen Intern Med* 1997; 12:669–671.
5. Marracino RK, Orr RD. Entitling the student doctor: defining the student's role in patient care. *J Gen Intern Med* 1998;13:266–270.
6. Kim N, Lo B, Gates EA. Disclosing the role of residents and medical students in hysterectomy: what do patients want? *Acad Med* 1998;73:339–341.
7. Magrane D, Jannon J, Miller CT. Obstetric patients who select and those who refuse medical students' participation in their care. *Acad Med* 1994;69:1004–1006.
8. Brennan TA, Hebert L, Laird NM, et al. Hospital characteristics associated with adverse events and substandard care. *JAMA* 1991;265:3265–3269.
9. Silver-Isenstadt A, Ubel PA. Erosion in medical students' attitudes about telling patients they are students. *J Gen Intern Med* 1999;14:481–487.
10. Magrane D, Jannon J, Miller CT. Student doctors and women in labor: attitudes and expectations. *Obstet Gynecol* 1996;88:298–302.
11. Williams CT, Fost N. Ethical considerations surrounding first-time procedures: a study and analysis of patient attitudes toward spinal taps by students. *Kennedy Inst Ethics J* 1992;3:217–233.
12. Kaldjian LC, Wu BJ, Jekel JF, et al. T.P. D. Insertion of femoral-vein catheters for practice by medical house officers during cardiopulmonary resuscitation. *N Engl J Med* 1999;341:2088–1091.
13. Orlowski JP, Kanoti GA, Mehlman MJ. The ethics of using newly dead patients for teaching and practicing intubation techniques. *N Engl J Med* 1988;319:439–441.
14. Berger JT, Rosner F, Cassell EJ. Ethics of practicing medical procedures on newly dead and nearly dead patients. *J Gen Intern Med* 2002;17:774–778.

15. Goldblatt AD. Don't ask, don't tell: practicing minimally invasive resuscitation techniques on the newly dead. *Ann Emerg Med* 1995;25:86–90.
16. Council on Ethical and Judicial Affairs of the American Medical Association. Performing procedures on the newly deceased. *Acad Med* 2002;77:1212–1216.
17. Benfield DG, Flaksman RJ, Lin TH, et al. Teaching intubation skills using newly deceased infants. *JAMA* 1991; 265:2360–2363.
18. McNamara RM, Monti S, Kelly JJ. Requesting consent for an invasive procedure in newly deceased adults. *JAMA* 1995;273:310–312.
19. Satterwhite WM, Satterwhite RC, Enarson CE. Medical students' perceptions of unethical conduct at one medical school. *Acad Med* 1998;73:529–531.
20. Council on Ethical and Judicial Affairs of the American Medical Association. Disputes between medical supervisors and trainees. *JAMA* 1994;272:1861–1865.

ANNOTATED BIBLIOGRAPHY

1. Marracino RK, Orr RD. Entitling the student doctor: defining the student's role in patient care. *J Gen Intern Med* 1998;13:266–270.
   Analyzes why medical students are often not introduced to patients as medical students.
2. Goldblatt AD. Don't ask, don't tell: practicing minimally invasive resuscitation techniques on the newly dead. *Ann Emerg Med* 1995;25:86–90.
   Berger JT, Rosner F, Cassell EJ. Ethics of practicing medical procedures on newly dead and nearly dead patients. *J Gen Intern Med* 2002;17:774–778.
   Two articles that cogently argue that permission should be obtained from next of kin before practicing invasive procedures on patients who have just died.

Ethical Issues in Clinical Specialties

CHAPTER 37

Ethical Issues in Pediatrics

Children are immature, they depend on their parents or guardians emotionally and financially, and they cannot make informed decisions about their own care. Therefore, decisions should be made differently in pediatrics than in adult medicine.

HOW ARE ETHICAL ISSUES IN PEDIATRICS DIFFERENT?

CHILDREN ARE NOT AUTONOMOUS

Because children cannot weigh risks and benefits, compare alternatives, or appreciate the long-term consequences of decisions, they are incapable of making informed decisions. Hence, autonomy is less important in pediatrics than in adult medicine. Children's objections to beneficial medical interventions do not have the same ethical force as adults' informed refusals. Because children are immature and vulnerable, they need an adult to make decisions for them and to look after their best interests. Parents are presumed to be the appropriate decision-makers (1).

Children must be protected from the consequences of unwise decisions by themselves or by others. Indeed, it is tragic if a child dies or undergoes serious harm because a simple, effective medical treatment was not provided.

PHYSICIANS SHOULD BE ADVOCATES FOR CHILDREN

Doctors are in a unique position to identify situations in which parental decisions or children's actions jeopardize children's health and well-being. Pediatricians are given special responsibilities in these situations because if they do not intervene, children might suffer serious, long-lasting harm.

PHYSICIANS SHOULD RESPECT CHILDREN'S POTENTIAL TO BECOME AUTONOMOUS ADULTS

Although young children are not autonomous, their potential autonomy as future adults deserves respect. Parents mold children, and parental values deserve great deference. However, when children reach maturity they might choose values that differ from those of their parents. Physicians need to help ensure that parental decisions do not close off a child's open future as a unique person.

As children grow, they become capable of making informed decisions and their involvement in care should increase. Pediatricians need to provide children with information about their conditions and opportunities to participate in decisions about their care, to the extent it is appropriate developmentally (1).

WHAT STANDARDS SHOULD BE USED IN MAKING DECISIONS FOR CHILDREN?

Because children cannot make informed decisions, beneficence or the child's best interest is the primary ethical guideline in pediatrics.

CHILDREN'S BEST INTERESTS

The concept of "best interests" emphasizes that children are persons separate from their parents, with their own interests and rights. In most situations parents' decisions and their ongoing involvement in children's care promote children's best interests. However, children's "best interests" are often difficult to interpret. People might disagree over which factors comprise a child's best interests, which outcomes and risks are acceptable, and how to weigh the benefits and burdens of interventions. Promoting some of the child's interests might set back other interests.

A child's best interests include both the duration and quality of life. However, although quality-of-life judgments seem unavoidable, they might be ethically problematic. It is difficult to predict a child's future quality of life. Healthy people tend to underestimate the quality of life of persons with chronic illness. Some people believe that Down syndrome is a fate worse than death, but children with this condition can experience happiness and parents often prize them. Chapter 4 discusses best interests in detail.

CHILDREN'S PREFERENCES

To the extent that children have the capacity to make informed decisions about their medical care, their choices should be respected. Chapter 10 discusses how to determine whether a patient has the capacity to make medical decisions.

Even when children are not capable of giving informed consent, their assent to interventions is still ethically important. It is disturbing to force interventions on children who are actively resisting them. A child's objections are not necessarily decisive. For instance, a child who objects to shots should still receive immunizations. However, forced therapy becomes more ethically problematic if children are older, the effectiveness of the intervention is less clear, or the side effects are more common, more serious, or longer lasting. The pediatrician should listen to and respond to the child's reasons for dissenting from treatment. If interventions are carried out despite the child's objections, it is appropriate for the pediatrician to offer an apology to the child (2).

PARENTS' AND FAMILY MEMBERS' INTERESTS

Although the child's best interests are of primary concern, parents and other family members have interests that must also be taken into account. What is best for an individual child can be understood only in the context of what is best for the family as a whole or for other family members. Parents cannot be expected to devote all their energy and resources to one child even though they should be expected to make some sacrifices. For example, parents might choose not to buy a house in the best school district but instead live closer to their jobs.

WHO SHOULD MAKE MEDICAL DECISIONS FOR CHILDREN?

THE PRESUMPTION OF PARENTAL DECISION MAKING

Parents are presumed to be the appropriate decision-makers for their children. Generally, love motivates them to do what is best for their children. In addition, parents have long-term relationships with and obligations to their children. In most cases parents concur with pediatricians' recommendations—for example, agreeing to antibiotics for strep throat, bronchodilators for asthma, and surgery for appendicitis.

American culture prizes parental responsibility, family integrity, and strong parent–child relationships. Parents or guardians have considerable latitude, but not complete discretion, in raising children. Within limits set by society, parents have discretion to inculcate their values in children and to make choices for rearing their children. For example, children must attend school but parents may choose the type of school.

Pediatricians speak of parental permission rather than consent in order to distinguish what people may decide for themselves from what they may decide for their children. Although informed adults have a right to refuse any medical intervention, parents do not have absolute power to refuse care for their children (1,2).

Emergencies

In an emergency, when a parent or guardian is not available and delay in treatment would jeopardize the child's life or health, the physician should provide appropriate treatment without parental permission (3). The rationale is that it would violate the child's best interests to delay emergency treatment until approval is obtained.

Exceptions to Parental Decision Making

Some parents might be estranged from their children or unwilling to be involved in their care. Other parents lack the capacity to make informed decisions because of alcohol or substance abuse, developmental disability, or irresponsibility. Strictly speaking, parents should make decisions for children unless a court has appointed someone else as guardian. The court process, however, might be too slow for medical decisions to be made promptly. In practice, physicians often make informal arrangements for another relative to make decisions when parents are absent or incapable of making decisions.

Disagreements Between Parents and Pediatricians

Pediatricians are understandably distressed when parents make medical decisions that are not in the child's best interests or when a child's care at home is deficient. Doctors need to try to persuade parents to accept effective interventions that have few side effects. Chapter 4 offers specific suggestions on how to resolve such disagreements. In addition, physicians, together with social workers and nurses, can mobilize emotional support and social resources to help the parents provide better care.

In rare situations physicians should ask the courts to override parental decisions—for example, when parents cannot be persuaded to accept life-saving therapy that has few side effects, such as antibiotics for bacterial meningitis in a previously healthy child.

Overriding parents through the courts, however, should be a last resort (4). Lifestyles that physicians might find objectionable, such as alcohol abuse or a disheveled home, do not in themselves constitute neglect. Even if a child with asthma or diabetes is not receiving medications regularly, disrupting the parent–child bond causes emotional distress for the child. Foster placement or institutionalization might be worse for the child than care from well-meaning parents who are trying to cope with difficult circumstances.

THE ADOLESCENT PATIENT

As children mature they develop the capacity to make informed decisions about their health care. By statute, adolescents 18 years old may give informed consent or refusal to medical care without parental involvement in almost all states. The law might also allow younger minors to make their own decisions about health care in some circumstances (5,6). State laws regarding the medical care of adolescents attempt to accommodate several conflicting policy goals, such as fostering access to treatment for important public health problems, respecting adolescents who are functionally adults, and encouraging parental involvement in their children's care. Because statutes vary both from one state to another and from one medical condition to another, pediatricians need to be familiar with the laws in their jurisdiction.

Mature Minors

"Mature minors" are capable of giving informed consent. Ethically, mature minors should be allowed to consent to or refuse medical treatment, just as adults can. Pediatricians need to evaluate adolescents' capacities to give informed consent and to help them obtain appropriate support from parents or other adults. Physicians need to assess an adolescent's understanding of the proposed intervention, the alternatives, the risks and benefits of each, and the likely consequences. Generally adolescents over 14 or 15 have such decision-making capacity, but younger children often have difficulty entertaining alternatives, appreciating the consequences of decisions, and appraising their future realistically. In most states a court must declare an adolescent a mature minor.

Emancipated Minors

Adolescents who are living apart from parents and managing their own finances, are married, have children, or have served in the armed forces are termed "emancipated" minors. Most states regard them as *de facto* adults capable of consenting to their own medical care. Some states require a judicial hearing and declaration of emancipation by the courts.

Treatment of Specified Conditions

Most states allow minors to assent to treatment without parental permission for sensitive conditions, such as sexually transmitted diseases (STDs), contraception, pregnancy, sexual assault, substance abuse, and psychiatric illness (7–9). The rationale is not that adolescents who seek treatment for such conditions are making informed decisions. Indeed, these conditions might impair judgment or result from unwise choices. Instead, the justification is that requiring parental permission would deter many adolescents from seeking treatment for important public health problems. As discussed later in this chapter, even when adolescents consent to such care themselves, it is generally in their best interests to involve their parents in their subsequent care.

Parental Requests for Treatment

Parents might request that the physician test an adolescent for illicit drug use or pregnancy without telling the child (10). Although concern generally motivates such requests, surreptitious testing is unacceptable because it violates the adolescent's emerging autonomy, undermines trust in the physician, and compromises future care.

THE PEDIATRICIAN'S RELATIONSHIP WITH CHILDREN AND PARENTS

Disclosing of information to children, protecting confidentiality, and truth-telling might raise ethical dilemmas. These actions are important because they show respect for children, lead to beneficial consequences, and foster trust in the medical profession.

DISCLOSURE OF INFORMATION TO CHILDREN

To obtain assent from children, pediatricians need to provide them with pertinent information in terms that they can understand. Children who do not want information or cannot understand medical details might still want to know what will be done to them.

Some parents do not want their children to know about serious diagnoses, such as cancer or human immunodeficiency virus infection (11). Pediatricians should elicit the parents' concerns and fears. Parents might believe that the child will not be able to handle bad news or that peers will reject the child. Physicians can explain how children might cope better, have fewer psychosocial problems, and adhere more closely to treatment if they understand their diagnosis and the proposed therapy. Parental requests for secrecy are particularly difficult when adolescents are capable of making health care decisions. Generally, physicians can persuade parents to allow disclosure of information to the child, provide developmentally appropriate information, and help the child cope with the news.

Physicians should never promise parents that the child will not learn about the diagnosis. Other members of the health care team might disclose that information. In addition, pediatricians should give forthright answers when children ask directly about their diagnosis. Deception would compromise the physician's integrity and patients' trust in the medical system.

CONFIDENTIALITY

As Chapter 5 discussed, confidentiality is not absolute. Pediatrics presents several unique issues involving confidentiality.

Exceptions to Confidentiality

Physicians and other health care workers must report cases of suspected child abuse or neglect to child protective services agencies. Parents' and children's privacy is overridden in order to protect vulnerable children from a high likelihood of serious harm. To be justified in reporting a case, physicians do not need definitive proof of abuse and neglect, only sufficient information to warrant a fuller investigation. In evaluating possible cases of child abuse, pediatricians should treat parents with respect, keeping in mind that most parents are trying their best to deal with a difficult situation. Intervention might enable parents to obtain enough assistance and support to prevent further abuse. In extreme cases protective service agencies may remove the child from parental custody.

Disclosure to Schools

Pediatricians might need to disclose health information to schools. Whenever information is disclosed, physicians should disclose only information that is truly needed. For example, a school need not know the diagnosis but only know that the child's absence was medically indicated. Pediatricians might also need to arrange for the child to receive medications at school. It is useful for pediatricians to discuss how parents, the child, and school personnel might respond to inquiries about the child's health in ways that maintain confidentiality.

Adolescents

Adolescents might wish to keep certain information confidential from their parents—for instance, that they are receiving care for mental health, STDs, pregnancy, or substance abuse (7,12). Assurances of confidentiality increase the willingness of adolescents to disclose sensitive information to physicians and to seek health care (9). Pediatricians should routinely discuss confidentiality with adolescents and offer them an opportunity to talk privately, apart from parents.

Many physicians provide absolute rather than conditional assurances of confidentiality, and such unconditional assurances increase adolescents' willingness to return for future care (13). However, as Chapter 5 discussed, overriding confidentiality is ethically appropriate and legally mandated in several situations. Moreover, most adolescents themselves believe that confidentiality should be overridden when a patient plans to commit suicide or has been physically or sexually abused (14). Physicians should not promise more than they can deliver. Hence, physicians should explain that confidentiality is not absolute and that exceptions are made, but only in limited situations (7).

Even when adolescents are allowed to consent to treatment for sensitive conditions, parents' involvement in their subsequent care will generally be beneficial. State laws vary on whether the physician may or must inform parents of the patient's care (5,6). Laws also vary according to the condition being treated, as Table 37-1 illustrates. For some sensitive conditions physicians are required to notify parents or are permitted (but not required) to do so. In other conditions physicians are prohibited from so informing parents without the minor's consent, and in still others doctors may use their judgment about disclosing to parents. When disclosure is mandated, laws generally allow an exception when the physician believes that disclosure will harm the patient.

TABLE 37-1

California Laws Regarding Notification of Patients after an Adolescent Has Consented to Treatment (15)

Condition	Requirement
Pregnancy, birth control, or STDs	May not inform parents unless the adolescent consents
Sexual assault	Must inform parents unless parent committed assault or rape
Drug or alcohol abuse	Must involve parents in care unless physician considers involvement inappropriate
	However, in federally funded programs, may not inform parents unless the adolescent consents
Minors living apart from parents and managing own finances	May notify parents
Emancipated minors who are married or in the armed forces	May not inform parents unless the adolescent consents

Because these laws are complex, physicians might need to consult a specialist in adolescent medicine or the institution's legal counsel.

Generally, physicians should encourage adolescents to discuss medical decisions with their parents, who usually provide useful support and advice (7). It is often impossible to keep the parents from learning about the child's condition because of the condition's nature, the practicalities of obtaining treatment, or the payment for care. Doctors can offer to help adolescents disclose information to their parents. In some situations, however, disclosure might be counterproductive or dangerous, as when domestic violence is likely. In such situations it might be best for the child to confide in a trusted adult relative.

REFUSAL OF MEDICAL INTERVENTIONS

The physician's response to parents' refusal of treatment will depend on the clinical circumstances, the benefits and burdens of treatment, and, in some cases, on the child's wishes (16).

REFUSAL OF INTERVENTIONS OF LIMITED EFFECTIVENESS OR GREAT BURDENS

Parents may refuse interventions that have limited effectiveness, impose significant side effects, require chronic treatment, or are controversial. In such situations the parents' informed refusals should be decisive. Refusal of such interventions might be ethically appropriate even if the patient's life expectancy might be shortened.

REFUSAL OF EFFECTIVE INTERVENTIONS WITH FEW SIDE EFFECTS

Parents sometimes refuse treatments for life-threatening conditions even though these treatments are highly effective in restoring the child to previous health, are short term, and have few side effects (17). For example, Jehovah's Witnesses commonly refuse blood transfusions for children who undergo major trauma. Similarly, Christian Scientist parents often refuse antibiotics for bacterial meningitis. Physicians who are unable to persuade parents to accept such interventions should seek a court order to administer the treatment (18). A court order is important because it signifies that society believes that the parent's refusal is unacceptable. As one court declared, although "parents may be free to become martyrs themselves," they are not free to "make martyrs of their children (19)."

In some situations physicians defer to parental refusals of effective, safe interventions because conflict between the parents and the medical system would harm the child. For instance, some parents object to immunizations because of religious objections, concerns about side effects, or opposition to modern medicine. Immunizations are required for entrance into school, although many states allow parents to refuse on the basis of religious or other objections. Even when no exceptions are permitted, requirements for immunization might not be enforced. If the number of unimmunized children is small and herd immunity exists, it might not seem worth alienating the parents. However, if an epidemic does break out, public health officials rapidly enforce requirements for immunization.

REFUSAL OF EFFECTIVE THERAPY WITH SIGNIFICANT SIDE EFFECTS

The most difficult decisions involve interventions that are highly effective in serious illness but also highly burdensome, such as bone marrow transplantation in acute lymphocytic leukemia or combination chemotherapy in testicular carcinoma. In this situation the child's preferences might be important. If an older child or adolescent makes an informed decision to undergo such treatment, physicians should support that decision.

If parents continue to refuse such therapy after repeated attempts at persuasion, some physicians seek court orders to compel treatment. In doing so, physicians need to take into account the impact on long-term parental cooperation with the child's care. At the very least, physicians should listen to the parents' objections and show respect for their opinions and ongoing responsibility for the child.

CHILD'S REFUSAL OF INTERVENTIONS

In some cases children might refuse effective treatments. The physician's response should depend on the seriousness of the clinical situation, the effectiveness and side effects of treatment, the reasons for refusal, the parents' preferences on treatment, and the burdens of insisting on treatment. It is difficult to force adolescents to take ongoing therapies, such as insulin shots for diabetes or inhalers for asthma. The most constructive approach is to try to understand the patient's reasons for refusal, to address them, and to provide psychosocial support. In several cases adolescents have run away from home rather than accept cancer chemotherapy that has significant side effects (20). Because it is physically difficult as well as morally troubling to force such treatment on adolescents, these refusals have been accepted, particularly when the parents have supported the child's refusal.

HANDICAPPED INFANTS

The federal Child Abuse Amendments of 1984 and subsequent regulations, commonly called "Baby Doe Regulations," apply to decisions to withhold medical treatment from disabled infants less than 1 year old. Their intent is to ensure such interventions as surgery for duodenal atresia or tracheal-esophageal fistula in infants with Down syndrome. They limit the circumstances in which interventions may be withheld. Under these regulations, treatment other than "appropriate nutrition, hydration, or medication" need not be provided if (a) the infant is irreversibly comatose, (b) treatment would merely prolong dying, (c) treatment would not be effective in ameliorating or correcting all life-threatening conditions, (d) treatment would be futile in terms of survival, or (e) treatment would be virtually futile and would be inhumane. Decisions to withhold medically indicated treatment might not be based on "subjective opinions" about the child's future quality of life. In addition, hospitals are encouraged to establish ethics committees, called *infant care review committees*, to advise physicians in difficult cases.

The Baby Doe Regulations have been sharply criticized (21). Many terms, such as "appropriate" and "futile," are subject to conflicting interpretations. Parents are not included in decision making despite their customary role as surrogates. Commentators point out that the regulations are often not literally followed or strictly enforced. Physicians should appreciate that these regulations do not require physicians to provide treatment that, in their judgment, is inappropriate.

REFERENCES

1. American Academy of Pediatrics Committee on Bioethics. Informed consent, parental permission, and assent in pediatric practice. *Pediatrics* 1995;95:314–317.
2. Bartholome WG. A new understanding of consent in pediatric practice: consent, parental permission, and child assent. *Pediatr Ann* 1989;18:262–265.
3. American Academy of Pediatrics Committee on Pediatric Emergency Medicine. Consent for medical services for children and adolescents. *Pediatrics* 1993;92(2):290–291.
4. American Academy of Pediatrics Committee on Bioethics. Guidelines on foregoing life-sustaining medical treatment. *Pediatrics* 1994;93:532–536.
5. Hartman RG. Coming of age: devising legislation for adolescent medical decision-making. *Am J Law Med* 2002; 28:409–453.
6. Weddle M, Kokotailo P. Adolescent substance abuse: confidentiality and consent. *Pediatr Clin North Am* 2002; 49:301–315.
7. Society for Adolescent Medicine. Confidential health care for adolescents: position paper of the Society for Adolescent Medicine. *J Adolesc Health* 1997;21:408–415.
8. American Academy of Pediatrics Committee on Adolescence. The adolescent's right to confidential care when considering abortion. *Pediatrics* 1996;97:746–751.
9. Ford CA, Millstein SG, Halpern-Feisher BL, et al. Influence of physician confidentiality assurances on adolescents' willingness to disclose information and seek future health care. *JAMA* 1997;278:1029–1034.
10. American Academy of Pediatrics Committee on Adolescence. Screening for drugs of abuse in children and adolescents. *Pediatrics* 1989;84:396–397.
11. American Academy of Pediatrics Committee on Pediatric AIDS. Disclosure of illness status to children and adolescents with HIV infection. *Pediatrics* 1999;103:164–166.
12. Council on Scientific Affairs of the American Medical Association. Confidential health services for adolescents. *JAMA* 1993;269:1420–1424.
13. Ford CA, Millstein SG. Delivery of confidentiality assurances to adolescents by primary care physicians. *Arch Pediatr Adolesc Med* 1997;151:505–509.

14. Cheng TL, Savageau JA, Sattler AL, et al. Confidentiality in health care. A survey of knowledge, perceptions, and attitudes among high school students. *JAMA* 1993;269:1404–1407.
15. National Center for Youth Law. California Minor Consent Laws. January, 2003. Available at: http://www.youthlaw.org/
16. Fleischman AR, Nolan K, Dubler NN, et al. Caring for gravely ill children. *Pediatrics* 1994;94(4 Pt 1):433–439.
17. Asser SM, Swan R. Child fatalities from religion-motivated medical neglect. *Pediatrics* 1998;101:625–629.
18. Wadlington W. Medical decision making for and by children: tensions between parent, state, and child. *Univ Illinois Law Rev* 1994;1994:311–336.
19. Prince v. Massachusetts. 321 U.S. 158 (1944).
20. Traugott I, Alpers A. In their hands: adolescents' refusal of treatment. *Arch Pediatr Adolesc Med* 1997;151:922–927.
21. Kopelman LM, Irons TG, Kopelman AE. Neonatologists judge the "Baby Doe" regulations. *N Engl J Med* 1988; 318:677–683.

ANNOTATED BIBLIOGRAPHY

1. American Academy of Pediatrics Committee on Bioethics. Informed consent, parental permission, and assent in pediatric practice. *Pediatrics* 1995;95:314–317.
   Lucid discussion of distinctions between assent by children, permission from parents for care, and informed consent by adults.
2. Society for Adolescent Medicine. Confidential health care for adolescents: position paper of the Society for Adolescent Medicine. *J Adolesc Health* 1997;21:408–415.
   Thoughtful and current review, with practical suggestions on handling dilemmas regarding confidentiality.
3. Fleischman AR, Nolan K, Dubler NN, et al. Caring for gravely ill children. *Pediatrics* 1994;94:433–439.
   Discussion of end-of-life decision making in pediatrics.
4. Traugott I, Alpers A. In their own hands: adolescents' refusal of life-sustaining treatment. *Arch Pediatr Adolesc Med* 1997;151:922–927.
   Dilemmas that occur when adolescents are old enough to run away rather than accept life-sustaining interventions.
5. Hartman RG. Coming of age: devising legislation for adolescent medical decision-making. *American Journal of Law & Medicine* 2002;28:409-453.
   Explains legal issues regarding age at which adolescents may give their own consent for treatment.

CHAPTER 38

Ethical Issues in Surgery

Surgery differs from other specialties in clinically significant ways. First, surgeons intentionally cause short-term injury in order to achieve longer-term therapeutic goals. Patients undergo operative risks, experience pain, and emerge with scars. Although all medical interventions involve risk, many of surgery's side effects are certain rather than possible and occur before any benefit can be realized. Second, patients turn over control of their bodies to the surgical team. Events in the operating room are out of the patient's and family's view. Third, operations are not standardized in the sense that drug therapies have standard dosages. The surgeon's technical competency, judgment, experience, and confidence are crucial. Individual surgeons vary in their choice of incision, use of electrocautery and stapling, and selection of suture material or implanted devices. In an individual patient the surgeon might need to modify the operative approach because of anatomic variation. This chapter discusses how these distinctive clinical characteristics of surgery have important ethical implications.

HOW ARE ETHICAL ISSUES IN SURGERY DIFFERENT?

Several ethical guidelines are particularly salient in surgery.

First, acting in the patient's best interests takes on added importance because patients are completely dependent on the surgical team during operations. Patients cannot look out for their interests during surgery and neither can a family member or proxy.

Second, informed consent is especially important because surgery is a major bodily invasion. Some operations, such as mastectomy, colostomy, or amputation, dramatically alter patients' body image, sense of self, and daily functioning. Patients differ in what surgical risks they are willing to accept.

Third, learning procedural skills differs from learning cognitive skills. More senior physicians can supervise decision-making by trainees so that the risk of mistakes is greatly reduced. However, with procedural skills, the trainee has manual control of the procedure and can make a mistake before the supervising surgeon can intervene. After surgeons complete residency or fellowship, they need to learn new techniques, such as laparoscopic procedures, with little formal training.

Fourth, individual surgeons are held responsible for the outcomes of surgery. Deaths in the operating room or after surgery raise the question of whether the surgeon erred in judgment or technique. Postoperative deaths need to be reported to the coroner. After a serious adverse event, in surgical morbidity and mortality conferences surgeons must justify why they operated and how the case was managed (1). Increasingly, surgeon-specific clinical outcomes are tracked and made available to the public or insurers. Moreover, surgeons feel personally responsible for outcomes because of their "hands-on" involvement in care.

INFORMED CONSENT IN SURGERY

Patients need information that is pertinent to their decision to have an operation. As part of the informed consent process, surgeons need to discuss information about the operation, the benefits and risks, the likely consequences, and the alternatives.

DISCLOSURE OF ALTERNATIVE APPROACHES

Evidence-based medicine has demonstrated that for some conditions several options have similar outcomes. In benign prostatic hypertrophy, transuretheral resection of the prostate, medical treatment, and watchful waiting are all acceptable approaches. For localized breast cancer, lumpectomy followed by radiation offers survival rates similar to more extensive surgery with less disfigurement. A number of states legally require that women with breast cancer be informed of breast-conserving treatments (2). The importance that the patient places on side effects of different approaches will be decisive. Hence, the surgeon should discuss all standard options with the patient even if the doctor believes that one is superior. However, surgeons do not need to discuss alternative or unconventional therapies whose effectiveness has not been demonstrated or that a respected subset of physicians has not adopted.

DISCLOSURE OF THE OUTCOMES AND EXPERIENCE

For some operations low-volume hospitals and surgeons have markedly higher surgical mortality rates (3,4). Thus, the surgeon's experience with the operation is information that reasonable patients might consider relevant when selecting a hospital or surgeon. For major elective operations, patients might want to select a hospital or surgeon with low morbidity and mortality rates. Hence, surgeons should discuss with patients their experience and outcomes with an operation when outcomes for the procedure vary substantially by provider and by experience (5–7). This ethical obligation rests on both respecting patient autonomy and acting in the patient's best interests.

Provider-specific outcomes might be publicly available. New York State and Pennsylvania publish risk-adjusted hospital-specific and surgeon-specific outcomes for coronary bypass surgery. Surgeons might object to public disclosure of such outcomes data because of concerns about risk adjustment, random variation in relatively small samples, and changes in personnel or procedures. However, the antidote is for surgeons to provide more explanation to patients, not to withhold information.

Experience might also be an issue in teaching hospitals because of residents' and students' roles. In fact, outcomes in teaching hospitals have better outcomes for complex operations than nonteaching hospitals (8). Patients should be informed of trainees' role during surgery and how they will be supervised (7). Patients usually consider it very important to be told that a resident or a medical student is going to make the incision, hold retractors, perform rectal or pelvic examinations under anesthesia, or suture (9,10). Furthermore, patients consider such disclosure more important than medical students do (9). The faculty surgeon might say. "Dr X is a senior resident and will be performing portions of your operation; I will be assisting and supervising Dr X throughout (11)." Almost all patients also want to meet the resident before the operation (10). Patients generally respond favorably to having trainees participate in operations, and most patients believe that residents are adequately supervised and can respond quickly if complications develop, although patients also realize that inexperience in residents might lead to substandard care (10).

Disclosure is also an issue when experienced surgeons learn new techniques, such as laparascopic surgery (7). Initially, complication rates are higher with laparascopic procedures than with open techniques and operating times are longer. When surgeons get more experience, complication rates become comparable to those of open procedures. For patients it might be important to know a surgeon's experience with a new technique, particularly if the outcome would be significantly better with a more experienced surgeon. However, surgeons might be concerned that patients who learn that they are inexperienced with a technique will not trust them to do the operation.

CHANGES IN THE OPERATION CAUSED BY UNANTICIPATED FINDINGS

A surgeon might encounter unexpected findings that require a substantially different operation than was discussed during the informed consent process. For example, suppose that during a cholecystectomy, the surgeon finds a gastric mass that is suspicious for carcinoma. Should the surgeon biopsy the mass, and if so, should the surgeon resect the tumor if the biopsy shows carcinoma? The surgeon might believe that an opportunity to cure gastric carcinoma might be missed if biopsy and resection are not done. Furthermore, a second operation would subject the patient to additional risk. On the other hand, the patient might be shocked to find that the surgeon performed a more extensive operation than discussed even if the surgeon did so in order to benefit him.

How can surgeons resolve this dilemma between acting for patient's good and respecting the patient's autonomy? Some surgeons seek blanket consent to change the operation if unexpected findings occur. However, this contingency is so rare that it is not efficient to discuss it with all patients preoperatively. A sound approach is to contact the next of kin in the waiting area. If the family agrees with the surgeon's recommendations, the patient's best interests and autonomy are both served. It would also be acceptable to carry out the biopsy if the family cannot be immediately located and to resect the mass only if a family member's consent can be obtained.

Such cases of incidental findings need to be distinguished from cases in which the operation needs to be changed because of a complication. For instance, a surgeon might nick the spleen and a splenectomy might be required to control bleeding. In this instance the surgeon should proceed with splenectomy and explain to the patient after the operation that a splenectomy was done because of the intraoperative complication.

MAY A SURGEON DECLINE TO OPERATE?

In some cases a surgeon might determine that an operation is not indicated because the risks of surgery greatly outweigh the possible benefits (12). What should the surgeon do if the patient or referring physician insists on surgery? Different reasons for not operating need to be distinguished. Some reasons are patient-centered. The surgeon might believe that an operation will not benefit the patient. For instance, a patient with chronic abdominal pain might believe that the pain is caused by gallbladder disease and seek a cholecystectomy (12). However, if there is no objective evidence of gallstones, the surgeon might conclude that a cholecystectomy would be futile in a strict sense and decline to operate (*see* Chapter 9).

In other situations the surgeon might judge that although the operation is not futile, the risks are prohibitive, as the following case illustrates.

CASE 38.1 Decision to not operate in a very high-risk patient.

A 64-year-old man admitted for a myocardial infarction continues to have chest pain, ischemic changes on his cardiogram, and congestive heart failure. He is found to have multiple diffuse coronary lesions that cannot be revascularized. He also develops a urinary tract infection from a Foley catheter. Despite antibiotics, he subsequently develops pyelonephritis, intrarenal abscesses, and septic shock. The patient becomes confused and unable to participate in decisions. Percutaneous drainage guided by computed tomography is not feasible. The family appreciates that the surgery is very risky, but they believe it offers the patient the only chance of survival. However, the surgeon believes that the patient's coronary disease is so unstable that he is unlikely to survive an open procedure.

Surgeons are traditionally permitted great discretion not to operate when they determine that surgery would not be in the patient's best interests. Surgeons often justify a refusal to operate by the shorthand declaration, "This patient is not a surgical candidate." Such surgical decisions are rarely challenged and discussed, but internists' unilateral decisions to withhold medical interventions are often extensively debated.

Is there an acceptable ethical basis for this distinction between surgeons and internists? Surgeons are considered more responsible for the harmful consequences of operations than internists are for the harmful effects of drugs they prescribe. In both situations the physician is responsible for the recommendation to carry out an intervention or not. However, making a surgical incision causes much more certain and direct harm to the patient than writing a prescription does. Furthermore, because surgery requires manual manipulations, it is undesirable to require surgeons to perform operations they consider inadvisable. An operation by an unwilling surgeon might place the patient at additional risk because of lapses of concentration or lack of confidence.

Surgeons need to appreciate that patients have different thresholds for risk. Some might accept severe short-term harms and unfavorable odds of success. Surgeons should decline to operate only if the risks are dramatically greater than the likely benefits, as opposed to only slightly increased. Surgeons must guard against misrepresenting information to patients because of their own bias. For example, they should never overstate an operation's risks because they recommend against it. Furthermore, they must be careful to base decisions on medical outcomes, not their personal judgments that the patient's quality of life is unacceptably poor.

Other reasons for not operating might be surgeon-centered. In some cases surgeons question whether the risk of contracting human immunodeficiency virus (HIV) infection or hepatitis C during an operation is acceptable in view of the limited benefits to the patient. For example, an orthopedic surgeon might believe that a total hip replacement on a patient with the acquired immunodeficiency syndrome presents an unacceptable risk of occupational HIV infection because bone fragments might penetrate even a double layer of gloves. In other cases a surgeon might be reluctant to take on complex, high-risk cases that might worsen their complication rates or length of hospital stays or make it more difficult to secure contracts from managed care organizations. Yet another factor might be unreimbursed care (12). Surgeons might believe that they have accepted more than their fair share of charity cases. In these situations the surgeon's self-interest must be acknowledged as a natural and legitimate concern. However, they must be put into perspective and addressed directly. Ultimately, the ethical ideal is for physicians to make patients' best interests paramount if they can do so without a grave setback to their own self-interest. To clarify patients' best interests, surgeons can consider what they would recommend if the patient did not have HIV infection (but another disease with a similar prognosis) or had good health insurance.

Some patients decline an operation recommended by a surgeon, choose to have surgery by someone else, and after an unsatisfactory outcome return to the first surgeon to request that the complications be fixed. In deciding whether to operate in such a case, surgeons need to be aware of their feelings, which might include anger, resentment, and pride and which might stand in the way of objective judgment. Surgeons have the option of not reestablishing the doctor–patient relationship in this situation. In many cases it will be desirable to refer patients to colleagues who can start afresh without qualms. In contrast, surgeons would be responsible for addressing the complications of an operation that they had performed.

REQUESTS TO CARRY OUT SURGERY IN WAYS THAT INCREASE RISK

Patients might consent to an operation but refuse specific interventions or techniques. Such restrictions might make their operation riskier and more complicated. These decisions need to be distinguished from patient refusals of the operation itself.

CASE 38.2 Emergency surgery on a Jehovah's witness.

A 54-year-old Jehovah's Witness is admitted after a motor vehicle accident with a ruptured spleen, a hemoglobin of 6%, hypotension, chest pain, and ischemic changes on electrocardiogram. He refuses blood transfusions but agrees to surgery, understanding that he might die without transfusions. The surgeon declares, "I accept his right to refuse transfusions, but he can't make me operate with one hand tied behind my back."

In this case the patient has a clear indication for splenectomy. In this patient's religion, surviving the accident is less important than avoiding the taint of transfusions, which would result in everlasting damnation (*see* Chapter 11). Operative risk increases with more severe anemia, reaching 33% when hemoglobin falls below 6 g per dl (13). Severe anemia also places this patient at greater risk for myocardial infarction and renal failure. The hospital course will be more complicated without transfusion support, and the length of stay and overall cost will probably be greater.

Some surgeons might be angry because of the need for additional time and effort and the reduced margin for error. Many surgeons intuitively make a distinction between respecting the patient's refusal of transfusions and following the patient's request to have the surgery under restrictive conditions. Philosophers distinguish negative and positive rights. Negative rights are claims to be left alone; they protect patients from unwanted interventions on their bodies. Positive rights require others to act in certain ways. Negative rights are generally considered stronger than positive rights. Thus, it makes sense to grant patients a strong right to refuse unwanted interventions but to permit much weaker claims to specify how surgeons carry out their work.

Faced with requests to carry out operations with specific restrictions, surgeons generally have a legal right to decline to operate and to transfer care to another surgeon. In many cases a more fruitful approach is to consider how to minimize additional risks from withholding transfusions. Use of cell savers, hemodilution, and administration of erythropoeitin might reduce perioperative risk (14). Moreover, surgeons should keep in mind the ethical ideal of putting the patient's best interests paramount. A skilled and experienced surgical team offers the patient the best chance at a favorable outcome.

In some cases the patient expresses objections to certain aspects of the proposed operation only because the physician brings up the issues.

CASE 38.3 Patient refusal of emergency colostomy.

A 74-year-old man is admitted to the hospital with an acute abdomen. He is found to have free air under the diaphragm. The surgeon believes that the patient has perforated a peptic ulcer or a carcinoma of the colon. The surgeon explains that if the perforation is in the colon, she will perform a colostomy, which might not need to be permanent. The patient adamantly refuses a colostomy. "A friend had one and had one complication after another. He was so ashamed of that bag. I'd rather be dead than go through that humiliation." There is no time for the patient to talk to people who have adapted well to a colostomy. Technically, an end-to-end anastamosis is possible, but it has a much higher risk of complications.

The surgeon consults a colleague about the case. He says, "In an emergency I never discuss the details of the surgery. All that the patient needs to know is that he needs an operation to save his life and that the risks of surgery are small compared with the alternatives. Too much information can be dangerous because there is no time to correct misunderstandings. All this discussion about a colostomy is probably moot. Chances are he'll have a perforated ulcer. Even if he perforated his colon, you might be able to take the colostomy down later. I wouldn't do an end-to-end anastamosis. How would you justify it at a morbidity and mortality conference if he got a complication?"

In Case 38.3 the ethical dilemma is that the patient might be making an irreversible decision that he would greatly regret later. The surgeon believes that the patient's refusal is based on an unrealistic appraisal of a colostomy. In elective situations most patients can be persuaded to accept a colostomy, but in an emergency there is no time for extended discussions. A surgeon dedicated to acting in the patient's best interests would want to do the less risky operation, knowing that most patients adapt to a colostomy. From this perspective, it would be terrible if the patient refused surgery because of an outcome that might not happen or might be only temporary. The colleague's concern about the morbidity and mortality conference is not just a desire to avoid personal criticism; the professional standard of care is based on what a reasonable surgeon would do under the circumstances.

In contrast, a surgeon dedicated to patient autonomy will respect the patient's refusal of colostomy even if that decision might not be fully informed. From this viewpoint, even if the operation were skillfully performed and successfully treated the perforation, it would be tragic if the patient had to live with a mutilation of his body that he did not consent to. A patient's preferences about therapy depend not only on the likelihood of survival but also on the surgery's nature and the quality of life afterward (15,16). A patient might consider a colostomy so unacceptable that he would rather die than have the operation.

The surgeon in Case 38.1 has several options. One option is to refuse to operate unless the patient agrees to a colostomy if needed. However, this option might leave the patient worse off than having an end-to-end anastamosis. Also, if the on-call surgeon declines to operate, it might be difficult to find a colleague to take over the case without delay.

A better approach is to try to persuade the patient to accept the colostomy. This can often be done despite severe time constraints. The surgeon can ask the patient to talk his decision over with his family, friends, primary care physician, or the chaplain, and the surgeon could explain to them why a colostomy is preferable. In addition, the surgeon might be able to persuade the patient by paradoxically giving him control. "If you decide that you won't accept the colostomy after talking to your family and your primary care doctor, I'll agree to do the surgery in the other, riskier way. I won't force you to have an operation you don't want. But before you decide, I'd like to understand better what about the colostomy troubles you. I'd also like you to understand why I think the colostomy is the best operation for you." If persuasion fails, it is ethically appropriate for the surgeon to agree to do an end-to-end anastamosis, based on the patient's informed decision.

In trying to persuade patients, some surgeons might be tempted to misrepresent what they will do in the operating room. For example, they might say they will try to do an end-to-end anastamosis if possible even though they actually intend to do a colostomy. For reasons discussed in Chapter 6, such misrepresentation is problematic and undermines both patient trust and the physician's integrity.

In summary, the unique clinical circumstances of surgery impose special ethical obligations on surgeons regarding informed consent, decisions not to operate, and patient requests to carry out the operation in certain ways.

REFERENCES

1. Bosk CL. *Forgive and remember: managing medical failure*. Chicago: University of Chicago Press, 1979.
2. Nattinger AB, Hoffman RG, Shapiro R, et al. The effect of legislative requirements on the use of breast-conserving surgery. *N Engl J Med* 1996;335:1035–1040.
3. Halm EA, Lee C, Chassin MR. Is volume related to outcome in health care? A systematic review and methodologic critique of the literature. *Ann Intern Med* 2002;137(6):511–520.
4. Birkmeyer JD, Stukel TA, Siewers AE, et al. Surgeon volume and operative mortality in the United States. *N Engl J Med* 2003;349(22):2117–2127.
5. Kizer KW. The volume-outcome conundrum. *N Engl J Med* 2003;349(22):2159–2161.
6. Arnold RM, Shaw BW, Purtillo R. Acute high-risk patients: the case of transplantation. In: McCullough LB, Jones JW, Brody BA, eds. *Surgical ethics*. New York: Oxford University Press, 1998:97–115.
7. Gates EA. New surgical procedures: can our patients benefit while we learn? *Am J Obstet Gynecol* 1997;176(6): 1293–1298.
8. Dimick JB, Cowan JA Jr., Colletti LM, et al. Hospital teaching status and outcomes of complex surgical procedures in the United States. *Arch Surg* 2004;139(2):137–141.
9. Silver-Isenstadt A, Ubel PA. Erosion in medical students' attitudes about telling patients they are students. *J Gen Intern Med* 1999;14:481–487.
10. Kim N, Lo B, Gates EA. Disclosing the role of residents and medical students in hysterectomy: what do patients want? *Acad Med* 1998;73:339–341.
11. McCullough LB, Jones JW, Brody BA. Informed consent: autonomous decision-making of the surgical patient. In: McCullough LB, Jones JW, Brody BA, eds. *Surgical ethics*. New York: Oxford University Press, 1998:15–37.
12. Sugarman J, Harland R. Acute yet non-emergent patients. In: McCullough LB, Jones JW, Brody BA, eds. *Surgical ethics*. New York: Oxford University Press, 1998:116–132.
13. Carson JL, Duff A, Poses RM, et al. Effect of anaemia and cardiovascular disease on surgical mortality and morbidity. *Lancet* 1996;348(9034):1055–1060.
14. Loubser PG, Stoltz SM, Schmoker JD, et al. Blood conservation strategies in Jehovah's Witness patients undergoing complex aortic surgery: a report of three cases. *J Cardiothorac Vasc Anesth* 2003;17(4):528–535.
15. McNeil BJ, Weichselbaum R, Pauker SG. Speech and survival: tradeoffs between quality and quantity of life in laryngeal cancer. *N Engl J Med* 1981;305:982–987.
16. McNeil BJ, Weichselbaum R, Pauker SG. Fallacy of the five-year survival in lung cancer. *N Engl J Med* 1978; 299:307–401.

ANNOTATED BIBLIOGRAPHY

1. McCullough LB, Jones JW, Brody BA, eds. *Surgical ethics*. New York: Oxford University Press, 1998.
   Monograph written jointly by a surgeon and an ethicist that covers ethical issues in various surgical contexts.
2. Gates EA. New surgical procedures: can our patients benefit while we learn? *Am J Obstet Gynecol* 1997;176: 1293–1298.
   Argues that surgeons should disclose their own experience and outcomes during the informed consent process.

CHAPTER 39

Ethical Issues in Obstetrics and Gynecology

Ethical dilemmas in obstetrics and gynecology are particularly difficult because care for a pregnant woman and care for her fetus are inextricably linked. Furthermore, decisions about reproduction and sexuality rest on values that are intensely private but often socially contested.

HOW ARE ETHICAL ISSUES IN OBSTETRICS AND GYNECOLOGY DIFFERENT?

REPRODUCTIVE HEALTH IS HIGHLY PERSONAL, BUT THIRD PARTIES SEEK TO INFLUENCE IT

Decisions in obstetrics and gynecology involve intimate and personal topics, such as sexuality, reproduction, and childrearing. Many women want control of their reproductive decisions and have strong preferences in family planning and childbirth. At the same time, public leaders and religious groups might hold strong views regarding children, family, and women's appropriate role. These third parties might seek to shape women's decisions about reproductive health. Currently, debates over abortion in the United States are passionate and highly politicized. On the one hand, some seek to reaffirm traditional attitudes toward women, reproduction, and sexuality, and on the other hand, feminist critics assert that society and physicians exercise inappropriate control over women through policies regarding reproductive health care. Some women also believe that doctors and society have transformed the experience of pregnancy and childbirth into an overly technological and medicalized procedure.

REPRODUCTIVE HEALTH INVOLVES PHILOSOPHIC QUANDARIES THAT SCIENCE CANNOT RESOLVE

Decisions about reproduction inevitably raise philosophic or religious questions that science cannot resolve.

- Is the fetus a person with moral and legal rights?
- When does personhood begin: at conception, viability, birth, or some other time?
- Does the pregnant woman have an ethical right of reproductive liberty that encompasses a right to abortion?

Theologians, philosophers, public officials, and the public have debated these conundrums without reaching agreement or common ground. Consensus is unlikely to emerge, and public policies need to be developed despite deep disagreements.

NEW REPRODUCTIVE TECHNOLOGIES RAISE UNPRECEDENTED DILEMMAS

Assisted reproductive technologies (ARTs) allow pregnancy to occur in unprecedented ways. With ARTs and gamete donation, different persons can fill the roles of genetic, gestational, and childrearing parents. Dramatic dilemmas have arisen over the disposition of frozen embryos after a couple has separated, ART for postmenopausal women, and "surrogate motherhood," in which the gestational mother has no genetic link with the fetus and will not raise the child after birth. Such dilemmas force people to reconsider fundamental, often unspoken beliefs about parental responsibility and roles.

THE OBSTETRICIAN MIGHT HAVE TWO PATIENTS, THE PREGNANT WOMAN AND THE FETUS

Fetal movements and fetal heartbeat can be visualized with ultrasound and other imaging techniques. Doctors can diagnose many conditions in utero, such as congenital abnormalities or fetal distress. Furthermore, physicians can treat the fetus through interventions on the mother, such as prenatal vitamins, tocolytic agents in premature labor, corticosteroids in prematurity, and fetal blood transfusion for Rh isoimmunization. In light of this ability to diagnose and treat fetal disorders, it seems reasonable to consider the fetus a patient, along with the pregnant woman, provided that she intends to carry the fetus to term and presents for prenatal care (1). Thinking of the fetus as a patient helps prevent inadvertent injury to the fetus by reminding physicians and pregnant women to consider how care for the woman might affect the fetus (2).

Everyone hopes that children will be born healthy. It is tragic when a child is born with a serious preventable illness or congenital anomaly. The pregnant woman has some moral responsibility to take steps to reduce harm and provide benefit to the child who will be born (3). Physicians have a responsibility to represent the interests of such future children, who cannot represent themselves. These moral responsibilities are based on the desire to prevent harm to children who will be born; they do not require a belief that the fetus is a person with rights (3).

The idea that the fetus is a patient is limited by the fact that interventions directed to the fetus are also interventions on the pregnant woman that might cause side effects in her or affect other aspects of her life (2). In premature labor terbutaline causes tremor and anxiety in the pregnant woman. Long-term bed rest for premature labor might prevent the pregnant woman from caring for her other children or working at a job that supports her family. Most pregnant women accept side effects, inconvenience, and disruption of their life for the sake of the child who will be born. However, pregnant woman need not adopt every intervention that might benefit the fetus, regardless of the degree of benefit, risks, or impact on her life. Responsibilities to a fetus who will become a child have limits; logically they should not exceed responsibilities that parents have to living children (4). Parents are not obligated to provide all potentially beneficial interventions to children after birth or to minimize all harms to them.

INFORMED CONSENT IN OBSTETRICS AND GYNECOLOGY

Several situations in obstetrics and gynecology raise particular ethical issues regarding consent.

PROVISION OF INFORMATION ABOUT FAMILY PLANNING AND ABORTION

Some physicians have strong moral and religious objections to these interventions (5). They believe it would violate their conscience to write a prescription for birth control or perform an abortion. Institutions should make reasonable accommodations to conscientious objections, and patients should be referred to facilities that provide care (see Chapter 24).

REPRODUCTIVE HEALTH FOR ADOLESCENTS

Girls under 18 years of age, who are often sexually active, might seek care for contraception, sexually transmitted diseases, or pregnancy. Many people believe that allowing minors to obtain such care without parental consent undermines family values and encourages promiscuity and irresponsibility.

In most states, however, adolescents may seek reproductive health care without parental consent. The rationale is that it is preferable for adolescents to have access to such care rather than to forego care because they are reluctant or unable to obtain parental approval. Usually it is in the adolescent's best interest to involve parents in their care, and physicians should encourage them to do so. However, in some cases adolescents might have compelling reasons for not involving parents—for example, in cases of domestic violence or incest. Chapter 37 discussed ethical issues in adolescent medicine in detail.

ROUTINE PRENATAL TESTING

During pregnancy women commonly have screening tests for rubella, syphilis, gonorrhea, Rh type, and diabetes. The Centers for Disease Control and Prevention (CDC) now recommend routine prenatal human immunodeficiency virus testing (6). In many ambulatory tests the patient usually assents rather than gives full informed consent. Each test's risks, benefits, and alternatives are not discussed, and testing is carried out unless the patient objects. Another way to describe routine testing is that women may opt out of testing but do not need to give affirmative consent. Going beyond routine testing, most states require mandatory prenatal testing for syphilis (7). The ethical justification for routine and mandatory prenatal screening tests are prevention of harm to children who will be born, the failure of voluntary testing to achieve the desired level of testing, and the belief that the infringement of the woman's autonomy is acceptable.

OBSTETRIC EMERGENCIES

Some obstetric decisions need to be made in crisis situations. An uncomplicated pregnancy at term might unexpectedly and rapidly become an emergency if severe fetal distress develops or if the umbilical cord is wrapped around the fetus's neck. A cesarean section might need to be carried out within minutes in order to prevent severe, irreversible harm to a child. As with any emergency situation, the informed consent process may be truncated if delaying care to obtain consent would cause serious harm and if most patients would agree to the intervention if fully informed. In an emergency a cesarean section may be performed on the basis of the pregnant woman's assent rather than informed consent. That is, the patient agrees to the doctor's recommendations without being informed of all the procedure's risks and benefits. Almost all pregnant women agree to recommended emergency cesarean sections (8).

STERILIZATION

Sterilization without a woman's consent is a grave violation of her autonomy. In the early 1900s nonvoluntary eugenic sterilization was carried out in the United States on women who had mental retardation, resided in psychiatric institutions, and were prisoners (9,10). African-American women were disproportionately subjected to nonvoluntary sterilization. In response to these abuses, many states have enacted procedural requirements such as waiting periods to ensure that sterilization decisions are voluntary and informed (9,10).

Sterilization is commonly considered for severely mentally disabled persons. It might be in the best interests of a person who will never have the capacity to make informed reproductive decisions or to provide basic care for a child (11). Generally, a court hearing is required in order to sterilize a woman who is not capable of giving informed consent (9,10).

ELECTIVE CESAREAN SECTION AT TERM

Traditionally, obstetricians have opposed pregnant women's requests for elective cesarean section deliveries at term. Most obstetricians believed that this procedure presented unacceptable risks to the mother and child. In addition, many believed that convenience and the mother's preferences were not adequate reasons for a surgical procedure. Recently, attitudes have shifted dramatically (12). New evidence suggests that elective cesarean sections at term might benefit the mother and fetus (12). Operative and anesthetic advances have decreased risks to the mother. Many obstetricians report that they would choose this procedure for themselves or their partner (13).

ABORTION

Debates over abortion in the United States are contentious. Pro-life advocates contend that the fetus is a person with a right to live and that abortion constitutes a form of murder. Pro-choice advocates claim that women have a right to control their bodies and their reproductive choices and often contend that a fetus becomes a person only after birth. Disagreements over abortion are associated with different views on women's roles and the meaning of their lives (14). Although pro-life activists tend to view motherhood as the "most important and satisfying role" for a woman, pro-choice activists tend to believe that motherhood is "only one of several roles, a burden when defined as the only role" for a woman (15). Debates have become increasingly polarized (1,14).

The Supreme Court has made several important rulings on abortion. In *Planned Parenthood v. Casey* (1992) the Supreme Court affirmed the landmark 1973 *Roe v. Wade* decision, which protected a woman's right to choose to abort her fetus. In *Casey* the court held that states may ban abortion after fetal viability, as long as exceptions were made to protect the woman's health or life and as long as the restriction's "purpose or effect [was not] to place substantial obstacles in the path of a woman seeking an abortion before the fetus attains viability (16)." Many states require parental notification if a minor seeks an abortion; these states must have a procedure for adolescents to seek judicial authorization for the procedure instead of parental notification. Physicians need to understand the laws in their state.

Some requests for abortion are particularly problematic. For example, a pregnant woman might seek an abortion on the basis of the sex of her fetus even though there is no sex-linked genetic disease. The woman might come from a culture in which male children are more prized or might desire a son or daughter after having all children of the opposite sex. Although parents commonly have a preference about the child's sex, a physician is not morally justified to perform an abortion on a healthy fetus solely because of its sex (17). There is little ethical justification for treating females and males differently in this situation. If the physician cannot persuade the woman to withdraw her request, the doctor is justified in withdrawing from the case.

MATERNAL–FETAL CONFLICT

Most pregnant women agree with their physician's recommendations for interventions that benefit the fetus. However, in some cases women might reject such recommendations despite continued attempts at persuasion.

PATIENT REQUESTS FOR INTERVENTIONS WHOSE RISKS OUTWEIGH THE BENEFITS

Pregnant women might request interventions whose balance of benefits to risks physicians consider unfavorable. For example, young pregnant women at low risk for genetic abnormalities might request amniocentesis or chorionic villus sampling. Such women might place a high value on information about the fetus and reassurance that the pregnancy is progressing normally, even though there is little likelihood of a serious abnormality (18). Moreover, women might want to know of congenital abnormalities even if they would still carry the fetus to term. However, if the risk for serious congenital abnormalities is very low, it might be less than the risk of complications such as miscarriage.

How should the physician respond to such requests? The physician can check that the mother understands the procedure's benefits and risks and the availability of other tests for congenital abnormalities, such as alpha fetoprotein screening. In addition, the physician can help the woman deliberate about the decision and make a recommendation. Ultimately, however, the woman's choice should be decisive.

CARE OF PREGNANT WOMEN WITH OTHER MEDICAL PROBLEMS

When pregnant women have serious medical problems, such as cancer, depression, or seizures, physicians are understandably concerned that treatments for those conditions might adversely effect the fetus. However, such concern for the fetus must not lead physicians to withhold effective therapies from the woman. First, physicians need accurate information about therapies' effects on the fetus, and physicians often overestimate the risks. Second, in conditions such as tuberculosis or epilepsy, aggressive treatment for the pregnant woman promotes the physical health of the child who will be born (19). Furthermore, it will be in the child's best interests for the mother to be healthy. Finally, the pregnant woman should make informed decisions about the care of her medical problems. She should decide what risks to the fetus are acceptable in view of the intervention's overall benefits. It is inappropriate for physicians to withhold effective interventions from the mother or to insist that the pregnant woman obtain an abortion as a condition of treatment.

SUBSTANCE AND ALCOHOL ABUSE DURING PREGNANCY

Many states have enacted laws to try to prevent harm caused by prenatal substance abuse. As of 2003, 24 states permit involuntary civil commitment of pregnant women who use certain illegal drugs (20). In a few states drug abuse during pregnancy triggers child abuse laws (20,21). Depending on the state, there may be an evaluation of parenting ability or a presumption of neglect. No state mandates drug screening during pregnancy. Physicians and hospitals may not conduct drug testing of pregnant women for criminal prosecution without a warrant or an explicit consent (21). Except in South Carolina, courts have refused to apply existing criminal laws on child endangerment or delivery of drugs to a minor to drug-using pregnant women. Punitive approaches to drug and alcohol abuse during pregnancy might be counterproductive, deterring women from seeking prenatal care or being candid with physicians (20,22). Focusing on substance abuse treatment is more likely to benefit the fetus's and the mother's health than punishment is (23,24).

FORCED CESAREAN SECTION DELIVERIES

If a pregnant woman cannot be persuaded to accept a cesarean section that the physician believes is required, some doctors seek court authorization for the operation. The trend in recent court rulings holds that a competent pregnant woman may refuse a cesarean section even if a viable fetus's welfare is at stake (22,25–27). Courts note that competent adults may refuse treatment, that cesarean sections are a significant bodily invasion, and that the medical need for the procedure is often overstated. In many cases in which court orders were sought for cesarean section, the woman delivered vaginally without complications (22,28). In addition, forced cesarean sections compromise women's trust in physicians and discriminate against women who do not speak English and women of color.

ASSISTED REPRODUCTIVE TECHNOLOGIES

Because physicians take an active and essential role in ARTs, they feel a moral responsibility for the well-being of the child who might be born (29). Many physicians would hesitate to provide infertility treatments to women with drug addiction, serious developmental delay, or severe psychiatric illness because they believe the woman would not be a good parent. Other physicians might be reluctant to assist single, unmarried, or lesbian women because they believe that only married women should be parents.

Concern for the well-being of children who will be born is laudable. Physicians should help women and couples who seek ARTs appreciate the difficulties of infertility treatments and childrearing. The physician might also make recommendations on the basis of the patient's situation, needs, and goals. Furthermore, it would be irresponsible for physicians to provide ARTs to women who are incapable of giving informed consent or to women who have abused their children. However, physicians should distinguish concerns that are based on clinical evidence from their personal views of parenthood and family. Some characteristics, such as marital status, have little power to predict whether a person would be a good parent (29). Many married couples fail as parents, but many persons who are single or have nontraditional relationships succeed.

Some women over 40 seek infertility treatment (29). Although many such women are committed to raising a child, have strong social support, and have carefully considered their decision, some writers believe that the natural span of childbearing years should be respected (30). Because having a child is such a private decision, it is problematic for third parties to impose their views of who is worthy of being a parent.

STUDENT PARTICIPATION IN GYNECOLOGIC AND OBSTETRIC CARE

Pelvic examinations done under anesthesia offer opportunities for students to master a difficult skill. Because a woman's muscles are relaxed under anesthesia, a more thorough examination is possible. Senior physicians sometimes ask students to perform pelvic examinations on an anesthetized patient in the operating room without her consent. Some persons believe that explicit consent is not needed because, by agreeing to the surgery, the patient implicitly consents to examinations by medical students. However, agreeing to surgery is not tantamount to consenting to a pelvic exam by an unknown medical student who is not providing ongoing care. In one study all the women surveyed believed that students should ask specific permission to perform a pelvic examination on an anesthetized patient (31). Although patient consent to participation by trainees in their care is always important (*see* Chapter 38), it is particularly important for pelvic examinations because of patient privacy. Under a recent California law, trainees may not perform a pelvic examination on an anesthetized or unconscious patient without informed consent unless the examination is within the scope of care for the patient (32).

In summary, obstetrics and gynecology raise ethical issues that might be particularly controversial. Physicians need to help women understand various options' risks and benefits. Doctors also need to appreciate that the patient's values might differ from their own, try to understand how the woman's decision might make sense from her perspective, and negotiate a mutually acceptable plan for care.

REFERENCES

1. McCullough LB, Chervenak FA. *Ethics in obstetrics and gynecology*. New York: Oxford University Press, 1994.
2. Dickens BM, Cook RJ. Ethical and legal approaches to "the fetal patient". *Int J Gynecol Obstet* 2003;83:85–91.
3. Steinbock B. Maternal–fetal relationship: ethical issues. In: Reich, WT, ed. *Encyclopedia of bioethics*, Revised ed. New York: Simon & Schuster Macmillan, 1995:1408–1413.
4. Murray TH. *The worth of a child*. Berkeley, Los Angeles, London: University of California Press, 1996:96–114.
5. Cantor J, Baum K. The limits of conscientious objection–may pharmacists refuse to fill prescriptions for emergency contraception? *N Engl J Med* 2004;351:2008–2012.
6. Wolf LE, Lo B, Gostin LO. Legal barriers to implementing recommendations for universal, routine prenatal HIV testing. *J Law Med Ethics* 2004;32:137–147.
7. Acuff KI. Prenatal and newborn screening: state legislative approaches and current practice standards. In: Faden RR, Geller G, Powers M, eds. *AIDS, women and the next generation*. New York: Oxford University Press, 1991: 121–165.
8. Lescale KB, Inglis SR, Eddleman KA, et al. Conflicts between physicians and patients in non-elective cesarean delivery: incidence and adequacy of informed consent. *Am J Perinat* 1996;13:171–176.
9. Dubler NN, White A. Fertility control: legal and regulatory issues. In: Reich WT, ed. *Encyclopedia of bioethics*, Revised ed. New York: Simon & Schuster Macmillan, 1995:839–847.
10. American Academy of Pediatrics Committee on Bioethics. Sterilization of minors with developmental disabilities. *Pediatrics* 1999;104:337–340.
11. Diekema DS. Involuntary sterilization of persons with mental retardation: an ethical analysis. *Ment Retard Dev Disabil Res Rev* 2003;9:21–26.
12. Minkoff H, Chervenak FA. Elective primary cesarean delivery. *N Engl J Med* 2003;348:298–302.
13. Al-Mufti R, McCarthy A, Fisk NM. Survey of obstetricians' personal preference and discretionary practice. *Eur J Obstet Gynecol Reprod Biol* 1997;73(1):1–4.
14. Murray TH. *The worth of a child*. Berkeley, Los Angeles, London: University of California Press, 1996:142–166.
15. Luker K. *Abortion and the politics of motherhood*. Berkeley: University of California Press, 1984.
16. Planned Parenthood of Southeastern Pennsylvania v. Casey. 112 US 674 (1992).
17. The New York State Task Force on Life and the Law. *Assisted reproductive technologies*. New York: The New York State Task Force on Life and the Law, 1998:165–169.
18. Kuppermann M, Nease RF, Learman LA, et al. Procedure-related miscarriages and Down syndrome-affected births: implications for prenatal testing based on women's preferences. *Obstet Gynecol* 2000;96(4):511–516.
19. Eller DP, Patterson CA, Webb GW. Maternal and fetal implications of anticonvulsant therapy during pregnancy. *Obstet Gynecol Clin* 1997;24:523–534.
20. Jos PH, Perlmutter M, Marshall MF. Substance abuse during pregnancy: clinical and public health approaches. *J Law Med Ethics* 2003;31:340–350.
21. Harris LJ, Paltrow L. The status of pregnant women and fetuses in U.S. criminal law. *JAMA* 2003;289:1697–1699.
22. Johnsen DE. Maternal–fetal relationship: legal and regulatory issues. In: Reich WT, ed. *Encyclopedia of bioethics*, Revised ed. New York: Simon & Schuster Macmillan, 1995: 1413–1418.
23. Chavkin W. Mandatory treatment for drug use during pregnancy. *JAMA* 1991;266:1556–1561.
24. Board of Trustees AMA. Legal interventions during pregnancy: court-ordered medical treatments and legal penalties for potentially harmful behavior by pregnant women. *JAMA* 1990;264:2663–2670.

25. Curran WJ. Court-ordered cesarean sections receive judicial defeat. *N Engl J Med* 1990;323:489–492.
26. Levy JK. Jehovah's Witnesses, pregnancy, and blood transfusions: a paradigm for the autonomy of all pregnant women. *J Law Med Ethics* 1999;27:171–189.
27. Goldblatt AD. Commentary: no more jurisdiction over Jehovah. *J Law Med Ethics* 1999;27:190–193.
28. Nelson LJ, Milliken N. Compelled medical treatment of pregnant women: life, liberty and law in conflict. *JAMA* 1988;259:1060–1066.
29. The New York State Task Force on Life and the Law. *Assisted reproductive technologies.* New York: The New York State Task Force on Life and the Law, 1998:177–213.
30. The President's Council on Bioethics. *Reproduction and responsibility: the regulation of new biotechnologies.* Washington: The President's Council on Bioethics, 2004.
31. Bibby J, Boyd N, Redman C, et al. Consent for vaginal examination by students on anaesthetised patients (letter). *Lancet* 1988;2(8620):1150.
32. Cal Bus & Prof Code §2281 (2003).

ANNOTATED BIBLIOGRAPHY

1. The New York State Task Force on Life and the Law. *Assisted reproductive technologies.* New York: The New York State Task Force on Life and the Law, 1998.
The President's Council on Bioethics. *Reproduction and responsibility: the regulation of new biotechnologies.* Washington: The President's Council on Bioethics, 2004.
Two works that contain ethical and policy analyses regarding assisted reproductive technologies.
2. Dickenson DL, Fulford KWM. *Ethical issues in maternal–fetal medicine.* New York: Cambridge University Press, 2002.
Discusses ethical issues in obstetrics from a feminist and British perspective.
3. McCullough LB, Chervenak FA. *Ethics in obstetrics and gynecology.* New York: Oxford University Press, 1994.
Monograph with a philosophical orientation on ethical issues in obstetrics and gynecology.
4. Minkoff H, Chervenak FA. Elective primary cesarean delivery. *N Engl J Med* 2003;348:298–302.
Argues that elective cesarean delivery at term is a medically and ethically acceptable option.
5. Jos PH, Perlmutter M, Marshall MF. Substance abuse during pregnancy: clinical and public health approaches. *J Law Med Ethics* 2003;31:340–350.
Analysis of ethical and legal issues regarding substance abuse during pregnancy.

CHAPTER 40

Ethical Issues in Psychiatry

Some patients with severe psychiatric illness might cause serious harm to themselves and others, but they might not be capable of making informed decisions about health care or controlling their behavior. Effective treatment of the psychiatric illness might restore their decision-making capacity and control over their actions. Rather than respect their choices, physicians need to protect such nonautonomous patients against the consequences of their decisions and actions.

HOW ARE ETHICAL ISSUES IN PSYCHIATRY DIFFERENT?

SEVERE PSYCHIATRIC ILLNESS MIGHT IMPAIR THE PATIENT'S AUTONOMY

Patients with severe psychiatric illness might be unable to make informed decisions, care for themselves, distinguish right from wrong, or control their thoughts, impulses, and actions. They might have so little insight into illness that they are not considered morally or legally responsible for their actions. When their illness is severe, such patients might have different values, preferences, and judgments than when their illness is treated.

TREATMENT MIGHT RESTORE THE PATIENT'S AUTONOMY

Treatment of the underlying psychiatric illness often restores the patient's decision-making capacity and control over his or her behavior. Thus, a short-term infringement on the patient's freedom, such as involuntary hospitalization, might restore the patient's autonomy in the long term.

PHYSICIANS HAVE A UNIQUE OPPORTUNITY TO PREVENT SERIOUS HARM

Physicians are in a unique position to identify patients who are rendered nonautonomous by psychiatric illness, to protect them from harm, and to prevent harm to third parties. Society therefore has authorized physicians to intervene primarily to protect third parties from harm and also to help such patients obtain treatment.

PSYCHIATRIC THERAPIES RAISE ETHICAL CONCERNS

By altering how people think and feel, effective psychiatric medications might change a person's personality and identity. Some patients complain that medication transforms them into people who are no longer their true selves. Some patients even say that they would rather live with mild symptoms than take medications that alter their brain and their essential characteristics. In contrast, others believe that effective psychiatric therapies, by removing delusions, disturbed thinking, mood disorders, and other undesired characteristics, restore a person's true self. Still others criticize the use of selective serotonin reuptake inhibitors by persons who do not have serious psychiatric illness to try to improve their mood, confidence, or social functioning (1). To these critics self-improvement and accomplishment should result from hard work, not medications.

Involuntary psychiatric interventions, such as forced hospitalization, present even stronger ethical concerns because they deprive patients of liberty. In the past many psychiatric patients were involuntarily subjected to extreme measures, such as lengthy confinement in inhumane mental institutions and psychosurgery.

CONFIDENTIALITY ENCOURAGES THERAPY

In therapy patients reveal their innermost emotions, fears, and fantasies. Maintaining confidentiality respects the personal and sensitive nature of such information and encourages patients to seek care for mental illness and to be candid with physicians. In addition, confidentiality protects patients from stigma and discrimination, which patients with psychiatric illness might face even if their disease is in remission. Recent federal privacy regulations, as well as some state laws, give special protection to psychotherapy notes by requiring specific patient authorization to disclose them.

ACCESS TO PSYCHIATRIC CARE

Despite recent efforts to achieve parity between insurance coverage for medical and psychiatric problems, many patients have limited access to mental health care. Managed care plans often restrict the therapy's frequency or duration. Many patients with severe psychiatric illness are uninsured, and public mental health services are underfunded. Finally, such patients might have concurrent problems, such as homelessness, alcoholism, or substance abuse, that make it difficult for them to obtain care.

INVOLUNTARY PSYCHIATRIC COMMITMENT

Involuntary commitment is a dramatic exception to the ethical guideline of respecting people's liberty. Because it infringes on freedom so profoundly, involuntary psychiatric commitment must be carefully justified.

RATIONALE FOR INVOLUNTARY COMMITMENT

Intervention is warranted to prevent persons who are incapable of making informed decisions and of controlling their actions from causing serious, irreversible harm to themselves or to others. Depriving such patients of their liberty for a short time might allow them to regain their autonomy (2). After their depression, bipolar disorder, or schizophrenia is treated, most patients no longer choose to kill themselves or harm others.

STANDARDS FOR INVOLUNTARY COMMITMENT

Criteria for involuntary commitment differ among states but typically require that patients be, because of mental illness,

- dangerous to themselves—for example, suicidal, or
- unable to care for themselves—for example, unable to provide food, clothing, and shelter, or
- dangerous to others—for example, through a threat, an attempt, or an overt act of harm.

In addition, patients in several states may be involuntarily committed if a severe deterioration in their condition is likely without treatment and they cannot give consent to treatment. Under such laws the rationale for commitment is the patient's need for treatment rather than the patient's danger to self or others (2).

PROCEDURES FOR INVOLUNTARY COMMITMENT

Because involuntary commitment procedures vary across the states, physicians need to be familiar with the law in their states. The following provisions are typical. Initially, patients may be held against their will on an emergency basis for brief periods (typically a few days). During an emergency patients can also be treated against their will to prevent serious physical injury to themselves or others or, in some states, to prevent an irreversible deterioration of their condition. A judicial hearing must be held to determine whether the patient may be confined for a longer period.

Legal hearings are time consuming, and many physicians believe that they are an unwarranted intrusion of the legal system into medical practice. However, many laypeople have a sharply different perspective. Because involuntary psychiatric hospitalization is a serious deprivation of liberty and has been abused in the past, the public demands rigorous safeguards.

Physicians might threaten to initiate commitment proceedings unless the patient "voluntarily" consents to hospitalization. This practice is coercive and ethically questionable (2). Voluntary hospitalization helps physicians by reducing paperwork and eliminating the need for a judicial hearing. However, patients might not realize that by agreeing to voluntary hospitalization, they are waiving their right to a judicial hearing to determine whether commitment is appropriate. A more respectful strategy is to first tell patients that plans for involuntary hospitalization will be instituted and explain their right to a judicial hearing. After patients understand the commitment procedures, they may be offered an opportunity to sign into the hospital voluntarily (2).

OUTPATIENT COMMITMENT AND INVOLUNTARY TREATMENT

In many states patients with psychiatric illness can be subjected to involuntary outpatient treatment if they at serious risk for relapse because of nonadherence to treatment (3). Such persons can be ordered to undergo outpatient treatment even though they are currently not gravely disabled or violent. Recent highly publicized cases of violence perpetrated by psychiatric patients have sparked interest in outpatient commitment. The rationale for outpatient commitment is to prevent persons from lapsing again into a cycle of deterioration and involuntary hospitalization (4,5). Such mandatory treatment may be carried out in several ways (4,6). It may be a condition of obtaining housing and social service payments. Courts may order it as a condition of avoiding jail or inpatient commitments. Advocates argue that mandatory outpatient treatment is more humane and less restrictive than repeated involuntary hospitalizations. Critics contend, however, that such programs divert attention and resources from the underlying problem of inadequate outpatient services, restrict patient freedom, undermine the voluntary delivery of ambulatory psychiatric care, and deter patients from seeking mental health care (7). Furthermore, critics charge that there is no rigorous evidence that such programs improve public safety.

Outpatient commitment is controversial because two strong ethical guidelines are in conflict. On the one hand, psychiatrists should respect patients who are still competent to make medical decisions by accepting their decisions and by not coercing them. On the other hand, psychiatrists should also intervene to prevent a high likelihood of serious harm to patients, particularly if they can prevent the patient from relapsing into a state of diminished autonomy. The issue is complicated because limited access to outpatient psychiatric care might make less restrictive alternatives impractical.

SUICIDAL PATIENTS

When patients attempt or threaten suicide, physicians have an ethical obligation to intervene. It is essential for physicians to understand the rationale for suicide intervention and to be able to assess the seriousness of suicide threats.

RATIONALE FOR SUICIDE INTERVENTION

The ethical justification for suicide intervention is preventing serious, irreversible harm to persons with impaired decision-making capacity. Suicidal patients are almost always impaired by severe depression or other severe mental illness (8). Their actions therefore are not autonomous choices but rather are the product of their mental illness. Interventions to prevent suicide provide time to treat the underlying mental illness or let it enter a remission. Empirical studies demonstrate the effectiveness of suicide prevention. If persons are prevented from committing suicide, only about 10% to 20% subsequently kill themselves (8).

Even strong proponents of patient autonomy recognize the need to intervene to prevent nonautonomous persons from seriously harming themselves (9). In contrast, it is ethically problematical to restrict the liberty of autonomous persons in order to prevent them from harming themselves.

Interventions to prevent suicide include arranging for voluntary psychiatric treatment, mobilizing assistance from family and friends, removing the means of suicide, getting patients to promise to call for help before they take their lives, and, as a last resort, imposing involuntary commitment. To varying degrees, these interventions restrict patient liberty. Infringements should be minimized while still protecting the patient from harm. In some cases it might be unclear whether patients who are threatening suicide are making an autonomous decision or not. It is ethically prudent to intervene temporarily to ascertain if the threat is serious and if the patient's decision-making capacity is impaired. If involuntary commitment is deemed necessary, it should be continued only as long as necessary to protect the patient.

Physicians need to appreciate that they do not have the power to prevent all patients from committing suicide. After discharge, patients who are determined to kill themselves can find the means and opportunity to do so. In addition, some patients with terminal illnesses, whose decision-making capacity is unimpaired, might make a deliberate and firm decision to end their lives. The ethics of so-called "rational suicide," particularly physician-assisted suicide, is hotly debated (*see* Chapter 19).

WHEN IS A PATIENT SUICIDAL?

Many people make suicidal gestures that, although representing a "cry for help," might not warrant involuntary commitment. Because such persons can be successfully treated through less restrictive measures, such as outpatient care or voluntary hospitalization, physicians must determine which patients truly need involuntary hospitalization.

When patients are severely depressed or mention suicide, physicians should ask specific questions to determine the likelihood of a serious suicide attempt. Fears that raising the topic of suicide will suggest it to depressed patients or will encourage persons to kill themselves are unfounded and deter physicians from gathering crucial information and initiating effective treatment. Many depressed patients feel relieved to discuss suicide with a caring and nonjudgmental physician.

The following are persons who are more likely to attempt suicide or to succeed in killing themselves (2,10).

- Persons who have an intent to commit suicide, a specific plan for doing so, and the means to carry out the plan. Access to lethal and violent means of suicide indicates particularly high risk. Similarly, it is more serious when the proposed method of the suicide attempt makes rescue unlikely, as when patients have arranged to be alone for an extended period.
- Persons who have made preparations, such as giving away possessions or saying good-bye.
- Persons who view their situation as hopeless or have ideas of reuniting with a deceased person.

MITIGATING THE ADVERSE CONSEQUENCES OF INVOLUNTARY HOSPITALIZATION

When suicidal patients are involuntarily hospitalized, they might view the physicians who committed them as adversaries who can no longer be trusted. Such feelings might make psychiatric therapy difficult. Physicians should try to minimize the confrontational aspects of the situation and stress shared therapeutic goals. An experienced psychiatrist has suggested saying: "It would be a shame if you killed yourself while your depression clouded your judgment. Let's get you undepressed; then, if you still want to kill yourself, I know I can't stop you (2)." Such a statement demonstrates concern, suggests that therapy might effectively lead to remission of the mental illness, and reassures patients that ultimately they are in control.

PATIENTS WHO ARE DANGEROUS TO OTHERS

Patients with serious psychiatric illness might tell physicians about plans to kill or injure third parties, actual attempts, or overt acts of harm. Thus, the physician might be in a unique position to prevent serious harm to the threatened person. Social norms and criminal sanctions might not deter psychiatric patients who cannot control their violent impulses. In this situation the landmark Tarasoff case established that confidentiality should be overridden in order to prevent serious harm to third parties (11).

THE TARASOFF CASE AND THE DUTY TO PREVENT HARM

A university student, Prosenjit Poddar, confided to his psychologist that he was planning to kill a woman, readily identifiable as Tatiana Tarasoff, who had rejected him romantically. The therapist and his superiors at the student health service decided that Poddar should be committed involuntarily and asked the campus police to detain him. The police did so but released him because he appeared rational. The director of psychiatry ordered therapy notes and correspondence with the police destroyed and ordered no action to place Poddar under involuntary detention. Subsequently Poddar went to Tarasoff's home and stabbed her to death.

In a suit by Tarasoff's parents, the California Supreme Court ruled that a therapist who determines, or should have determined, that the patient presents "a serious danger of violence to another" has a "duty to exercise reasonable care to protect others against dangers emanating from the patient's illness (11)." Thus, the court found a duty to protect potential victims, not just warn them. The court rejected the defendant's arguments that the defendant had owed no duty of care to Tarasoff, that predictions of violence by psychiatric patients are inherently inaccurate, and that confidentiality is essential to psychotherapy. The court ruled that the special relationship between patients and their doctors or psychotherapists supports "affirmative duties for the benefit of third persons." In this case fallibility of predications of violence was not an issue because the therapists had determined that Poddar was dangerous. Furthermore, the confidentiality of psychotherapy communication must be balanced against the need to avert danger to others. "The protective privilege ends where the public peril begins (11)."

Therapists feared that the decision would undermine the doctor–patient relationship. They predicted that patients would be deterred from seeking mental health services and disclosing their violent thoughts, that warning potential victims would be ineffective, and that issuing a warning would effectively end therapy with a patient (12). However, these effects have not occurred to any significant degree (12).

Most states require therapists to protect identifiable persons threatened with serious violence by psychiatric patients (12). Generally, the duty is limited to identifiable patients and actual threats. In most states therapists can meet this legal duty by warning the potential victim or the police or by hospitalizing the patient (12).

STEPS TO PREVENT HARM

The duty to prevent harm to potential victims of psychiatric patients requires several steps (13,14). First, the physician needs to evaluate the threat of violence. As with asking about suicide, physicians need to appreciate that asking about violence does not give patients the idea of harming others or encourage them to do so. It might be useful to ask whether the patient has ever seriously injured another person or has ever thought about harming someone else (14).

Predictions of violence by physicians can be quite inaccurate. In one study 53% of patients whom clinicians predicted would be violent in fact committed violent acts over the subsequent 6 months; in comparison, 36% of patients whose psychiatrists had no concerns about violence committed violent acts (15). Violence was more serious in those patients whose psychiatrists had predicted would be violent. For women, however, the accuracy of predictions of violence was no greater than that expected by chance alone. Doctors need to do the best they can within the limits of clinical judgment. The standard of care is what a reasonable physician would do under the circumstances.

After determining that the threat of violence is severe and probable, the physician must decide how to respond. A number of actions might protect the victim, such as changing the patient's medications, increasing the frequency of therapy sessions, attempting to hospitalize the patient voluntarily or committing the patient involuntarily, having the patient give up weapons, and notifying the police (14). The law in many states specifically requires warning the threatened victim. Physicians should notify patients before they override confidentiality and explain why they are required to do so (14). Discussing with patients threats against third parties as part of therapy might help maintain a therapeutic relationship (16). Patients might permit the physician to warn the threatened person (2). Many patients are ambivalent about violence and might welcome help in finding other ways to express their emotions or deal with interpersonal conflicts. In addition, when beginning therapy with patients who have a history of violence physicians might discuss the situations in which confidentiality may be overridden (2).

REFUSAL OF PSYCHIATRIC TREATMENT

Patients who are involuntarily committed to psychiatric institutions might still be deemed competent to refuse psychiatric treatment. Because competency is determined with regard to specific tasks, a patient who is not competent to refuse commitment might still be competent to refuse medications. Confining patients but not treating them with effective medications has been criticized as "rotting with their rights on (17)." To critics it is cruel and pointless to withhold from severely impaired patients the very treatments that are likely to restore their autonomy. In this view short-term involuntary treatment, which might improve the underlying psychiatric illness, is a lesser infringement on the patient's freedom than prolonged involuntary hospitalization without treatment.

Nonetheless, many states have made it more difficult to administer treatments to involuntarily committed psychiatric patients. The rationale is that confinement without treatment can sometimes accomplish involuntary hospitalization's goal—prevention of harm to self or others. In addition, patients and the public might view psychiatric therapies' risks and benefits differently from physicians. Many psychiatric patients reject drugs because of side effects or because medications alter their brain and personality. Furthermore, past abuses have led the public to mistrust physicians' unilateral judgments that treatment is beneficial and necessary.

The ethical guideline of preventing harm has more moral force than the guideline of doing good (*see* Chapter 4). Thus, the obligation to prevent harms to nonautonomous psychiatric patients or to third parties is stronger than the duty to help psychiatric patients recover from their illness. Forced administration of medications to unwilling patients is intrusive, inhumane, and impractical in the long run. Even if psychiatric medications were forcibly administered to inpatients, patients can (and often do) discontinue therapies after discharge.

Several states have procedures to deal with such refusals of treatment by involuntarily hospitalized psychiatric patients. These states require a court hearing if a psychiatric patient who has been involuntarily committed refuses treatment (2). The court determines whether the patient is competent to make an informed decision to refuse treatment. If so, the refusal must be honored. If the patient is not competent, the court decides whether the treatment will be provided.

The patient's capacity to make informed decisions therefore is crucial to whether the patient's refusal of therapy will be respected. Chapter 10 discussed decision-making capacity. Assessing the decision-making capacity of psychiatric patients might be particularly difficult (18). People with major depression might underestimate the benefits of treatment and overestimate the risks (19). They might be convinced that the treatment will fail or that they will experience a serious side effect of therapy. Depressed patients might also believe that they deserve to suffer and that treatment might interfere with such suffering. Similarly, manic patients might believe that nothing is wrong with them and therefore reject treatment. Both depressed and manic patients can give seemingly logical reasons for their decisions yet be incapable of making informed decisions because they hold false premises about medical care and inaccurately assess the benefits and risks of treatment.

Empirical studies have described refusals of antipsychotic medications. In one study only 7% of inpatients refused antipsychotic medication for longer than 24 hours (20). Patients refused because of psychotic or idiosyncratic thought processes in 30% of cases, side effects of medications in 35%, denial of mental illness in 21%, and alleged ineffectiveness of medications in 12%. Cases were resolved in several ways. In 50% of cases the patient eventually took medication voluntarily. Typically, the nursing staff, psychiatrists, or family persuaded the patient. In 23% of cases either the psychiatrist discontinued antipsychotic drugs or the patient was discharged without medication—that is, the physician probably did not consider these medications essential. Finally, in 18% of cases the psychiatrists obtained a court order for involuntary administration of the medication. In all the cases that went to court, the judge authorized involuntary treatment.

REFUSAL OF MEDICAL TREATMENT BY PSYCHIATRIC PATIENTS

Patients with serious psychiatric illness might refuse recommended therapy for concurrent medical problems. As with other patients who refuse interventions, physicians should ask whether the patient has intact decision-making capacity. A psychiatric diagnosis *per se* does not imply that a patient lacks the capacity to make an informed decision about treatment. A competent patient's refusal should be respected if attempts at persuasion are unsuccessful. If the patient lacks decision-making capacity, decisions should be based on advance directives or made by surrogates (*see* Chapters 12 and 13).

Decisions might be especially perplexing when psychiatric patients who lack decision-making capacity actively resist treatment that is clearly in their best interests. Forced treatment might be difficult to carry out if patients actively protest or resist. It might also be counterproductive because issues of control and independence might be problems that patients need to resolve. Overriding patients' refusal might make it more difficult for them to take responsibility and control of other aspects of their lives. Finally, the possibility of forced treatment is illusory. In a structured inpatient setting, the staff might, through cajoling, negotiation, and threats, be able to ensure that the patient is taking the medicine. For example, health care workers might threaten to withhold visiting privileges, outings, or cigarettes. However, the patient might discontinue medicines after discharge.

In conclusion, when psychiatric patients are suicidal, unable to care for themselves, or are dangerous to others, physicians have ethical as well as legal obligations to prevent harm. This obligation might override the ethical guidelines of respecting patient autonomy and maintaining confidentiality. In fulfilling this duty, physicians also need to use their clinical skills and judgment to encourage effective treatment for the underlying psychiatric disorders.

REFERENCES

1. The President's Council on Bioethics. *Beyond therapy: biotechnology and the pursuit of happiness.* Washington: The President's Council on Bioethics, 2003.
2. Appelbaum PS, Gutheil TG. *Clinical handbook of psychiatry and the law*, 2nd ed. Baltimore: Williams & Wilkins, 1991.
3. Swartz MS, Monahan J. Special section on involuntary outpatient commitment: introduction. *Psychiatr Serv* 2001;52(3):323–324.
4. Monahan J, Bonnie RJ, Appelbaum PS, et al. Mandated community treatment: beyond outpatient commitment. *Psychiatr Serv* 2001;52(9):1198–1205.
5. Torrey EF, Zdanowicz M. Outpatient commitment: what, why, and for whom. *Psychiatr Serv* 2001;52(3):337–341.
6. Monahan J, Swartz M, Bonnie RJ. Mandated treatment in the community for people with mental disorders. *Health Aff (Millwood)* 2003;22(5):28–38.
7. Allen M, Smith VF. Opening pandora's box: the practical and legal dangers of involuntary outpatient commitment. *Psychiatr Serv* 2001;52(3):342–346.
8. Miller RD. Need-for-treatment criteria for involuntary civil commitment: impact in practice. *Am J Psychiatry* 1992;149:1380–1384.
9. Beauchamp TL, Childress JF. *Principles of biomedical ethics*, 4th ed. New York: Oxford University Press, 1994: 271–287.
10. Blumenthal SJ. Suicide: a guide to risk factors, assessment, and treatment of suicidal patients. *Med Clin North Am* 1988;72:937–971.
11. Tarasoff v. Regents of the University of California. 551 P2d 334 (Cal 1976).
12. Appelbaum PS. *Almost a revolution: mental health law and the limits of change.* New York: Oxford University Press, 1994:71–113.
13. Appelbaum PS, Zonana H, Bonnie R, et al. Statutory approaches to limiting psychiatrists' liability for their patients' violent acts. *Am J Psychiatry* 1989;146:821–828.
14. Anfang SA, Appelbaum PS. Twenty years after Tarasoff: Reviewing the duty to protect. *Harv Rev Psychiatry* 1996;4:67–76.
15. Lidz C, Mulvey EP, Gardner W. The accuracy of predictions of violence to others. *JAMA* 1993;269:1007–1011.
16. Simon RI. Clinical approaches to the duty to warn and protect endangered third parties. *Clinical psychiatry and the law.* Washington: American Psychiatric Press, Inc, 1987:307–336.

17. Appelbaum PS, Gutheil TG. "Rotting with their rights on": constitutional theory and clinical reality in drug refusal by psychiatric patients. *Bull Am Acad Psychiatry Law* 1979;7:306–315.
18. Gutheil TG, Bursztajn HJ, Brodsky A, et al. Affective disorders, competence, and decision making. *Decision making in psychiatry and the law*, 2nd ed. Baltimore: Williams & Wilkins, 1991:153–170.
19. Grisso T, Appelbaum P. *Assessing competence to consent to treatment: a guide for physicians and other health professionals*. New York: Oxford University Press, 1998:49–51.
20. Hoge SK, Appelbaum PS, Lawlor T. A prospective, multicenter study of patients' refusal of antipsychotic medication. *Arch Gen Psychiatry* 1990;47:949–956.

ANNOTATED BIBLIOGRAPHY

1. Gutheil TG, Appelbaum PS. *Clinical handbook of psychiatry and the law*, 3rd ed. Philadelphia: Lippincott Williams & Wilkins, 2000.
   Excellent book on ethical and legal issues regarding psychiatric patients. Contains practical clinical advice on managing patients with severe psychiatric disorders.
2. Appelbaum PS. *Almost a revolution: mental health law and the limits of change*. New York: Oxford University Press, 1994.
   Lucid discussion of the ethical and policy issues regarding involuntary commitment and treatment.
3. Dickenson D, Fulford KWM. *Two minds: a casebook of psychiatric ethics*. New York: Oxford University Press, 2000.
   Case discussions of ethical issues in psychiatric diagnosis, symptom interpretation, and social control from a British perspective.
4. The President's Council on Bioethics. *Beyond therapy: biotechnology and the pursuit of happiness*. Washington: The President's Council on Bioethics, 2003.
   Critique of the widespread use of psychiatric medications for enhancement rather than for major psychiatric illness.

CHAPTER 41

Ethical Issues in Organ Transplantation

Kidney, liver, heart, and lung transplantation can allow patients with end-stage disease to return to active lives. In organ donation interventions are performed on one person in order to benefit another. Thus, consent for donation and preventing harm to donors are essential to maintain public trust that physicians never compromise one patient's care to benefit someone else. The need for organ transplantation far exceeds the supply of donated organs; in May 2004 more than 85,000 people were on waiting lists for transplants. Thus, difficult decisions about allocating donated organs cannot be avoided. This chapter discusses the donation of organs, the selection of recipients, and the cost of transplantation.

DONATION OF CADAVERIC ORGANS

ETHICAL CONCERNS ABOUT CADAVERIC DONATION

Harm to Donors

At the onset, concerns were raised that cadaveric organ transplantation hastened or caused the donor's death. Criteria were developed for determining death in patients whose brains had ceased to function but whose hearts were still beating (*see* Chapter 21). Misunderstandings about brain death persist, and many people do not understand why organs may not be harvested from anencephalic infants and persons in a persistent vegetative state.

Conflicts of Interest

Because of concerns that potential organ donors might receive suboptimal care, decisions about the potential donor's care must be separate from decisions about procurement and transplantation. The physician for the potential donor may not be part of the transplantation team. Also, in the United States payments for donation are prohibited to prevent abuse and exploitation of potential donors.

The Autonomy of Organ Donors

Some people would not want to be organ donors, and their wishes need to be respected. It is controversial how much evidence of a donor's consent or refusal is required and whether surviving relatives may decline to donate even if the patient would have wanted to be a donor.

THE CURRENT SYSTEM FOR CADAVERIC DONATION

The United States has a voluntary altruistic system for organ donation. The Uniform Anatomical Gift Act allows people to use an organ donor card to grant permission to use their organs for transplantation after their death. This card is usually attached to a person's driver's license. However, few Americans have signed such cards. One reason is fear that persons who have agreed to organ donation will receive suboptimal care (1). Although the donor card has legal authority, in practice permission for organ donation is sought from the next of kin after the donor's death (2). Hospitals must report all inpatient deaths to local organ procurement organizations, which contact eligible families to request donation (3).

Only about 50% of relatives of patients with brain death give permission for organ donation (1). Many families do not understand the concept of brain death, and some perceive the organ procurement process as insensitive (1). Some cultures reject organ donation (4,5). For instance, some Asian or Latino families believe that bodies or spirits can suffer after death if organs are removed.

NONHEART-BEATING CADAVER DONORS

Most cadaver donors are declared dead by brain criteria and have effective circulation until the harvesting of organs. A few donors are declared dead by cardiorespiratory criteria (1,6,7). In one approach, donors are terminal patients whose life-sustaining interventions will be withdrawn. They are transported to the operating room, where life support is withdrawn, death is declared using cardiorespiratory criteria, and organs are promptly retrieved (1,6–8). This approach has been criticized because relatives might not have sufficient opportunity to be with dying patients. In addition, anticoagulants and vasodilators administered to preserve the organs might hasten or cause death. In a second approach, donors are patients in whom cardiopulmonary resuscitation (CPR) fails or who are dead on arrival in the emergency department. Catheters are inserted into patients immediately after death is pronounced and organs are perfused to keep them viable (6,7). Later, physicians seek permission for transplantation from relatives. However, consent is not obtained for insertion of catheters and perfusion of organs (1,7). Surveys show that the public strongly objects to such procedures being carried out without permission.

PROPOSALS TO INCREASE THE DONATION OF CADAVERIC ORGANS

Many proposals have been made to increase cadaveric organs donation, and some have been adopted in other countries. However, some of these proposals might undermine public trust in transplantation, which in the long term might make people less willing to donate.

Mandated Choice

Persons would be required to state their preferences about organ donation when renewing drivers' licenses or filing income taxes (9). This requirement would relieve relatives of the stress of making decisions about donation. In surveys most Americans support this policy.

Following Donor Cards

Physicians would retrieve organs from people who had signed donor cards even if the next of kin objects. Legally, this policy would merely implement existing statutes. Ethically, it is consistent with respecting patient autonomy and advance directives. However, some family members might feel outraged if organs are harvested over their objections.

Presumed Consent

Currently, organs are harvested only if the patient or family has given explicit consent. Under this proposed policy, organs would be harvested unless the patient or family specifically objects (10). However, 52% of respondents in a U.S. survey disapproved of this approach (11).

Financial Incentives for Donation

A regulated market in organs has been proposed to increase the supply of organs (12). Critics charge that such a market would undermine altruism, treat the human body as a commodity, and result in exploitation, fraud, or coercion, particularly in underdeveloped countries (13,14). Furthermore, commercially motivated renal transplantation in developing countries might pose risks to recipients because of a significantly higher rate of human immunodeficiency virus (HIV) and hepatitis B infection (15). In the United States buying and selling of organs is illegal because of objections to commodifying vital organs and concerns about exploitation. However, one state provides partial burial expenses for cadaveric donors. In addition, proposals have been made to give living organ donors incentives, such as medical leave, life insurance, and highest priority for transplantation if they should need it (16). Proponents distinguish these modest incentives and tokens of appreciation from cash payments.

DONATION OF ORGANS FROM LIVE DONORS

Transplantation of kidneys and portions of liver and lung from live donors is increasing. In 2002, 43% of kidney transplants were from living donors. Live donors include both "emotionally related donors"—such as relatives, friends, and coworkers (17)—and strangers. Donation from strangers is technically feasible because human leukocyte antigens (HLA) compatibility does not enhance survival of liver and lung transplants and is less important in transplants from living kidney donors than from cadaveric donors. The quality of organs from live donors is higher because of thorough screening and shorter ischemia time compared to cadaveric donors. Transplants from live donors do not delay cadaveric transplants to other patients on the waiting list because the total number of transplants is increased. Hence, persons on the waiting list suffer no adverse consequences.

ETHICAL ISSUES REGARDING LIVE DONATION

Harm to Donors

Surgeons might violate the guideline of "do no harm" when they perform an operation on a healthy person for another person's benefit. The highly publicized death of a living liver donor in New York in 2002 dramatized the grave risks of donation. In addition to serious medical problems such as bile leak, donors suffer pain and lost income.

To limit risks, persons may not serve as living donors if they have medical conditions that significantly increase operative risk or if they have abnormal organ function. In the case of kidney donation, persons are excluded as donors if they have a condition that might impair renal function in the future. To further reduce risk of living liver donation, some have advocated that this procedure be carried out only at experienced centers (18,19).

In many impoverished countries paying live donors is widespread (13). In India living kidney donors said that they were financially worse off after surgery despite having received payments (20). Although some writers have advocated a regulated market to increase the number of organs from living donors, the likelihood of exploitation, coercion, and abuse is a compelling reason to reject such proposals.

Motives of Donors

Donation to relatives and friends is understandable because people are expected to help and care for others with whom they have close relationships. However, donating to a stranger raises concerns. On the one hand, forming a close emotional bond to a stranger in need can be an extraordinary form of altruism and humanitarianism. On the other hand, it can also be driven by a desire for publicity or financial gain, by internal psychological conflicts, or by psychopathology. Thus, offers by strangers to donate need to be carefully reviewed to rule out such problematic motives.

Consent from Donors

Because a live donor undergoes serious risks in order to benefit another person, it is essential that the decision to donate be free and informed. Altruism does not fit a model of rational utilitarian deliberation about personal risks and benefits. The live donor finds a reward in making a sacrifice to benefit someone else. Consent might not be informed because many live donors choose to donate immediately, before they learn of the risks of donation. Also, consent might not be free. Relatives might feel social pressure to donate. Donors might also feel internally compelled to donate.

People commonly base important decisions on emotion rather than reason. Donors should be able to explain their decision to donate, however, in a coherent manner, which takes into account the risks. The donor needs to understand the procedure's risks, even though the donor might give less weight than most people to the possibility of a serious risk. The donor should make a choice that remains stable after the donor receives more information and has time to reflect. Also, the decision should be consistent with the donor's core values.

The "gift of life" through live donation entails obligations and burdens (21). Generally, gifts impose reciprocal obligations and expectations on the recipient. The gift of an organ is so extraordinary that it can never be repaid and might therefore become a "tyranny (21)." A live kidney donor might take a "proprietary interest" in the recipient's life (21). The recipient's sense of indebtedness might make it difficult for him or her to remain independent of the donor. For these reasons, many transplantation programs generally do not reveal the identities of donors and recipients to each other.

Use of children as live donors raises ethical concerns because they cannot give consent for themselves and depend on others to protect their interests. Although adults may make extraordinary sacrifices for others, they may not require children to do so. Hence, children should be live donors only as a last resort if no suitable adult donor can be identified. To assure that a child donor's interests are protected, approval from the courts should be sought.

Confidentiality of Recipient

The recipient might have a medical condition that might affect the potential donor's willingness to donate. For example, the recipient might have a condition such as cancer that might recur in the transplanted organ and reduce the likelihood of long-term success. Moreover, some donors might feel that patients whose liver failure was caused by alcoholic cirrhosis or HIV infection brought about their illnesses through their own actions and choices. According to the principle of informed consent, prospective donors should receive information that is pertinent to their decision to donate. However, patient confidentiality is also important; potential recipients should give permission to disclose such information to potential donors (22).

THE CURRENT SYSTEM FOR LIVE DONATION

Live donors undergo extensive education and medical and psychosocial evaluation (23,24). This process ensures that decisions to donate are informed, free, and altruistic, and that the donor is medically suitable.

Some eligible donors who do not wish to donate might need help in carrying out their wishes—for example, in the face of family pressure to donate. The transplant team might need to say that the potential donor has been ruled out as unsuitable, without providing more specifics. Such nondisclosure is justified because the person might face pressure to donate and recrimination if the true reason were known (21). It is ethically problematic, however, to misrepresent the potential donor's medical condition to provide a reason not to donate (23).

SELECTION OF RECIPIENTS

Because the number of people needing transplants far exceeds the number of donated organs, difficult decisions about allocating organs must be made.

HISTORICAL BACKGROUND

When dialysis was developed in the 1960s, only a limited number of dialysis machines were available and committees ranked candidates according to their perceived social worth (25). Responding to concerns that selection was based on prejudice and unwarranted value judgments, Congress decided to fund dialysis for all patients with end-stage renal disease. In transplantation, however, allocation decisions cannot be avoided because the limiting factor is a lack of organs.

Because people donate cadaveric organs without knowing who will receive them, a fair allocation procedure is essential to maintain public trust in transplantation (14,26). In the United States the federal government and the United Network for Organ Sharing (UNOS), a nonprofit organization with which the government contracts to operate the system for distributing organs, set the rules for allocating cadaveric organs.

The following section discusses general ethical principles for allocating organs. Specific selection criteria are too detailed to be discussed here but can be found on the Web site of the UNOS at www.unos.org. Different considerations receive priority for different organs (27,28).

BENEFICENCE

From a utilitarian perspective, scarce organs should go to those patients who will receive the greatest net medical benefit. Relevant outcomes include the likelihood and duration of survival and the patient's quality of life. Although this criterion appears objective, it involves complex value judgments.

Psychosocial factors such as poor adherence to medical regimens, substance abuse, and lack of family support might compromise outcomes of transplantation. Recent injection drug use and a history of nonadherence are commonly regarded as contraindications to transplantation (29–31). Many physicians consider it pointless to transplant a scarce organ that is very likely to be rejected because of nonadherence to immunosuppressant drugs. Critics, however, contend that psychosocial factors might "cloak biases about race, class, social status, and other factors that, if stated openly, would not be tolerated (26)." Furthermore, such obstacles might be overcome with rehabilitation and psychosocial support (28).

JUSTICE

The guideline that scarce resources should be distributed fairly or equitably is indisputable in the abstract but difficult to specify. Several ways to operationalize equity have been considered.

Time on the Waiting List

The precept of "first-come, first-served" seems intuitively fair if there are no other compelling reasons to distinguish among candidates. However, time on the waiting list can be manipulated by placing patients on the waiting list earlier in the course of illness or at several regional transplantation networks (14,32). Better-educated and wealthier patients are more likely to be on multiple waiting lists.

Medical Need

In liver and heart transplantation, patients who would die soon without transplantation are given priority over more stable patients (33). The rationale is to assist those in greatest need. In 2002 the prioritization system for cadaveric liver transplantation was revised to use a severity of illness score [the Model for End-Stage Liver Disease (MELD) system] based on objective laboratory tests that predict the risk of death while on the waiting list more accurately than clinical judgment does. However, significant geographical disparities remain, with sicker patients in larger organ-procurement areas waiting longer for transplants than patients in smaller organ-procurement areas (34).

Ability to Pay

Transplantation is generally performed only on patients who can pay for it. Medicare covers kidney transplantation for all Americans, and most private insurers and most state Medicaid programs cover liver and heart transplantation (35). Americans who lack health insurance must raise money for transplantation of organs other than kidneys through means such as public appeals.

Allocating organs by ability to pay, although routinely practiced, has been strongly criticized (14). It seems unfair to ask all people, rich and poor alike, to be organ donors if the poor or uninsured would not be eligible recipients. Also, people might be less willing to donate organs if they perceive that the distribution system favors the wealthy.

Previous Transplantation

The success rate in transplanting a second organ after a transplanted organ fails is substantially lower than in first-time transplants (36). The guideline of promise keeping or loyalty is often used to justify retransplantation; having made a commitment to the patient, the surgeons cannot now abandon the patient. Critics contend, however, that retransplantation might be "an obdurate, publicly theatricalized refusal" to accept the inevitable limits of human life and an unwillingness to say "enough is enough (37)."

Citizenship

Should people who are not long-term U.S. residents receive organs harvested in the United States (14)? Particular objections have been directed at foreigners who come to the United States specifically to obtain a transplant. It seems unfair, however, to exclude foreign nationals who contribute to the U.S. economy and who would be asked to serve as organ donors.

Geographic Location

In response to significant disparities in waiting times for liver transplantation, it has been proposed that organs be allocated on a national basis to those with the greatest medical need, with less emphasis on keeping organs in the geographic area in which they are donated (3). This proposed change would provide more organs to large referral centers, which transplant sicker patients and have better outcomes. However, opponents object that such redistribution is unfair because it penalizes states that make efforts to increase donations and might also worsen outcomes because of increased cold ischemia time (3).

Ethnic Background

Even though African Americans are more likely than Caucasians to develop chronic renal failure, they have less access to renal transplantation. They are less likely to be evaluated for transplantation, to be placed on waiting lists, and to find a suitable donor (38,39). Also, waiting times on transplantation lists are longer for African Americans. The point system for prioritizing cadaveric kidneys gives priority to HLA matching, which improves graft and patient survival. However, this makes it more difficult for African Americans to receive cadaveric kidneys. Although African Americans donate cadaveric kidneys at the same rate as Caucasians, they have a greater need for renal transplantation. Because the prevalence of ABO and HLA antigens differs among ethnic groups, African Americans are less likely to find a highly matched Caucasian donor. Thus, the allocation procedures to maximize benefit through optimal graft survival conflict with equitable access to transplantation. Proposals have been made to modify the point system to increase equity while only slightly increasing renal graft loss (40,41).

DIFFERENCES IN ALLOCATING VARIOUS ORGANS

The ethical guidelines of beneficence and justice are balanced differently for different organs (33). For renal failure, dialysis is an effective alternative to transplantation and the level of HLA matching is a predictor of cadaveric graft survival. Hence, urgency is not considered and HLA matching is given weight. In contrast, in liver failure, because there is no alternative to transplantation, the highest priority is given to patients in the most critical condition. HLA matching is not considered because it has little impact on outcomes for this procedure. These different ethical considerations might conflict. For example, liver recipients with the most urgent need have worse outcomes and greater costs than more stable patients.

PATIENT BEHAVIORS THAT CAUSE DISEASE

Patients with end-stage alcoholic cirrhosis disease initially were not considered for transplantation because it was believed that active drinkers would not take immunosuppressive medications regularly. However, selected alcoholics who receive liver transplantation have short-term and long-term survival rates comparable to those of patients with other liver diseases even though a few recipients have a relapse of alcoholism and are noncompliant with immunosuppression (42). Thus, the issue is not whether such transplantation is medically feasible but whether it should be done. Some argue that patients who develop end-stage liver disease "through no fault of their own" should have higher priority than persons with alcoholism (43). In this line of thinking, patients should be held responsible for behaviors that would deprive others of scarce resources. Others contend that the public might be less willing to donate organs if they are given to alcoholics. On the other hand, restrictions on liver transplantation for alcoholics have been strongly criticized (44). Critics argue that because alcoholism has genetic and environmental components that are beyond the person's control, it would be unfair to hold a patient responsible for it. Moreover, criteria for disqualification are inconsistent and arbitrary and treatment for alcohol dependence is not routinely offered (45). Furthermore, judgments of moral responsibility are not made for other illnesses. For example, smokers are not precluded from heart transplants.

COST OF TRANSPLANTATION

Because of the soaring cost of medical care, the cost effectiveness of organ transplantation cannot be ignored. In 2002 average billed charges for a kidney transplant were $143,000, for a liver transplant $314,000, and for a heart transplant $392,000 (46). The annual costs of follow-up care after transplantation are comparable to the costs of other high-technology medical interventions, such as cancer chemotherapy (35).

The cost of organ transplantation can also be viewed in the context of allocating resources in a health care system that denies many persons access to basic care. Critics charge that "allowing ourselves to become too caught up in such problems as the shortage of transplantable organs while . . . millions of people do not have adequate or even minimally decent care" is "medically and morally untenable (47)."

In summary, although organ transplantation can return patients with end-stage illness to active lives, it raises difficult issues of informed choice in donation and fair allocation of scarce resources. These dilemmas need to be addressed openly in order to maintain public trust in transplantation.

REFERENCES

1. Herdman R, Potts JT. *Non-heart-beating organ transplantation: medical and ethical issues in procurement.* Washington: National Academy Press, 1997.
2. Wendler D, Dickert N. The consent process for cadaveric organ procurement: how does it work? How can it be improved? *JAMA* 2001;285(3):329–333.
3. Committee on Organ Procurement and Transplantation Policy. *Organ procurement and transplantation: assessing current policies and the potential impact of the HHS final rule.* Washington: National Academy Press, 1999.
4. Perkins HS. Cultural differences and ethical issues in the problem of autopsy requests. *Tex Med* 1991;87:72–77.
5. Tolle SW, Bennett WM, Hickam DH, et al. Responsibilities of primary physicians in organ donation. *Ann Intern Med* 1987;106:740–744.
6. Youngner SJ, Arnold RM. Ethical, psychosocial, and public policy implications of procuring organs from non-heart beating cadaver donors. *JAMA* 1993;269:2769–2774.
7. Institute of Medicine. *Non-heart-beating organ transplantation: protocols and practice.* Washington: National Academy Press, 1999.
8. Youngner SJ, Arnold RM, Schapiro R, eds. *The definition of death.* Baltimore: The Johns Hopkins University Press, 1999.
9. Council on Ethical and Judicial Affairs of the American Medical Association. Strategies for cadaveric organ procurement: mandated choice and presumed consent. *JAMA* 1994;272:809–812.
10. Kennedy I, Daar AS, Sells RA, et al. The case for "presumed consent" in organ donation. *Lancet* 1998;351: 1650–1652.
11. Kittur DS, Hogan MM, Thukral VK, et al. Incentives for organ donation? *Lancet* 1991;338:1441–1443.
12. Radcliffe-Richards J, Daar AS, Guttmann RD, et al. The case for allowing kidney sales. *Lancet* 1998;352: 1950–1952.
13. Scheper-Hughes N. Keeping an eye on the global traffic in human organs. *Lancet* 2003;361(9369):1645–1648.
14. Childress JF. Ethical criteria for procuring and distributing organs for transplantation. *J Health Polit Policy Law* 1989;14:87–113.
15. The Living Non-Related Renal Transplant Study Group. Commercially motivated renal transplantation: results in 540 patients transplanted in India. *Clin Transplant* 1997;11:536–544.
16. Arnold R, Bartlett S, Bernat J, et al. Financial incentives for cadaver organ donation: an ethical reappraisal. *Transplantation* 2002;73(8):1361–1367.
17. Spital A. Ethical and policy issues in altruistic living and cadaveric organ donation. *Clin Transplant* 1997;11: 77–87.
18. Cronin DC, Siegler M. Ethical issues in living donor transplantation. *Transplant Proc* 2003;35(3):904–905.
19. Cronin DC, 2nd, Millis JM, Siegler M. Transplantation of liver grafts from living donors into adults—too much, too soon. *N Engl J Med* 2001;344(21):1633–1637.
20. Goyal M, Mehta RL, Schneiderman LJ, et al. Economic and health consequences of selling a kidney in India. *JAMA* 2002;288(13):1589–1593.
21. Fox RC, Swazey JP. *Spare parts.* New York: Oxford University Press, 1992:31–42.
22. Roland ME, Lo B, Braff J, et al. Key clinical, ethical, and policy issues in the evaluation of the safety and effectiveness of solid organ transplantation in HIV-infected patients. *Arch Intern Med* 2003;163(15):1773–1778.
23. Abecassis M, Adams M, Adams P, et al. Consensus statement on the live organ donor. *JAMA* 2000;284(22): 2919–2926.
24. Adams PL, Cohen DJ, Danovitch GM, et al. The nondirected live-kidney donor: ethical considerations and practice guidelines: A National Conference Report. *Transplantation* 2002;74(4):582–589.
25. Fox RC, Swazey JP. *The courage to fail: a social view of organ transplants and dialysis*, 2nd ed. Chicago: University of Chicago Press, 1978.
26. Robertson JA. Patient selection for organ transplantation: age, incarceration, family support, and other social factors. *Transplant Proc* 1989;21:3431–3436.

27. UNOS. The UNOS statement of principles and objectives of equitable organ allocation. *Semin Anesth* 1995;14: 142–166.
28. Council on Ethical and Judicial Affairs of the American Medical Association. Ethical considerations in the allocation of organs and other scarce medical resources among patients. *Arch Intern Med* 1995;155:29–40.
29. Evans RW, Manninen DL, Dong FB, et al. Heart transplantation recipient and donor selection criteria: the results of a consensus survey. In: Evans RW, Manninen DL, Dong FB, eds. *The national cooperative transplantation study: final report.* Seattle: Battelle-Seattle Research Center, 1991:31-1–31-24.
30. Evans RW, Manninen DL, Dong FB, et al. Kidney transplantation recipient and donor selection criteria: the results of a consensus survey. In: Evans RW, Manninen DL, Dong FB, eds. *The national cooperative transplantation study: final report.* Seattle: Battelle-Seattle Research Center, 1991:30-1–30-24.
31. Evans RW, Manninen DL, Dong FB, et al. Liver transplantation recipient and donor selection criteria: the results of a consensus survey. In: Evans RW, Manninen DL, Dong FB, eds. *The national cooperative transplantation study: final report.* Seattle: Battelle-Seattle Research Center, 1991:32-1–32-24.
32. Sanfilippo FP, Vaughn WK, Peters TG, et al. Factors affecting the waiting time of cadaveric kidney transplant candidates in the United States. *JAMA* 1992;267:247–252.
33. Hauptmann PK, O'Connor KJ. Procurement and allocation of solid organs for transplantation. *N Engl J Med* 1997;336:422–431.
34. Trotter JF, Osgood MJ. MELD scores of liver transplant recipients according to size of waiting list: impact of organ allocation and patient outcomes. *JAMA* 2004;291(15):1871–1874.
35. Evans RW. Organ transplantation costs, insurance coverage, and reimbursement. In: Terasaki PI, ed. *Clinical transplants 1990.* Los Angeles: UCLA Tissue Typing Laboratory, 1990:343–352.
36. Ubel PA, Arnold RM, Caplan AL. Rationing failure: the ethical lessons of the retransplantation of scarce organs. *JAMA* 1993;270:2469–2474.
37. Fox RC, Swazey JP. *Spare parts.* New York: Oxford University Press, 1992:204–205.
38. Young CJ, Gaston RS. Renal transplantation in black Americans. *N Engl J Med* 2000;343(21):1545–1552.
39. Epstein AM, Ayanian JZ, Keogh JH, et al. Racial disparities in access to renal transplantation—clinically appropriate or due to underuse or overuse? *N Engl J Med* 2000;343(21):1537–1544, 2 p preceding 1537.
40. Gaston RS, Danovitch GM, Adams PL, et al. The report of a national conference on the wait list for kidney transplantation. *Am J Transplant* 2003;3(7):775–785.
41. Roberts JP, Wolfe RA, Bragg-Gresham JL, et al. Effect of changing the priority for HLA matching on the rates and outcomes of kidney transplantation in minority groups. *N Engl J Med* 2004;350(6):545–551.
42. Bellamy CO, DiMartini AM, Ruppert K, et al. Liver transplantation for alcoholic cirrhosis: long term follow-up and impact of disease recurrence. *Transplantation* 2001;72(4):619–626.
43. Moss AH, Siegler M. Should alcoholics compete equally for liver transplantation? *JAMA* 1991;265:1295–1298.
44. Cohen C, Benjamin M. The Ethics and Social Impact Committee of the Transplant and Health Policy Center. Alcoholics and liver transplantation. *JAMA* 1991;265:1299–1301.
45. Masterton G. Psychosocial factors in selection for liver transplantation. Need to be explicitly assessed and managed. *Br Med J* 2000;320(7230):263–264.
46. Hauboldt RH, Ortner NJ. 2002 Organ Tissue and Transplant Costs and Discussion. Available at: http://www.transplantliving.org/beforethetransplant/finance/costs.aspx. Accessed June 29, 2004.
47. Fox RC, Swazey JP. *Spare parts.* New York: Oxford University Press, 1992:208–209.

ANNOTATED BIBLIOGRAPHY

1. Council on Ethical and Judicial Affairs of the American Medical Association. Ethical considerations in the allocation of organs and other scarce medical resources among patients. *Arch Intern Med* 1995;155:29–40. Overview of the topic.
2. Committee on Organ Procurement and Transplantation Policy. *Organ procurement and transplantation: assessing current policies and the potential impact of the HHS final rule.* Washington: National Academy Press, 1999. Review of proposed federal regulations to improve allocation of scarce organs (particularly livers) for transplantation.
3. Cohen C, Benjamin M, The Ethics and Social Impact Committee of the Transplant and Health Policy Center. Alcoholics and liver transplantation. *JAMA* 1991;265:1299–1301. Moss AH, Siegler M. Should alcoholics compete equally for liver transplantation? *JAMA* 1991;265:1295–1298. Two articles that argue for and against liver transplants in alcoholics, respectively.
4. Delmonico FL, Arnold R, Scheper-Hughes N, et al. Ethical incentives—not payment—for organ donation. *N Engl J Med* 2002;346:2002–2005. Argues that modest financial incentives to reward organ donation are ethically defensible, whereas payment for organs is not.
5. Scheper-Hughes N. Keeping an eye on the global traffic in human organs. *Lancet* 2003;361:1645–1648. Passionate criticism of payments and black markets for organs for transplantation.
6. Adams PL, Cohen DJ, Danovitch GM. The nondirected live-kidney donor: ethical considerations and practice guidelines: A National Conference Report. *Transplantation* 2002;74:582–589. Overview of kidney transplantation from live donors.

CHAPTER 42

Testing for Genetic Conditions

T he Human Genome Project, which completed DNA sequencing of all human chromosomes in 2002, has the ultimate goal is of developing tests and therapies for illnesses that have a genetic component. Genomics refers to the DNA sequence of chromosomes; genetics refers simply to the science of inheritance. For some genetic diseases, such as sickle cell anemia, phenylketonuria, and Tay-Sachs disease, screening tests have been available for years. DNA-based testing has recently become available for conditions such as cystic fibrosis (CF), familial colon and breast cancer, hemochromatosis, and polycystic kidney disease.

DNA testing for predisposition to adult-onset genetic diseases must be distinguished from carrier screening and prenatal testing. In adult-onset conditions, DNA screening might lead to further diagnostic and therapeutic interventions for the person who is tested. In contrast, carrier screening for recessive conditions has no therapeutic implications for the persons tested but might affect their future reproductive decisions. Prenatal genetic testing raises additional ethical controversies over procreation and abortion.

With ongoing advances in genomics, physicians in all specialties will increasingly be asked to advise patients about genetic testing. This chapter discusses DNA-based screening tests' clinical limitations, genetic discrimination, informed consent for genetic testing, and confidentiality of test results.

WHAT IS DIFFERENT ABOUT GENOMICS?

Although genetic or genomic information is commonly viewed as qualitatively different from other clinical information, on closer examination this claim is untenable.

GENES RARELY DETERMINE DISEASE OR BEHAVIOR

The popular press has characterized the human genome as a "blueprint" for life or as a "future diary." These metaphors imply that a person's DNA sequence determines that person's future. Genomic information is often considered to have greater predictive power than other types of medical information. Single-gene mutations that have complete penetrance cause some severe diseases, such as sickle cell anemia or Huntington disease, but most genes have incomplete penetrance or variable expressivity—that is, their presence does not reliably predict the occurrence of disease. Furthermore, most common conditions are polygenic. For example, whether a person develops hypertension and diabetes will likely depend on several genes, as well as on environmental factors such as diet, exercise, and exposure to viral illness. No matter how clearly we understand human genetics, education and environment as well as heredity determine health and illness.

THEORIES OF INHERITANCE HAVE BEEN ASSOCIATED WITH CONTROVERSIAL SOCIAL BELIEFS

Ideas about genetic inheritance were used in the late 19th and early 20th centuries to support ideas of racial superiority as well as discriminatory social policies. Eugenic laws were passed forbidding marriage or mandating sterilization of people categorized as feebleminded, insane, and criminals (1). In addition, miscegenation laws and restrictive immigration policies were enacted (1). The science used to support such discriminatory policies was deeply flawed (1,2).

During the 1970s many states enacted sickle cell anemia screening programs that contained "blatant medical and scientific errors," such as labeling sickle cell anemia an infectious disease or a sexually transmitted disease and confusing sickle cell disease with the trait (3). Persons with sickle cell trait, who have no impairment or increased risk for disease, were denied employment, health insurance, and schooling. In addition, targeting of these programs at African Americans fueled accusations of genocide (4). Because of this adverse historical legacy, genetic research and testing might be viewed with suspicion or concern. Some people fear that genetics might be used today to justify discriminatory social policies (5).

GENETIC ADVANCES MIGHT UNDERMINE TRADITIONAL MORAL BELIEFS

Critics fear that advances in genetic science might contradict moral and religious teachings about human nature and undermine human dignity (6). For example, some oppose preimplantation genetic diagnosis as fostering a desire for the "perfect" baby, disrespecting persons with disabilities, violating the natural order, and undermining the awe of procreation (6).

Advances in genetics might also change beliefs about individual responsibility. People generally are not considered responsible for inherited conditions. Identification of genes that predispose to alcoholism or drug addiction might weaken the idea that persons with these conditions lack will power or are irresponsible. Instead, evidence of genetic predisposition might strengthen the view that such persons are patients who need medical treatment.

GENETICS PROVIDES INFORMATION ABOUT RELATIVES AS WELL AS THE PROBAND

All genetic information, whether a family history or a DNA test, provides information about relatives as well as the patient. Ethical dilemmas might arise about the confidentiality of genomic information if the proband refuses to share information that would enable relatives to take effective steps to prevent or treat a serious disease.

WHEN IS DNA-BASED GENETIC TESTING APPROPRIATE?

Every clinical test should meet several criteria in order to be adopted in clinical practice (7). Analytic validity means that the test is reliable and accurate. Clinical validity means that the test predicts the presence or absence of clinical disease or condition. In technical terms, the test must have high positive and negative predictive value. Clinical utility means that testing must lead to better outcomes for the patient. The potential benefits of testing must outweigh the risks, and the balance of benefits to risks must be acceptable to the patient. For most conditions a screening test is justified only if there is an intervention that will prevent the disease or if treatment is more effective when started early in the disease (8). Earlier diagnosis alone is not usually considered a justification for screening for risk factors. However, some patients might desire screening for a serious illness even when there is no prevention or treatment because, if positive, they would change their life plans.

Thus, genomic screening tests are most justified if the disease is serious, the test has very high positive and predictive value, and prevention or treatment is effective. However, many DNA tests are ordered in situations that do not meet these criteria (9). The following examples illustrate diseases for which DNA-based genetic tests are appropriate, as well as conditions for which testing is not warranted, even though testing for a specific mutation is technically feasible.

HEREDITARY NONPOLYPOSIS COLORECTAL CANCER (HNPCC)

This autosomal dominant syndrome is caused by mutations in mismatch-repair genes. The most common mutations, MLH1 and MSH2, occur in 2.7% of cases of newly diagnosed colorectal cancer (10). In persons with these mutations, the lifetime risk of colorectal cancer is as high as 85% (11). Also, cancers are more likely to be earlier-onset and synchronous. Screening colonoscopy, which should start around age 20 to 25, has been shown to cut the risk of colorectal cancer in half and decrease overall mortality by 65% (10). In addition to MLH1 and MSH2, many other mutations can cause this syndrome. Hence, testing for only these two mutations has a sensitivity of only 65% and false-negative tests are common.

BRCA1 AND BRCA2

These autosomal dominant genes for susceptibility to breast cancer account for about 2% to 3% of cases of breast cancer. In families with a high incidence of breast and ovarian cancer, mutations in BRCA1 are associated with up to an 85% lifetime risk of developing breast cancer and a 40% risk of ovarian cancer (12).

BRCA testing has important limitations. False-negative tests might occur if a specific mutation has not been identified in an index case in the family. This lack of sensitivity occurs if the test used did not detect a BRCA mutation or if a different gene caused the pattern of illness in the family. The test's limitations are due in part to the patent holder's licensing restrictions, which have discouraged other laboratories from developing tests that screen for additional mutations (13). Another limitation is uncertainty over optimal care for women who are found to have BRCA mutations. Screening mammography should begin earlier for affected women, but the currently available preventive measures, prophylactic mastectomy and oophorectomy, are major interventions that carry significant medical and psychosocial ramifications.

HEMOCHROMATOSIS

Hemochromatosis is a syndrome of cirrhosis, diabetes, and gonadal failure due to iron overload. About one in 200 persons of Northern European descent is homozygous for the mutation C282Y. The value of DNA screening is unproven because of low penetrance even among heterozygotes for this mutation and variable expressivity of disease.

FACTOR V LEIDEN

This abnormal clotting factor, which occurs in 5% of Northern Europeans, confers an increased risk of venous thromboembolism. In women taking oral contraceptives, there is a 30-fold increase in relative risk. However, population screening is controversial because the absolute risk is very low.

GENOMIC TESTING IN CHILDREN

Testing children for increased risk for adult-onset diseases raises concerns because children bear the risk of stigma and discrimination but cannot give informed consent. Such testing is best deferred to adulthood whenever possible. However, testing in childhood might be justified in exceptional cases in which treatment or prevention would lead to a clinically significant benefit for the child.

GENETIC DISCRIMINATION

Screening for genetic disorders might lead to stigmatization and discrimination. Asymptomatic persons at increased risk for adult-onset genetic conditions might regard themselves, or be regarded by others, as impaired, unwhole, or flawed despite their good health. Persons with asymptomatic genetic abnormalities have been reported to suffer discrimination in employment or health insurance (14–16). Furthermore, the belief that it is "irresponsible and immoral for people who could transmit disability to their offspring to reproduce (3)" might cause severe stigma. Because of past abuses in the United States, fears of discrimination resulting from genetic testing need to be taken seriously.

INSURERS

In the current U.S. health care system, health and life insurance companies have incentives to use genetic testing to avoid adverse selection. Patients who learn that they are at risk for genetic diseases naturally want to be well insured. If insurers cannot identify such high-risk persons, they would sell increased coverage at relatively low rates to people who know they are at increased risk for future illness. Insurers therefore want to know any pertinent medical information that the applicant knows. Companies often refuse to insure people at increased risk for diseases, exclude the diseases from coverage, or set prohibitive premiums. In response to such concerns, most states have prohibited genetic discrimination in health insurance (17).

Widespread genetic testing might be incompatible with the current system of risk rating and exclusion of high-risk persons from coverage (18). With increases in genetic screening, more and more people will be found to be at risk for some genetic disease. If all such persons were in effect excluded from coverage, the very purpose of health insurance—to pay for health care when illness strikes—would be negated.

EMPLOYERS

Employers also have incentives to utilize genetic screening. Excluding employees who are likely to become sick will increase future productivity and cut health insurance premiums. Employers might also want to identify workers at genetic risk for occupational diseases because it might be cheaper to exclude them from the workplace than to reduce occupational exposure.

Genetic testing, however, could be a tragedy for employees identified as at risk for adult-onset conditions (19). They might be unable to find employment, even if they are asymptomatic and able to work productively. In turn, they would be unable to obtain employment-linked health insurance. Several states have enacted legislation banning employment discrimination on the basis of genetic information (17,19).

ANTIDISCRIMINATION LAW

The Americans with Disabilities Act (ADA) bans discrimination against persons who have conditions that result in significant impairment or who are regarded as having a significant impairment. Under the ADA preemployment medical inquiries and examinations are prohibited until after a job offer has been made. Results may not be used to exclude an applicant from the job unless the "exclusion is shown to be job related, consistent with business necessity, and not amenable to reasonable accommodation (20)." In regulations to implement the ADA, the Equal Employment Opportunity Commission (EEOC) has stated that the ADA covers persons who have suffered discrimination based on genetic information—for example, because of a genetic predisposition to a disease (16). The EEOC advisory interpretation does not cover carriers of recessive or sex-linked genetic diseases (18). However, the courts have not adjudicated this issue, and the Supreme Court has narrowed the protections provided under the ADA.

INFORMED CONSENT

Careful attention to informed consent can maximize genetic testing's benefits while minimizing the risks. DNA-based genetic testing differs from most other blood tests because it has significant psychosocial risks (21). Breaches of confidentiality might cause stigma and discrimination. Even if they are asymptomatic, persons found to be at risk for adult-onset illness might regard themselves as abnormal or be regarded as such by family members, teachers, or employers. In addition, patients might experience psychological distress after learning either positive or negative test results; generally the distress is mild, however (22).

IMPORTANCE OF INFORMED CONSENT

Informed consent is particularly important for genetic testing because persons differ on whether the benefits of testing outweigh the risks. Some persons at risk will want more prognostic information, even if its significance is uncertain and no proven preventive or therapeutic intervention is available. Others will decline testing because they do not perceive themselves to be vulnerable or are concerned about losing health insurance (23).

Truly informed consent for genetic testing will thus be difficult. Genetic concepts and probability are difficult to comprehend. Misunderstandings about genetic testing and the interpretation of results are widespread among health professionals and laypeople alike (9). The availability of multiplex testing, which allows the detection of several genetic conditions from a single blood sample, will further complicate consent.

NONDIRECTIVE GENETIC COUNSELING

Nondirectiveness has been a core tenet in genetic counseling, but people interpret the term differently. It commonly means that all sides of an issue are presented without bias, that the counselor's personal views should not influence the client's decision, and that the client's or couple's decision is respected (24). Historically, the ideology of nondirectiveness developed as a reaction to eugenicist policies and from the desire to distance prenatal genetic diagnosis from controversies over abortion (25).

Empirical studies question whether genetic counselors are in fact nondirective (26). In one study 28% of genetic counselors said they would recommend testing or screening to a client (24). Another study found that genetic counselors gave advice an average of almost six times per session and that clients did not object (27). Fewer than 20% of clients thought they were definitely being steered in a particular direction. Other writers suggest that most problems with nondirectiveness could be solved through better communication skills (28). Counselors can respond to clients' direct questions about what to do by expressing empathy and suggesting issues to consider in making the decision rather than by giving a direct recommendation. Moreover, advice can be framed tentatively as a suggestion rather than as a directive.

The stance of nondirectiveness is ethically problematic for several reasons. First, when patients request advice it might be incompatible with a caring doctor–patient relationship. Second, it might violate ethical guideline of beneficence. Outside the prenatal context, physicians recommend highly predictive screening tests for serious illness for which effective preventive measures or early treatment are available. Finally, the physicians have some obligation to be directive if patients make a decision that is ethically troubling (25). Physicians should encourage patients to share genetic test results with relatives who might be at high risk for a serious disease, and in some situations they might have an obligation to override confidentiality.

RECOMMENDATIONS

Because of the shortage of formally trained genetic counselors (29), physicians will need to help patients make decisions about genetic testing. They need to learn enough about genetic tests to provide sound information and advice.

Provide Pretest Education

To the extent that a DNA-based genetic test is not just another blood test, education about the limitations of testing and psychosocial risks is desirable before testing is carried out. Such pretest education is particularly appropriate for predictive tests that have questionable clinical validity and utility and for conditions that have no effective prevention or treatment.

Make a Recommendation for Testing

Physicians should make a recommendation for genetic testing for susceptibility to adult-onset diseases, just as they would for other screening tests. Both evidence-based medicine and the patient's values and situation should guide these recommendations. In some situations genetic tests are highly predictive of future disease and effective prevention or early treatment is available. Doctors should recommend such tests. In other situations genetic testing will provide little or no guidance for clinical decisions. Physicians should recommend against such testing. Some patients might still want nonrecommended testing (30); their informed choices should be respected.

CONFIDENTIALITY

Genetic testing provides information about relatives as well as about the person being tested. DNA-based genetic testing might have more predictive power than other types of genetic information. Persons identified as having a predisposition to an adult-onset genetic illness have a moral duty to inform relatives who might also be at risk. Similarly, persons identified as carriers of an autosomal recessive condition have a moral duty to disclose such information to their partner or spouse when making reproductive decisions. An ethical dilemma can arise for physicians when the patient objects to such disclosure.

WHEN IS OVERRIDING CONFIDENTIALITY JUSTIFIED?

The guidelines in Chapter 5 for determining whether an exception to confidentiality is justified can be applied to genetic testing. Suppose a colon cancer patient with a strong family history of colon cancer is found to have a mutation for HNPCC but refuses to inform her relatives. The potential harm to identifiable third parties is serious and the likelihood of harm is high. There is no less invasive means for warning relatives at risk because the presence of an MLH1 or MSH2 mutation has much greater predictive power than simply the family history of cancer. Breaching confidentiality allows relatives at risk to take effective steps to prevent harm—namely, initiation of annual screening colonoscopy at an earlier age. Thus there are good reasons to override confidentiality in this situation (31,32). On the other hand, the proband might feel wronged by the breach of confidentiality. In genetic testing the proband's identity can usually be inferred. Another problem is that the person notified might feel that his or her privacy has been violated or might not want to know that he or she is at risk (33).

Some have argued that overriding confidentiality to prevent infectious disease can be distinguished from this case because the person with a genetic condition does not cause the risk (34). However, the rationale behind overriding confidentiality is the prevention of serious and likely harm to unknowing third parties, regardless of the risk's cause. As in most cases in which confidentiality is overridden, it is impossible to identify and contact those at risk if the proband does not cooperate.

Only two cases involving overriding confidentiality of genetic information have reached appellate courts, and the rulings differ on whether the physician has a duty to warn relatives at risk and whether the physician may rely on the proband to warn relatives (35,36). Thus, physicians cannot simply follow the law but need to rely on their ethical judgment.

In most cases of genetic predisposition to adult-onset conditions, overriding confidentiality is unjustified because the test's predictive power is low or there are no effective preventive measures (32). In autosomal recessive conditions such as CF, there are no compelling reasons to override confidentiality. Relatives who might be carriers are at no risk for illness, and their offspring will be at risk only if their partners are also carriers.

RECOMMENDATIONS

Discuss Disclosure during Pretest Counseling

Discussing the importance of disclosure during informed consent process for testing can prevent most dilemmas about disclosure to relatives and spouses.

Urge Disclosure of Positive Results to Relatives or Spouses

Physicians should urge patients to disclose positive results to relatives or spouses when the information is pertinent to their health. In this situation nondirective counseling is highly problematic. Physicians can elicit patients' concerns about sharing test results and help them resolve those concerns. For example, patients who do not want to have contact with estranged relatives might be willing to have the physician contact them.

Disclosure Against the Patient's Wishes Should Be a Last Resort

In some situations there might be compelling reasons to disclose results of genetic testing to relatives over the patient's objections. Such disclosure should be done only as a last resort after attempts have failed to persuade the patient to allow notification and after the physician has told the patient that notification will occur and has given the patient the option to notify relatives directly. Furthermore, if the person at risk should be offered the information; if he or she has indicated that he/she does not want to know the information, these wishes should be respected.

In summary, physicians will increasingly be asked to help patients weigh genetic testing's benefits and risks. Physicians have an obligation to learn about the new applications of molecular genetics to clinical medicine. In advising patients about genetic testing, physicians need to be aware of testing's clinical limitations, the risk of discrimination, the importance of informed consent, and the need for confidentiality. Physicians as well as society as a whole can take steps to maximize genetic testing's benefits and promise while minimizing the harms.

REFERENCES

1. Kevles DJ. *In the name of eugenics*. Berkeley: University of California Press, 1985:96–112.
2. Gould SJ. *The mismeasure of man*. New York: W.W. Norton & Company, 1981.
3. U.S. Congress Office of Technology Assessment. *Cystic fibrosis and DNA tests: implications of carrier screening*. Washington: U.S. Government Printing Office, 1992:128–129.
4. Stoto MA, Almario DA, McCormick MC. *Reducing the odds: preventing perinatal transmission of HIV in the United States*. Washington: National Academy Press, 1999:28.
5. Nuffield Council on Bioethics. *Genetics and human behavior: the ethical context*. London: Nuffield Council, 2002.
6. President's Council on Bioethics. *Beyond therapy: biotechnology and the pursuit of happiness*. Washington: President's Council on Bioethics, 2003.
7. Secretary's Advisory Committee on Genetic Testing. Enhancing the Oversight of Genetic Tests: Recommendations of the SACGT. Available at: http://www4.od.nih.gov/oba/sacgt/gtdocuments.html. Accessed April 8, 2004.
8. U.S. Preventive Services Task Force. *Guide to clinical preventive services*. Baltimore: Williams & Wilkins, 1989.
9. Giardiello FM, Brensinger JD, Petersen GM, et al. The use and interpretation of commercial APC gene testing for familial adenomatous polyposis. *N Engl J Med* 1997;336:823–827.
10. Lynch HT, de la Chapelle A. Hereditary colorectal cancer. *N Engl J Med* 2003;348(10):919–932.
11. Calvert PM, Frucht H. The genetics of colorectal cancer. *Ann Intern Med* 2002;137(7):603–612.
12. Wooster R, Weber BL. Breast and ovarian cancer. *N Engl J Med* 2003;348(23):2339–2347.
13. Cho MK, Illangasekare S, Weaver MA, et al. Effects of patents and licenses on the provision of clinical genetic testing services. *J Mol Diagn* 2003;5(1):3–8.
14. Hudson KL, Rothenberg KH, Andrews LB, et al. Genetic discrimination and health insurance: an urgent need for reform. *Science* 1995;270:391–393.
15. Lapham EV, Kozma C, Weiss JO. Genetic discrimination: perspectives of consumers. *Science* 1996;274:621–624.
16. Miller PS. Genetic discrimination in the workplace. *J Law Med Ethics* 1998;26:189–197.
17. Clayton EW. Ethical, legal, and social implications of genomic medicine. *N Engl J Med* 2003;349(6):562–569.
18. Rothstein MA. Genetic privacy and confidentiality: why it's so hard to protect. *J Law Med Ethics* 1998;26:198–204.
19. Rothenberg K, Fuller B, Rothstein M, et al. Genetic information and the workplace: legislative approaches and policy changes. *Science* 1997;275:1755–1757.
20. Americans with Disabilities Act of 1990. 42 USC §§12181,12182.
21. Grady C. Ethics and genetic testing. *Adv Intern Med* 1999;44:389–411.
22. Marteau TM, Croyle RT. Psychological responses to genetic testing. *Br Med J* 1998;316:693–696.
23. Lerman C, Narod S, Schulman K, et al. BRCA1 testing in families with hereditary breast-ovarian cancer. *JAMA* 1996;275:1885–1892.
24. Bartels DM, LeRoy BS, McCarthy P, et al. Nondirectiveness in genetic counseling: a survey of practitioners. *Am J Med Genet* 1997;72:172–179.
25. Caplan AL. Neutrality is not morality: the ethics of genetic counseling. In: Bartels DM, LeRoy BS, Caplan AL, eds. *Prescribing our future: ethical challenges in genetic counseling*. New York: Aldine De Gruyter, 1993:149–165.
26. Williams C, Alderson P, Farsides B. Is nondirectiveness possible within the context of antenatal screening and testing? *Soc Sci Med* 2002;54(3):339–347.
27. Michie S, Bron F, Bobrow M, et al. Nondirectiveness in genetic counseling: an empirical study. *Am J Hum Genet* 1997;60:40–47.
28. Kessler S. Psychological aspects of genetic counseling: nondirectiveness revisited. *Am J Med Genet* 1997;72:164–171.
29. Andrews LB, Fullarton JE, Holtzman NA, et al., eds. *Assessing genetic risks: implications for health and social policy*. Washington: National Academy Press, 1994.
30. Benkendorf JL, Reutenauer JE, Hughes CA, et al. Patients' attitudes about autonomy and confidentiality in genetic testing for breast-ovarian cancer susceptibility. *Am J Med Genet* 1997;73(3):296–303.
31. Andrews LB, Fullarton JE, Holtzman NA, et al., eds. *Assessing genetic risks: implications for health and social policy*. Washington: National Academy Press, 1994.
32. The American Society of Human Genetics Social Issues Subcommittee on Familial Disclosure. Professional disclosure of familial genetic information. *Am J Hum Genet* 1998;62:474–483.
33. Wickle JTR. Late onset genetic disease: where ignorance is bliss, is it folly to inform relatives? *Br Med J* 1998; 317:744–747.

34. Sulmasy DP. On warning families about genetic risk: the ghost of Tarasoff. *Am J Med* 2000;109:738–739.
35. Safer v. Pack. 677 A.2d 1118 (N.J. App.).
36. Pate v. Threlkel. 662 So.2d 278 (Fla. 1995).

ANNOTATED BIBLIOGRAPHY

1. Marteau TM, Croyle RT. Psychological responses to genetic testing. *Br Med J* 1998;316:693–696.
   Comprehensive review of patient responses to genetic testing.
2. Rothstein MA. Genetic privacy and confidentiality: why it's so hard to protect. *J Law Med Ethics* 1998;26:198–204.
   Thoughtful discussion of problems with measures to prohibit genetic discrimination within the current U.S. insurance system.
3. Rothenberg K, Fuller B, Rothstein M. Genetic information and the workplace: legislative approaches and policy changes. *Science* 1997;275:1755–1757.
   Analyzes recent policy developments regarding workplace discrimination based on genetic information.
4. The American Society of Human Genetics Social Issues Subcommittee on Familial Disclosure. Professional disclosure of familial genetic information. *Am J Hum Genet* 1998;62:474–483.
   Position paper on whether genetic information should be disclosed to relatives over the objections of the patient.
5. Offit K, Groegner E, Turner S, Wadsworth EA, Weiser MA. The "duty to warn" a patient's family members about hereditary disease risks. *JAMA* 2004;292:1469–1473.
   Analyzes the dilemma of whether to inform relatives at risk for late-onset genetic diseases.
6. Clayton EW. Ethical, legal, and social implications of genomic medicine. *N Engl J Med* 2003;349(6):562–569.
   Recent comprehensive review of the topic.

CHAPTER 43

Ethical Issues in Public Health Emergencies

In 2001 the attacks on the World Trade Center and the Pentagon and the subsequent outbreaks of inhalational anthrax raised concerns about bioterrorism. The federal government developed a vaccination strategy in case of a smallpox outbreak initiated by terrorists. In 2003 severe acute respiratory syndrome (SARS) rapidly spread to many countries through international travel. These incidents dramatize how serious public health emergencies might require large-scale public-health interventions. Measures such as quarantine, isolation, and compulsory vaccination raise public policy dilemmas about how to protect the public health while still respecting individual freedom and treating different groups equitably (1–5).

This chapter focuses on the clinical dilemmas that physicians will confront because some patients will disagree with public health measures. Some will not accept restrictions on their freedom of movement and others will want preventive measures that are not recommended.

RECENT PUBLIC HEALTH EMERGENCIES

In October 2001 cases of inhalational anthrax occurred in several states. In Washington, D.C., congressional staff who were exposed to anthrax contained in a letter were offered prophylactic antibiotics within hours. In contrast, prophylactic antibiotics for postal workers were delayed, even after several workers were hospitalized with what was determined to be anthrax pneumonia. Concerns were raised that working class, predominately African-American postal workers received less timely prophylactic care than predominately Caucasian congressional staff. Across the country, during the season of upper respiratory infections and influenza, many people presented to emergency departments and physician offices with concerns about inhalational anthrax. Prescriptions for ciprofloxacin, the recommended drug for inhalational anthrax, increased so much that a shortage of this antibiotic was feared. The anthrax outbreaks illustrate how knowledge about an outbreak is incomplete and evolving, how perceptions of discrimination might arise, and how people might request preventive measures beyond those recommended by public health officials.

In 2002 the Centers for Disease Control and Prevention (CDC) developed plans for smallpox vaccination of first responders to an outbreak. At first the union for emergency medical technicians (EMTs) pressed for vaccination of the families of EMTs, arguing that they could be exposed to smallpox through clothing worn by EMTs (6). However, wider vaccination before an outbreak was rejected because the vaccine was in limited supply and because of risks to immunosuppressed third parties. Ironically, vaccination of first responders later fell far short of target levels because of the risk of cardiac adverse events. The smallpox vaccination program illustrates how preventive interventions might need to be triaged and how persons might demand greater access to such measures than public health guidelines recommend.

The SARS epidemic in 2002–2003 illustrated how emerging infections might spread rapidly from country to country in the era of international airplane travel. Public health responses varied markedly in different nations (7,8). In China officials locked patients and health care workers in hospitals that experienced many cases of SARS. In Canada, in contrast, exposed persons were quarantined in their homes.

HOW ARE ETHICAL ISSUES IN PUBLIC HEALTH DIFFERENT?

FOCUS ON THE PUBLIC GOOD RATHER THAN ON THE INDIVIDUAL PATIENT

Public health focuses on assessing benefit and risk to the public rather than to the individual patient (1,9). It might be appropriate for public health officials to impose compulsory public health measures to respond to a serious, probable threat to the public. Such measures might restrict freedom of movement, as through quarantine or isolation. In addition, mandatory interventions may be imposed, such as testing, treatment, and vaccination. Thus, the autonomy and liberty of individual patients may be overridden in an emergency for the public good. This is a sharp difference from ordinary clinical practice, in which individual patients decide whether to accept or decline an intervention based on their own assessment of the benefits and risks of the intervention.

INDIVIDUAL AUTONOMY MIGHT BE OVERRIDDEN

Public officials must observe ethical guidelines when imposing mandatory interventions in response to a serious and probable harm to the public health (1,3,4,9). The intervention should be effective in addressing the threat and be the least restrictive alternative that will do so. There should be procedural due process for persons deprived of their freedom and autonomy. That is, persons who are subjected to compulsory measures should have the right to an open, impartial, and timely appeal of their case. Furthermore, the benefits and burdens of the public health interventions should be equitably distributed across society, consistent with the threat's epidemiologic features. In the past, public health measures were sometimes applied discriminatorily and persons and groups affected by epidemics were often stigmatized (5,10). However, no group should bear an unjust share of the burdens of public health interventions or gain an unjust share of the benefits. Even the perception that some groups are being treated unfairly will undermine public support for compulsory measures.

Public health policies in an emergency fall within the authority of public health officials, not individual clinicians. Physicians should presume that public measures are reasonable and fair if they are developed through appropriate decision-making procedures. If doctors have questions or disagreements, they should raise them with officials rather than take it on themselves to override guidelines. Public health officials generally welcome such input from frontline physicians.

Ultimately, public health officials have police powers to enforce public health mandates. However, mandatory measures have costs and adverse effects that need to be taken into account. Isolation and quarantine raise difficult social, financial, and logistic challenges (11). Public health investigations, particularly in unprecedented outbreaks, usually require affected persons' cooperation, and the use of force might undermine such cooperation. Hence, public health officials generally invoke compulsory measures only as a last resort after less drastic measures have failed to control an outbreak. It is not necessary to have 100% enforcement of isolation or quarantine in order to stem an outbreak (11).

WEAKER EVIDENCE BASE

The evidence base for interventions in public health emergencies might be weaker than the evidence base for clinical practice. Knowledge about new conditions such as SARS or inhalational anthrax is incomplete and develops over time. Accurate diagnostic tests might not be available at the start of an outbreak. For fatal or serious conditions, there can be no definitive clinical trials of new vaccines or therapies because it would be unethical to administer the infectious agent to volunteers. Moreover, public health officials might need to act quickly on the basis of uncertain and incomplete information.

PATIENT DISAGREEMENTS WITH PUBLIC HEALTH POLICIES

In public health emergencies physicians in clinical practice will encounter patients who believe that infringements on their autonomy are unwarranted or unfair. Two different scenarios might arise: Patients might request interventions beyond those recommended or patients might refuse public health measures.

REQUESTS FOR INTERVENTIONS NOT RECOMMENDED IN PUBLIC HEALTH GUIDELINES

CASE 43.1 Patient who requests antibiotics.

During the anthrax outbreaks in the fall of 2001, a 48-year-old man requests a prescription for ciprofloxacin. He is a Federal Express driver who has had no exposure to anthrax but is concerned that he is at high risk for exposure in light of the cases of anthrax transmitted through the mail. "Look at what happened to those postal workers in Washington. Two of them died, and there were delays in getting them antibiotics. If I see white powder, I want to take the antibiotics right away." After the physician explains that there are concerns about a national shortage of the antibiotic of choice if a massive outbreak occurs, the patient retorts, "That's ridiculous. Look at those office workers in Congress who weren't even exposed. They got cipro in a few hours. They weren't told there was a shortage."

In ordinary clinical practice, when patients request interventions that are not indicated, physicians generally attempt to persuade the patient (*see* Chapter 32). Nevertheless, physicians often accede to such requests as long as the intervention does not present undue risk to the patient. In contrast, in a public health emergency it might not be appropriate or feasible to provide requested interventions that fall outside the guidelines (12).

Protect the Public Health

In public health emergencies physicians have a primary obligation to act for the common good. Unlike in ordinary clinical practice, physicians need to consider how a decision for one patient might significantly affect the spread of an epidemic, public trust, and perceptions of fairness. If many patients receive nonrecommended interventions, the press is likely to report the story. In turn, people might believe that the guidelines are being unfairly implemented or that the magnitude of the threat is greater than officials acknowledge. As a result, trust in public health officials might be undermined.

A particular case might be a justified exception to public health policies or might show that a policy needs to be modified. The burden of proof in an emergency is on those who argue that an exception or modification is warranted. An exception must be fair in the sense that it would also apply to all patients in a similar clinical situation, not just in that particular case. If such a widespread exception would not be feasible from a public health perspective, it is difficult to justify making an exception for an individual patient.

Physicians should clarify how strictly public health guidelines are to be enforced; officials might accept less than full compliance. In Case 43.1 it might be plausible to write a prescription for ciprofloxacin for someone in a high-risk occupation. Guidelines in this context reflect recommendations, as opposed to mandatory rules. In other situations, however, public health interventions are tightly controlled and the physician might have little or no discretion. For instance, early in the smallpox vaccination program, explicit criteria for eligibility were set because of a shortage of vaccine.

Physicians should help patients understand that in a public health emergency decisions need to be based on public health considerations as well as their personal preferences. The impact on the well-being of other persons and the public is paramount. Although resource constraints exist in ordinary clinical care (*see* Chapter 30), they usually are not the determining factor in decisions.

Act in the Patient's Best Interests

In so far as it is possible, physicians should maintain their usual role of acting in the patient's best interests while observing public health guidelines that are strictly enforced.

Elicit and address patient concerns and emotions. Fear and a sense of loss of control are natural human reactions to public health emergencies and they need to be acknowledged. Also, physicians should acknowledge the uncertainty inherent in a situation where knowledge is evolving. Trying to reassure people by telling them not to worry is unlikely to be effective. Patients might be more willing to pay attention to public health after their own needs are addressed.

Use the doctor–patient relationship to benefit patients. As was demonstrated in the SARS epidemic, patients can often be reassured if they believe they can see the physician promptly if their condition worsens or fails to improve (13). Also, patients can be reassured by knowing what warning signs they should watch for.

Address patient concerns in other ways. It might be possible to address the patient's concerns and needs without affecting public health. For example, if access to ciprofloxacin were strictly limited, the physician could prescribe antibiotics that are not in such short supply and that might also be effective. When patients have a prescription and access to follow-up care, their sense of control might be increased to the extent that they decide not to take the drug.

REFUSAL OF PUBLIC HEALTH INTERVENTIONS

CASE 43.2 Patient who rejects quarantine.

During the SARS epidemic in 2002, a 48-year-old businessman presents with fever, cough, and malaise. Five days before, he returned from a trip to a country where SARS cases have been reported but he was not near the area in which the cases occurred. He says his symptoms are no different from what he commonly experiences after such long travel. Because SARS cases have been reported in his city, public health officials are requiring physicians to report such cases for consideration of home quarantine. He objects strongly. "If I had known that, I wouldn't have come in. I have a lot of meetings that I can't do over the phone. My business would go down the tubes if I were in home quarantine."

In clinical practice when patients refuse recommended interventions, their informed wishes are respected. However, in public health emergencies, individual autonomy is not paramount (1). Compulsory measures may be imposed to prevent transmission to others and to control an outbreak of a serious infection.

Protect the Public Health

Physicians need to be clear about the limits of their discretion in public health emergencies. In some situations doctors might have little control over public health measures. Reporting of emerging infections or infections related to bioterrorism might be mandatory and done directly by hospitals or clinical laboratories rather than by individual physicians. In other situations isolation and quarantine might be voluntary rather than mandatory; if this is the situation in Case 43.2, the physician may exercise discretion.

Act in the Patient's Best Interests (12)

Advocate for changes in guidelines or exceptions. Doctors should communicate disagreement with public health guidelines to responsible officials. For example, a policy of quarantine for all persons who have traveled to a particular country might not be warranted if cases of the disease have been reported only from a well-defined area of a large country. Justifications for exceptions need to have a sound public health basis. It would be ethically inappropriate to argue that patients who would suffer great economic losses should be exempted from home quarantine.

Establish common ground with the patients. When patients refuse public health measures, physicians can still find areas of agreement. For example, most patients do not want to infect their families. Also, business people might suffer greater harm to reputation and business relationships if they flout public health measures and others are infected as a result. Furthermore, cooperating with public health officials might enable patients to have access to special tests that are not otherwise available.

Mitigate the risks of mandatory public health interventions. Physicians can assuage the adverse psychosocial consequences of quarantine or isolation by keeping in telephone contact with patients and addressing their feelings of isolation. In addition, physicians can help address practical concerns—for example, by referring patients for social services and for legal assistance as needed.

Refrain from Deception

Patients might ask doctors to intentionally misrepresent their condition in order to exempt them from public health policies. For instance, patients might ask physicians to certify that they do not have a reportable condition. Such deception to third parties is ethically problematic for physicians (*see* Chapter 6). If doctors intentionally mislead third parties who have an ethical and legal right to information about the patient, they cannot be trusted to tell the truth in other situations. Moreover, the harms of such deception outweigh the benefits when the adverse consequences to other patients and the public are taken into account.

In summary, in public health emergencies time for physicians to deliberate about a particular case might be limited. Further public health emergencies are to be expected. Before a crisis occurs, physicians should think through in advance how they would respond to foreseeable dilemmas that arise when patients disagree with public health recommendations or requirements.

REFERENCES

1. Childress JF, Faden RR, Gaare RD, et al. Public health ethics: mapping the terrain. *J Law Med Ethics* 2002; 30(2):170–178.
2. Gostin LO. When terrorism threatens health: how far are limitations on human rights justified. *J Law Med Ethics* 2003;31(4):524–528.
3. Gostin LO. Public health law in an age of terrorism: rethinking individual rights and common goods. *Health Aff (Millwood)* 2002;21(6):79–93.
4. Gostin LO, Sapsin JW, Teret SP, et al. The Model State Emergency Health Powers Act: planning for and response to bioterrorism and naturally occurring infectious diseases. *JAMA* 2002;288(5):622–628.
5. Gostin LO, Bayer R, Fairchild AL. Ethical and legal challenges posed by severe acute respiratory syndrome: implications for the control of severe infectious disease threats. *JAMA* 2003;290(24):3229–3237.
6. Board on Health Promotion and Disease Prevention, ed. *Scientific and Policy Considerations in Developing Smallpox Vaccination Options: A Workshop Report.* Washington, D.C.: National Academies Press; 2002.
7. Institute for Bioethics Health Policy and Law. Quarantine and Isolation: Lessons Learned from SARS. May 13, 2004. Available at: http://mmrs.fema.gov/News/SarsWatch/2004/may/nsars2004-05-13.aspx. Accessed July 18, 2004.
8. Knobler S, Mahmoud A, Lemon S et al., eds. *Learning from SARS: Preparing for the Next Disease Outbreak.* Washington, D.C.: National Academies Press; 2004.
9. Gostin LO. *Public Health Law: Power, Duty, Restraint.* Berkeley: University of California Press; 2000.
10. Person B, Sy F, Holton K, Govert B, et al., NICD/SARS Emergency Outreach Team. Fear and stigma: the epidemic within the SARS outbreak. Available at: http://www.cdc.gov/ncidod/EID/vol10no2/03-0750.htm.
11. Centers for Disease Control and Prevention. Community Containment Measures, Including Non-Hospital Isolation and Quarantine. Jan 8, 2004. Available at: http://www.cdc.gov/ncidod/sars/guidance/D/index.htm. Accessed July 18, 2004.
12. Lo B, Katz MH. Clinical decision-making during public health emergencies: ethical considerations. In press.
13. Maunder R, Hunter J, Vincent L, et al. The immediate psychological and occupational impact of the 2003 SARS outbreak in a teaching hospital. *Cmaj* 2003;168(10):1245–1251.

ANNOTATED BIBLIOGRAPHY

1. Childress JF, Faden RR, Gaare RD, et al. Public health ethics: mapping the terrain. *J Law Med Ethics* 2002;30:170–178.
   Presents ethical framework for public health policies.
2. Gostin LO, Sapsin JW, Teret SP, et al. The Model State Emergency Health Powers Act: planning for and response to bioterrorism and naturally occurring infectious diseases. *JAMA* 2002;288:622–628.
   Proposes model state legislation to grant emergency powers to public health officials while still respecting individual liberties.
3. Lo B, Katz MH. Clinical decision-making during public health emergencies: ethical considerations. Under review.
   Analyzes ethical dilemmas that frontline clinicians face during public health emergencies.

Cases for Discussion

CASE 1. Choosing among therapeutic options for prostate cancer.

An asymptomatic 52-year-old teacher is diagnosed with prostate cancer on the basis of a prostate-specific antigen of 5.4 (normal < 4.0) and a needle biopsy that shows several foci of adenocarcinoma with a Gleason score of 3 + 3 = 6. Options for treatment include surgery, radiation, or "watchful waiting." Suppose that you are the attending surgeon.

QUESTIONS FOR DISCUSSION

1. You are hosting a visiting physician from China, who says he does not understand why Americans regard informed consent as so important: "I can understand that in your country, you tell patients they have cancer. But why don't you then just do what is the best treatment for them rather than going through what you call informed consent?" How would you explain (a) the purposes of informed consent and (b) the ethical reasons for informed consent?

2. An intern asks you how to determine what information about surgery he needs to discuss with the patient. "I just read a chapter in a surgery textbook, and I'm not sure how much information I am supposed to tell him to get informed consent," he says. "There's no way I can tell him everything! What do I need to discuss with him?" How would you answer the intern's question?

3. Suppose, on the basis of your critical reading of the published evidence, you believe that surgery offers the best outcome for this patient. How do you take into account this judgment in your discussions with the patient?

4. One resident has read articles reporting that patients don't understand basic information that physicians discuss with them and says, "Why do we bother with the informed consent? Patients don't understand what we say and don't remember any of it." How do you respond to the resident's objections?

5. A student asks if patients need to be told of the role that students and residents play during surgery and in postoperative care. One of the residents says, "We don't need to tell the patient about that. They have given implied consent to have residents and students participate in their care by choosing to come to a teaching hospital." Do you agree or disagree? Give the ethical considerations for your position. How have the courts used the term "implied consent"?

CASE 2. Refusal of treatment by a patient with inoperable cancer.

A 64-year-old man has inoperable pancreatic cancer and obstructive jaundice. He had an internal drainage tube placed in the common duct in an attempt to decompress his biliary tree and prevent sepsis. However, he developed cholangitis, which was treated with antibiotics. He entered hospice care, and over the next 2 weeks he had progressive jaundice, abdominal pain, nausea, pruritis, anorexia, and weight loss. His life expectancy is a few weeks. His drainage tube obstructs and he is admitted with another episode of biliary sepsis. As his physician, you discuss with him plans for care. He is lucid and shows no sign of mental impairment during your conversation.

QUESTIONS FOR DISCUSSION

1. The patient says he does not want cardiopulmonary resuscitation (CPR) if he suffers a cardiac arrest. In a number of studies, no patients with metastatic cancer who suffer a cardiopulmonary arrest leave the hospital alive after attempted resuscitation. Would you write a Do Not Attempt Resuscitation (DNAR) order? How would you explain your decision?

2. What would you do if his wife or family disagrees with his refusal of CPR? What is the ethical rationale for your decision?

3. The patient also refuses antibiotics for biliary sepsis, saying: "There isn't any point in going through this again only to have another infection next week or the week after." The intern exclaims, "How can we not give him antibiotics? He'll die without them, and we have an ethical duty to save lives." Do you agree to withhold antibiotics? What is the ethical rationale for your position?

CASE 3. Refusal of blood transfusions by a Jehovah's Witness.

A 34-year-old man is hospitalized after an automobile accident that ruptures his spleen. A devout Jehovah's Witness, he refuses transfusion. He does agree to a splenectomy and states emphatically, "I wish to live, but with no blood transfusions." He also refuses blood components and court-ordered transfusions. He declares, "It is between me and Jehovah, not the courts. I'm willing to take my chances. My faith is that strong." He is lucid throughout the conversation.

QUESTIONS FOR DISCUSSION

1. His hematocrit drops to 14.1%. One of the residents says, "How can we just stand by when we could bring him back to full health with transfusions? Aren't doctors supposed to act for the good of the patient? How can it be good for a young, healthy man to die needlessly?" Do you agree with the resident? What is the ethical rationale for your position?

2. The patient's wife was a Jehovah's Witness but left the faith. "I know that he says he doesn't want a blood transfusion, but I also know he loves his children," she says. "He could never agree to a transfusion, but he couldn't bear to leave us either. Can't you override his decision? That's what he would really want you to do." How do you respond to the wife? Explain the ethical rationale for your approach.

3. The surgeon is reluctant to operate without transfusion support. "What's the point of taking someone to the operating room to have him die on the table?" he says. "If he wants to refuse transfusions and die in the emergency room, that's his right. But he can't force me to operate and be responsible for his death." Do you agree or disagree with the surgeon? What is the ethical rationale for your position?

CASE 4. No clear reason for refusal of medically effective treatment.

A 45-year-old woman has a 1/2-cm breast mass that is found to be malignant on needle aspiration. With either mastectomy or lumpectomy plus radiation, she has an excellent chance of being cured of her cancer. She refuses any form of therapy, saying that she wants to try natural healing through herbal remedies, megavitamin therapy, spiritual healing, and relaxation techniques.

QUESTIONS FOR DISCUSSION

1. One resident objects, "How do we just stand by when she would most likely be cured of her cancer with surgery? Aren't we supposed to act in the patient's best interests? How can it be in the patient's best interests to lose the chance to have her cancer cured?" Another resident says, "Wait a minute, we're supposed to respect patient autonomy. It's her body and her life, and it's her decision." How do you respond to these viewpoints? What is the ethical rationale for your position? How would you carry out your position in practice?

CONFIDENTIALITY

CASE 5. Reporting a patient with syncope to the Department of Motor Vehicles.

A 76-year-old retired teacher with a history of coronary artery disease is hospitalized after a syncopal episode. He is found to have ventricular tachycardia. He had two previous syncopal episodes during the past 3 years. An automatic implantable cardioverter defibrillator (AICD) is implanted. During the first year after implantation, about 10% of patients experience syncope or near-syncope because of defibrillation.

QUESTIONS FOR DISCUSSION

1. A nurse in a clinic asks if the patient needs to be reported to the Department of Motor Vehicles. How do you respond? What ethical considerations support your position?

2. Suppose that your patient is a 47-year-old bus driver instead of a retiree. The patient tells you that he is willing to try anything, even take temporary leave from work, as long as you don't report him to the Department of Motor Vehicles. "Doc, if you take my license away, I can't support my family," he pleads. "I need this job." How do you respond? What ethical considerations support your position?

CASE 6. Use of anabolic steroids by an athlete.

A colleague asks your advice on a difficult case. A 19-year-old college swimmer reveals that she has started to take oral anabolic steroids, which she obtains through friends at the gym where she lifts weights. She says that she is aware of the long-term side effects but plans to use the drugs only while she is competing in intercollegiate athletics. She doesn't want to lose her scholarship; because many of her competitors are using steroids, there is no other way for her to be competitive.

QUESTIONS FOR DISCUSSION

1. Your colleague asks whether she should tell the coach of the swim team about the patient's steroid use, saying, "Maybe she can discourage her from taking these drugs. It's so dangerous for her, and her health can't be worth winning a few races. We need to act in her best interests." How do you respond? What ethical considerations support your position?
2. Another colleague, who joins your discussion, suggests: "She should be reported to the intercollegiate athletic officials. It isn't fair to swimmers at other schools for her to have an advantage. If she wants to risk her health, that's her business, but let's keep the playing field level." How would you respond? What ethical considerations support your position?
3. A third colleague says, "If you tell anyone, it should be her parents. If I were her mother, I'd certainly want to know." What is your view on talking to her parents? What ethical considerations support your position?

CASE 7. Disclosure of genetic illness to relatives

A 40-year-old auto mechanic is found to have a localized breast cancer, which is treated with lumpectomy and radiation. Because of a family history of both ovarian and breast cancer in several first-degree relatives, she is tested for BRCA-1 and is found to be positive for a mutation that is known to confer a greatly increased risk for these cancers. As her physician, you discuss the implications of this autosomal recessive condition for her 34-year-old and 36-year-old sisters and urge her to disclose her test results to them so they also can be tested for BRCA1. A relative who has the same mutation has a lifetime 85% risk of breast cancer and a 50% risk of ovarian cancer. An affected relative will probably want to begin screening mammography earlier than is usually recommended and also want to consider interventions such as bilateral mastectomy, tamoxifen, and experimental therapies. Your patient refuses to disclose her results to her sisters or allow you to do so. "We had a major falling out when mom died," she tells you. "They did some things that I'm not sure I can ever forgive. I just don't want to get involved with them at this point in my life."

QUESTIONS FOR DISCUSSION

1. A nurse is outraged at the patient's refusal to inform her sisters that they might be at high risk for cancer. "We should pick up the phone and call them," she says. "This is more serious than tuberculosis and we notify contacts of TB patients. What if her sisters get tested later and have inoperable cancer?" How do you respond to the nurse? What ethical considerations support your position?

DECISION-MAKING CAPACITY

CASE 8. Refusal of colonoscopy.

A 72-year-old retired lawyer comes into the hospital with lower abdominal pain. He is found to have guaiac positive stools and anemia. You plan to do a colonoscopy, but the patient refuses. During your conversation, you learn that the patient spends all day closed inside his house where the electricity has been turned off due to outstanding bills.

One intern says that it is appropriate to seek a court order, saying, "This guy can't even pay his bills, how can we expect him to make decisions about his health care?" Another intern responds, "Look, I have trouble paying my bills on time. I hope that no court would override my medical decisions."

The patient's only relative is a niece who lives in a distant state. She says that he is somewhat cantankerous and has always been independent and stubborn. She is unable to persuade him over the phone to have the colonoscopy. She tells the doctors, "If you believe that he's not able to make decisions for himself, I would certainly give permission for you to the tests and treatments he needs. I want the best care for him."

QUESTIONS FOR DISCUSSION

1. What will happen if it is determined that the patient is competent to make medical decisions? If he is determined to lack decision-making capacity?
2. What questions would you ask the patient to better evaluate whether he is competent to make decisions about his care?
3. The intern says, "I was told that we have to get a psychiatry consultation to declare a patient incompetent." Do you agree or disagree? What ethical considerations support your position?

DECISIONS FOR INCOMPETENT PATIENTS

CASE 9. Mechanical ventilation in end-stage lung disease.

A 72-year-old retired grocery store owner with end-stage interstitial lung disease presents to the Emergency Department (ED) for shortness of breath that began 4 hours ago. On room air, she is breathing at a rate of 36, is cyanotic, and has an O_2 saturation of 54%. She is afebrile and has no signs of consolidation. Her chest x-ray shows no infiltrates. She pulls nasal canulae or mask delivering oxygen off her face. Her daughter is unable to get her to keep the supplemental O_2 on. The patient is unable to have a coherent conversation. At baseline her FEV1 is 0.8 liters and her room air blood gas is PH 7.38, pO_2 51 mm Hg, PCO_2 55 mm Hg.

QUESTIONS FOR DISCUSSION

1. The daughter says that her mother knows that she has end-stage lung disease and has told her ambulatory physician several times that she does not want to be intubated. The patient has also told the daughter that she would not want intubation. Her daughter reports, "She knows what intubation is. She had it several years ago when she had pneumonia. But she knows that her lungs have just gotten worse and worse. She's ready to die when the time comes, but she wants to die with dignity, without machines or tubes." However, she has never completed a durable power of attorney for health care, and there is no Do Not IntubateDo (DNI) order in the computerized record system. You are unable to get the ambulatory records, and the on-call physician does not know the patient. Your resident says doctors must provide treatment for potentially reversible conditions, saying, "This is probably an aspiration pneumonia, from which she could recover. Without a written advance directive or DNI order, we have to intubate her." Do you agree? What are the ethical justifications for your position?
2. One intern says, "We have to intubate her. All we know is what the daughter is telling us. How can we be sure that she is accurately reporting what her mother wants? You never can trust family members; maybe she is trying to get an inheritance. Whenever there is any doubt, we have to err on the side of preserving life." The other intern responds, "But that means we would never trust any family to make decisions for an incompetent patient, except when patients complete a health care proxy. That doesn't seem right." Do you agree with the first intern? What are the ethical justifications for your position? How might the intern's concerns be addressed in emergency situation?

CASE 10. Stroke and aspiration pneumonia.

A 74-year-old retired gas station owner with Alzheimer disease and coronary artery disease is admitted with a stroke. Three days after admission he has a dense hemiplegia, is unable to speak coherently, and has difficulty swallowing. An ECG also shows an acute myocardial infarction with many premature ventricular contractions. He develops an aspiration pneumonia that is treated with antibiotics. At his baseline he often does recognize family members and needs help with all activities of daily living. He has not given any written advance directives.

QUESTIONS FOR DISCUSSION

1. His wife and daughter report that he had said many times that becoming demented and living in a nursing home would be a fate worse than death. He had helped care for an uncle with Alzheimer disease and had said that not being able to recognize people and take care of himself would be intolerable. The wife and daughter request that he be transferred out of the intensive care unit (ICU) and allowed to die. They want a Do Not Attempt Resuscitation (DNAR) order, no intubation, no feeding tube, and no antibiotics for infections. "Just keep him comfortable and let him die in peace," they say. They report that in the emergency room they agreed to active treatments because they were told that his stroke might be reversible and that he might return home. However, he has not improved after 3 days. They are unable to care for him at home because of his wife's medical problems and his daughter's job. They also cannot afford to hire full-time help. The nurses comment that they seem devoted to him.

2. How would the ethical analysis be different if the patient had completed an advance directive appointing his wife as proxy?

CASE 11. Stroke and aspiration pneumonia.

Assume the same medical facts as in Case 3, but the patient has made no statements about his preferences for care. His wife and daughter believe that he would not want to receive continued ICU care after failing to improve from his stroke. "He never really talked about what he would want in this situation for himself," his wife explains. "But he was a man who prided himself on his independence and dignity. He never wanted anyone to help him when he was injured or sick. He was always immaculately dressed. He would never even go out to pick up the newspaper in the morning before getting dressed because he didn't want anyone to see him in his robe or pajamas. It's hard enough for him to have us help him. He would be mortified to have strangers help him with his bathing and dressing. We've been married over 50 years, and I know in my heart he wouldn't want to live like this."

QUESTIONS FOR DISCUSSION

1. The intern says that without some indication of the patient's own preferences, either written or oral, it is inappropriate to discontinue antibiotics or write a DNAR-DNI order. "What the wife is saying is pure speculation," the intern points out. "He may still improve from his stroke." Do you agree with the intern? What are the ethical justifications for your position?

CASE 12. Stroke and aspiration pneumonia.

Assume the same medical facts as in Case 3, but the patient has made no statements about his preferences for care and has no family members. He has lived in a nursing home for several years and has no friends who visit him regularly. The nurses did not know him before he became demented.

QUESTIONS FOR DISCUSSION

1. One of the interns says, "We have to continue ICU care because we don't know what the patient would want in this situation. Without any surrogate, we have to give maximal treatment. How can we say that it's better for him to be dead than to live like this, when we don't know him?" Do you agree with the intern? What are the ethical justifications for your position?

CONFUSING ETHICAL DISTINCTIONS

CASE 13. Withdrawal of mechanical ventilation.

A 72-year-old retired grocery store owner with end-stage interstitial lung disease was intubated in the ED. Later you obtain old records, which document extensive discussions with her primary physician that she does not want to be intubated or have resuscitation attempted. You also speak with the primary physician, who confirms that the patient did not want to be intubated and says, "This is exactly what she most feared—that she be on a ventilator with nothing readily reversible."

QUESTIONS FOR DISCUSSION

1. An ICU nurse says, "I would have no problem if we hadn't intubated her in the first place. But we can't just turn off the ventilator or extubate her. She would die in a couple of minutes. That would be killing her, pure and simple, just as if we injected potassium." Do you agree with the nurse? What are the ethical justifications for your position?

2. Because the patient will be dyspneic, you want to administer morphine and also provide sedation. An intern objects, saying that it could reduce her respirations or lower her blood pressure, which would kill her: "That would be active euthanasia, and that's wrong." Do you agree? What are the ethical justifications for your position?

DO NOT ATTEMPT RESUSCITATION ORDERS

CASE 14. Do Not Attempt Resuscitation orders during endoscopy.

A 58-year-old woman with dysphagia is found to have inoperable carcinoma of the esophagus. She realizes her poor prognosis and opts for palliation. With the concurrence of her family, she agrees to a DNAR and DNI order. Because she has difficulty maintaining adequate oral intake, she agrees to endoscopic placement of an intraluminal esophageal stent.

QUESTIONS FOR DISCUSSION

1. The gastroenterologist who performs the procedure insists that the DNAR order be lifted during the procedure, saying, "I understand that she has chosen palliative care. However, if she has a cardiac arrest during the endoscopy, it is due to the medications that we give for conscious sedation. Our ability to resuscitate patients in this situation, even those with inoperable cancer, is close to 100%. The situation is completely different from a cardiopulmonary arrest that occurs spontaneously in the course of illness." Do you agree with the gastroenterologist that the DNAR order should be suspended during the procedure? What are the ethical justifications for your position?

CASE 15. Pneumonia and Alzheimer disease.

A 74-year-old man with severe Alzheimer disease is transferred from a nursing home for treatment of pneumonia. Except for mild hypercholesterolemia and osteoarthritis of the knees and hips, he has no active medical problems and takes no medications regularly. He has no living relatives or friends, and before becoming demented he had not indicated what he would want done in such a situation. His baseline state in the nursing home is that he requires assistance with all activities of daily living, including eating. He usually does not recognize nursing home staff, but he does smile when watching television. The nursing home physician says that he does not know what the patient would want but that it seems reasonable to administer antibiotics but not to provide interventions such as mechanical ventilation.

QUESTIONS FOR DISCUSSION

1. The resident on the team says, "He should be DNAR. It doesn't make any sense to resuscitate someone with such a terrible quality of life. It would be futile." Do you agree with the resident's view? What are the ethical justifications for your position?

FUTILE INTERVENTIONS

CASE 16. Multiorgan failure.

Mr. D is a 72-year-old homebound man with multisystem failure admitted to a community hospital for pneumonia, a myeloproliferative disorder, and failure to thrive. He develops stupor and adult respiratory distress syndrome (ARDS), for which he requires mechanical ventilation. He is transferred to a referral center, where he develops renal failure requiring dialysis and recurrent episodes of hypotension and sepsis. No primary site of infection has been identified.

His major problem now is abdominal pain and distention, which requires fentanyl. A CT scan shows dilated extrahepatic bile ducts but no intrahepatic dilatation or other abnormalities. His liver function tests are only mildly and occasionally elevated. The patient's daughter believes that an operation on his biliary tract would cure his abdominal problem and that relief of his abdominal distention would in turn allow him to be weaned off the ventilator. Surgery believes that there is no abdominal problem that surgery would improve and that general anesthesia would be lethal. Two attempts at endoscopic retrograde cholangio-pancreatography (ERCP) were unable to visualize the ampulla of Vater. Interventional radiology is unwilling to attempt percutaneous biliary drainage because there is no intrahepatic duct dilatation.

The patient has given no advance directives. The patient's wife tends to defer to the daughter in discussions and agrees with her. His family believes that if he had widespread cancer or were in a permanent coma he would not want life-prolonging treatment, but they point out that this is not currently the case. They refuse to agree to a DNAR order or limitation of medical interventions.

QUESTIONS FOR DISCUSSION

1. The surgical chief resident says that it would be "crazy" to operate on this patient and remarks, "There is no reason to operate. It would be futile. We won't take her to the Operation Room, no matter what the family wants." Do you believe that exploratory laparotomy would be futile and that the surgery team may refuse to do the procedure? What are the ethical justifications for your position?

2. The gastrointestinal(GI) service declines to make another attempt at ERCP. The GI fellow says, "We've already tried the procedure twice. There's no point in trying again. The family can't force us to do something that's futile." Do you believe that ERCP would be futile and that the GI team may refuse to do the procedure? What are the ethical justifications for your position?

3. The nephrology service believes that continuing dialysis is futile, saying, "What's the point of dialyzing him? That's not going to allow him to leave the ICU." Do you believe that continued dialysis would be futile and that the nephrology team may refuse to do the procedure? What are the ethical justifications for your position?

4. The resident believes that CPR would be futile and says, "If he has a cardiac arrest, there's no way he would survive. We don't need the family's agreement to withhold CPR. We can write a medical DNAR order." You try to find evidence to support the claim that CPR would be futile in this situation. Do you believe that CPR would be futile and that the medical team may write a DNAR order against the wishes of the family? What are the ethical justifications for your position?

5. When you sign out the patient to the night float resident, she notes that the last time she covered, the patient suffered an episode of hypotension, which she treated with fluids, vasopressors, and antibiotics. "What if that happens again, but he doesn't respond and develops progressive hypotension despite maximal therapy?" she asks. "Do you still want me to do CPR if he suffers a cardiac arrest?" In that situation would it be appropriate to withhold CPR despite the family's wishes? What are the ethical justifications for your position?

PHYSICIAN-ASSISTED SUICIDE AND ACTIVE EUTHANASIA

CASE 17. Head and neck cancer.

A 57-year-old machinist has head and neck cancer that has progressed despite radiation and chemotherapy. She cannot swallow foods and secretions and has to sit upright at night to spit out her secretions. She asks her physician for a prescription for a lethal dose of sleeping pills and says, "It's barbaric that the medical system does not allow me to retain the last shreds of my dignity. Why can't I have the same humane, compassionate treatment that we give our pets at the end of their *lives? I do not want to wait for pneumonia or starvation to deliver me. I want to end my life freely and rationally. I am not depressed, but it is inhumane to ask me to live this way." Her husband agrees with her decision.*

QUESTIONS FOR DISCUSSION

1. What actions should a physician who supports physician-assisted suicide take before deciding that it is appropriate to write a prescription for a lethal dose of medication in this case?
2. What actions should a physician who opposes physician-assisted suicide take in addition to refusing the patient's request?
3. How does the moral responsibility of the physician differ when writing a lethal prescription compared to injecting a lethal dose of medication, such as potassium?

CASE 18. Failed suicide attempt.

The patient with head and neck cancer is found at home by her husband after a suicide attempt. She has ingested a combination of tricyclic antidepressants, barbiturates, and alcohol and has left a long explanatory suicide note. She had held a good-bye party for her friends and then ingested the medications while he played her favorite music. As they agreed, they left her alone for 3 hours. When he returned with a friend, they were shocked to find her grunting for breath but not conscious. Horrified that she was suffering, they called 911.

In the field she is found to have an O_2 saturation of 70% and is intubated. In the ED she is placed on mechanical ventilation and given intravenous fluids and vasopressors. The patient's primary physician confirms her diagnosis, her recent deterioration, and the absence of depression or other psychiatric illness, saying, "She didn't want to be a burden on her family or spend her last days waiting for an infection. I personally wouldn't do what she did, but I respect her choice. There is no question that she thought about this long and hard."

QUESTIONS FOR DISCUSSION

1. Would you continue mechanical ventilation, fluids, and vasopressors? One ED resident says, "If we withdraw support, we'll be abetting a suicide. That's illegal and morally wrong. What message does it send to other patients if the emergency room helps people kill themselves?" Do you agree with this position? What are the ethical justifications for your position?
2. While the medical and nursing staff are discussing the case, the patient begins to awaken. She is weaned off vasopressors, and 2 hours later she is extubated. As per ED protocol, a psychiatrist talks with her. She says, "Of course, I'll do this again as soon as I get home and can figure out how to do it right. We'll have to get on the Internet and find out. Don't you understand that waiting for some medical catastrophe to occur is an inhumane way to die? Wouldn't you do the same thing? Do you expect me to lie about my intentions to make you all feel less guilty?" As the psychiatrist, do you place her on an involuntary hold because she is actively suicidal? What are the ethical justifications for your position?

CASE 19. Withdrawal of mechanical ventilation.

A 72-year-old retired grocery store owner with end-stage interstitial lung disease has mechanical ventilation withdrawn based on evidence that she would not want such treatment. She is placed on oxygen via nasal canulae and morphine and diazepam drips to palliate her dyspnea and anxiety. On 10 mg morphine per hour and 2 mg diazepam per hour, the patient appears comfortable, without any tachypnea, use of accessory muscles, tachycardia, or restlessness. Her respiratory rate is 12 per minute. She does not respond when called or when an intravenous line is restarted.

QUESTIONS FOR DISCUSSION

1. The patient's family requests that you increase the drips: "She said many times she didn't want to linger or to have a prolonged death." Do you agree with the family's request? What are the ethical justifications for your position?

REFUSAL TO CARE FOR PATIENTS

CASE 20. Caring for a patient with acquired immunodeficiency syndrome.

A 34-year-old man with acquired immunodeficiency syndrome (AIDS) (CD4 level 47) is admitted to your service with Pneumocystis carinii pneumonia. His IV has infiltrated, and you are asked to restart it.

QUESTIONS FOR DISCUSSION

1. How would you feel if you suffered a needlestick injury while caring for an HIV-infected patient?
2. One of the interns on the admitting team refuses to take care of this patient. What are the ethical considerations if:
   a. The intern says he is inexperienced at starting IVs and thinks that a more experienced physician should care for the patient.
   b. The intern is a deeply religious person who believes that homosexuality is a sin. Because the patient is gay, the intern does not want to care for him.
   c. The patient is an injection drug user. An injection drug user at the hospital had earlier mugged the intern in his internship. The intern is still experiencing flashbacks about that earlier incident and does not want to be subjected to more stress.

ETHICAL DILEMMAS FACING STUDENTS AND HOUSE STAFF: LEARNING ON PATIENTS

CASE 21. Outcomes of coronary artery bypass and graft.

Suppose your favorite uncle has been recommended to have coronary artery bypass and graft (CABAG) by his primary care physician and cardiologist in New York. From your clinical epidemiology course you recall that the mortality rates for this operation vary from under 1% to over 8% and that New York State publishes mortality rates for hospitals and for individual surgeons.

QUESTIONS FOR DISCUSSION

1. Do you want to know the outcomes experience for the hospital or for the surgeon who would operate on your uncle? What are your reasons?

CASE 22. Carrying out an invasive procedure.

Recall the first time you did a lumbar puncture (LP) (or central line, major suturing, or other major procedure).

QUESTIONS FOR DISCUSSION

1. How did you feel before doing your first invasive procedure?
2. One of your classmates says that by coming to a teaching hospital, patients have given implied consent to having students and residents do procedures. Thus there is no need to tell the patient that a student will be performing a procedure. Do you agree, and why?
3. What would you do if before your first LP, the resident calls to say go ahead and do it yourself, because he and the interns are in the emergency room with critically ill new patients. The LP needs to be done today. How would you respond?

CASE 23. Unethical behavior of an attending physician.

On a clerkship you observe what you consider flagrantly unethical behavior by one of your attending physicians. On several occasions, his speech is slurred and you smell alcohol on his breath He also fails to round on his patients for days at a time, without having anyone cover for him, and does not return your pages or those of your resident.

QUESTIONS FOR DISCUSSION

1. What are the ethical reasons for reporting the situation to an appropriate senior physician?
2. What are some of the risks in reporting the situation?
3. In practical terms, how might you proceed?

DISCLOSING ERRORS

CASE 24. Muscle weakness due to inadequate potassium replacement.

A 42-year-old man is admitted to you with diabetic ketoacidosis. After treatment with intravenous flu-ids and an insulin drip, the patient's glucose declines from 745 to 289 mg per dl after 4 hours. However, the patient develops progressive leg weakness and difficulty breathing and requires transfer to the ICU for mechanical ventilation. In reviewing the case, you check the computer for labs results and realize that the patient had a potassium of 2.3 mmol per L. No potassium replacement had been given during the treatment of the ketoacidosis.

QUESTIONS FOR DISCUSSION

1. If you were the subintern on the case, what would your feelings be?
2. In your experience, how have colleagues reacted to mistakes?
3. What would your concerns be about telling the attending physician about this mistake?
4. Would you tell the attending physician about the episode?

CASE 24, continued.

The patient's family asks what happened. They say that the patient has been hospitalized several times for ketoacidosis but has never required mechanical ventilation.

QUESTIONS FOR DISCUSSION

1. A nurse asks you what she should tell the patient and family, saying that they are very con-cerned about what happened. How do you respond? What are the ethical reasons for your response?

ETHICAL ISSUES IN PEDIATRICS

CASE 25. Treating adolescents without parental consent.

A 15-year-old high-school student comes to the physician because of dysuria and a discharge from his penis after intercourse without a condom. He wants to be tested and treated but does not want his par-ents to know about his problems. "They would completely freak out if they knew I was having sex," he says.

QUESTIONS FOR DISCUSSION

1. You ask a colleague whether you can treat the patient without his parents' authorization. She says that you may do so, provided that he is capable of giving informed consent to treatment. Do you agree with her advice? What are the ethical justifications for your position?
2. The patient is so concerned about his parents' finding out that he asks you to write on the encounter form that the visit is for shoulder pain. "I don't want them getting a bill that tells them why I came in." How do you respond to this request? Give the ethical considerations for your decision.

CASE 26. Treating children despite refusals.

A 10-year-old boy is taken to the ED with vomiting and right lower quadrant abdominal pain and is found to have appendicitis.

QUESTIONS FOR DISCUSSION

1. The patient says that he does not want surgery, saying that the pain is getting better and he does not want to have a scar the rest of his life. His parents are willing to authorize surgery for him. The resident on the team says, "We're not going to operate on a patient who is screaming that he doesn't want surgery. That's assaulting the patient." Do you agree with the resident? Give the ethical considerations for your decision.

2. Suppose instead that the parents refuse surgery. (An aunt who was baby-sitting brought the child to the ED.) The parents are devout Christian Scientists who believe that their child will recover with prayer therapy. The intern says that parents are not permitted to make irrational decisions, so the surgery should proceed as recommended. Do you agree with the intern? Give the ethical considerations for your decision.

Subject Index